NEW SOVIET GYPSIES

Nationality, Performance, and Selfhood
in the Early Soviet Union

BRIGID O'KEEFFE

New Soviet Gypsies

Nationality, Performance, and Selfhood in the Early Soviet Union

UNIVERSITY OF TORONTO PRESS
Toronto Buffalo London

ISBN 978-1-4426-4650-6 (cloth)

Printed on acid-free, 100% post-consumer recycled paper with
vegetable-based inks.

Publication Cataloguing information is available from Library
and Archives Canada

University of Toronto Press acknowledges the financial assistance to its
publishing program of the Canada Council for the Arts and the Ontario Arts
Council.

University of Toronto Press acknowledges the financial support of the
Government of Canada through the Canada Book Fund for its publishing
activities.

The University of Toronto Press is pleased to acknowledge the financial
support for this book provided by the Jordan Center for the Advanced
Study of Russia at New York University.

For my mother, Margaret O'Keeffe,
and in loving memory of my father,
Liam O'Keeffe (1940–2005)

Contents

List of Illustrations   ix

A Note on Terminology and Transliteration   xi

Acknowledgments   xiii

Introduction   3

1 Backward Gypsies, Soviet Citizens: The All-Russian Gypsy Union   27

2 A Political Education: Soviet Values and Practical
Realities in Gypsy Schools   66

3 Parasites, Pariahs, and Proletarians: Class Struggle and
the Forging of a Gypsy Proletariat   103

4 Nomads into Farmers: Romani Activism and the
Territorialization of (In)Difference   145

5 Pornography or Authenticity? Performing Gypsiness on
the Soviet Stage   191

Epilogue and Conclusion: "Am I a Gypsy or Not a Gypsy?":
Nationality and the Performance of Soviet Selfhood   239

Glossary of Terms and Abbreviations   255

Notes   257

Bibliography   303

Index   319

List of Illustrations

1 Representatives of the Romani choir directed by Ivan
  Grigor'evich Lebedev in 1910.   31
2 Romani woman telling fortunes.   106
3 Front cover of the first issue of *Romany zoria*, 1927.   109
4 Children of a nomadic Romani camp in Ukraine, circa 1935.   150
5 The founding of the State Gypsy Theatre Romen, 1931.   192
6 Romani choir in the era of NEP.   200
7 Scene from A.V. Germano's play *Life on Wheels*, at
  the Theatre Romen.   222
8 Ivan Rom-Lebedev, in costume for his leading role in
  A.V. Germano's play *Life on Wheels*, at the Theatre Romen.   224

A Note on Terminology and Transliteration

As an official nationality, Roma were categorized in the Soviet Union as Gypsies (*tsygane*). Roma self-identified and were identified by the state as Gypsies. The ethnonym "Roma" was scarcely employed in the Soviet Union in Russian-language sources of the period – even by Romani activists. Throughout this book, I deploy both ethnonyms – Gypsies and Roma – with a distinct purpose in mind. In order to accurately reflect contemporaries' vocabulary as well as the stereotypes of Roma that prevailed in the Soviet Union, I reproduce the grammatical variants of "Gypsy" when reporting direct speech, referencing official state categories, and describing the documented perspectives of historical actors. When speaking for myself, I employ the terms "Roma" (nominative plural) or "Romani" (adjective).

I have used the Library of Congress system of transliteration except when referring to names and geographical places conventionally known to English readers in more familiar guise. Thus, for example, I refer to Tolstoy rather than Tolstoi and to Riazan rather than Riazan'.

Acknowledgments

Many people helped me as I wrote this book, in ways both big and small. At New York University, I enjoyed the mentorship of truly phenomenal colleagues. Yanni Kotsonis has generously supported this project from start to finish, demonstrating unwavering confidence in me even at times when I doubted myself. With buoyant good humour, he has offered me over the years both trenchant critiques and the dogged encouragement to write this book as I saw fit. It is through conversations with Jane Burbank that I first became fascinated with Russian and Soviet approaches to governing a multi-ethnic population, and interested in the history of empires generally. Jane actively supported this project in countless ways, not least in providing careful readings, helpful criticism, wide-ranging advice, and ceaseless enthusiasm. Bruce Grant cheerfully read drafts and encouraged me to think in new ways about the writing of history. His boundless energy and insatiable curiosity have provided me with much inspiration, and I remain awed by his example of model academic citizenship. For their friendship as much as for their expert guidance, I simply cannot thank Yanni, Jane, and Bruce enough.

Brooklyn College has also proved a welcome home for the writing of this book, and my colleagues in the History Department have been staunch and energetic supporters of my research. Special thanks are owed to David Troyansky, who tirelessly went out of his way to ensure that my research, writing, and publication of this book were possible. Swapna Banerjee, Chris Ebert, and Jocelyn Wills have provided sound advice and moral support, never failing to share with me their time and insight. The Brooklyn College History Department has brightened my life in all manner of unexpected ways. Its corridors and classrooms pulse with an energy I have not found in any other academic setting. To say that I am fortunate in my colleagues and students is a gross understatement.

I am enormously grateful for the generous financial support provided me by a number of institutions. Subvention funding for the publication of this book was provided by the Brooklyn College History Department as well as the Jordan Center for the Advanced Study of Russia at New York University. Fulbright-Hays, International Research and Exchanges Board (IREX), American Councils for Teachers of Russian (ACTR), PSC-CUNY Research Foundation, and Council for European Studies grants made my research possible. A postdoctoral fellowship at Miami University's Havighurst Center for Russian and Post-Soviet Studies also provided a hospitable home and invaluable time with which to work on my manuscript. At the Havighurst Center, I am especially grateful to Karen Dawisha, Steve Norris, and Neringa Klumbyte for their wisdom, spirit, and friendship. I am likewise appreciative of the hospitality shown me at the Russian archives I visited. I am especially indebted to the staffs of the State Archive of Smolensk Oblast', the Orel State Literary Museum of I.S. Turgenev, the Russian Institute of the History of Art, and the Russian Ethnographic Museum for offering me special courtesy and remarkable cheer.

While conducting research in Russia and writing this book in New York, I forged friendships with an extraordinary group of colleagues with whom I look forward to working in the years to come. For their camaraderie, I thank Caroline Arnold, Wilson Bell, Auri Berg, Desi Allevato, Sarah Cornell, Arch Getty, Sean Guillory, Christoph Gumb, Maya Haber, Mobina Hashmi, Mara Heifetz, Chia Yin Hsu, Andy Janco, Ryan Jones, Jenny Kaminer, Lauren Kaminsky, Danielle Kellogg, Kelly Kolar, Greg Kveberg, Olga Livshin, Steve Maddox, Ben Sawyer, Karl Steel, Christian Teichmann, Vanessa Voisin, Karen Weber, and Mike Westren. Fiercer allies could not be found than in Ben Loring, Josh Sanborn, and Oscar Sanchez. I am particularly grateful to Maya and Oscar; I dearly hope that they each understand why.

Two friends in particular have gone far out of their way to help me see this project to completion without losing my head. The generosity of Steve Norris and Tracy McDonald leaves me in awe. Steve is the very definition of a *mensch* – an obvious point with which my colleagues in the field will readily and boisterously agree. Tracy is as much a formidable scholar as she is a faithful friend. Whatever the topic of our discussion, I have learned something and I have laughed. Whatever draft of mine she has read, Tracy has helped to improve it. For the countless ways Tracy and Steve have helped me in the years of our friendship, I thank them – but with the painful awareness that such thanks could never do justice to the good will and good humour they have both shown me. I would be literally lost without them.

For their friendship as much as for their making me feel at home in Russia, I also thank Tania and Masha Shmigel'skaia; Nona, Karina, and Margo Shahnazarian; Ania Ustivitskaia; Nina Peskareva; Nastia Maksimova; Liudmila Borisovna; Joseph DeVeny; Iverson Long; Lauren and Senya Makaleev; Nona Lambert; and Anna Popova.

For their willingness to read and provide comments on earlier versions of this manuscript (in whole or in part), I thank Eliot Borenstein, Alaina Lemon, Larry Wolff, Chris Otter, Michael David-Fox, Lewis Siegelbaum, and Susan Smith-Peter. I am grateful to Valerii Aleksandrov, Nadezhda Demeter, Martin Holler, Marina Kerimova, Nikolai Kirei, Nathaniel Knight, and Olessia Vovina for their help on matters both practical and analytic.

At The University of Toronto Press, I thank Richard Ratzlaff for his tremendous expertise and inexhaustible energy. Richard is, quite simply, an amazing editor. He can be relied upon always for his unfailing integrity and generosity of spirit. Meanwhile, the incredibly helpful and insightful reviewer reports provided by two anonymous readers continue to energize me even upon completion of the revisions they suggested. I thank them for their professionalism and collegiality.

I am overwhelmed with appreciation for family and old friends who have supported me in this endeavour even when perplexed by its often inconvenient demands. I thank the Brymer, Centers, Clovis, Dockery, MacMahon, McMillan, Mueller, O'Keeffe, Power, Tinker, VanKannel, and Vencill families, as well as Beth Lucas, Jason Calicchia, Cal Carlisle, Scott Ciolek, and Chris Fields. In recent years, Deva, Katie, Eoin, and Patrick have valuably instructed me in the powers of imagination and storytelling. Layla, Georgie, and Ernie have lavished me with joy, wisdom, and comfort of the type no human could ever possibly provide.

Of my fortunes in life, none compare to my parents, Margaret and Liam O'Keeffe, and my sisters, Siobhan O'Keeffe Clovis and Deirdre O'Keeffe Mueller. It is from them that I have learned the truly important things in life – the value of laughter not least of all. In this book as in daily life, I gratefully see each of their influences.

My parents were the first to believe me, so long ago, when I told them with the comical seriousness of a child that I was a writer. It is, moreover, primarily because of them that writing and books captivated me in the first place. My mother showed me how words could sing and even dance. My father taught me that pens were spades with which to dig, and words – tools with which to build. Their library fuelled my imagination, but it is the stories that they themselves told me that continue to inspire. In his own peculiar way, my father gave me the initial idea for this project long before I was even aware of a sprawling place on the map known as the Soviet Union. Although I so desperately wish that he could have lived to see me complete it, I am both comforted and honoured to hear trace echoes of his inimitable voice in the pages that follow. With uncommon grace, my mother has made sure in recent years that my father's history is not forgotten and his stories are retold. Little does she seem to know that her own tales are as riveting or as full of humour as his, especially when delivered in unusual fonts. For their inspiration as much as for their love, it is to my parents that I dedicate this book.

Last but not least, I offer special thanks to Zac Centers, whom I love beyond measure. Every day he sets my life to music and, God help him, listens to me sing.

NEW SOVIET GYPSIES

Introduction

"Every man has taxes to pay, and powers to exert, the Gipsies none of the least; if he does not know how to make use of them, let the state teach him, and keep him in leading strings till the end is attained. If the root of this depravity lies so deep, in the first generation, that it cannot be removed immediately, a continuation of the same care will, in the second or third descent, be sure of meeting its reward. Now let us reflect on a Gipsey, when he has discontinued his Gipsey life, consider him with his fecundity and numerous family, who being reformed, are made useful citizens, and we shall perceive how great want of economy it was to throw him away as dross."

– Heinrich Moritz Gottlieb Grellmann,
Dissertation on the Gipsies, Being an Historical Enquiry,
Concerning the Manner of Life, Economy, Customs,
and Conditions of These People in Europe, and Their Origin (1783)

"We are completely unconscious people, completely illiterate," pleaded three Romani citizens of the Soviet Union in 1933 in a letter to the General Procuracy. Confronting a death sentence imposed upon them for their alleged theft of ten horses from a collective farm, the desperate threesome offered several justifications for what they hoped would be prosecutors' clemency. In the first place, they claimed, it was not they who had stolen the horses at all. Rather, the real criminals were a different band of Gypsies with whom they had initially been arrested for the theft. Once thrown inside a jail cell together, the three explained, the real criminals had terrorized, beaten, and threatened to kill them if they did not assume the blame for the theft. While the guilty horse thieves had been set free, the unfortunate threesome now faced the death penalty in line with the infamously draconian 7 August 1932 Soviet law criminalizing the theft of socialist property. The three had never imagined such a horrific punishment when they pled guilty for a crime they had not committed, they explained. Having never been indicted previously, they admittedly lacked knowledge of the Soviet legal system. Backward Gypsies, they insinuated, could scarcely be expected to know even the basics of Soviet law.

While insistent on their own pitiable benightedness, these seemingly doomed Roma nonetheless claimed absolute certainty that the Soviet legal system had failed them. "The Court," they argued, "did not take into account that we, as Gypsies, were oppressed and almost completely deprived of all civic rights as a nation under the tsarist regime and that there was a view of us then that we were capable only of committing crimes." In a fierce, if not subtle, strategic move, the three transferred emphasis from their declared innocence of the crime to their insistent status as representatives of a backward and historically maligned minority people. Defining themselves as Gypsies, the three underscored that they were "completely unconscious" and "completely illiterate" members of a nationality long persecuted and despised under the tsars. They insisted that they were not horse thieves, but instead minority victims of centuries of imposed backwardness and chauvinism. They pointedly asked the Procuracy, "Are we really such socially dangerous people who cannot be reformed, who must be physically destroyed?" No, the three answered, they were not. Rather, they were reviled, uneducated Gypsies intent on realizing their full potential as Soviet citizens. If granted clemency, they promised, they would "in the future be useful in their work for socialist construction."[1]

On 30 December 1933, assistant prosecutor of the Soviet Union Borisov stayed the execution of the three alleged Romani horse thieves pending further investigation into their claims.[2] Although the ultimate fate of the three is unknown, their plea for clemency captures many of the key dynamics of Soviet nationality policy explored in this book. Arrested and sentenced to death for a crime long associated in the popular imagination with Gypsies, the three Romani citizens argued for their exoneration by not only performing common stereotypes of Gypsies, but also deploying the ideological premises of Soviet nationality policy. Mobilizing the trope of the swindling Gypsy, the accused insisted that it was "other Gypsies" – naturally – who had stolen the horses. As for themselves, they claimed to literally embody nearly all the pathologies that Soviet officialdom feared to be innate in Gypsies. They staunchly defined themselves as backward, unconscious, illiterate, ignorant, and marginalized from Soviet society. Their purported backwardness as Gypsies, however, served as their platform for claiming special consideration and help in their path towards becoming conscious, socially useful Soviet citizens. Invoking the key premise of Bolshevik nationality policy, they demanded that the Soviet state consider their status as representatives of a nationality oppressed and developmentally stunted by the tsarist empire – if not, as their plea rather mutely suggested, by its Soviet successor. Leniency was owed to them, the three claimed, if not for their innocence, then for the fact that they were backward Gypsies still redeemable as conscious Soviet citizens. As backward minorities, they were entitled to the state's patient guidance and material help on their road to becoming New Soviet Gypsies. In steadfastly claiming an ignorance and marginality ostensibly inherent to their nationality, the three adeptly mobilized the Soviet nationality regime in a desperate attempt not only for freedom, but also for their lives. In their insistent demand that the Procuracy spare them as "backward Gypsies," these three accused Romani horse thieves were already proving themselves to be adept Soviet citizens, conscious of their duty to transform themselves into socially useful labourers and striving towards full integration into Soviet life. The logic of Soviet nationality policy afforded them the opportunity and the means with which both to potentially benefit from their ascribed "backwardness" as Gypsies and to claim status as Soviet citizens in-the-making.

Roma and the Soviet Nationality Regime

In the wake of the October Revolution, the Bolsheviks demanded the creation of a New Soviet citizen – one who was conscious, disciplined, socially useful, rational, literate, cultured, and energized by a purportedly masculine vigour to advance the cause of the collective as much as the individual.[3] Seemingly the antithesis of modern citizens, Gypsies figured menacingly in the Bolshevik imagination as the personification of backwardness and inscrutability. As perceived icons of indifferent marginality, disorder, indolence, parasitism, criminality, illiteracy, philistinism, irrationality, and a feminine slavishness to the flesh, Gypsies threatened Bolsheviks' ideal vision of New Soviet Men and Women. The accursed "Gypsy question" was thus an inescapable Bolshevik problem. How, the Bolsheviks were ultimately forced to ask themselves, could idle swindlers be refashioned as disciplined labourers and aimless nomads converted into productive farmers? Indeed, how could backward Gypsies be transformed into Soviet citizens?

With the slogan "national in form, socialist in content," the Bolsheviks assaulted what they termed the cultural backwardness of Gypsies and other officially recognized national minorities throughout the 1920s and 1930s with expansive nation-building projects and nationality-based "affirmative action."[4] This Soviet nationality regime was designed to assimilate minority peoples to Soviet culture and the socialist economy – to transform them into citizens. At least theoretically, early Soviet nationality policy entitled non-Russians to a host of declared benefits that included, most notably, the purported accoutrements of nationhood: territories, alphabets, schools, theatres, and a range of other national institutions. Suffused with socialist content, these national forms were intended by the state to accustom minority citizens to a distinctly Soviet way of life, integrating them into the polity as conscious citizens.

While nationality policy was designed as a lever for the transformation of "backward" minorities into integrated Soviet citizens, the Soviet civilizing mission not only demanded but also depended upon the quotidian participation of its minority citizens. Indeed, this book argues that the primary agents in the refashioning of so-called "backward Gypsies" into conscious Soviet citizens were Roma themselves. In their engagement of the Soviet nationality regime, Roma assimilated Sovietism – that is, the complex of Soviet culture, social customs, and economic relations by which all Soviet citizens were to be bound to one another in the Bolsheviks' vision of a modern, rational, and unified state. In mobilizing the Soviet nationality regime, minority citizens demanded the affirmative action entitled to them, but also deployed Soviet values and participated in Soviet culture, politics, and the socialist economy. In this way, Soviet nationality policy facilitated Roma's self-fashioning as conscious, integrated Soviet citizens in the 1920s and 1930s. Thus, while it was the Bolsheviks who initially designed Soviet nationality policy, it was Roma and their fellow minority peoples themselves who made it work.

Defined by the Soviet state as both an official nationality and a woefully backward people, Roma offer a representative view of minority citizens who actively participated in the shaping of the early Soviet nationality regime and of their own Soviet selves. Throughout the 1920s and 1930s, Roma mobilized the categories "nationality" and (minority) "backwardness" as they crafted an array of both institutions and narratives through which they refashioned themselves as conscious Soviet citizens. Minority status, let alone ascribed backwardness, served Roma and other official nationalities as invaluable tools with which to profitably engage in the intertwined projects of building socialism and self-sovietization. Nationality policy offered Roma and their fellow minority peoples a stake in the building of socialism and a manipulable framework of self-sovietization. In this general sense, Roma's experience as a Soviet nationality was devoutly typical.

By no means the only minority targeted as culturally backward, Roma nonetheless distinctively figured in the Soviet imagination as an exceptionally intractable people who threatened the state's designs for a modern, rationalized state and conscious citizenry. Alaina Lemon has rightly noted that "the Russian romance with Gypsies has no equivalent force in most other countries."[5] Exotic fixtures of late imperial Russian culture, Gypsies flitted famously (almost obligatorily, it seems) through the works of classic Russian authors from Pushkin to Tolstoy to Blok. In the imperial capitals of Moscow and St. Petersburg, Russian elites and foreigners alike gawked with rapturous delight as Gypsies performed music and dances beloved for their sentimental whimsy and "hot-blooded" vivacity. Long before the October Revolution, Gypsies fuelled Russian visions of a liberty-loving people of primordial wandering and fire-burning sensuality. They appeared in the Russian mind as steppe-roaming human mysteries to be both pitied and envied for their lack of civilization. Especially in the guise of Pushkin's Zemfira, they also seemingly personified primal sexuality – exciting, unrestrained, but dangerous. Gypsies were seen both positively and negatively as a people who could not, would not be tamed.[6]

Yet while Gypsies inspired in tsarist elites romantic and lusty flights of fancy, they instead represented in the minds of Bolsheviks pathology, danger, and backwardness writ large. In the eyes of Soviet officials no less than of the wider Soviet public, Gypsies had escaped the forward march of history, surviving only by means of feeding off the toil and ignorance of the societies upon whom they preyed. In this view, Gypsies stubbornly clung to an unparalleled freedom from the constraints of social and cultural propriety, the necessity of labour, and the imposed duties of belonging to a modern state. As a population, they appeared uncommonly underdeveloped civilizationally and extraordinarily deviant sociologically. Gypsies haunted the Soviet imagination as a people frighteningly at odds with socialist modernity. Gypsies were feared not only as a phantom of the tsarist past, but also as a strikingly real dilemma of unique socio-cultural disfiguration. As a hyperreal vision of backwardness both personified and ethnicized, Gypsies posed the extraordinary challenge of how to transform a population that was illiterate and unlettered, peculiarly nomadic and parasitic, fragmented territorially and ethnically, diseased and dirty, free-loving and free-wheeling, and obstinately content in their morass of societal alienation and ill repute. In this sense, then, Roma were not representative of the Soviet Union's officially recognized minority peoples. Rather, they were considered by officials themselves as an extraordinary, astonishingly peculiar case of minority backwardness – indeed, as a dangerously problematic ethnic oddity. Although legally an official nationality like any other, Gypsies inspired in practice a multilayered, deeply rooted bias unique to them as a minority people in the Soviet Union. Popularly defined as unruly nomads, parasites, and marginals, Gypsies seemingly jeopardized the Soviet Union's modernizing goals as a top contender for the empire's singularly "most backward" minority people.

As I demonstrate throughout the book, Gypsies' ascribed backwardness – despite its distinctive and marked extremity – proved an asset as often as it did a handicap for Roma engaging the Soviet nationality regime. Roma relentlessly invoked their own supposedly extreme backwardness in their claims on nationality policy and in their diverse efforts to reinvent themselves as Soviet citizens. They shrewdly and strategically deployed overwhelmingly negative tropes of Gypsy backwardness in their efforts at Soviet self-fashioning. In so doing, Roma not only performed and reproduced denigrating stereotypes of Gypsies, but also fashioned themselves into settled, literate, labouring, and integrated Soviet citizens. Indeed, the more Roma performed Sovietism as "backward Gypsies" within the ready framework of nationality policy, the more they legitimized themselves as conscious Soviet citizens.

Citizenship, Nationality, and Self-Fashioning in the Early Soviet Union

While loath to admit any ideological similarities between themselves and their tsarist forebears, the Bolsheviks launched their Revolution in October 1917 with a base understanding of citizenship that they shared with many of the former empire's ministers and officials. As Yanni Kotsonis has argued, many tsarist officials in the post-Emancipation era strived towards the creation of a community of citizens bound to one another, at the very least, by their shared obligations to the state. In this vision of autocratic citizenship, the individual was not only "honored" by the duties that marked his or her inclusion in the civic community, but also transformed through his or her participation in the state. In this obligation-laden vision of citizenship, the individual developed consciousness and, indeed, self-actualized via the performance of his or her duties to the civic whole. Fully realized, the conscious citizen would therefore ideally recognize the state not as an external and likely repressive force, but instead as a constituent and potentially liberating source of self.[7]

Similar to their imperial Russian predecessors, the Bolsheviks envisioned the creation of a harmonious, unified whole through the cultivation of the individual citizen. In their October Revolution, the Bolsheviks proceeded from the premise not only that humankind could be entirely remade, but also that they would succeed in reforging a compositely backward population into a modern citizenry fully implicated in the state. Soviet citizenship was predicated on the notion that the individual's participation in the state – no matter how coerced – inescapably compelled the embodiment of the state in the self. According to this totalizing and totalitarian ideal, the individual citizen gained the full dignity of consciousness through the earnest embrace of Soviet ideology and willing fulfilment of obligations to the civic whole.[8]

Among the civic obligations necessarily shouldered by all Soviet citizens, the duty to actively transform themselves into New Soviet Men and Women was paramount. Nationality, class, sex, or any other legal mark of distinction never sufficed as absolution from this central obligation. The Soviet civilizing mission resolutely demanded that individuals become the stalwart agents of their own sovietization. Russian peasants, Kyrgyz nomads, and Romani fortune tellers were required alongside all their fellow Soviet citizens to embody the state's transformative power and willingly submit to expert guidance as they traversed an accelerated path of development from their presumed backwardness to socialist, Soviet modernity.[9] Agents of their own transformation, New Soviet citizens became the living, breathing incarnation of Soviet power. As such, they were expected to actively contribute to the building of socialism as well as to appreciate the moral value of labouring, learning, and disciplining themselves in the service of the collective as much as the individual. According to the Bolshevik ideal, it was not merely participation in building socialism that defined the fully realized Soviet citizen, but also his or her consciousness of having meaningfully contributed to the advancement of an exalted Soviet civilization built by enlightened and self-mastering individuals.[10]

In practice, however, Soviet citizenship demanded nothing less and ultimately nothing more than individuals' participation in the construction of both socialist society and their own Soviet selves.[11] Responding to this inescapable demand, individuals fashioned themselves as Soviet citizens through their participation in Sovietism *regardless* of what variously motivated their actions. In the realm of the quotidian, individuals' performance of Sovietism ostensibly signalled their active civic belonging and ideological commitment to Soviet socialism, but – to the dismay of many a Bolshevik, not to mention many a historian – that performance could never reliably serve as a barometer of their belief in Soviet ideology. This book thus defines Soviet citizenship as a performative effect of individuals' requisite participation in Sovietism. It understands this participation as having been variously motivated within a system built on the foundations of both ruthless coercion and exultant visions of a rational, liberating socialist future. No matter what animated Soviet men and women to affirm the system that unavoidably shaped their daily lives, it was participation in Sovietism rather than belief that transformed them into citizens.[12] For Roma and their fellow minority peoples, Soviet nationality policy not only issued a distinctive demand for that participation, but also offered a flexible arena for achieving it. No matter their intentions, their performance of Sovietism *as minorities* transformed them into citizens.

In the practical calculus of Soviet citizenship and citizen-making in the 1920s and 1930s, non-Russian nationality played a crucial and exclusive role. After all, the means of Soviet self-actualization available to Roma and their fellow minority citizens differed in a very important respect from those available to Russians in the early Soviet period. Castigating Russia as the historic oppressor nation of the tsarist era, the Bolsheviks denied Russians the nationality-based "affirmative action" that they promised to officially designated minority peoples – Roma included. Bolshevik nationality theory postulated that Russians did not deserve the privileged mechanisms of nation-building granted to the Soviet Union's minority peoples because Russians had for too long advanced themselves at the criminal expense of the minority peoples whom they oppressed.[13] In practical terms, this by no means translated into a silencing of the Russian language or even of Russian culture. The Bolsheviks' strategic priority of minority advancement did mean, however, that Russians were absolved of *ethnic* backwardness and thereby allotted an abbreviated repertory of self-fashioning tools of which the most salient was class.[14] Unlike Roma and their fellow minority peoples, Russians could not invoke nationality as a means of claiming state aid or other special consideration along their path to redemption as enlightened Soviet citizens.

For those minority peoples entitled to Soviet nation-building, nationality was an inescapable but also potentially advantageous source of Soviet selfhood, not to mention of political, social, and material advancement. Indeed, the early Soviet nationality regime produced more than an institutional capacity to repress citizens on account of nationality. It also opened possibilities for Soviet citizens to advance themselves namely as "backward" minorities, thereby empowering Soviet subjectivities. Not merely a Bolshevik straitjacket designed to repress nationalism, nationality policy enticed or else forcibly summoned minority peoples to nest – however comfortably – among their fellow citizens within the metaphoric Soviet communal apartment. As an unavoidable framework within which minority peoples were expected to acclimate to Soviet values and integrate into the socialist economy, the Soviet nationality regime accommodated both minority repression and self-advancement.[15]

Since the dissolution of the Soviet Union in 1991, historians have re-examined Soviet nationality policy from multiple angles, thereby broadening our understanding of how the Soviet nationality regime enabled not only the suppression or erasure, but also the promotion and even creation of national languages, cultures, and territories.[16] Yet studies of Soviet nation-building have tended to concentrate on Soviet institutions and officialdom as the mobilizers of the Soviet nationality regime more so than on the minority peoples whom nationality policy was intended to transform. Focusing on the social and political lives of Roma, this book illuminates the centrality of nationality to minority citizens' Soviet self-fashioning. Roma's varied engagement of the Soviet nationality regime highlights minority peoples' crucial participation not only in the shaping of national languages, institutions, territories, and historical narratives, but also in the transformation of their own selves into integrated Soviet citizens. Rather than take minority mobilization of the Soviet nationality regime for granted, this book demonstrates the multiple ways in which minority peoples actively refashioned themselves as Soviet through their layered performance of nationality. It shows *how* Roma transformed themselves into integrated citizens via their deployment of the Soviet politics of nationality.

As a study of Soviet self-fashioning, this book contributes as well to a recent historiography that has reappraised the centrality of ideology in everyday Soviet life. Positing ideology neither as a totality imposed upon a passive population, nor as a regime of beliefs and practices rejected outright by citizens in the arena of the conscious mind, this historiography understands ideology as the fundamental component of a new Soviet culture and, ultimately, of new Soviet selves.[17] The New Soviet Person is conceptualized neither as a lionized ideal type nor as a despicable caricature of the Bolsheviks' utopian vision of social engineering, but instead as a real human being of variable personality and circumstance who, as both product and producer of Soviet ideology, was called upon to realize himself or herself as one with the evolving socialist collective. The Soviet subject thus emerges not as a pawn whose mind and body is held captive by the totalitarian ideology in which it is steeped, but instead as a historical agent who pursues his or her interests (including Soviet self-fashioning) with the tools and conceptual framework of Soviet ideology. In this framing, Soviet subjectivity and ideology are rightly conceptualized as symbiotically related. One could not claim to be a New Soviet Person, indeed a conscious Soviet citizen, without actively engaging, if not internalizing, Sovietism.

Given the preponderance of the empire's minority citizens and the centrality of nationality policy to early Soviet modernization efforts, perhaps no Soviet idiom bore as much potential for self-fashioning utility – if not existential meaning – as that of nationality. All citizens were not only required to identify themselves as members of a distinct nationality, but also compelled to recognize the special significance of minority status. In the Bolshevik worldview, nationality was no mere identity. Nationality was a diagnosis. Subscribing to Marxist evolutionary thinking, the Bolsheviks defined few minority peoples as "advanced" – that is, literate, cultured, clean, sedentary, and labouring. The Bolsheviks instead diagnosed most nationalities as "backward" repositories of the dangerous vestiges of irrational and primitive modes of social, economic, and cultural organization. Thus, for many of the empire's minority citizens, their nationality neatly categorized them as illiterate, superstitious, childlike, dirty, diseased, brutish, patriarchal, and generally devoid of consciousness. Nationality – and the backwardness it implied in official understandings of many non-Russian peoples in the empire – was thus conceived as an obstacle for minority peoples to ultimately overcome on the path to the Soviet goal of universalization. Once the transformation of the entire population into a modern citizenry bound by the common values of the Soviet Union's peerless socialist civilization was achieved, the salience of nationality in the lives of minority peoples would recede, trumped by the universal and unifying values of Sovietness.

Yet, while nationality typically functioned in the early Soviet present as a diagnosis of an all-encompassing benightedness, it also served as a prognosis for minority peoples' promisingly brilliant future as literate, cultured, clean, and socially useful citizens fully integrated into Soviet life. Both nationality and its faithful attendant – backwardness – were purportedly guaranteed entitlements to state aid and guidance for minority citizens travelling along the path to Soviet redemption. As Roma and many of their minority compatriots quickly discovered, non-Russian nationality potentially translated into alphabets, schools, money, tax breaks, land, publishing houses, theatres, industrial workshops, preferential educational admissions, and government jobs. These tangible fruits of the Bolsheviks' nationality policy were to ease the transition of benighted minorities from the depths of their oppressed backwardness to the heights of Soviet civilization as self-actualized citizens. While the mere fact of non-Russian nationality spelled minority citizens' duty to transform themselves, nationality policy was proffered as an enticing palliative for their short-term growing pains and a liberating arena of Soviet self-fashioning.[18]

In the long term, the benefits promised minority peoples by nationality policy were to transcend materiality. Nationality policy was, after all, as much a spiritual enterprise as it was a mechanism to build political loyalties, create a rational socialist economy, and modernize the Soviet Union's institutional landscape. Its end goal was not merely developed Soviet nations, but also mature Soviet citizens bound by common Soviet values and integrated into the socialist economy. As such, nationality policy was formulated not only to introduce "backward" minority peoples to Sovietism, but also to implicate them in Sovietism. Whether minority peoples actively sought nationality policy's entitlements or had Soviet-sponsored "national forms" forced upon them, minority citizens were called upon in either case to mobilize, legitimize, and internalize the "socialist content" contained therein. While national theatres, schools, and workers' cooperatives were to institutionally transmit Soviet values, minority peoples were to assimilate those values body and soul as New Soviet Men and Women – that is, as conscious citizens. In practice, this book shows, nationality policy worked as a pliable tool of minority peoples' Soviet self-fashioning, Roma included.

Many Roma actively and even enthusiastically answered the Soviet clarion call to sovietize themselves and others via the vehicle of the

Soviet nationality regime. Throughout the interwar period, Roma of varied backgrounds and circumstance engaged Soviet nationality policy not merely as citizens, but also emphatically as Gypsies. While they joined their fellow citizens in mastering the grammar and cadences of "Bolshevik speak," they availed themselves of a series of specific vocabularies afforded them as an official nationality, as a backward people, and as Gypsies.[19] Roma deployed the idioms of nationality, backwardness, and Gypsiness as they crafted the narrative and institutional forms of nationhood offered them as a minority people. Shouldering both the diagnosis and prognosis attached to their national status as Gypsies, they pursued the reformation promised and required of them as purportedly backward minority citizens. For many Roma, I argue, nationality proved an asset in the sense both of short-term material and cultural advancement and of long-term Soviet self-realization as integrated citizens. It served as an opportunity to craft both what it meant to be a Gypsy and what it meant to be Soviet. Nationality offered Roma a productive space within which to tailor, revise, and even reinvent themselves first as Gypsies, but ultimately as Soviet citizens. Asserting themselves as "backward Gypsies," Roma fashioned themselves into Soviet citizens – and did so regardless of their sincerity or intentions.

Questions of Authenticity and Performance

Tracing as it does Roma's varied manipulation of Gypsiness in particular and the parlance of Soviet nationality generally, this volume calls into question conceptions of identity – especially of ethnic and Soviet identities – as elemental, binding, and rigid.[20] In examining Roma's varied mobilization of nationality in the early Soviet Union, it is instructive to consider Rogers Brubaker's warning that even among contemporary scholars who employ a constructivist approach to understanding ethnicity, race, and nation, there nonetheless remains "the tendency to treat ethnic groups, nations, and even races as things-in-the-world, as real substantial entities with their own cultures, identities and interests." Analysis of how ethnicity is not only made but also mobilized by historical actors, Brubaker suggests, is furthered when ethnic groups are treated rather as "collective cultural representations, as widely shared ways of seeing, thinking, parsing social experience, and interpreting the social world."[21]

Brubaker's caution is particularly relevant when considering that Soviet citizens were required not only "to participate as if one believed" in socialism, but also as if they believed in nationality as a fundamental source of self.[22] In a culture saturated with politicized ethnicity, Soviet citizens – Roma included – mobilized nationality in their everyday lives on a monumental scale. Analysis of this mobilization need not and should not presuppose that Soviet citizens internalized the cultural meanings ascribed to their nationality or invested existential meaning in their official status as Gypsies, Russians, Ukrainians, or Kazakhs. Without denying the plausibility of individual Soviet citizens embracing nationality as an abiding source of self, analysis of the Soviet nationality regime must first account for nationality as a state-prescribed yet flexible means of positioning one's self within both the Soviet collective and its evolving socialist culture. It is within such a vein that this book examines how Roma mobilized Gypsiness in the early Soviet Union as they pursued the state-mandated process of fashioning themselves as Soviet. For the Roma whose words, actions, and lives I have studied, Gypsiness served as a mutable stance within a state that required citizens to self-identify as belonging to a distinct nationality. Following the example of the historical actors whose lives are explored in the pages that follow, I treat Gypsiness less as a matter of authenticity than as a matter of representation.

Thus, in my analysis of how Roma fashioned their Soviet selves via the nationality regime, I am not concerned with the question of whether they, as individual historical actors, earnestly believed in the varied meanings ascribed to the category "Gypsy" or located existential value in their nationality. These are questions, in any event, to which the sources are incapable of providing definitive answers. I analyse instead the performative effect of Roma's engagement of the Soviet nationality regime as Gypsies. This framework of performance not only allows for a realistic confrontation of the historical sources and their interpretive limits, but also accounts for the fact that participation in the mandates of everyday Soviet life neither disqualified nor guaranteed a subject's internalization of Soviet ideology.[23] Although sincere internalization of the values and practices of Sovietism may have been the mandated Bolshevik ideal, it was participation in them that remained the fundamental necessity at the level of quotidian social practice. Roma and their fellow citizens need not have sincerely internalized any of the Bolshevik idioms – nationality, class, or citizenship, for example – in order to mobilize and thus legitimize them via everyday acts of articulation and representation.[24] This book neither seeks nor pretends to measure the sincerity or cynicism of Roma as they asserted themselves as "backward

Gypsies" or deployed any other category or premise of Soviet ideology. It focuses instead on Roma's required participation in the Soviet system as essential to their self-fashioning as integrated Soviet citizens.

Studies of Soviet subjectivity have often centred on questions of historical actors' authenticity and intentions.[25] Recent preoccupation with adjudicating the sincerity of Soviet citizens, while perhaps motivated by a desire to escape unfairly typecasting them as either powerless ideological sponges or as self-interested winkers immunized from Soviet ideology, has nonetheless inspired an analytical tendency to "essentialize" the Soviet self.[26] In this regard, the seminal work of Jochen Hellbeck represents both the possibilities and limitations that such an approach entails. Hellbeck's analysis of Soviet diaries as "laboratories of the soul" revealed the often torturous musings of Soviet citizens struggling to fashion themselves as conscious Soviet citizens fully integrated with the revolutionary collective. His work is a helpful reminder of the agency of Soviet citizens confronting the state's demand that they reforge themselves – in terms not only of their outward behaviour, but also of their souls.

Strikingly problematic, however, is Hellbeck's insistence on a flattened, singular "illiberal socialist subject" ideologically invested in the purification of his or her Soviet soul. In the place of the old historiographical caricatures of Soviet citizens – the automaton, the kitchen-table resister, and the ideologically disinvested self-seeker, for example – Hellbeck offers a new one: the Soviet self ardently yearning for sublimation within the state, earnestly struggling to ideologically recast his or her soul.[27] While Hellbeck's analysis illuminates how individual Soviet diary writers may have navigated the duty to self-sovietize in the Stalinist 1930s, it does not offer a reliable blueprint for conclusively gauging the extent to which Soviet citizens believed in, did not believe in, or were indifferent towards the Soviet culture they helped to create. As Stephen Kotkin earlier emphasized in his own study of Soviet subjectivity, historians cannot escape the reality that all Soviet citizens were required by the state to "participate as if one believed."[28] Given this profound reality, no less its saturation of all manner of historical sources, it appears that the question of belief is neither the most productive line of historical inquiry into Soviet subjectivities, nor the most fair to historical subjects themselves.

In a combined effort to fully appreciate the diversity of Soviet selves, to resist arbitrarily typecasting its historical subjects, and to contend with the practical limits of its sources, this study frames Roma's participation in the Soviet nationality regime as a matter of performance, rather than a question of belief. As such, it builds from the so-called "performative turn" that has energized the humanities in recent decades and, still more recently, the anthropological and historical study of the former Soviet Union.[29] Representative of a larger trend towards understanding the performance of symbolic action as indicative of agents' sociocultural milieus rather than of their (in-)sincerity and intentions, Alexei Yurchak has persuasively argued in his rich analysis of everyday life during late socialism that Soviet citizens' participation in the rituals and metanarratives of Soviet life cannot be explained via the analytical binaries of sincerity and cynicism or ideological investment and ideological immunization. Rather, citizens' performance of Sovietism must be seen as "constitutive" of their subjectivity.[30] Consonant with this view, the present volume argues that Roma's participation in Sovietism not only legitimized Soviet ideology, but also legitimized their own selves as Soviet citizens. Belief – no matter how "varied, contradictory, full of ostensibly mutual exclusive conceptions, partial, selective, sowed with doubts, predicated on the suspension of disbelief, related to opportunism, and mocked" – never figured as a mandatory factor in securing the performative effect of individuals' participation in Sovietism.[31] Regardless of motivation or belief, Roma transformed themselves into "backward Gypsies" as well as conscious Soviet citizens through their performance of the categories and values that were authorized not only by state officials, but also by their very own participation in Sovietism. For many of the Roma featured prominently in this study, performing Gypsiness proved no less a learned, mutable behaviour than performing Sovietness. In order to become Soviet, they first had to become Gypsies.

Roma: Histories and Representations

In his *Gypsies of the USSR* (1931), Soviet ethnolinguist A.P. Barannikov estimated the world's Romani population at 800,000. Despite their relatively small number, Barannikov maintained, Roma were known – often infamously – throughout the entire world. After centuries of seemingly endless migration, Roma had settled in Europe, Asia, Africa, the Americas, and Australia. And yet, he claimed, until quite recently Roma had for centuries figured in the European imagination as a "living mystery." Not only were Romani culture and language inscrutable to European populations, but also Roma's origins themselves remained unclear. Did Roma even have a homeland? If so, what prompted them to abandon it?[32]

Only through the study of the Romani language, Barannikov insisted, had nineteenth-century European scholars begun to unravel the "mystery" of Roma's origins. Long considered by the scholars of "bourgeois Europe" as a criminals' argot rather than a national language, he explained, Romani provided the key to tracing Roma's historical migration patterns. Citing the pioneering philological studies of the German scholars A.F. Pott (1802–77) and Franz von Miklosich (1813–91), Barannikov explained that the discovery of Romani's Sanskrit roots first led scholars to chart Roma's migrations from ancient India through Central Asia, the Middle East, the Balkans, and ultimately into wider Europe and beyond.[33]

The historical exegesis of Romani migrations that Barannikov provided Soviet readers in the early 1930s in many ways mirrors the introductions to works written on Romani history and culture produced in the West in recent decades.[34] Heirs to the nineteenth-century comparative philology of Pott, Miklosich, and others, scholars still today rely on Romani – an Indo-European language of many dialects – to illuminate the pathways first charted by proto-Romani–speakers more than a millennium ago. While a great deal of Romani history remains obscure (if not inaccessible) to researchers in the present day, many scholars still embrace the general typology of Roma's origins in India and subsequent centuries-long migratory pattern along the Silk Road, through the Byzantine Empire, and onward from the Balkan Peninsula into Europe and, ultimately, the wider world.[35]

The reasons for proto-Romani–speakers' exodus from northwest India in approximately the eleventh century have long inspired scholarly debate. Whereas European "Gypsiologists" in the eighteenth and nineteenth centuries advanced theories of innate Gypsy nomadism and Gypsies' eternal "pariah status" as explanations for the medieval exodus, Romani Studies scholars have recently provided alternative theories of Roma's origins in India. According to Romani scholar Ian Hancock, for example, the predecessors of today's Romani populations who departed northwest India in the early eleventh century were spurred not by the supposedly inherent nomadism often historically ascribed to them, but instead more likely by the military incursions of Afghani and Turkic forces (the Ghazvanids). Hancock also refuses the highly influential theories of nineteenth-century European scholars who insisted that Roma's Indian ancestors were "untouchables" – the prostitutes, entertainers, beggars, thieves, and slaves of India's lowest castes. Hancock and other contemporary scholars of Romani history have argued that these theories of Roma as perpetual pariahs amount to little more than a projection of Romani poverty and European prejudices onto the distant past. More likely, they argue, Roma's diasporic ancestry comprised upper-caste, skilled warriors and mixed-caste camp followers who first aligned in efforts to resist and repel invading Islamic forces.[36] As Hancock himself concedes, debates over the origins of the Romani diaspora are unlikely to abate anytime soon.[37]

No matter what prompted them to travel the Silk Road, Roma's ancestors ultimately spent several centuries in Persia, Armenia, and the Byzantine Empire – a reality seemingly reflected in the preponderant influence of Persian, Armenian, and Greek on Romani language dialects. In approximately the thirteenth and fourteenth centuries, Roma arrived in the Balkan lands. While some settled, others continued north further into Europe and later, to the west. Extant records chronicle the arrival of Romani groups throughout the fifteenth century in France, Spain, England, Scandinavia, and Poland.

As elsewhere, Roma's arrival into Russia occurred intermittently, over time, and in waves. Scholars have delineated three substantial periods of Romani migration into Russia. As early as the fifteenth century, Roma migrated from the Balkans and Wallachia into present-day Ukraine. Meanwhile, Roma also began in the fifteenth century to enter Russia from the north – that is, by first travelling through Polish and Baltic lands. The immigration of Roma into Russia through Poland intensified in the seventeenth century as increased state persecution in Germany and elsewhere prompted Roma to move east in search of safe haven. By the eighteenth century, the Russian empire was home to a substantial population of both sedentary and nomadic Roma. This population expanded greatly in the late nineteenth century, following the emancipation of Romani slaves in Wallachia and Moldavia in 1855–1856. After several centuries of enslavement in the Danubian Principalities, tens of thousands of emancipated Roma departed for Hungary and the Russian Empire. Further Romani migration into Russia – particularly from Germany, Austria-Hungary, Romania, and the Balkans – continued throughout the turbulence of the early twentieth century and especially in the context of World War I and the Russian revolutions of 1917.[38] By the time of the first Soviet census in 1926, the Bolshevik state counted at least 61,234 Roma among its population, though it recognized these numbers as a low estimate tempered both

by the state's ability to register nomadic Roma and some Roma's un-
willingness to self-identify as belonging to a maligned nationality.[39]

Yet, as this admittedly cursory historical overview of Romani migrations already suggests, it would be a grave error to assume the
homogeneity of the Romani diaspora. Anything but a homogeneous
population, Roma are profoundly diverse – differing not only in language or country of citizenship, but also in terms of culture, history,
religion, lifestyle, occupations, and intraethnic affiliation. The case of
Roma in the former Soviet Union illustrates this inescapable and often
profoundly consequential reality. Though the Soviet state defined its
Romani populations as all belonging to one official nationality – that
is, Gypsies (tsygane) – Roma themselves spoke different dialects of Romani (if they spoke Romani at all) and often found little, if anything, in
common with their fellow Romani citizens. Matters of language, culture, geography, and willingness to engage the Soviet civilizing mission
distinguished and at times even bitterly divided Romani groups in the
Soviet Union. As will be explored later in this book, intraethnic conflicts
imposed very real life and death consequences on Roma living in the
early Soviet period.

Within the former Soviet Union, at least ten Romani dialects are spoken by a Romani population that is further subdivided into groups
that have been described by some as "tribes" or "nations."[40] The larg-
est Romani groups in Russia have historically been the Russka, Servi,
and Vlax Roma. Russka Roma are defined as those whose ancestors immigrated to Russia from Germany and Poland and who settled in the
northern and central regions of European Russia. Roma who arrived in
present-day Ukraine and the southern regions of European Russia in
the fifteenth century after travelling first through the Balkans and Wallachia are known as Servi. The label Vlax – derived from the geographical
term Wallachia – is applied to speakers of the Vlax dialects of Romani.
Having immigrated to Russia in the late nineteenth and early twentieth
centuries primarily from the Romanian Principalities and the Austro-
Hungarian Empire, Vlax Roma in the former Soviet Union include such
self-identifying groups as the Lovara, Kelderara, Ungri, and Machvano.
Yet the Soviet Union was home to other, smaller Romani groups as well,
including Crimean Roma, the Bosha of Transcaucasia, the Liuli of Central Asia (primarily the Uzbek and Tadzhik SSRs), and others.[41]

Given its source base, this book focuses primarily on the fates
of Russka and Vlax Roma living in the RSFSR. Yet Russka and Vlax
voices do not register in the archives on equal footing – and not merely

because of the linguistic, occupational, and cultural differences that distinguished the two groups. By the time of the October Revolution, generations of Russka Roma had long since settled on Russian territory. In Moscow and St. Petersburg especially, the descendants of the Russka Roma who had first immigrated to Russia in the fifteenth through eighteenth centuries were already markedly integrated into Russian society and culture by the late nineteenth century. Indeed, nineteenth-century Russia's fascination with so-called Gypsy choirs had enabled a high degree of social mobility for Russka Romani performers, leading to the development of a self-styled Romani elite in imperial Russia's capitals. Fluent in Russian language and culture (if not in Romani), these Russka elites often prided themselves on their ostensible cultural distance from other, less educated or integrated Roma – especially nomads. In the early Soviet period, many Russka elites actively engaged the Soviet civilizing mission and even joined the ranks of Soviet officialdom.

Vlax Roma, by contrast, were relative newcomers to Russia by the time of the October Revolution, while some arrived on Soviet soil only in the 1920s. Many – especially the most recent immigrants – did not speak Russian well, if at all. Instead, they spoke Romani dialects barely intelligible even to those Russka elites who could speak Romani. Whereas Russka elites had long since established themselves in Moscow and St. Petersburg, Vlax Roma often resided in makeshift tents on the outskirts of the cities and seemed, by stark comparison, bereft of education and culture. Occupationally, Vlax Roma tended towards metalworking and trade, rather than towards artistic performance and state service as did prominent Russka. In the eyes of the Russka elite – and ultimately, of Soviet officialdom – Vlax Roma figured threateningly as potentially irredeemable "backward Gypsies" who obstinately clung to the most despised features of stereotyped Gypsy culture: secretiveness, criminality, patriarchy, illiteracy, filth, and an overriding lack of consciousness.

Thus, it was not merely Roma themselves who perceived differences between the Soviet Union's Russka and Vlax populations. Despite the fact that Soviet officials most often spoke of Gypsies as a homogenous and decidedly "backward" nationality, they also at times distinguished between "our Gypsies" or "Russian Gypsies" (Russka) and "foreign Gypsies" (Vlax). Used by Soviet officials in this way, the label "foreign" had as much to do with Vlax Roma's country of origin or citizenship status as it did with notions of Vlax Roma as the stubborn and socially alien preservationists of backward Gypsy culture.[42]

Although Soviet officialdom stereotyped Vlax Roma specifically as dangerously "socially foreign" in the 1920s and 1930s, it need be underscored that all Romani citizens of the Soviet Union were defined in both the official and popular imagination according to the common stereotypes applied to Roma throughout their history in Europe and into the present day. While surely well known to any reader, these stereotypes deserve brief examination – if for no other reason than that so many Roma who feature in this history often performed these stereotypes while also defying them.

European art, literature, and folklore – including its Russian variants – have long featured Roma as rootless nomads always on the margins of society, isolated from the political, economic, and cultural order of their purported "host populations." With their tambourines, ragged clothing, filth-streaked faces, and bare feet, stereotyped Roma have often aroused both the hostility and admiration of their ostensible others. At one and the same time, Roma inspire images of beguiling thievery, crushing poverty, dangerous disease, pitiable illiteracy, exotic beauty, unbridled licentiousness, nefarious kidnapping, carefree whimsy, and pathological dishonesty. In the European imagination, Roma have been decried as disease-bearing, illiterate, and uncivilized parasites as often as they have been desired for their tempting mystery, fiery passion, and rebellious rejection of "civilization" and "modernity." In accord with such hyperreal visions, the possibility of "the Gypsy" as sedentary, educated, productive, honest, chaste, or simply "ordinary" has most often been relegated to the realm of fantasy.[43]

Wittingly or not, even contemporary practitioners of Romani Studies have contributed to the longevity of some of these stereotypes. Within studies that self-consciously reject essentialist and homogenizing accounts of "the Gypsies," one may still find categorical reference to Roma as stubbornly marginal, resistant to assimilation, rootless, nomadic, otherworldly, and indifferent to the past.[44] Some scholars, meanwhile, represent Roma as the voiceless footnotes to other people's history. Within a framework that examines Roma as eternal victims of state-sponsored persecution or as objects of non-Roma's fascination, revulsion, pity, and activism, Roma scarcely if ever emerge as historical agents in their own right.[45] All too often in scholarly and popular accounts of Roma, it is forgotten or else willingly denied that – to borrow Alaina Lemon's apt phrasing – "there never actually lived an abstract Gypsy."[46]

This book challenges the all-too-common accounts of Roma that deny the purported subjects of their inquiry their rightful claim to human complexity and historical agency. In its focus on Roma as individuals in a variety of circumstances, exhibiting a range of behaviours, and fluent in multiple and at times overlapping cultural milieus, my analysis emphatically rejects the stereotypes that have long fuelled both the scholarly and popular imagination both within and without the former Soviet Union – from the Gypsy as romantic, freewheeling wanderer to the Gypsy as the staunchly antisocial, hoodwinking, filth-loving deviant. It thus calls into question the very same stereotypes that also framed the options (or lack thereof) that Roma faced in their everyday life in the early Soviet Union. While this book addresses the ways in which Soviet nationality policy empowered and otherwise conditioned Soviet subjectivities, it *also* demands historical understanding of Roma that does not resign "the Gypsies" to indifferent marginality and insistent alterity. Roma's minority status in the former Soviet Union or anywhere else does not excuse the simplistic, essentialist accounts that have long presupposed, either implicitly or explicitly, the purported "truth" that Gypsies are "a people living as best they can, outside history."[47]

Indeed, this book welcomes the more rare scholarly voice that has fully challenged us to see not only that Roma defy easy typecasting, but also that Roma – individual historical actors – "are and speak of themselves as connected to local places and pasts."[48] While conducting research for this book in the archives of the former Soviet Union, I found it generally impossible to avoid taking this challenge seriously. Despite the yellowing crinkle of brittle archival documents and the painful blur of imperfect microfilms, the agency of the Roma whose lives are studied here shone through crisply and unmistakably. While the bulk of my sources were authored by and/or concerned with the fates of the Soviet Union's urban Russka Romani elite, I nonetheless encountered a diverse range of Romani voices testifying to an extensive variety of life circumstances, personal histories, and experiences as citizens in the early Soviet Union. More often than not, the archival record revealed not only Roma who were as "ordinary" as any other Soviet citizen could claim to be, but also Roma who were stubbornly insistent on belonging to the Soviet community of citizens, not to mention its tsarist Russian precursor. Had Soviet officialdom fully appreciated these realities, the history explored in this book would likely have been profoundly different.

Organization

Each chapter in this book focuses on how Roma constructed, mobilized, and performed Gypsiness within the framework of the Soviet nationality regime as a means of fashioning themselves as Soviet citizens during the 1920s and 1930s. Where appropriate, individual chapters briefly examine Roma's prerevolutionary history in late imperial Russia, or look ahead to their experiences during and after World War II. Throughout, considerable attention is paid to how shifts in Soviet state priorities produced shifts in Soviet nationality policy that, in turn, affected how and why Roma spoke of and presented themselves as either Gypsy, Soviet, or both. During the 1920s, many Roma awakened to the potentially beneficial possibilities afforded them as minority citizens of the Soviet Union. Yet, as was made clear to Roma by the diminishing opportunities afforded them as Gypsies on the eve of World War II, the value of Gypsiness as an ingredient of their own Sovietness was neither static nor guaranteed. In the second half of the 1930s, most Roma who actively engaged the Soviet nationality regime recognized the waning significance and depreciated asset of Gypsiness as both a claim and a stance and responded accordingly. In describing, representing, and working on themselves, they increasingly invoked their own ongoing mastery and itemized personification of Soviet values. They relied less on the Soviet Union's dwindling state-sponsored Romani institutions and on the category of Gypsy nationality itself as effective tools of self-fashioning.

Chapter 1 explores the All-Russian Gypsy Union, a mutual-aid organization established in 1925 by Romani youth activists who claimed to speak for all of the empire's Roma. The heirs of Moscow's prerevolutionary Romani intelligentsia, Gypsy Union activists endeavoured not only to define what it meant to be a Gypsy in the Soviet Union, but also to organize and direct a civilizing mission directed specifically at their supposedly benighted Romani brethren. As they learned to effectively manoeuvre the Soviet nationality regime, Gypsy Union activists honed the political, cultural, and social skills necessary to assimilate themselves and others to Sovietism.

Chapter 2 focuses on Romani activists' efforts to establish Romani-language primary schools, adult literacy centres, a Romani alphabet, Romani-language textbooks, and teacher-training courses for Roma. These underfunded educational initiatives imparted to Roma not only lessons in literacy or hygiene, but also lessons in navigating the opportunities and pitfalls of the Soviet nationality regime. Though few in number, resource-poor, and short-lived, Romani educational initiatives provided students with a Soviet political education in ways both intended and unintended by the Romani activists and state officials who designed them.

Efforts to "introduce" Moscow's Roma to the world of socially useful labour are explored in chapter 3. The Soviet state regarded those professions traditionally associated with Roma – trading and fortune telling, for example – as socially dangerous pursuits in defiance of legitimate socialist labour. Meanwhile, Gypsies themselves were popularly imagined as social parasites in need of rehabilitation before they could be properly integrated into the socialist economy. In the late 1920s and 1930s, national cooperatives, a Romani-language journal, the rhetoric of class struggle, involuntary resettlement, and penal labour were all tools employed to transform urban Roma from "parasites" into disciplined, socially useful workers.

Chapter 4 examines the Soviet struggle to sedentarize and collectivize Romani nomads in Krasnodar, Smolensk, Volgograd, and other provinces of the empire. The "unproductive" service nomadism of many Roma threatened bureaucratic efforts to rationally organize and mobilize both the Soviet Union's rural population and its economy's agricultural sector. Although Soviet officials theorized national Gypsy collective farms as contained sites of immobilizing, rehabilitating, and assimilating Romani nomads to productive, sedentary agricultural life, they largely refused to prioritize the construction and development of such farms – leaving Romani agricultural settlers to fend for themselves on the neglected sidelines of the socialist economy.

Chapter 5 explores the varied fates of professional Romani choral performers whose popular art was deemed decadent, bourgeois, socially harmful, and even pornographic in the wake of the October Revolution. It focuses in particular on how Leningrad's Ethnographic Theatre and Moscow's Gypsy Theatre Romen confronted the vague demand that they stage the "enthographically authentic Gypsy" whose songs and dances synced with Soviet culture. With varying degrees of success, both theatres struggled to reconcile the contested tradition of Gypsy performance with the ideological shifts of the Stalinist 1930s. For Romani performers, the early Soviet stage proved a perilous, but crucial site of their refashioning into cultured actors and Soviet citizens. Ultimately, the Soviet stage served no less as a site of self-fashioning as it did a key mechanism of promoting stereotypes of Gypsies as thieves, illiterates, and whores – no matter how potentially redeemable.

The combined epilogue and conclusion build from an examination of a series of autobiographies penned by the Soviet Union's most celebrated Gypsy writer, A.V. Germano (1893–1955). Written for bureaucratic consumption between the mid-1920s and early 1950s, Germano's autobiographic texts are representative of the process by which Roma who engaged the distinctly ethnicized version of the Bolshevik civilizing mission sovietized themselves by fashioning themselves first as Gypsies. Germano's evolving life story reflects not only changes in Soviet ideology and nationality policy, but also the shifting opportunities available to Roma to fashion themselves as Soviet citizens within the framework of the Soviet nationality regime. It highlights the Soviet nationality regime as potential field of play in which Germano, for example, deftly contended with shifting opportunities to transform himself into a Gypsy, a conscious Soviet citizen, and even into a self-declared Russian.

Before moving forward, however, it is worth pausing a moment to contemplate the epigraph with which this book begins, words taken from the eighteenth-century German scholar Heinrich Grellmann's *Dissertation on the Gipsies* (1783). With a healthy dose of Enlightenment optimism and an abiding faith in the capacity of the state to reform even a people so often presumed to be "dross," Grellmann reflected on the "problem" that Gypsies posed as perceived by many a modern European state, and not least by the Bolsheviks in the early Soviet Union. The question for Grellmann as well as for the Bolsheviks was how to transform a people seen as pathologically alienated from state, economy, society, and culture into "useful citizens." In still more simple Soviet parlance, this "problem" was articulated in the 1920s and 1930s as the question of how to refashion so-called backward Gypsies into conscious, integrated Soviet citizens. The answer, as this book will show, was found in none other than New Soviet Gypsies themselves.

1 Backward Gypsies, Soviet Citizens: The All-Russian Gypsy Union

In 1926, the People's Commissariat of Enlightenment (Narkompros) conceded that Gypsies posed serious challenges to the Soviet Union's all-encompassing modernization aims. In a memorandum detailing its recent successes in educating minority peoples, Narkompros singled out the empire's Gypsies as a people so peculiar, perplexing, and "backward" that they had thus far escaped the focused attention of political-enlightenment workers. "This nationality," Narkompros officials explained, is:

> extremely scattered – it leads a nomadic way of life and for now has settled only in small part. It lacks ... a written language and is almost universally illiterate; it is isolated from surrounding nationalities; as a consequence of economic needs and poverty, a number of Gypsies tend to such antisocial pursuits as horse-stealing, thievery, begging, and the like; and this provokes distrust among the settled population.

Yet despite their overwhelming "backwardness" and subversive tendencies, Narkompros declared, Gypsies were "still another people (*narodnost'*) that has begun to awake to conscious civic life and to lay their claim to cultural-enlightenment activity."[1]

That the Soviet Union's Gypsies were undergoing a national awakening – or any awakening at all – initially came as encouraging news to Narkompros and other Soviet officials. Soviet nationality policy, after all, did not provide officials with a detailed plan for the transformation of "backward" Gypsies into conscious Soviet citizens. Yet nationality policy did promise minority peoples a generous platform from which *even Gypsies* could transition from backwardness to Sovietism.

Staunchly assimilationist in its logic, the Soviet nationality regime demanded that minority peoples not only slough off centuries of historic backwardness, but also submit to an accelerated program of sovietization tailored to their purportedly specific ethnic needs. Nationality policy theoretically guaranteed minority peoples a banquet feast of rich offerings to aid them in their transformation from backward nationalities into Soviet citizens. From printing presses to territories, from minority-language schools to theatres, national institutions – flush with socialist content – were offered to minority citizens as attractive tools of Soviet self-fashioning, not to mention as compensation for the developmentally stunting oppression they suffered under the imperial Russian regime. The state-sponsored flowering of national cultures in the short term, it was argued, would usher in a supranational socialist unity that would bind like-minded and "advanced" Soviet citizens.[2]

In the first years of Soviet rule, few officials expected representatives of an unheard-of Romani intelligentsia to step forward as political entrepreneurs, let alone to demand that the Soviet state fulfil its promises to all nationalities, and to Roma in particular. Fewer still expected that an organization by the name of the All-Russian Gypsy Union would challenge reigning notions of what it meant to be Soviet. It even occurred to a few officials in Moscow that the appearance of a group of Romani intellectuals preaching the word of Lenin could be nothing more than a conjurer's trick, a typical Gypsy ruse. For a brief period in the mid-1920s, however, many Soviet officials welcomed the All-Russian Gypsy Union and its Romani youth activists as a potentially convenient answer to the empire's thorny "Gypsy question."

This chapter examines the short-lived All-Russian Gypsy Union and the political struggles of its organizers, the heirs of Moscow's prerevolutionary Romani intelligentsia. A product of the largely unscripted opportunities offered minority peoples by Soviet nationality policy, the All-Russian Gypsy Union provided Romani activists a space within which they fashioned themselves into citizens on a civilizing mission and developed the political, cultural, and social skills necessary for engaging the Soviet nationality regime. In their brief tenure as All-Russian Gypsy Union members, Romani activists assimilated the language and mores of Sovietism and learned to make effective political use of both their minority status and ascribed backwardness. Through their embrace of Soviet nationality policy, Moscow's Romani activists assumed the Bolshevik mission to incarnate the merger between civilizer and civilized. Shrewdly asserting themselves not only as "backward Gypsies," but also as Soviet citizens, All-Russian Gypsy Union activists integrated themselves and others into the Soviet project. Although Gypsiness was officially regarded as the antithesis of the advanced civilization promised Roma by the October Revolution, the All-Russian Gypsy Union and its Romani activists nonetheless came to embody the Soviet ideal of a modern citizenry composed of conscious, self-mastering, and enlightened individuals. The All-Russian Gypsy Union starkly reveals the creative capacity of minority peoples to energetically deploy Bolshevik nationality policy in both the pursuit and achievement of their own Soviet self-fashioning.

Late Imperial Russia's Romani Intelligentsia

In memoirs composed for a late socialist audience, I.I. Rom-Lebedev vividly recalled his first glimpse of "a live Gypsy." Then a small child living with his maternal Russian grandmother in fin-de-siècle Vilnius, Rom-Lebedev was startled one day when a swarthy male stranger unexpectedly knocked at his grandmother's door. After exchanging pleasantries with the home's matriarch and offering sweets to the children, this "dark-faced" man abruptly departed, taking Rom-Lebedev's sisters with him. Though this encounter terribly confused Rom-Lebedev at the time, he soon learned that the visitor, I.G. Lebedev, was none other than his own father. This, then, was not merely Rom-Lebedev's first memory of "a live Gypsy." It was his first memory of his very own father.[3]

Prior to being reunited with his father in Vilnius, Rom-Lebedev had imagined Gypsies through the lens of one of his toys – a Gypsy marionette with a face "as dark as coal," a "thick, dishevelled beard," and a sack filled with the terrorized faces of abducted children. Troubled by this menacing image, he often manipulated the puppet's strings, making it dance. "Because the Gypsy submitted to me and obediently danced," Rom-Lebedev explained, "I was not afraid of him."[4] This fictional Gypsy presumably kept Rom-Lebedev company in the newfound absence of his sisters.

Two years later, in 1911, Rom-Lebedev travelled to Moscow to be reunited with his parents and siblings. Ten years old at the time, he initially found the transition to be startlingly painful. Rom-Lebedev's was a double burden of estrangement. He felt himself a stranger in his own family and an alien among Gypsies. In Vilnius, Rom-Lebedev had feared Gypsies as mysterious cheats and fearsome criminals. Now he lived at the heart of one of Moscow's "Gypsy regions" – Petrovskii Park – and played in a courtyard that doubled as the social centre for his female Romani neighbours. "What kind of Gypsy are you?" the women ritually asked Rom-Lebedev, chiding him for not understanding the Romani language. The young Rom-Lebedev did not speak Romani, nor did his brothers and sisters. Only when his parents argued or discussed important matters behind closed doors, he recalled, did he and his siblings hear Romani words spoken in their home.[5]

Rom-Lebedev's parents, Ivan Grigor'evich and Mariia Nikolaevna Lebedev, rarely spent time at home with their children. Busy entertainers who worked late into the night, the Lebedevs capitalized on the "Gypsy mania" that had ensnared late imperial Russia's nobles, intellectuals, and merchants.[6] Ivan Grigor'evich directed one of Moscow's most famed Romani choirs in which Maria Nikolaevna starred as a soloist. The Lebedevs' celebrated choir performed nightly at Moscow's luxurious Strel'na restaurant – a premier venue of late imperial Russian nightlife where the empire's elites and entrepreneurs commingled as they consumed not only expensive meals and libations, but also the beloved exotica of Gypsy music.[7] The young Rom-Lebedev thus witnessed the daily routine of the "entire Gypsy population of the neighbourhood" trailing his parents each evening as they headed towards Strel'na and its clientele.[8]

Looking back on his childhood, Rom-Lebedev recognized that his family – the rare type within his milieu that categorically spoke Russian instead of Romani – stood somehow apart from its Romani neighbours. Rom-Lebedev's parents rarely invited neighbours into their home or socialized with their fellow choristers outside of the restaurant. Though Rom-Lebedev to a certain degree attributed his family's aloofness to his father's authoritative position as choir director and stern demeanour, he also astutely understood that his family was a member of an internal elite – the Romani intelligentsia. Propriety insisted that the Lebedevs distance themselves from their less cultivated, more conspicuously Gypsy neighbours.

Thus, the Lebedevs typically invited Romani neighbours to their home only for holiday celebrations. At the Lebedev home, Christmas, New Year's, and Easter were times not only of social gathering, but also of social distinction. Guests greeted Rom-Lebedev's parents with a bow before being invited to a table that was set according to "Gypsy tradition." Together they ate, drank, celebrated, and discussed the choir's

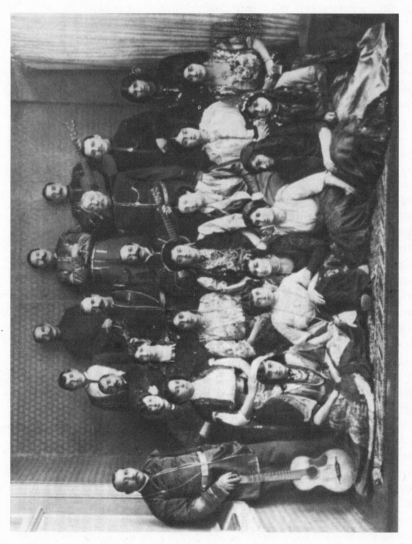

Representatives of the Romani choir directed by Ivan Grigor'evich Lebedev in 1910. From Ivan Rom-Lebedev, *Ot tsyganskogo khora k teatru "Romen"* (Moscow: Iskusstvo, 1990).

business matters. "For some reason," Rom-Lebedev noticed, "none of the guests ever sang or danced. To do so was considered unsophisticated (*ne intelligentno*)."[9]

Yet the Lebedevs and other Romani intelligentsia families were not alone in their concern with self-presentation and social distinction. Petrovskii Park was alight with strivings towards cultural sophistication. "Choir Gypsies" who worked at Moscow's premier restaurants, Rom-Lebedev explained, "considered themselves to be close to high society." In their daily interactions with society's luminaries, members of Russia's elite Romani choirs learned to pattern their lifestyle according to the dictates of aristocratic custom. So saturated were their lives with the ways of Russia's elites, Rom-Lebedev maintained, that "choir Gypsies involuntarily 'acquired polish,' assimilated good manners, knew how to behave themselves at a table, knew how to eat, drink, and dress finely ... and even tried to converse with each other in a cultivated way (*po-intelligentnomu*)." While these may have been only "superficial signs of culture (*intelligentnost'*)," Rom-Lebedev argued, "this manner of socializing affected the upbringing of Gypsy children." After all, Russia's Romani choir elites did more than teach their children table manners and outfit them in expensive clothing. They also enrolled them in exclusive gymnasia. It was the children of fin-de-siècle Moscow's Romani choirs, Rom-Lebedev emphasized, who benefited most from this social striving. Children, after all, were formally educated while "the parents remained semiliterate."[10]

The emergence of a Romani intelligentsia in Russia's urban capitals can be traced back to the establishment of professional Romani choirs in the late eighteenth and early nineteenth centuries. Count A.G. Orlov established the first professional Romani choir in Russia outside of Moscow in 1774. Directed by a Rom, I.T. Sokolov, Orlov's choir rapidly acquired fame among Muscovite nobles and wealthy merchants. Moscow's elites eagerly invited the choir to perform at balls and other lavish celebrations. Orlov rewarded the choir's performers by freeing them from servitude in 1807. Previously Orlov's privately owned serfs, these Romani performers were now free to settle in Moscow.[11]

Professional Romani choirs proliferated throughout the nineteenth century as their performances of Russian folk songs and "Gypsy romances" brought prestige to their wealthy patrons. In restaurants and private homes across the empire, Romani choirs performed for those who could afford the high price of their entertainment. The Romologist

Bernard Gilliat-Smith portrayed the veritable "cult" of Romani choirs in imperial Russia in this way:

> After dinner at a club with some friends some one says 'Let's go to the Gypsies,' and the whole party drives to certain restaurants in the vicinity of the Gypsy quarter, a 'chief' is called, who produces a choir of some thirty to forty men and girls. Those who have the best voices sing the famous so-called 'Gypsy Romances,' accompanied by the choir, singing and strumming guitars. If you so desire, one of the Gypsy girls will come and sit with you and entertain you for several hours with conversation, occasionally humming your favorite tunes, while you feast your eyes on her and drink unceasingly. A huge amount of roubles is paid to the chief for this entertainment.[12]

Romanticized and exoticized in the literary works of Pushkin, Dostoevsky, Turgenev, Tolstoy, and other Russian writers, Gypsies appealed to Russian elites with the intoxicating "wildness" of their singing, dancing, and appearance. It became stylish for Russian noblemen to marry Romani women.[13] The popularity of Romani choirs was so great that Lev Tolstoy described Russia's nineteenth century as a time "when no music was loved more than Gypsy, when Gypsies sang old Russian choral songs."[14]

Responding to the nobility's great demand, many nomadic and previously enserfed Roma found employment in Romani choirs and settled in Moscow and St. Petersburg. Family connections dictated the composition of the professional choirs, and a series of surnames dominates the history of Romani music in imperial Russia. The Sokolov, Vasil'iev, Shishkin, Pankov, Masal'skii, Il'inskii, and Baurov families emerged as Russia's first Romani choir dynasties, and were later joined by the Poliakov, Paninin, Dul'kevich, and Lebedev families. The heads of these families directed the choirs that bore their names and served as leaders among the Romani communities of St. Petersburg and Moscow. In business as well as in private matters, a choir director's word was final. The members of Romani choirs lived together as in a "little commune," typically occupying most of a building's apartments.[15]

The directors of prestigious Romani choirs in late imperial Russia were dedicated to preserving aristocratic decorum in the performances of their charges. The reputedly "puritanical" directors of elite Romani choirs hawkishly guarded the honour of female performers and forbade all employees from drinking alcohol alongside clients.[16] Maintaining the "purity" of their choirs was one way for Romani elites to define themselves against the "primitive" Gypsies of the Russian imagination. For imperial Russia's Romani elites, their demonstrable commitment to propriety and civility markedly distinguished them from those other Gypsies living in Russia's capitals and posing as professional entertainers – those lowbrow members of "wild, semi-nomadic choirs" who allegedly read fortunes more often than they sang.[17]

Yet for Romani choir elites in late imperial Russia, perhaps nothing signified their own respectability more than their well-groomed appearance. This attention to fine dress had deep roots. Russia's first professional choir, the Sokolov, had from its beginnings donned the same styles worn by their clientele, establishing a tradition of Romani choirs' preference for "European" dress.[18] In Rom-Lebedev's view, this was the only logical choice. "At the end of the eighteenth century," he wrote, "Gypsies in Russia already wore Russian caftans, shirts, waistcoats, boots, caps, and drank tea from Tula samovars." In fact, he continued, it was "only nomadic Gypsy women" who wore iconic brightly coloured, wide-flowing skirts – the kind that allowed them to "freely walk the roads."[19] Thus, Russia's first Romani choirs displayed "Gypsy women festively dressed, in gold embroidered shawls fastened to one shoulder, in necklaces and earrings made from fine gold coins" and men in "white caftans with gold braids."[20]

By mid-century, patrons began complaining that the choirs' female performers in particular did not dress like real Gypsies, leading some choir directors to further cater to their clients' demand for the exotic. Many, like Rom-Lebedev's father, struck a compromise. The women in his choir dressed in brightly coloured skirts chosen to resemble those supposedly worn by their "wild" nomadic counterparts. Female soloists, however, performed in expensive evening gowns and lace or silk shawls. The men of Lebedev's choir wore tuxedos, dyed their mustaches, and slicked back their hair. These "were not Gypsies," Rom-Lebedev wrote, "but gentlemen!"[21]

While growing up in Moscow, Rom-Lebedev was surrounded by Gypsiness though not defined by it. His parents, Rom-Lebedev later understood, doggedly attempted to shield him from the subservience of "Gypsy restaurant life." He and his siblings were educated in elite schools, tended to by domestic servants, and given fine clothes. They grew up alongside the like-minded children of other prosperous Romani choir directors in Moscow. Rom-Lebedev, his siblings, and peers watched as their parents invited wealthy merchants and other high-society figures into their homes but closed their doors to "unsophisticated" Gypsies. The children of Russia's Romani intelligentsia were raised to regard nomadic Roma as dirty and less civilized, and knew that the Romani beggars and fortune tellers who crowded Moscow's train stations regarded them, the choir elites, as "bootlickers."[22]

The Vanguard of the Gypsy Proletariat

The February Revolution of 1917 scarcely interrupted the lives of Moscow's Romani elites. When the Bolsheviks seized power in October, however, life quickly changed for Russia's Romani choirs. "Restaurant life," Rom-Lebedev lamented, "having securely fed entire generations of Moscow's and Petersburg's choir Gypsies, was suddenly cut short."[23] Romani elites in Russia's urban centres were hard-pressed to align with the Bolshevik's dictatorship of the proletariat and to disassociate themselves from imperial Russia's nobles and merchants. Having catered to the "bourgeoisie" for over a century, Romani elites and their craft were now ideologically suspect. For them, revolution, civil war, and War Communism spelled disaster. The restaurants where they had once performed nightly closed, and their clients were anathematized. The Bolsheviks demanded not sentimental romances, nor exotic women for bourgeois eyes to feast on, but instead dedication to Soviet socialism and a new revolutionary culture. Russia's Romani choirs quickly dissolved, leaving their performers to scramble in search of alternative livelihoods.

Rom-Lebedev recalled bitter disputes arising among the members of his father's now defunct choir. They debated the prospects for finding a place for Gypsy music in the new Soviet culture, and debated, too, just who exactly these Bolsheviks and proletarians were. A number of choir performers, according to Rom-Lebedev, fell back on "traditional" professions that choir elites had formerly disdained as the questionable livelihoods of less civilized Roma: horse-trading and gambling. Some resumed former nomadic lifestyles, while others took to travelling for the first time.[24] A few Romani choir elites fought on the side of the Whites in the Civil War, and others emigrated to Yugoslavia, France, or Morocco. Many of the choir elites' children, however, chose to work in factories, further pursue their education, or join the Red Army.[25]

Still others did not give up on finding a way to integrate Gypsy music into the evolving Bolshevik culture. The first to reap success in this venture was N.N. Kruchinin, the son of N.I. Khlebnikov, a renowned

Romani choir director of the late nineteenth century. Khlebnikov was one of a few Romani choir leaders of his time who had graduated from secondary school. Recognized by his peers as a particularly cultured person, Khlebnikov insisted that his own son receive a higher education. As a young adult, Kruchinin refused to perform in his father's choir, considering such work an "insurmountable [professional] barrier for a cultured person." Though Kruchinin pursued an acting career, he "zealously" collected the songs and folklore of Russian Roma in his spare time.[26] In 1916, he began directing his own choir and organized a concert series known as "Evenings of Gypsy Singing." His work studying Romani folklore and music also led him to join the ethnographic department of the Rumiantsevskii Museum.[27]

After the revolution, Kruchinin approached officials at Narkompros to inform them of the "impoverished situation of the Gypsy choirs, of the meaning of Gypsy art within the general musical life of the country, about classical scholars' opinion of [Gypsy] art."[28] In 1920, he organized members of prerevolutionary Romani choirs into a new ensemble under his lead and registered his Studio of Old Gypsy Art in the musical department of Narkompros. Kruchinin's Studio distanced itself from the "bourgeois decadence" associated with prerevolutionary Romani choirs, and the ensemble's performances quickly came to be known for their "academic character."[29] In between musical numbers, Kruchinin and his performers would recite classical poetry with Gypsy themes and lecture audiences on Gypsy music's influence on Russian composers, writers, and poets. Members of Kruchinin's choir were required to study music as well as Romani history and culture.[30]

Ultimately, it was the introduction of Lenin's New Economic Policy (NEP) that allowed other Romani performers to reassert their art, and not necessarily in the "academic" fashion of Kruchinin's choir. In this regard, one of the earliest and most successful of the resurgent Romani choirs established during NEP was that of E.A. Poliakov. Born in 1871, Poliakov was heir to the Romani choir dynasty that his forbears had firmly established in both Moscow and St. Petersburg. At the age of sixteen, Poliakov began performing at Moscow's most prestigious venue for Gypsy music, the restaurant Iar, and soon began directing his own choir. For nearly thirty years, Poliakov's choir performed at Iar and mixed daily with Russian society's luminaries. In the wake of the October Revolution, however, Iar was shuttered and Poliakov's choir collapsed. For a few years, Poliakov grudgingly worked as a labourer in a bakery, though he bitterly longed to return to the stage.[31]

Fortunately for Poliakov, NEP led to the reopening of restaurants, cafes, and taverns. The scourge of disillusioned Bolsheviks, the NEPmen, spent freely on entertainment. Realizing that there was again a chance to make a living as a choir director, Poliakov gathered the former members of I.G. Lebedev's choir and his own. Once again, imperial Russia's Romani choir elites profitably sang and danced in Moscow's premier restaurants – Iar, Strel'na, Praga, and Ermitazh. Choir members joined the Circus and Variety trade union, and as the Poliakov choir grew in popularity, they began performing in concert halls and other fashionable venues throughout the Soviet Union.[32]

Within Poliakov's choir stirred a youthful cohort – the children of the Romani intelligentsia – ready to avail themselves of new opportunities offered "backward minorities" by Soviet nationality policy.[33] In his memoirs, Rom-Lebedev described his friends as "militant" youths energized by revolutionary fervour and a desire to lead their fellow Gypsies onto the path of Soviet enlightenment. Rom-Lebedev recalled, "We fiercely struggled against the relics of the past, of intransigence, of habits hindering the new from taking hold in the lives of the old Gypsy choirs."[34] These young "militants" argued with their parents and even left home – all vain efforts, they decided, in attempting to transform the outdated ways of their choir elders. They soon opted to take an institutionalized approach to assaulting Gypsy "backwardness."

In January 1923, Rom-Lebedev and his friends registered with their regional Party committee and organized a local Communist Youth League (Komsomol) cell exclusively for Roma in Moscow. They committed to spreading enlightenment among "backward Gypsies" and to battling fortune telling, begging, and other anachronistic "relics" of Gypsiness.[35] With the help of their trade union, the new Komsomol members created a red corner for their cell in Petrovskii Park. They decorated their red corner with posters on "Gypsy themes" and filled it with old books and journals that they had taken from home. To the youths' dismay, Moscow's Roma greeted their enthusiasm with silence. "In those first days," Rom-Lebedev recalled, "we amused ourselves with games of checkers and dominoes. We looked through the yellowed journals, trying to kill time in our completely empty [red] corner."[36]

The youths patiently invited neighbours to visit their red corner and to join them in discussions of Roma's future in the Soviet Union. Soon, Petrovskii Park's Roma began trickling into the novice Komsomol cell. Visitors competed in games of checkers, examined the propaganda posters, and borrowed from the cell's makeshift library, but rarely expressed interest in the youths' vision for a Gypsy cultural revolution. The Komsomol youths nonetheless soldiered onward and even organized a small Romani contingent for Moscow's May Day celebrations. With a banner reading "Gypsy Workers of the World, Unite!" the youths marched alongside other minority groups in an attempt to represent Roma as "useful, loyal," and integrated Soviet citizens.[37]

Given their political marginality, lack of resources, and pitifully small numbers, Rom-Lebedev and his fellow youth activists soon accepted that their plans to revolutionize the lives of "backward Gypsies" were "grandiose and practically infeasible." They also recognized that they could do little but dream without the help and resources of the Soviet bureaucracy. In coming to this realization, Moscow's Romani activists took keen notice of a recent growth of state-sponsored organizations devoted to the "cultural advancement" of various national minorities. "Naturally," Rom-Lebedev explained, "among the [youths] arose the question: why not organize a mutual-aid society in Moscow that would conduct work among Gypsies?"[38]

The youths decided to pose this question to their community and convened a general meeting of Petrovskii Park's Roma. The Romani youths did their best to convince their audience that, as one activist later put it, "Gypsies must also participate" in the creation of a new, Soviet way of life.[39] It was thus necessary, the Komsomol youths instructed, for Roma to organize and educate themselves. Yet, while the activists gained their neighbours' support for the creation of a Romani mutual-aid society, others rebuffed them. When they took their ideas to Moscow's horse markets to convince Romani traders to join in their efforts, for example, the traders brushed the youths aside. The young activists, however, continued to spread their message through the city's various Romani networks, winning a few new sympathizers along the way.[40]

Notably, the move towards the formal creation of a mutual-aid organization for Moscow's Roma was initially a joint effort on the part of the Komsomol youths and their elders in Poliakov's choir. In early January 1924, ten members of Poliakov's choir met to discuss the establishment of the Society for the Organization of the Proletarian Backward Gypsy Masses of Moscow and Moscow Province. Electing Poliakov and another choir elder as the group's cochairmen, the organization's founding members established their primary goal as the "union of the backward proletarian Gypsy masses on the territory of Moscow Province in a society of the collective creativity of labour."

Two weeks later, the activists drafted their first application to the Moscow City Soviet (Mossovet) for approval of their proposed association. Here, the activists conceived of their organization as the central command for the Soviet Union's battle with Gypsies' immeasurable "backwardness" – their nomadism, aversion to labour, illiteracy, and even physical degeneration. The society proposed to open elementary schools for Romani children and literacy programs for adults. It sought to establish clubs, libraries, and industrial workshops where Roma could learn trade skills. The activists also promised to prepare nomads for "the transition to a settled way of life." They limited their activism to Moscow Province, but declared, "All Gypsies – not excluding other nationalities – can become members of the society."[41]

In this, their first appeal for official recognition, the activists explicitly embraced the goal of integrating Roma into a broader Soviet culture, but did so by implicitly playing on reigning stereotypes of their nationality. While their focus was clearly trained on Roma's education and adaptation to a productive and settled way of life, the drafters of the application did not speak directly of illiteracy or nomadism as endemic to Roma. They proposed the creation of industrial workshops without specifically mentioning begging, horse-trading, black-market speculation, fortune telling, or other subversive professions attributed to "backward Gypsies." They also downplayed Roma's language particularities. While arguing for schools and other educational facilities, for example, they did not advocate Romani-language instruction. Yet perhaps most glaring was the organizers' omission of any reference to Soviet nationality policy. Whether for these reasons or others, Mossovet ignored the activists' proposal.[42]

With their proposal caught in the grips of a bureaucratic stranglehold at Mossovet, Romani activists busily reorganized their society and refined their approach to Soviet officialdom. The Romani youths quickly assumed leadership of the so-called "Action Committee of Member-Founders of the Gypsy Proletarian Society."[43] In late summer, they elected a newcomer, A.S. Taranov, as their chairman. Unlike the majority of Romani activists in Moscow, Taranov was neither a native Muscovite nor a performer with ties to Russia's prerevolutionary Romani choirs. Hailing from Siberia, the young Taranov had volunteered to serve in the Red Army, joined the Communist Party in 1922, and recently graduated from Moscow's Communist University of the Toilers of the East. Meanwhile, all ten of the action committee's members described themselves as proletarians, three had served in the Red

Army, three were Communist Party members, and three were Komsomol members. While the eldest were aged fifty-four and fifty-five years
respectively, the majority of Romani activists were in their twenties
or thirties.[44] Together, they fashioned themselves the vanguard of the
Gypsy proletariat.

Under its new youth leadership, the Society decided to bypass Mossovet and seek recognition from higher up. In the summer of 1924, the
activists approached the Central Executive Committee of the USSR
(TsIK) and the Nationalities Department of the All-Russian Central Executive Committee (VTsIK) with their designs for a Romani mutual-aid
society. By this time, Romani activists had learned how best to capture
the attention of Soviet bureaucrats. In particular, they had recognized
the utility of emphasizing "Gypsy backwardness" and invoking the
ideological underpinnings of nationality policy.

Thus, in a revised statement addressed to Soviet officials, the activists
justified the need for their Society by itemizing the dangerous afflic-
tions of "the Gypsy proletarian masses." Romani choral performers,
the activists explained, suffered in so far as their livelihood was an art
that had long since been corrupted by bourgeois ideology. Out of sync
with Soviet culture, they argued, the "backward art" of Gypsy choirs
alienated not only performers, but also their audiences from the Soviet
reconstruction of life. Moreover, they explained, the "Gypsy proletarian masses" were not familiar with the ways of labour, thus lending
themselves to "defects such as robbery, thievery, fraud, and prostitution." Given their "nomadic way of life," Gypsies were constantly travelling and "involuntarily spreading" their infectious backwardness and
devious ways – thereby threatening "the peasant and working population" and the stability of the empire itself. The activists concluded that
the "only acceptable" option for transforming backward Gypsies into
productive Soviet citizens was to endow their organization with the
power and means to re-educate the "Gypsy proletarian masses."[45]

In a modified version of the proposed organization's statutes, the
activists emphasized the purported needs of Gypsies as a backward
minority people. Their main goal remained the "the raising of [Gyp-
sies'] cultural level" – a task they sought to achieve through the creation
of educational institutions, a club, industrial cooperatives, agricultural
communes, and a mutual-aid register specifically for Roma. For the
first time, the activists declared their intention to publish newspapers,
journals, and other literature in the Romani language. Lastly, the Society committed itself to conducting "a moral struggle with the social evil

present among its own members, such as: drunkenness, fortune telling, gambling, and others."[46]

With the support of the Nationalities Department of VTsIK, the action committee again approached Mossovet in August 1924 to inquire about the status of their languishing application. To the Romani activists' dismay, a disdainful secretary informed them that Mossovet would not approve their application given the Society's "speculative goals." The "appalled" Romani activists argued at length against the perceived injustice of Mossovet's distortion of their aims to no avail. Yet the activists still had reason to hope. Having recently enlisted the help of the Nationalities Department of VTsIK, they were convinced that Mossovet's "abnormal attitude" towards Roma would be corrected and that recognition of their Society would quickly follow.[47] Despite their continued efforts, however, the Romani activists' aspirations were stymied for at least another eight months as their requests continued to be ignored.[48] Frustrated by the Soviet bureaucracy, the vanguard of the Gypsy proletariat waited impatiently for its desired cultural revolution.

Waking Sleeping Beauty

In his memoirs, activist N.A. Pankov referred to 23 July 1925 as a "great day in the history of the Gypsy people."[49] On that day, and following a year and half since the Romani activists' first organizational meeting, the People's Commissariat of Internal Affairs (NKVD) approved the establishment of the All-Russian Gypsy Union (Gypsy Union) in Moscow. The Gypsy Union's newly approved statutes declared the activists' mission to refashion Gypsy nomads, beggars, speculators, and drunkards into conscious, integrated Soviet citizens. The sovietization of backward Gypsies was to be achieved through the creation of a variety of national institutions – Gypsy schools, cooperatives, agricultural communes, and a theatre. Finally, in exchange for official sanction, Gypsy Union leaders submitted to bureaucratic policing and oversight on the part of the NKVD and the Nationalities Department of VTsIK.[50]

In August, the Gypsy Union convened its first official meeting and held elections for its leadership positions. Members re-elected Taranov and Rom-Lebedev as chair and secretary respectively, and promoted eleven new members to the Gypsy Union's central governing board. The list of board members easily could have been mistaken for an outdated advertisement for imperial Russia's Romani choirs. Nearly all of the Gypsy Union's leaders descended from Russia's prerevolutionary choral dynasties. The children of imperial Russia's Romani intelligentsia had retained their parents' elitist aspirations and adapted them to the new Soviet culture.[51] Confidently, this self-declared "group of cultured, toiling Gypsies" set out to civilize their "backward" brethren.[52]

Yet if their brief organizational experience had taught the Gypsy Union's founders anything, it was that they were in no position to achieve their ambitious goals without the state's institutional and material support. Experience had also proven that their own purported "Gypsy backwardness" was their sole source of bargaining power vis-à-vis Soviet bureaucrats. Yet the Gypsy Union's leaders also realized that in lobbying for state resources, they needed to underscore not only Gypsies' ascribed backwardness, but also their own intimate knowledge of nationality policy and its generous offerings.

With these considerations in mind, the Gypsy Union's governing board drafted a memo to the Presidium of VTsIK entitled "On Work Among Gypsies." In their opening salvo, Moscow's Romani activists praised the Soviet government for its visionary efforts to liberate "backward nomadic and seminomadic peoples" from the chains of tsarist oppression. Lenin's nationality policy, they intoned, had laid the groundwork for "all national minorities ... to build their own culture" and "to stand on equal footing with the country's revolutionary cadre." Yet for all of nationality policy's successes in bringing backward minorities from the darkness of tsarist oppression into the light of Soviet civilization, the Gypsy Union activists insisted, "one nationality ... has not yet been given proper attention." They referred, of course, to Gypsies – a "ragged, dark, dirty" people, they claimed, who aimlessly wandered the empire, pathetically scrounging for sustenance. And it was Gypsies – they and their constituents – who most desperately needed nationality policy's salvation.

Seeking their readers' sympathy, the Gypsy Union's leaders blamed Gypsies' "backwardness" and "isolation" neither on Soviet officials nor on Gypsies themselves. They instead indicted the capitalist-imperialist world, invoking the long history of Gypsies' own personal "Golgotha." As told by Romani activists, the story of Gypsies' "complete and utter bloody slaughter" began with their arrival in western Europe in the seventeenth century. Here, Gypsies' "black colour" and suspicious multilingualism prompted their persecution, enslavement, and even attempted "extermination." Imperial Russia, they argued, treated Gypsies no differently. Under the tsars, they wrote, "our landlords excelled in the art of persecuting Gypsies." These, the Gypsy Union claimed, were the origins of Gypsies' pitiable life of nomadism, fortune telling, begging, and thievery. Hounded by their enemies, Gypsies isolated themselves in self-defence and suffered the scourge of backwardness as a result.[53]

Here, the activists emphasized Gypsies' particular historic legacy of oppression and marginality that both spanned Europe *and* rooted itself in prerevolutionary Russian soil. The implications of their rhetoric of Gypsies' extremity of backwardness were far-reaching. They insisted that Gypsies in Russia were not only cruelly persecuted and developmentally stunted, but also untainted by the patronage of and co-optation by tsarist elites. Unlike "more advanced" nationalities within the Soviet Union like the Germans or Finns, Gypsies could claim a position of both severe backwardness *and* historic purity.[54] Although Roma shared access to this rhetorical strategy with other minorities considered extraordinarily backward, the Gypsy Union activists inflected their analysis with stress on Gypsies' incomparable history of pan-European persecution. Thus, they implied that the Soviet state owed Gypsies not only the preferential treatment promised all minority peoples, but also a special and deserving generosity in state aid towards their advancement as a people plagued by a distinct and honourable historic suffering. Not for the last time, the Gypsy Union activists would marry their claims of Gypsies' exceptional backwardness to a rhetoric of historical innocence. Unfortunately, they insisted, the October Revolution had little affected the lives of Soviet Gypsies, and thus the Gypsy Union had inherited the historic role of leading their "backward" brethren in their "struggle for new life." It was high time for the state to join the Gypsy Union in vigorously eradicating the legacy of Gypsies' dignified suffering at the hands of capitalist oppressors – both in imperial Russia and abroad. It was time, at long last, for the unrestrained realization of Soviet nationality policy's promises to Gypsies.

In an unabashed claim on state resources, the Gypsy Union repeatedly referenced Soviet nationality policy as the only potential cure for Gypsies' countless ills. Striving towards the "involvement of the Gypsy masses in the course of social life," the Gypsy Union's leaders committed to "the destruction of the factual inequality in which our nationality finds itself vis-à-vis other national minorities." This political, social, cultural, and economic inequality was untenable in a state ideologically devoted to forcing all nationalities to be free from "backwardness." After all, the Gypsy Union instructively declared, "Soviet power, as the Union of workers and peasants of all nationalities, demands the equal participation of all nationalities in the construction of the economy and the state." No nationality could be ignored or excluded – not even Gypsies. Therefore, activists argued, the state had no choice but to help the Gypsy Union in uplifting Gypsies from the depths of their benightedness. Who else but Gypsies themselves, the activists implied, could possibly reach the "Gypsy masses" and lead them through the cultural transformation demanded of all the empire's backward peoples?[55]

In work plans created in ensuing months, Gypsy Union members relentlessly invoked backwardness, marginality, and darkness when describing and claiming to speak for Gypsies. "With the exception of a few individuals," they claimed, "our people (*narodnost'*) has been completely alien" to "social movements" and has always "stood to the side (*stoiala v storone*), never making known its own interests." Gypsies, the activists declared, "had laid not a single brick" in the construction of society. As a nationality, Gypsies were not merely "backward" or marred by an inherent "antisocial" tendency. They were, the activists bluntly declared, only at the "first stage of human development." In sum, the Gypsy Union's leaders concluded, Gypsies personified all those terrible qualities of the human condition that the Soviet Union sought to eradicate. It was time, they announced, for a Gypsy "cultural renaissance (*vozrozhdenie*)."

The activists' heightened rhetoric extended to their new phrasing and justification of their agenda. Whereas in earlier statements, Romani activists had serenely expressed the desire to open schools for children and to organize literacy programs for adults, the Gypsy Union now militantly committed itself "to struggle with universal illiteracy" among Roma. It was no longer simply necessary to establish a club, red corners, and libraries. Now, the activists realized the explicit need "to develop" Roma's "social and cultural self-awareness" and to inspire in them an "aspiration for self-improvement (*stremlenie k samosovershenstvovaniiu*)." Romani women, in particular, needed to be liberated "from the yoke of family and from man's domination." Once unshackled from traditional patriarchy, the Gypsy Union argued, Romani women could realize their own power, reject fortune telling and begging, and engage in socially useful work. Indeed, the Gypsy Union needed to smash all centuries-old traditions before "backward Gypsies" could transform themselves into productive citizens.[56]

Lest the activists come off as too confident, they declared even the necessity for their own self-improvement. The activists admitted that even among many of the Gypsy Union's most committed members, there existed not even "an elementary understanding of the workers' state and the history of the Party." The more or less "advanced" among them were therefore to lead others in coming to a deeper understanding of the Party and its history. Their goal was also to ensure that "a comrade could generally manage with a book or newspaper, could learn how to draw up a plan, summary, and report." The wider political enlightenment spread among the Gypsy Union's members, it was agreed, the more effective they would be in planting "a political and social seedbed of culture" from which Roma would emerge reborn into Soviet life. In order to plant this seedbed, the Gypsy Union needed to establish schools, literacy programs, a theatre, and a central club for "rest and rational entertainment."[57]

Gypsy Union activists, however, soon faced the problem of having to explain why they were more effective in refining their rhetorical skills than they were in producing practical results. In early 1926, Gypsy Union members appraised their first six months and conceded the slow pace of their enlightenment work. While they had helped organize three Romani-language schools in Moscow and enrolled Romani adults in literacy and workers' training courses, the activists had accomplished little in terms of establishing a central Romani club, red corners, or a theatre. As for their "struggle with nomadism," Gypsy Union activists could only vaguely attest to having provided the Central Committee of the Communist Party and the People's Commissariat of Agriculture (Narkomzem) with "relevant material" regarding the settlement of Roma in an unnamed "southern region."

In matters of internal organization, the Gypsy Union had much more to boast about. Within Moscow, the Gypsy Union delineated three regions of concentrated Romani settlement that were each headed by a regional leader selected from the central governing board. Altogether, the Gypsy Union claimed 330 Muscovite members in its sixth month of existence. Yet the Gypsy Union's influence had already extended beyond Moscow Province. By early 1926, Gypsy Union activists vaunted affiliate groups in Leningrad, Chernigov, Vladimir, and Smolensk. As explained by Gypsy Union activists, the development of regional satellite groups was unavoidable, given that Roma throughout the empire had enthusiastically written to the Gypsy Union's central command in Moscow announcing their dedication to establishing local affiliates.[58] One such letter, signed "Gypsy S." and addressed to "Moscow's Gypsy organization," pleaded for instructions on how best to organize "comrade Gypsies" in the provinces. Like those who had inspired him,

"Gypsy S." also underscored the backwardness of his people.[59] While the fate of "Gypsy S." remains unclear, Roma in both the Ukrainian and Belorussian SSRs organized Gypsy Union cells – at least on paper – in 1926. At one of the Belorussian Gypsy Union's organizational meetings, members agreed: "The Gypsy nation (*natsiia*), like the fairy-tale Sleeping Beauty, had been woken from deep slumber by the enchantress-revolution."[60] Now it remained for the Romani activists to institute practical changes necessary for the cultivation of New Soviet Gypsies. For this to occur, however, the Gypsy Union desperately needed money.

The Struggle for Resources and Legitimacy

Once given official sanction, Gypsy Union members did not hesitate to campaign for state funding. In October 1925, the Gypsy Union requested support from the Council of People's Commissars (Sovnarkom) in the sum of 59,600 rubles. Sovnarkom, in turn, awarded the Gypsy Union 5,000 rubles and a meager promise of tax breaks.[61] Understandably, the Gypsy Union's leaders felt hard-pressed to carry out their ambitious goals in the absence of adequate state funding. Their aim, after all, was the refashioning of Romani life – a feat that simply could not be achieved on the cheap. Finding themselves early on in the position to beg the Soviet bureaucracy to subsidize even the most basic organizational supplies, Gypsy Union members wondered how they were to finance the transition of Romani nomads to a settled way of life.

Much to their dismay, the Gypsy Union's "cultured" activists soon found themselves wandering between bureaucratic offices with their hands outstretched in supplication.[62] Yet, in their solicitous wanderings, Gypsy Union activists proved remarkably adept in establishing a discursive template for all Soviet discussions of the "Gypsy problem" in the interwar period. Although ultimately unsuccessful in obtaining sufficient state subsidies for their work, Gypsy Union activists rigidly demanded that the state redeem the guarantees it offered to Roma in the form of its nationality policy. In the process, they defined themselves as integrated Soviet citizens as much as they characterized themselves as members of a "backward" nationality.

In early 1926, Gypsy Union activists begged Soviet officialdom to consider the conditions in which they worked. They insisted that the greatest obstacle to their work was a pitiable lack of resources. Even as letters from Roma poured in from all corners of the Soviet Union expressing the desire to establish Gypsy Union affiliate groups, Moscow's

Romani activists could scarcely balance the Gypsy Union's books. Without adequate state funding, activists argued, the Gypsy Union was incapable of achieving even a single one of its ambitious goals.[63] The Gypsy Union fruitlessly sought help from every direction. They asked for money from central state and regional authorities. To the great frustration of Romani activists, Soviet officialdom seemed unwilling to bear the burdensome financial costs of transforming backward nomads into conscious, productive citizens.[64]

Threatened with insolvency, the Gypsy Union soon began pursuing an enlightenment effort that required little spending of its own. In early summer 1926, Taranov joined efforts with a newcomer to the Gypsy Union, M.T. Bezliudskii, in drafting a memo to the Presidium of VTsIK that, it was hoped, would be impossible for Soviet officials to ignore. "The most radical method for uniting, organizing, and raising the cultural level of toiling Gypsies living throughout the USSR," Taranov and Bezliudskii wrote, "is their transition from a nomadic way of life ... to productive, [settled] agriculture."[65] The unease with which Soviet officials approached the specific question of Romani nomadism was no secret to the Gypsy Union's activists. They well understood that Soviet officials primarily imagined Gypsies in terms of a uniquely subversive, irrational, and unruly form of nomadism.[66] Even if Soviet officials remained indifferent to the Gypsy Union's political-enlightenment efforts in Moscow, Romani activists reasoned, they could not ignore the threat of thousands of "parasitic" Gypsies "scattered" and "wandering aimlessly" across the empire.

In this effort, the Gypsy Union's leaders likely recruited Bezliudskii because of the effect that his personal story would presumably have on any Soviet official entrusted with the task of rationalizing the empire's seemingly illegible Romani populations.[67] Bezliudskii was neither a native Muscovite nor a child of late imperial Russia's Romani intelligentsia. Born in Riazan Province in 1901, Bezliudskii led a nomadic lifestyle until he joined the Red Army in 1919. He served as a soldier until 1926, during which time he learned how to read and write.[68] Symbolically, Bezliudskii personified that which most frightened officials confronting the "Gypsy problem": nomadism. At the same time, his conversion to settled life, state service, and literacy ostensibly confirmed the Soviet belief in the malleability of humankind – the very same belief that underpinned Soviet nationality policy. Perhaps even more so than the "choir Gypsies," Bezliudskii could claim to be "of the Gypsy masses" while at the same time he occupied a more "civilized" position above them. Bezliudskii and other activists like him could prove immensely useful in settling the empire's Romani nomads and integrating them into Soviet culture and the socialist economy.

In refocusing their energies on the issue of nomadism, Taranov and his fellow Romani activists had gambled wisely. In August 1926, Narkomzem and the Nationalities Department of VTsIK joined with the Gypsy Union to forge the Commission on the Settlement of Toiling Gypsies.[69] Bezliudskii occupied the Gypsy Union's seat on the Commission, whose task was to integrate Romani nomads into socialist construction as settled farmers and workers.[70] As the Gypsy Union leader A.V. Germano later described the Commission's efforts, the goal was to convince Gypsies that there was "no point in nomadism" in so much as "persecution and oppression no longer exist in the USSR." In that Soviet nationality policy promised all national minorities a redemptive future as integrated citizens, Germano claimed, it was no longer necessary for Gypsies to "alienate themselves from cultured life."[71]

On the Commission's recommendation, TsIK and Sovnarkom issued on 1 October 1926 the first of several directives that would ultimately lead to the establishment of Romani collective farms. Titled "On Measures to Bring About Nomadic Gypsies' Transition to a Working, Settled Way of Life," this decree consisted of two brief points. The first obliged TsIK and Sovnarkom to adopt measures that would prioritize the issuance of subsidized land grants to any Gypsy seeking to settle and undertake agriculture. The second required regional and local authorities to privilege Gypsy settlers with the material and institutional aid required by their transition to sedentary, agricultural life.[72] In this way, the Soviet government made its first official promise to its "backward Gypsy" charges in entirely vague terms.

The Commission's work did not end with the decree's issuance. In late October, the Commission entrusted Bezliudskii and his fellow Gypsy Union activists with the vital task of "going out to the people" in order to gauge the willingness of Roma to settle and take up agriculture. The Gypsy Union was likewise responsible for collecting "precise data" on the location, household size, profession, and property holdings of potential Romani settlers. When confronted with a Romani family willing to settle, Gypsy Union plenipotentiaries were to explain the process of land allocation and potential resettlement. They also could promise potential Romani settlers state-issued monetary grants of 400 rubles per household to aid them in their sedentarization. The Gypsy Union was expected to fulfil these urgent orders "in a very short amount of time."[73]

Since June, the Gypsy Union had already been attempting a long-distance census of the Soviet Union's Romani population. With only limited success, Romani activists had solicited information from local authorities on the number of Roma living in the empire's provinces and about the kind of political-enlightenment work being conducted among them. Those regional authorities who had responded to the Gypsy Union's requests in the summer of 1926 universally attested to the fact that organized enlightenment campaigns directed at the Romani populations were not being carried out in the provinces. Several expressed the difficulty of providing a head count of Roma living in their jurisdictions, attributing this to the Gypsies' "scattered nature (*razbrosannost'*)." Several others referenced Gypsies' engagement in speculation, begging, and thievery.[74] Ultimately, the Gypsy Union's armchair fact-finding mission achieved little in constructing an "information order" to aid in the systematic and rational settlement of "scattered" Romani nomads.[75]

As Gypsy Union activists saw it, a crucial component of their task and a necessary ingredient of their information gathering was a propaganda campaign designed not only to inform Roma of the opportunities available to them as Soviet citizens, but also to impress upon all non-Roma the necessity of bringing enlightenment to "backward Gypsies." To this end, in January 1927 Taranov published a short article in *Izvestiia* in which he outlined the sources of "Gypsy backwardness," the Gypsy Union's historic role, and the promise offered the "Gypsy masses" by Soviet nationality policy. Gypsies, he wrote, had been "completely neglected and scattered by the tsarist government." Oppressed by "landlords and capitalists," Taranov explained, Gypsies had whiled away centuries in "nomadism and poverty." Having resorted to begging, fortune telling, and thievery to obtain their daily bread, Gypsies were forcibly divorced from society, and thus from settled life and literacy. Yet, Taranov revealed, "Soviet power put an end to the oppression of the backward Gypsy people." In response to the Bolsheviks' campaign of minority liberation, he announced, the Gypsy Union had been established in 1925 with the "goal to bring together the disorganized Gypsy masses, to give them settled life, to introduce them to Soviet society (*obshchestvennost'*)." The Gypsy Union itself was evidence that "Soviet power" would help "the Gypsy people to join the organized, working masses of the Great Soviet Union."[76]

Gypsy Union leaders recognized, however, the difficulties inherent in their efforts to propagandize among their estranged Romani brethren.

They conceded that Soviet designs for the rational reordering of society, economy, politics, and culture were simply "incomprehensible to the Gypsy masses." The word of *Izvestiia* apparently did not resonate with illiterate deviants who seemed to know nothing of the Communist Party, let alone of the Gypsy Union. Activists were further frustrated in their efforts by what they perceived as Roma's historical mistrust of state authority. "Many Gypsies fear giving information about themselves when questioned by local authorities," Taranov explained to his fellow activists. "There are even those who do not show up when called by the local police." The Gypsy Union's leaders thus adopted a new approach to their propaganda campaign. They decided to intensify their efforts in "going out to the people" and to distribute posters advertising the state subsidies offered to Roma seeking to settle and take up agriculture.[77]

In ensuing months, the Gypsy Union printed and distributed 2,000 posters written simultaneously in both Russian and Romani and addressed "to the Gypsy population of the RSFSR." At its most basic level, the poster was intended to introduce "backward Gypsies" to Bolshevik rule and to Soviet nationality policy in particular. Yet the poster was also a proclamation of the Gypsy Union's historic role as the self-appointed leader of the "poor and illiterate Gypsy population living and wandering across Soviet Russia." Providing a cursory review of Bolshevik efforts to liberate all the empire's minority peoples from backwardness, the Gypsy Union's poster announced that the Soviet state, through its nationality policy, "strives to improve the life of the liberated, small peoples, to give them the opportunity to freely and peacefully work, to have their own corner, their own land holding." In its insistence that all minority peoples transform themselves and contribute to socialist construction, the Gypsy Union explained, the Soviet state attempted "to enlighten them, to make them literate, so that they themselves may better their own lives." Meanwhile, it was the job of the Gypsy Union to bring Soviet power into the lives of the backward and isolated Gypsy masses – especially the nomads among them.[78]

Nomadic peoples, the poster explained, occupied a special place in the Bolsheviks' benevolent design to revolutionize the lives of "backward minorities." Despotic tsars, it was implied, had unceasingly oppressed the empire's "nomadic tribes," imprisoning them in economic irrationality and social alienation. The Bolsheviks, however, were now inviting once hapless nomads to enjoy the plentiful fruits of civilized, settled life. "With the help of Soviet power," the Gypsy Union declared, "nomadic tribes are beginning to settle on land, to take up agriculture. They have their own land, their own farmstead, woods, villages, their own schools." In fact, the Gypsy Union continued, the Bolsheviks' astonishing success in settling the empire's nomads had already made it possible to imagine a near future in which no minority people would remain so backward as to continue a nomadic way of life. "With every year the number of nomads decreases," the Gypsy Union revealed, "and soon there will be none."

"Backward Gypsies," however, defied the otherwise unstoppable force of progress unleashed by the Revolution. Scattered throughout the empire, Gypsies remained alienated from Soviet culture and productive labour. "To this day," the activists continued, "the majority of Gypsies subsists on fortune telling, begging, trading at the horse-markets, and sometimes even on horse-stealing. But with every day their situation becomes still worse and more difficult." The poster itself was intended as a harbinger of revolutionary changes still to come. Progress marched forward regardless of whether "backward Gypsies" liked it; their anachronistic way of life would no longer be tolerated. The Gypsy Union explained, "Fines are imposed for fortune telling" and "horse-stealing is strictly punished." Meanwhile, "government specialists, whom peasants trust more than they do Gypsies, have appeared at the horse markets." All of these measures, the Gypsy Union insisted, were designed with the purpose of saving Gypsies from themselves, redirecting them onto a path of enlightened self-transformation.

The point of the Gypsy Union's poster was not merely to announce punitive measures designed to discipline a benighted people divorced from Soviet culture and the socialist economy. The poster also trumpeted the Gypsy Union activists' solemn assumption of their duty to guide their "backward" brethren in their transformation into conscious Soviet citizens. A rallying cry designed to arouse a somnolent people, the poster exhorted Roma to refashion their lives according to the dictates of a state that promised them equality, enlightenment, and the dignity of both productive labour and citizenship. In unleashing this battle cry, the Gypsy Union simultaneously announced itself both as the native friend of all the empire's Roma and as the midwife of a cultural revolution designed specifically to meet the needs of "backward Gypsies." Though any such transformation would inevitably frighten a people too backward to even recognize their way of life as anachronistic, the Gypsy Union confidently appealed to all those "who would like to live otherwise, who are disturbed by their darkness and illiteracy."

The Gypsy Union promised to be their trusty guide on the path to Soviet salvation. "Comrade Gypsies!" the poster bellowed. "The Union calls you to take a more active participation in its work."

Gypsy Union activists took great pains to describe the monumental nature of the work that lay before them, and before all the empire's Roma. Gypsy thieves and swindlers, the poster explained, had long inspired "bitterness" among their neighbours, sometimes even inciting anti-Gypsy violence. Meanwhile, Gypsy nomads starved through harsh winters and, in their ignorance and shamelessness, ordered their children to "dance on the streets for kopecks" and to "beg for bread." The Gypsy Union, however, had a plan to change all of this.

For nomads, the Gypsy Union promised free land. The benevolence of Soviet power had already made it possible for the Gypsy Union to partner with state officials in forging the Commission on the Settlement of Toiling Gypsies. This commission, the poster explained, "registers Gypsies who wish to pursue agriculture" and "gives them land and monetary help in the sum of 400 rubles per holding." The Soviet state, seeking to liberate Gypsies from the degradation and inhumanity of the backwardness imposed on them by the tsars, offered this generous opportunity to "every Gypsy family wishing to work the land." Without hassle, every voluntary Gypsy settler could obtain land free of charge. The poster insisted that there was no longer any obstacle to a Gypsy nomad's assimilation to settled life and integration into the Soviet economy.

The Gypsy Union promised more than land, however. In Moscow, the poster explained, the Gypsy Union had established industrial workshops to teach Gypsies trade skills. The Gypsy Union had also opened schools for Romani children and literacy courses for adults. Children and adults alike were already learning to read and mastering productive trades. With their new, state-sponsored alphabet, even "backward Gypsies" could learn in their supposedly "native" tongue. The Gypsy Union thus vowed to ease the transformation of beggars, fortune tellers, wanderers, and thieves into integrated Soviet citizens. "Gradually transitioning Gypsies to agriculture, exterminating illiteracy, teaching them a trade, organizing them," the Gypsy Union explained itself, "the Union thus raises the self-awareness of our backward people and places it on equal standing with the other peoples who already participate in the construction of our Soviet state."[79]

Ultimately, however, it remained unclear how people here described as "illiterate" were to read and interpret such a document. While the

Gypsy Union could somewhat rely on the "cultured" among them to establish contact with individual nomadic groups and on local authorities to help spread the document's message, this poster could aspire to reach only very few of those Roma who were indeed illiterate and isolated from surrounding populations. With this in mind, the Gypsy Union printed and distributed two additional posters, entitled "What Has the October Revolution Given Gypsies?" and "From Nomadism to Settled Life." Illustrated depictions of Soviet nationality policy's promise, these posters conveyed in simpler, graphic terms the call for nomadic Roma to settle and become agricultural labourers.[80]

Yet the difficulty of reaching out to illiterate nomads was but one of many problems facing the Gypsy Union and threatening its very survival. In early January 1927, officials at VTsIK began to question whether the Gypsy Union was capable of fulfilling the crucial tasks set before it. In particular, they doubted that the Gypsy Union would successfully lead Romani nomads to settle, undertake agriculture, and integrate into the socialist economy. Either VTsIK's Nationalities Department would have to reorganize the Gypsy Union in such a way as to enable its Romani activists to fulfil the Herculean task of settling all of their nomadic brethren, or – as it seemed more likely – the Gypsy Union would have to be shut down.[81]

Meanwhile, the Commission on the Settlement of Toiling Gypsies had hoped to receive by 1 January 1927 a complete report from the Gypsy Union regarding Romani nomads and their willingness to settle. That report never arrived. By June 1927, the Commission was forced to admit that the Gypsy Union's "information order" was incomplete at best.[82] Worse still, the cumulative efforts on the part of the Commission as a whole, and of the Gypsy Union in particular, had yielded a worrisome portrait of the empire's "Gypsy masses." Several regional authorities had replied to the Gypsy Union's requests for information with the news that they knew of no Gypsies who wanted to convert to settled life and agriculture. The Riazan Province Executive Committee informed central state authorities that the "fundamental reason" for Gypsies' refusal to settle and take up agriculture was their "lack of resources required for the establishment of a farmstead."[83]

Perhaps most disturbing was Roma's general response to the question: "Do you wish to resettle collectively?" The vast majority of those who expressed a desire to receive land plots uniformly rejected the option for collectivized agriculture. While a few Romani families were willing to settle "collectively with their comrades," the overwhelming majority preferred to receive individual plots of land.[84] Here, the Romani correspondents were doing more than contradicting long-standing (and persistent) stereotypes of Gypsies as devoutly and deviantly communal. The Roma who rejected collectivization seemed to express – unwittingly or not – Roma's opposition to the Soviet ideal of communal life. While this discouraging reality could not legitimately be blamed on the Gypsy Union, Soviet officials nonetheless began to regard the Gypsy Union still more sceptically, if not outright disdainfully. As disappointing reports continued to flow in from the provinces, Soviet officials became increasingly convinced that the Gypsy Union was unfit to meet the challenges posed by a nationality seemingly hell-bent on remaining in darkness and rejecting the light of Soviet civilization.[85]

As early as January 1927, Sovnarkom officials informed the Gypsy Union's governing board of their doubts that the Gypsy Union could successfully lead the struggle to sedentarize Romani nomads.[86] In March, the Moscow Control Commission's Workers' and Peasants' Inspectorate (MKK-RKI) subjected the Gypsy Union to a surprise inspection and evaluation of its internal operations. Although by this time the Gypsy Union had claimed success in helping to establish schools, literacy programs, workers' cooperatives, and a journal for Roma, inspectors' criticism of certain aspects of the Gypsy Union's work and organization would later be used to justify its liquidation. The MKK-RKI inspection report, for example, alleged that the Gypsy Union governing board consisted of "nine profiteers, four stage variety performers, five white-collar workers, one member of the Communist Party, one candidate for CPSU membership, and one Komsomol member." Throughout the entire Soviet Union, the Gypsy Union could claim only 674 members, 417 of whom lived in Moscow. "Eighty-seven per cent" of Moscow's Gypsy Union members were "speculators on the horse market, nineteen per cent stage variety performers, and one per cent peasant-speculators." An organization originally designed for the advancement of the "proletarian Gypsy masses" seemed to fully lack a proletarian element. Perhaps worst of all, the Gypsy Union's industrial department owed sizeable debts while several members appeared criminally involved in illegal "commercial operations." From the vantage point of Sovnarkom and VTsIK, the Gypsy Union was inarguably poised for self-destruction if not forced liquidation.[87]

In response to this severe criticism, the Gypsy Union governing board met several times in the summer of 1927 to debate the best approach to carrying out work among the empire's "backward Gypsies" – especially among nomads. Faced in previous months with the threat of forced closure, the Gypsy Union's enlightenment and sedentarization work had come to a standstill. As a result, Rom-Lebedev explained to fellow activists in July, the Gypsy Union's reputation had suffered severely – not only in the eyes of Soviet officialdom, but even worse – in the eyes of their Romani brethren. It was time, he urged, for the Gypsy Union to reform itself. The governing board would have to be reduced in size and staffed only by "cultured comrades." Any activity suspected of being illegally commercial would be suspended. In order to continue its operations and repay its debts, the Gypsy Union would request another 5,000-ruble grant from Sovnarkom.[88] Finally, Moscow's Romani activists realized the need to redouble their efforts to lead nomadic Roma to the salvation of settled, agricultural life. Yet they also decided that sedentarization would require a more coordinated bureaucratic effort and a significant increase in state expenditure. Already by this time, however, Soviet officialdom had concluded that the Gypsy Union's seemingly quixotic civilizing mission was a losing proposition.

Shaming the State, Sovietizing the Self

In late August 1927, Rom-Lebedev reported to fellow activists on the Gypsy Union's continued efforts to bring civilization to the empire's Roma in the form of settled agriculture. This work was "fundamental," Rom-Lebedev explained, because "only through Gypsies' introduction to agriculture and a settled way of life will it be possible to exterminate our people's antisocial way of life, raise their cultural level, and improve their material situation." Unfortunately, Rom-Lebedev conceded in subtle terms, state authorities served as the main obstacle to this revolution. The land and other state subsidies promised to Gypsies in 1926 were not fully available even to those who applied for them according to established procedure. Soviet officials did not pay enough attention to those Gypsies who were writing to the Gypsy Union "from every corner of the USSR" and expressing their "desire to transition to settled agriculture." As for the Gypsy Union's potential for satisfying the desires of Romani nomads, Rom-Lebedev admitted, "We can do nothing for them." The Gypsy Union could only press VTsIK, Sovnarkom, and Narkomzem to move forward in seriously fulfilling the promises that the Commission had made to "backward" Gypsy nomads.[89] The Gypsy Union leadership thus decided to employ a new strategy: activists would now shame the state into submitting to their demand that "backward Gypsies" be tended to as outlined by nationality policy. In shaming the state, the activists defined Gypsies as "backward" citizens whose Soviet self-realization was being criminally stymied by bureaucrats who were still unwittingly steeped in bourgeois, anti-Soviet ideology.

The Gypsy Union's leaders confidently pursued this new campaign. In their eyes, the naked facts of Gypsies' dolorous living conditions and of nationality policy's failures were on their side. Their correspondence with rural and nomadic Roma clearly evidenced Soviet officials' disheartening refusal to honour the state's promises to an undeniably "backward" people. In September, for example, the Gypsy Union received word from four Romani families near Pskov who, despite having received plots of land from their local authorities, were finding it impossible to reconstruct their lives according to the Soviet template of communal prosperity. "By our origins," the Romani settlers explained:

> we, each of our four families, are poor, nomadic Gypsies who until now have exclusively wandered. At present, under our socialist construction, we, emerging from the oppression and enslavement of tsarism, strive with all our soul toward settled, productive life and now, having ... received [our] plot of land ... we, given our poverty, cannot build a life for ourselves [zastroit'sia] ... We are forced to live under the open sky. Therefore we turn to you, and to the higher authorities, to you who stand in defence of poor, oppressed Gypsies.

Adding that several among them had served in the Red Army, these families asked the Gypsy Union to provide them with the funds needed to build living quarters, a granary, and a barn.[90] Faced with its own insolvency, however, the Gypsy Union was powerless to satisfy their request.

The Gypsy Union was also powerless to help a group of nomadic Roma in the North Caucasus who had spontaneously decided to settle and organize a collective farm even before the Commission on the Settlement of Toiling Gypsies had been created. Led by a Rom and former Red Army Soldier, A.P. Krikunov, this group referred to itself as a "national society of citizens" who believed that "Soviet power is our power." Although local authorities had initially helped them to secure land, Krikunov and his followers soon began attracting other Romani nomads to their settlement. The commune now needed more land in order to establish a "purely national village" that could accommodate those newly arrived "brother nomads" who "still live[d] in the darkness of wild life."[91] Krikunov thus begged the Gypsy Union to help the commune obtain more land from regional authorities. Though the Gypsy Union was happy to oblige, regional authorities in the North Caucasus refused to transfer more land to the Krikunov commune. Further information was needed, local bureaucrats explained, before land and monetary subsidies could be allotted to the Krikunov village.[92] So long as officials in Moscow refused to enforce the 1926 decree on Romani sedentarization, the Gypsy Union could offer nothing but moral support to the Krikunov settlers as they attempted their own conversion to Sovietism.

Powerless, frustrated, and bankrupt, Gypsy Union leaders began a new funding campaign in the fall of 1927, issuing scathing letters to TsIK secretary Avel' Enukidze, the CPSU central committee, and the Nationalities Department of VTsIK. In these letters, the Romani activists amplified their rhetoric, staking still more explicit claims on the Soviet state and its nationality policy. In refusing the Gypsy Union adequate funding, Romani leaders explained, the state had robbed them of the ability to save the Soviet Union's Gypsies from nomadism and starvation. In their unjustifiable refusal to finance the Gypsy Union's work, they insisted, Soviet officials had not only contradicted Bolshevik nationality policy, but also mirrored the tsarist regime's bourgeois, chauvinistic approach to governing Gypsies.[93]

For nearly three years, the Gypsy Union testified, activists had faithfully agitated among Gypsies only to have their efforts frustrated by sceptical and intolerant state officials. The greatest obstacle to the Gypsy Union's work, its leaders claimed, "has been Soviet and Party organs' distrust towards us." Soviet officials had consistently regarded Gypsy Union activists "with irony and mistrust," never taking them seriously or showing them respect. "We, of course, knew," the activists continued, that such an attitude was "an inheritance from a bourgeois order that had taught the population to look upon Gypsies as inveterate tramps from whom nothing good could ever be expected except for thievery, begging, and various other human vices." While conceding that Gypsies had earned this reputation to a degree, the Gypsy Union's leaders asked Soviet officials to consider the root causes of Gypsies' reprehensible way of life. In the final analysis, they maintained, Gypsies could not be fully blamed for their seemingly interminable misery.

Central to Gypsy Union leaders' rhetorical effort to shame Soviet officialdom was their portrait of Gypsies as a pathetically backward and victimized minority who not only deserved but also desperately needed the oft-propagandized benefits of Soviet nationality policy. After all, the activists explained, "the Gypsies once had their own culture." Unwilling to submit to slavery, however, they had fled India centuries ago. Fundamentally progressive, then, in their rejection of oppressive authority, Gypsies suffered endlessly as a result of their steadfast resistance to illegitimate authority. The pages of their as-of-yet unwritten history would thus be "covered all over in the blood" spilled during their ongoing "struggle for independence."

The problem remained, the Gypsy Union asserted, that Gypsies' battle with their "highly-cultured" oppressors had not ended in 1917. Rather, their centuries-old struggle for humanity continued in the Soviet present. "How do Gypsies live today?" the Romani activists asked. "Cold, filth, poverty, and hunger are their constant life companions." Riddled by disease resulting from a torturous moral and material poverty, Gypsies now faced "degeneration and extinction." It was truly unacceptable, Romani activists railed, for "Soviet power" to neglect a "backward" nationality "that, because of its illiteracy, isolation, and darkness, cannot by itself realize the necessity for a change in its own way of life." Before it was too late, the state needed to help the Gypsy Union save Gypsies from themselves. Officials simply could not afford to liquidate the Gypsy Union.[94]

"With the closure of the Union," the activists threatened, "the matter of Gypsies' regeneration can be considered terminated." The Gypsy Union, being the first and only of its kind, had thus far served as the only institution that commanded any authority among the empire's Gypsies. It had served as the cultural and political nexus for backward Gypsies who were only now beginning to understand the Soviet struggle for new life. As such, it had won their hard-earned, non-transferable trust. "Today every Gypsy feels himself a member of a definitive organization," the Gypsy Union explained. "He is beginning to be active, he takes pride in his Union membership book and morally feels himself a full citizen in the Soviet state." Upon the union's closure, they argued, this new citizen Gypsy would "remain as before rejected ... despised by all, and a homeless tramp."

This was the closest the Gypsy Union had yet come in demanding that only Gypsies could enlighten their own – a notion that clearly lent itself to the charge of "bourgeois nationalism." Yet the activists chose to defend their point in practical, not nationalist terms. Appraising the work of the Commission on the Settlement of Toiling Gypsies, the Gypsy

Union maintained that all failures were those of the Soviet bureaucracy and all successes were their own. They argued that only when Gypsy Union representatives "went out to the people" had Gypsy nomads willingly submitted to being counted, questioned, and lectured on the Soviet government's offer to settle them. When regional authorities attempted the same, the Gypsy Union argued, Gypsies "uniformly fled into the forests, hiding their nationality by any means possible." When Narkomzem officials distributed questionnaires, "Gypsies feared filling them out and only with the help of the [Gypsy Union was] that task successfully executed." Nomadic Gypsies, by their very "backwardness," could not be expected to recognize any authority other than the Gypsy Union.

Activists also argued that they had achieved far more than Soviet officials recognized. In addition to their efforts to sedentarize nomads, they had helped to establish a variety of Romani educational institutions in Moscow. "Much more could have been done," they claimed, "if Soviet and Party institutions ... had regarded our needs attentively, and without mistrust." Instead, the activists charged, they had been maligned, abused, and thwarted by officials who refused to account for Gypsies' "particularities." Decrying such behaviour as unabashedly politically incorrect, the Gypsy Union's leaders declared, "No one in the Soviet state should deprive us, Gypsies, of the right to build up the well-being of our dark, backward tribe ... On the contrary, we should be helped in this work." Nationality policy entitled all "backward" minorities to the opportunity to advance under Soviet tutelage, they argued, and no degree of backwardness, illiteracy, or poverty could justify the Gypsy Union's closing. Rather, it was Gypsies' very "darkness (*temnota*)" that obliged the state to help the Gypsy Union "make Gypsies into citizens."[95]

Replete as they were with rhetorically forceful pleas, the activists' letters did not save the Gypsy Union. In November 1927, the NKVD decided that even though the Soviet government had provided the Gypsy Union with adequate funding, Romani activists had not succeeded in adopting "concrete measures in the struggle with the Gypsies' conservative style of life" and in particular with "fortune telling, begging, gambling, drunkenness, and other particularities of the Gypsy population." The Gypsy Union had scarcely raised Gypsies' cultural level and failed to attract the Gypsy masses to join in its work. The NKVD thus declared the Gypsy Union a "lifeless organization" that was so deep in debt, so marred by internal divisions, and so lacking in a proletarian

element that there was no point in saving it.[96] In the eyes of Soviet officialdom, the Gypsy Union, though perhaps a worthwhile experiment,
was a complete failure. The NKVD formally announced the Gypsy
Union's liquidation in February 1928.[97]

Moscow's Romani activists nonetheless refused to abandon their
struggle. Later that year, they issued a final memorandum to the Presidium of VTsIK. They stated their position in clear terms: "Ten years
of revolution have passed unnoticed in the history of the Gypsy people
and up to now the Gypsy question remains outside the sphere of the
attention of State and Society."[98] Their civic duty, as they saw it, was to
inform the Soviet government of both the economic and the ideological
reasons why it could no longer ignore the "Gypsy question."

In terms of its sheer number, activists maintained, the empire's
Gypsy population posed a serious threat to the Soviet economy. According to the Gypsy Union's statistics, at least 200,000 Gypsies lived
in the USSR. Of these, they deemed three-fourths to be "society's parasites" – that is, nomads who ostensibly produced nothing, and instead
only consumed. The Gypsy Union estimated that it cost the Soviet
state 13.5 million rubles each year to support nomadic Gypsies.[99] Yet
allowing Gypsy nomads to continue blindly with their parasitic existence was as unnecessary as it was costly. Nomadic Gypsy camps, the
activists explained, were "embryos of communism" and therefore the
transition of nomads to settled agriculture could "easily" be achieved.
Further demonstrating their political acumen, they invoked NEP's end
and praised state efforts to transition the peasantry to collectivized agriculture. They argued that the example of recent Gypsy settlers could
"serve as a useful example" for recalcitrant Russian peasants. Here the
Gypsy Union took the old populist trope of the peasant as the natural
bearer of communism and turned it quite awkwardly on its head. It
was the backward, illiterate Gypsy, they argued, who would take the
communal ideals of his nomadic camp and bring them to the peasantry, thereby revolutionizing collectivized agriculture in the Soviet
Union.

In support of such claims, the activists defined Gypsies as history's
perennially "propertyless class" and as "the poorest part of our population." They claimed that Gypsies "had never in all their history been exploiters and even amongst themselves lacked a bourgeoisie." Instead,
Gypsies had always been victims of "mockery, rage, the arbitrary rule
of the police, violence, persecution, and burning at the stake."[100] In the
activists' rendering of them, Gypsies were not merely natural-born

communists. They were also ideological innocents whose agonizing history of oppression organically aligned them with the proletariat.[101]

Given its vow to uplift the empire's minority peoples, activists argued, the Soviet state could no longer afford to deprive Gypsies of nationality policy's benefits. "Our constitution and nationality policy (*politika natsional'nykh men'shinstv*)," the activists opined, "speaks of the self-determination of nations, of assistance to the cultural-economic development of national minorities. Confirming this, the Central Executive Committee of the USSR, in its own decree of 30 November 1927, says that from now on the matter of developing the national culture of all peoples will be well provided for by all power and support of the Soviet Union." Yet despite these promises, the activists claimed, nothing had yet been done for the empire's Gypsies. "Not only have they been deprived of government care," the activists bitterly complained, "this semistarving, impoverished tribe is even deprived of the rights of citizenship, and for ten years of the October Revolution neither Party nor Soviet organs have done anything real for Gypsies ... For ten years their voices have remained cries in the wilderness." Alas, only the Gypsy Union had tried to alleviate Gypsies' desperate cries.[102]

To support such claims, the activists excerpted letters received by the Gypsy Union in its three short years of existence. They quoted despairing Roma who had been refused the land promised to them by law and others who longed to exchange their "Gypsy" poverty and ignorance for Soviet prosperity and enlightenment. In Minsk, a Rom claimed, "We live like lost wolves, [we] know nothing, and [to live with us] is considered worse than with dogs." A correspondent from Pskov expressed his belief that central state authorities could know nothing of how provincial authorities mocked and turned away Gypsies – if they had known, this Rom explained, they would have done something to help the poor, humiliated Gypsies by now.[103]

These letters, the activists continued, attested to a situation in the Soviet countryside that was more frightening still – anti-Gypsy pogroms.[104] Roma in Smolensk Province threatened that without the state's help:

We will understand nothing and will be savages and again will remain oppressed as we were before, and maybe even worse, because the peasantry has begun to look on Gypsies more and more with hate, and namely Soviet authorities have completely forgotten about us and we find no defence; they beat, thrash, and mutilate us and no one stands up for us ...

Give us life! It has already been ten years of Soviet rule. It is time to think about Gypsies.[105]

For Gypsy Union activists, these letters laid bare the defencelessness of their uncivilized brethren. Illiterate, hungry, backward, landless, and oppressed – this, they argued, was how Gypsies lived in the Soviet Union, ostensibly the most progressive state on earth.

Although they clearly indicted Soviet authorities for failing the empire's backward Gypsies, Romani activists granted that Soviet officials, like themselves, had thus far been limited by constraining circumstances beyond their control. The Soviet failure to civilize Gypsies was, they conceded, to some degree understandable. In a conciliatory tone, the activists acknowledged that the Soviet state "had demonstrated benevolence toward Gypsies, in particular in its decree on land settlement." The failure to integrate Gypsies as conscious Soviet citizens, activists claimed, could be explained by three fundamental and undeniable facts. First, the Soviet state had thus far been engaged in a "titanic struggle" to transform an entire society into a worker's paradise on earth. Its efforts had been complicated by civil war, economic crises, and the overwhelmingly "grandiose" nature of its goals. Second, Soviet society cared very little for Gypsies and did not trouble itself with "the Gypsy problem." Third, the activists invoked their own backwardness, pointing to the "unenlightened darkness of the Gypsy masses."[106]

In conclusion, the activists wistfully described the Gypsy Union as "an oasis of activism in a desert of general passivity toward Gypsy matters."[107] Its liquidation, in their view, had been the gravest mistake yet perpetrated by Soviet officials tasked with rationalizing the empire's Romani populations. It was time, they claimed, for the Soviet state to right that wrong. It was time to create a new Gypsy society that would resume the Gypsy Union's work in leading "backward Gypsies" to settled, productive life as conscious Soviet citizens. With the help of the state, activists argued, this resurrected Gypsy Union could not fail. Such an organization, they pleaded, was the "single ... possibility to solve Gypsy questions within the plane of Soviet nationality policy."[108] Soviet officials, however, disagreed.

Backwardness as Sovietness

Although Soviet officials deemed the Gypsy Union a failure, there can be no doubt that Moscow's Romani activists benefited greatly from this short-lived experiment. In their tenure as Gypsy Union activists, they not only fashioned themselves as conscious Soviet citizens, but also developed as skilled and forceful politicians. The Gypsy Union's activists – the majority of whom descended from late imperial Russia's Romani choir dynasties – accomplished something for which they received little credit at the time. While these activists had watched their parents strive towards "the good life" in fin-de-siècle Russia, they adapted their inherited cultural aspirations to the Bolshevik version of the same goal. Although Gypsy Union activists arguably failed to transform the lives of the Soviet Union's vastly diverse Romani populations, they succeeded in achieving something quite different but no less important to that desired transformation. They reinvented themselves as Soviet citizens who claimed to speak for an entire people; effectively defined that people as a mass of neglected, uncivilized children; and rhetorically manipulated the Soviet nationality regime to suit their own political agenda.

In taking up the mantle of Gypsy backwardness, these Romani activists nimbly occupied a position that Soviet nationality policy had carved out for them. They understood themselves as "cultured" – as immeasurably distant from the parasitic Gypsy nomads who were said to threaten the Soviet state with their "backwardness" and deviance. Yet, while these activists considered themselves more Soviet than they were Gypsy, their Gypsiness proved their most valuable political tool. It was thus their "Gypsy backwardness" that they most dramatically emphasized in dealing with Soviet officialdom. Though not like their "others" – their "wild" and illiterate Gypsy brethren, Gypsy Union activists nonetheless claimed a unique understanding of "their own people." In a state whose reigning ideology was in part premised on the notion that minority peoples were entitled to refashion themselves as New Soviet Men and Women with all due help of the state, this position of insider authority could not so easily be dismissed. Realizing this, activists volubly defined themselves as backward members of a benighted, desperate, and eternally oppressed people as they strategically invoked nationality policy's promises. They liberally reproduced disparaging Gypsy stereotypes while at the same time adroitly demonstrating their civic understanding of both nationality policy and Soviet cultural values more broadly.

Although officials rarely granted them their demands, Gypsy Union activists gained from their frustrated efforts an incredibly valuable experience: a crash course in Soviet political education. In the matter of only a few years, they learned the fundamentals of being good Soviet citizens. Gypsy Union activists not only gained fluency in Bolshevism, but also mastered the particular Soviet idioms of nationality, backwardness, and Gypsiness. No matter how awkwardly or felicitously they deployed these idioms, the Gypsy Union's "backward Gypsies" effectively implicated themselves in Sovietism as they pursued their civilizing mission. No matter the level of their sincerity (a question, in any case, to which the sources are decidedly incapable of providing definitive answers), Gypsy Union members activated, reproduced, and shaped early Soviet ideology in their everyday engagement of nationality policy. No matter the sheer multiplicity of motives that must have propelled them to pursue the state-prescribed salvation of both their nationality and their own individual selves, Gypsy Union activists fulfilled, at the very least, their civic duty to "participate as if one believed."[109] In participating in the delegitimization of their own selves as inherently "backward Gypsies," the Gypsy Union activists simultaneously actualized themselves as hard-working, self-reflecting, conscious Soviet citizens.

While historians of Soviet subjectivity have devoted considerable attention to questioning the authenticity and intentions of historical actors, the case of the Gypsy Union suggests the need for an alternative approach to theorizing the sources of Soviet selfhood. Whether Gypsy Union activists earnestly believed in their civilizing mission, let alone in the wider Soviet project, is irrelevant to the question of their performance of Sovietism – that is, to their recasting themselves as Soviet subjects. Only the Gypsy Union activists' participation in the early Soviet nationality regime was essential to their remaking as the transmitters, producers, and products of Soviet ideology – internalization, although the state-mandated ideal, was not. The performative effect of the Gypsy Union activists' words and deeds did not depend upon sincerity and belief, or upon cynicism and dissimulation. These "backward Gypsies" required neither masks nor a yearning for their souls' purification to assimilate and reproduce the language and mores of Sovietism. Regardless of their motives or intentions, the Gypsy Union's Romani activists transformed "backward Gypsies" into conscious Soviet citizens, thereby rendering both their backwardness and Sovietness as "real."[110]

Ultimately, the Gypsy Union's leaders remained committed to their purpose even as their organization crumbled and faltered. As dutiful Soviet citizens, they assumed responsibility for the full transformation of Gypsy life in the Soviet Union, and linked their specific civilizing mission to the broader task of revolutionizing life on earth. When denied further opportunity to resurrect the Gypsy Union, its leaders therefore pursued their revolution via different means. Many Gypsy Union members joined in the formal work of the Soviet bureaucracy and several emerged as nationality-policy careerists. Though deprived of the Gypsy Union's institutional framework, Moscow's Romani activists ultimately found that Soviet nationality policy was a productive framework in and of itself. Throughout the 1930s, they instrumentally involved themselves in the establishment of Romani schools, collective farms, and industrial cooperatives. They oversaw the creation of a Romani-language literature and of the world's first Gypsy theatre. Armed with the political, cultural, and social skills obtained in their tenure as Gypsy Union leaders, these activists continued to shape what it meant to be a Gypsy, and what it meant to be a Soviet citizen.

Though hardly identified as such during its time, the Gypsy Union embodied the Soviet ideal of a modern citizenry. In that all citizens were ideally expected to consciously work at disciplining and sovietizing themselves, officials should have joyfully embraced the Gypsy Union. Here was a group of mostly educated "Gypsies" pleading for the opportunity to "civilize" a people feared by officials as incomprehensible and intractable. Skillfully manoeuvring the Soviet nationality regime, Gypsy Union activists performed both Gypsiness and Sovietness, achieving civic integration in the process. In asking their fellow citizens to recognize them as willing and able hands in the construction of Soviet socialism, the Gypsy Union's Romani activists demonstrated that even those who were perceived as "backward" could become fellow travellers on the road to socialist paradise. They, too, even in their supposedly inherent "backwardness," were actively becoming Soviet.

2 A Political Education: Soviet Values and Practical Realities in Gypsy Schools

Reflecting on his participation in the Gypsy Union's work, N.A. Pankov recalled his fellow activists as "very gifted, yet very young." Though unable to recognize their own youthful lack of life experience, Pankov explained, he and his comrades had confidently committed themselves to leading a cultural revolution among their own people – a people "only just beginning to come alive again" and one that could boast "neither culture nor experience in societal or economic affairs." In hindsight, the Union's closure was understandable, but still regrettable. Despite its flaws and arguable failures, Pankov maintained, the Gypsy Union had positively impacted "the masses," kick-starting their education as New Soviet Men and Women.[1]

From the very start of the Gypsy Union, Moscow's Romani activists had prioritized the education of what they referred to as the illiterate, benighted Gypsy masses. They focused particular attention on the creation of "Gypsy schools" for Romani children and, by extension, for Romani adults. Their efforts ultimately expanded to the creation of a Romani alphabet, Romani-language textbooks, a didactic national literature, and teacher training courses. Throughout the late 1920s and 1930s, Romani leaders worked closely with Soviet officials to assault "Gypsy backwardness" with weapons of literacy and education. They exhorted their "backward" students to undertake individual programs of enlightenment and self-transformation, but also to join them as teachers of Sovietism.

This chapter examines early Soviet Romani educational initiatives not only as attempts to teach Roma literacy and hygiene, but also as concerted efforts to transform backward Gypsies into conscious Soviet citizens. In the 1920s and 1930s, Romani students were consistently taught that they, as Gypsies, were fundamentally backward. Castigated as dirty, diseased, illiterate, and socially unuseful, Roma were relent-lessly instructed that they could advance themselves and become So-viet only after they surrendered to the therapeutic education designed for and afforded them as a peculiarly "backward" people.

Early Soviet Romani educational initiatives ultimately provided Roma more than mere lessons in ascribed backwardness. Romani stu-dents gained a basic political education in what it meant to be a con-scious Soviet citizen – tidy, rational, literate, and socially useful. They were also trained in the politics of the Soviet nationality regime. As teachers, activists, and officials illuminated the varieties of state aid af-forded "backward Gypsies" in their assimilation to cultured Soviet life, Romani students discovered nationality policy's theoretically generous offerings and mobilized its framework for self-sovietization. Although nearly all of the early Soviet Romani educational initiatives were termi-nated by the eve of World War II, many Romani students had already emerged from the practical and political education that they received in the late 1920s and 1930s as literate, integrated Soviet citizens. Al-though short-lived and radically impoverished, early Soviet Romani educational initiatives were national in form, socialist in content, and sovietizing in practice.

Purity and Danger in Moscow's Gypsy Schools

In late October 1925, the Moscow Department of Education (MONO) dispatched school inspector E. Zhvigur to scout possible locations for the establishment of Romani-language sections within existing Rus-sian elementary schools. Zhvigur quickly set his sights on two schools in Moscow's Krasnopresnenskii region. Though both schools lacked electricity, plumbing, and central heating, they were advantageously located in "the center of the Gypsy population." Concluding that a bet-ter location could not be found in the midst of Moscow's housing crisis, Zhvigur recommended that both schools devote two classrooms and a cloakroom to the organization of new sections for Moscow's Romani children.[2] Zhvigur's inspection marked the beginnings of MONO's ef-forts to fulfil the promise made to the Soviet Union's Roma by Nar-kompros's decree of 31 October 1918, "On National Minority Schools." Gypsies, like "all nationalities residing in the RSFSR," had a right to an education conducted in their native language.[3]

By this time, the Gypsy Union's leaders had already committed to pursuing all paths leading "towards the enlightenment of backward

Gypsies." They quickly aligned with MONO and Narkompros in a co-ordinated effort to provide Moscow's Romani children with a Soviet education in what was referred to as their native Romani language. Ideally, these so-called Gypsy schools would grant Romani children literacy "in the native tongue," foster in them the "skills of socialist labour," and enable the young pupils to "influence" their own parents "with the goal to accustom them to a working way of life."[4] The Gypsy schools, then, would provide Romani children with the same classroom indoctrination on matters of literacy, hygiene, socially useful labour, Bolshevik glory, and civic-mindedness as all Soviet children were to receive.[5] Although Romani children may have appeared to education officials and Gypsy Union activists as a particularly challenging case of "backwardness" to be remedied in the classroom, they and their parents were also to benefit from Lenin's logic: "Children learn in school how to brush their teeth and wash their hands. They inspect their own clothes and they ask their mothers and sisters that their own clothes be examined, and, as much as possible, put in order."[6] A specialized minority education was presumed not only a right owed to Romani children, but also a potentially expedient mechanism of acculturating the youths and their parents to Soviet culture.

In late 1925, representatives of the Gypsy Union and MONO met several times to discuss the future of Romani-language elementary education in Moscow. In early November, they convened a general meeting for the Romani population of Moscow's Butyrskii region that was designed to popularize the schools among Romani parents. The Gypsy Union and MONO discussed educational matters generally, acknowledged the supposed particularities of teaching Roma, addressed concerns about Romani children's need to be properly outfitted for school, held elections for a school council, and introduced the Romani parents to two Russian schoolteachers. By meeting's end, attendees and organizers had agreed that MONO's approach towards providing Romani children with an education was "satisfactory." MONO and Gypsy Union representatives also agreed to prioritize the provisioning of clothing and shoes to needy Romani children. Similar meetings were held for Romani parents in subsequent weeks in other areas of concentrated Romani settlement in Moscow, all with the intent to accustom parents to sending their children to schools ostensibly designed to meet the particular needs of their own nationality.[7]

In advance of the opening of Moscow's Gypsy schools, the Gypsy Union petitioned VTsIK to fund clothing for Romani schoolchildren as well basic classroom supplies.[8] Upon receipt of seven thousand rubles designated specifically for Romani students by the children's commission of VTsIK, MONO and the Gypsy Union agreed first to allocate seven hundred rubles on shoes and clothing "in that Gypsy children in large part [were] completely shoeless and unclothed."[9] This fateful decision sparked the first of several conflicts between Moscow's Romani parents and the organizers of Moscow's as-of-yet unopened Romani-language schools. When MONO purchased material for the manufacture of Romani pupils' clothing, school officials decided to give a group of Russian schoolgirls an instructive assignment: they were to sew dresses for their Romani counterparts. Romani mothers were outraged. Animated by their own cultural beliefs regarding pollution and the female body, the mothers demanded that the style of their children's dresses "absolutely must be Gypsy." In the end, the purchased material was delivered to the Romani mothers who patterned and cut the material before returning it to be sewed by the Russian schoolchildren.[10] This first conflict ended almost as quickly as it began, and plans moved forward towards the establishment of Romani-language schools in the capital.

In January 1926, the Soviet Union's first Gypsy schools formally opened in Moscow. All three took the form of nominally independent sections operating within pre-existing Russian elementary schools.[11] Students were instructed in reading, writing, arithmetic, drawing, crafts, music, hygiene, physical education, history, and civics.[12] The schools completely lacked textbooks composed in either the Russian or Romani language, and were staffed, with one exception, by Russian teachers. N.A. Dudarova, born in 1903 and having completed a secondary education, assumed the position of Moscow's only Romani schoolteacher.[13] Needless to say, the majority of lessons taught in these newly established Gypsy schools were conducted in the Russian language.[14] Combined enrolment for all three schools amounted to a mere eighty-six pupils in their first months of existence.[15] Considering even their modest estimate of 2,000 Roma living within Moscow Province, Gypsy Union activists could not deny the woefully limited reach of Moscow's Gypsy schools.[16]

Despite the schools' low enrolments, Gypsy Union activists confidently envisioned the future development of Gypsy schools and other educational institutions as incubators for New Soviet Gypsies. The development of Romani-language education in the Soviet Union was a goal that particularly animated the Gypsy Union activist N.A. Pankov.

The son of a horse-dealing father and a mother with a history of no-madism, Pankov was born in 1895 into St. Petersburg's Gypsy choir milieu. Although his parents did not prioritize education, Pankov was from an early age determined to join educated society. Without his parents' help, the young Pankov enrolled in a local parish school and upon graduation, "embarked on an intensive course of self-education." Not only did he master Russian, he also haunted Petersburg's libraries and lecture halls in pursuit of self-improvement. After the October Revolution, he worked briefly as a teacher in an orphanage, but in 1922 moved to Moscow and took up factory work. Ingratiating himself among Moscow's Romani intelligentsia, Pankov soon became actively involved in the Gypsy Union and quickly rose as one of its leaders.[17]

Perhaps, then, with his own limited formal education in mind, Pankov spoke before Narkompros officials in early February 1926 – just a few weeks after Moscow's first Gypsy schools had opened. In his appeal, Pankov outlined the drastic need to create schools, literacy courses, red corners, and other institutions of political enlightenment for the Soviet Union's Roma. Committing personally to the creation of Romani-language textbooks, Pankov is also said to have astutely responded to Narkompros officials' questions while dazzling them "with his striking Gypsy appearance and enthusiasm."[18] On 26 February 1926, Narkompros's Council of National Minorities issued a directive establishing the "necessity to begin enlightenment work among Gypsies."

Narkompros's decision was not made without reservation. While Narkompros officials outwardly committed themselves to an expansion of Romani education, they inwardly doubted that such an expansion could easily be achieved. As one Narkompros memo worriedly explained, Roma were fragmented, nomadic, illiterate, problematically lacking a written language, and socially marginalized by their pursuits as horse-thieves, beggars, and fortune tellers. Narkompros officials therefore looked hopefully to the Gypsy Union's leaders to assume much of the responsibility for enlightening "backward Gypsies." They emphasized the need to construct a written language for Roma, but decided that all enlightenment work among them should temporarily proceed in Russian.[19]

Teachers at Moscow's new Gypsy schools and Gypsy Union activists, however, initially found the lack of a written Romani language to be the least of their problems. For example, Comrade Rudakova, the director of one of the new Gypsy schools, faced the daily challenges made by a "Gypsy headman" suspicious of the new schools. "Exercising very

large influence on the backward masses of Gypsies," Rudakova reported, the headman Mikhai not only refused to recognize the Gypsy
Union, but also meddled with her Gypsy school by whatever means
possible.[20] MONO officials further reported that the Vlax Romani community under Mikhai's lead exhibited a very "peculiar" way of life.
Describing Mikhai's uncontested authority, school inspector Zhvigur
wrote, "all of the backward Gypsies fear and serve him." Romani children's school attendance, Zhvigur explained, "depends on the mood
of the headman. If the headman is displeased by something … he for-
bids all the Gypsies from sending their children to school."[21] Moreover,
when it came time for Rudakova to distribute new clothes and shoes
to her needy pupils, the "Gypsy headman Mikhai demanded that the
clothing be divided up and distributed by him in his own apartment."
As was his wont, Mikhai threatened that if he did not get his way, he
would not allow a single child under his authority to attend school.[22]
Some days Rudakova arrived at school only to find her classroom completely empty – her pupils forbidden to attend school by the capricious
Mikhai.[23]

Rudakova further complained of meddlesome Romani parents inter-
rupting her work. The parents of the Mikhai community, she explained,
were "very superstitious and backward."[24] On International Women's
Day, for example, school officials invited all of the Romani pupils'
parents to join their children in a holiday celebration. Of the Romani
parents invited, only mothers attended. On the following morning,
the Romani group's female students showed up for class without their
male counterparts. When the director approached the elder Mikhai
and asked why her male students were no longer attending school,
Mikhai indicated that the school had been "defiled" by the mothers'
visit. "Now our 'men' … cannot go there," Mikhai reportedly informed
the schoolteacher. Without regard for the pollution taboos held by the
Mikhai community, school officials and Romani activists pointed to the
Women's Day incident as still further evidence of the "ignorance" and
"superstitions" shared by "backward Gypsies."[25]

For MONO officials, Gypsy Union activists, and the Gypsy schools'
teachers, the Mikhai community exemplified the extreme backwardness afflicting Gypsies as a nationality. In their eyes, nothing indicated
Gypsies' ignorance and lack of culture more than their perceived aversion to proper hygiene. Although unhygienic living conditions were
the early Soviet norm rather than the exception, activists and educational officials hyped the ostensible severity of Gypsy filth, disease,

and slovenliness as a product of this nationality's ethnic backwardness rather than as a result of broader social and economic conditions.[26] As participants in the larger Soviet battle to wage war not simply on dirt, but also on the dangerous ideological impurities that unwashed hair and shoeless feet implied, these civilizing missionaries approached the Gypsy schools as the frontline in their effort to transform "filthy, grubby little savages" into clean, socially useful, and enlightened Soviet citizens.[27] Embracing Bolshevik visions of a distinctly Soviet modernity, they looked to the Gypsy schools as the key to immunizing "savage" pupils from the darkness, disease, and disorder of their inherently "backward" culture, and thus to developing the consciousness of future New Soviet Gypsies. Intended to purify a seemingly degenerate, diseased nationality, the Gypsy schools were to rear modern citizens who were not merely clean, literate, rational, tidy, and well dressed, but who also understood the political significance of their own cleanliness, literacy, rationality, and social usefulness.[28]

In the first years of the Gypsy schools' existence, teachers relentlessly taught Romani pupils the ABCs of hygiene. They presented lessons in teeth brushing, hair combing, and face scrubbing in the classroom, at parent-teacher conferences, and during observations carried out in visits to Romani families' homes. Initially, officials and activists feared that the tenets of proper hygiene might never be instilled in the "backward Gypsies" they were attempting to sovietize. In a 1926 report, Zhvigur reported that the Romani pupils – most of whom lacked shoes and underwear – attended school in filthy, threadbare clothing and with dirty, unkempt hair. "The parents do not pay any attention to their children's clothing," Zhvigur explained, "It is very difficult for sanitary practices to catch on." The Gypsy schools therefore needed to offer pupils instruction in "bathing ... teeth-cleaning, and hairdressing."[29]

For activists and school officials, the squalid conditions observed at Romani homes and the disregard for hygiene evinced by Romani parents and children alike signalled "backwardness" writ large. Worst of all was the shared sense that such seemingly irrepressible "backwardness" had already been deeply ingrained in the consciousness of Romani schoolchildren. In his *Gypsies Yesterday and Today* (1931), the activist A.V. Germano painted a purportedly representative scene from one of Moscow's Gypsy schools in tones that subtly conveyed disapproval and alarm. Asked to draw pictures of their homes, Germano reported, the children dutifully sketched their homes, family members, and even dogs. Yet the teacher's prodding of one child to describe her home environment inspired the girl to "joyfully shout" that her house was surrounded by both "Gypsies" and "filth."[30]

In the eyes of Gypsy Union activists and MONO officials, Roma's "filthy ways" signalled not only the moral poverty of backwardness, but also the physical threat of infectious disease. At MONO, concerns about Romani schoolchildren's health abounded. Medical examinations conducted at the schools revealed an alarming degree of illness and malnutrition. Many children were diagnosed with anaemia, tuberculosis, and even typhoid fever.[31] The Soviet press, meanwhile, echoed official and popular concerns about the unsanitary living conditions of "backward Gypsies" and the wide-ranging ill effects of "backwardness" suffered by Romani children. The magazine *Drug detei* (*The Children's Friend*), for example, lamented the impossibility for Romani children to enjoy a normal childhood – an impossibility resulting from the "epidemics, extreme poverty, and unkindly attitude of the surrounding population" that Romani children suffered onward from birth. "Even primitive cultural and sanitary conditions" were reportedly unknown to them, and thus they were victimized by high rates of sickness and childhood mortality. *Drug detei* concluded that Moscow's Romani parents, clearly lacking any understanding of hygiene, could neither provide their children with a good upbringing nor ensure their health. "The task of their education entirely falls on the school."[32]

How effective were the Gypsy schools in eradicating the dirt, disease, and disorder thought endemic to Roma? How successful were they in imbuing Romani schoolchildren with Soviet values? A year after Moscow's first Gypsy schools opened, MONO officials and the schools' teachers appraised their work. Their findings echoed Narkompros and Sovnarkom officials' conclusion that minority education "in large measure lag[ged] behind the average level of public education in the RSFSR." Sovnarkom officials blamed the failures of minority education on the "immense cultural and economic backwardness of the eastern peoples and the absence of the necessary cadre of cultural workers among them." Lacking written languages, textbooks, and qualified native pedagogues, Gypsies and their fellow "backward" ("eastern") nationalities thwarted Narkompros's efforts to establish successful minority educational programs. Alphabets needed to be created, textbooks composed and printed, and minority teachers trained before "backward" minorities such as Gypsies could appropriately and effectively be educated in national schools.[33]

Nonetheless, officials also recognized the Gypsy schools' few successes. In a January 1927 report, Zhvigur celebrated the improved relationship between school officials and the Romani parents of the Mikhai community. "The attitudes of the parents towards the school are good," Zhvigur reported. "Improvement has been especially noticeable since the literacy centre [for adults] began to operate. It is as though a competition of writing and reading is taking place between children and parents." In the fall of 1926, he explained, N.P. Rogozhev, a Rom and trained teacher, had joined the school's staff and organized literacy classes for Romani adults.[34] Steadily, Zhvigur insisted, the school and its officials were gaining influence over both children and parents. He explained that when attendance rates had sharply dropped earlier in the school year, Romani parents were called to account at a parent-teacher meeting and threatened with the school's closure. On the next day, nearly every pupil arrived on time for class. "This proves all the same," Zhvigur wrote, "that they have recognized the necessity of the school." Having taken into account "all the peculiarities and difficulties of the conditions of work among Gypsies," Zhvigur concluded that both the school and the Mikhai community were headed in the right direction.[35]

Dudarova's school, however, earned the highest praise as a model of Romani elementary education. Dudarova's stature as a Gypsy Union representative, active involvement in Moscow's Romani communities, and most importantly her very own Gypsy nationality were credited for the success of her school and students.[36] According to officials, Dudarova's Gypsy school had proven almost from the moment of its inception to be a seat of grassroots Romani activism. In the school's first month of existence, Dudarova informed MONO that her pupils' parents – despite their "backwardness" – took great interest in the work of the school, recognized its authority, were eager to organize adult literacy courses, and had even contributed their own money to meeting the school's needs.[37]

Yet Dudarova's school was not without problems. Many of her students lived at a considerable distance from the school. At least two children had dropped out due to a lack of clothing and shoes. While another five had supposedly left to attend Russian schools, Zhvigur reported that only one such child actually attended classes as the remaining four in question sat idly at home. Textbooks were scarce. Located in the basement of a Russian elementary school, Dudarova's classroom was dim and damp. Though Dudarova and her Romani students had tried to forge a relationship with their Russian counterparts, their efforts were not reciprocated. Dudarova took particular offence when her students were not invited to the Russian school's commemoration of Lenin's death.[38]

Dudarova faced further problems when she and a colleague, Volodina, first attempted to organize a literacy centre for Romani adults within their school. "With great difficulty," Dudarova and Volodina informed MONO in March 1926, "we organized two groups for the liquidation of illiteracy from among such a backward population as the Gypsies." Though school officials had initially granted them permission to conduct literacy courses for Romani adults inside the school, this offer was quickly rescinded on the advice of a local doctor. Speculating on the unsanitary conditions of the local Romani population and "fearing an epidemic," the doctor in question urged school officials to disallow Romani adults from infecting school classrooms (and hence, Russian schoolchildren) with their presumed disease. Their pained efforts to establish a literacy centre now potentially wasted, Dudarova and Volodina wrote to MONO insisting that the doctor's fears were unwarranted. MONO officials, fearing the termination of Dudarova and Volodina's frustrated efforts more so than they did a possible epidemic, ultimately intervened to override the decision of local school officials. Given the difficulties faced by Dudarova and Volodina to bring enlightenment to "such a backward population as the Gypsies," MONO officials seemingly decided that risking an outbreak of disease was but a small price to pay for Roma's education.[39]

As 1927 came to a close, officials and activists celebrated even the smallest of the Gypsy schools' triumphs, but could not fail to recognize the schools' apparent deficiencies and failures. Although the Gypsy schools had already become vehicles for teaching pupils literacy, hygiene, civics, and Soviet values, the problem remained that Moscow's Romani students were learning in the Russian, not the Romani language.[40] Without an alphabet, textbooks, or their own cadres of native-language schoolteachers, Romani schoolchildren were thus deprived of their right to an education in their presumed native language. It mattered very little, meanwhile, that only 64.2 per cent of Gypsies accounted for by the 1926 census claimed Romani as their native tongue – as opposed to the 87.1 per cent average of native-language speakers among their fellow minority peoples. Even most Gypsy Union activists themselves did not speak Romani fluently, if at all.[41] As a nationality, Gypsies were entitled to national-language education regardless of whether they spoke Romani. On the eve of Stalin's Great Break, Moscow's Gypsy schools were not yet Gypsy enough.

The ABCs of Backwardness

In 1928, a Narkompros memo explained that the "language peculiarities of individual nationalities demand the maximum attention …
There are nationalities that completely lack a written language (Gypsies, for example). Lessons are conducted according to the Russian
textbook, in the Russian language, and conversations are conducted in
the native language." For Gypsies and similarly unlettered and "backward" nationalities, the national school had thus far operated as nothing more than a "transitional stage for the assimilation of the Russian
language."[42] What was needed then, was a truly national school for
Gypsies – one in which students were taught in their purportedly native Gypsy language.

The linguistic problems afflicting Moscow's Gypsy schools had long
troubled officials and activists. When the schools first opened, however,
officials had prioritized the supposed threat of the Romani students'
bare feet and disease. While Russian served as the primary language
of instruction, Dudarova and Rogozhev taught Romani as a secondary subject. Without textbooks or even an alphabet, however, their lessons were conducted using an unsystematic method of transliterating
Romani with the Cyrillic alphabet. Despite these lessons in Romani,
however, a common language could not easily be found at Moscow's
Gypsy schools. At Dudarova's school, most Romani students were
not fluent in Russian. Not knowing Romani, Dudarova's Russian colleagues could only instruct students in Russian.[43]

At Rudakova and Rogozhev's school, matters were still more complicated. A recent arrival to the Soviet capital, the Mikhai community
had immigrated to the Soviet Union from Romania a mere few years
earlier as part of a larger Vlax Romani migration during and after
World War I. These Vlax immigrants were linguistically, occupationally, and culturally distinct from the Russka Roma who had settled in
northern Russia in the seventeenth and eighteenth centuries and whose
descendants now largely monopolized the Gypsy Union's leadership
positions. Having adopted a "settled way of life" only in 1925, the Vlax
Roma of the Mikhai community represented in the eyes of Moscow's
core Romani activists not only social and cultural foreignness, but also
the literal alterity of noncitizens.[44]

Meanwhile, the linguistic "foreignness" of the Mikhai community
translated into practical challenges at the schools. Not only did these
Vlax Romani schoolchildren barely speak a word of Russian, their

dialect of Romani also "differed considerably" from that of Russka Roma. Despite Rogozhev's fluency in Russka Romani, therefore, the Mikhai schoolchildren barely understood him.[45] To ease these linguistic barriers, in the fall of 1926 school inspector Zhvigur recommended the hire of a teacher fluent in the Romanian, not the Romani, language. In the meantime, Russian inevitably served as a poor linguistic substitute. "The children," Zhvigur explained, "poorly understand Russian, especially the youngest. There are even those of the first group with whom the [Russian] teacher must speak through an interpreter. This of course affects the pace of work."[46]

Meanwhile, still another section for Romani children had opened in September 1927. The twenty-five pupils at this school were described as "Moldavian Gypsies" who had presented school officials with a particularly troublesome language issue. The children did not know their "native tongue" of Romani well and therefore studied with Moldavian primers. "Ukrainization," school officials remarked, "was apparent." Their teacher even suggested that the pupils might best (or at least most conveniently) be categorized and educated not as Gypsies, but simply as Moldavians.[47]

In the absence of a native language common to all of Moscow's Romani schoolchildren, activists and officials alike insisted that one must be created for them. Given "the backwardness of Gypsy children," the activist A.V. Germano wrote, "classes for Gypsy children in general [Russian] schools are absolutely inconceivable."[48] Moreover, Germano argued, the very fact that Roma's native language had presented itself as a question was a product of centuries of oppression and imposed "backwardness." Having wandered the vast expanses of the earth without a written language of their own, Germano explained, Roma "had lost their genuine native language."[49]

The problem of Roma's national language, however, was not as simple as Germano suggested. Even in the late nineteenth century, Russian ethnographers had noted the declining use of Romani dialects among the tsarist empire's Romani population – especially among those Roma who were settled and assimilated into the Russian economy and culture.[50] While only 64.2 per cent of Roma claimed Romani as their native language in the 1926 Soviet census, many of the Russka Romani elite in Moscow and St. Petersburg – including, notably, the Romani activists of the Gypsy Union – scarcely spoke Romani, if at all. Explaining this phenomenon in 1931, A.P. Barannikov, a linguist and Orientologist based at the Russian Ethnographic Museum and Leningrad University, noted the marked linguistic differences separating settled and nomadic Roma on Soviet soil. "Good knowledge of the [Romani] language," he argued, "is maintained only among nomadic Gypsies and among those who arrived on the territory of the Soviet Union relatively recently." According to Barannikov, sedentary Roma had in large measure fulfilled a process of "linguistical denationalization," whereby even those with some fluency in Romani did not employ it as their primary language. Rather, they thought in Russian exclusively and often even struggled when faced with the task of speaking in Romani at any length. For most Roma, he claimed, "their real mother tongue is not Romani, but the dialect spoken by the surrounding population."[51]

Yet from its earliest days, the Gypsy Union had prioritized the creation of a Romani alphabet as well as the subsequent production of Romani-language textbooks, dictionaries, and periodicals. Gypsy Union activists regarded the ostensible restoration and modernization of their "native language" as necessary to overcoming backwardness and as a prerequisite of national dignity. They thus approached Narkompros officials with concerns that the Romani language could be lost entirely if action was not taken to preserve it from both bastardization and the mortality promised by its own unlettered "backwardness."[52] Pankov and Dudarova, meanwhile, spearheaded the Gypsy Union's efforts to create a Romani alphabet. M.V. Sergievskii, a linguist and professor at Moscow State University who was appointed by Narkompros to lead the effort to create an alphabet for and standardize the Romani language, soon joined them.

Pankov and Dudarova closely aligned with Sergievskii, a scholar of romance languages, and one of his graduate assistants, thereby forging an active study group on the Romani language. Pankov's memoirs recall his initial scepticism about working under the lead of a Russian scholar on the task of codifying the Romani language. Yet upon his first meeting with Sergievskii, Pankov felt reassured by the professor's scholarly dedication to the task and personal commitment to Moscow's Romani communities. "Despite his duties at the university, Narkompros, and other institutions," Pankov favourably recalled of Sergievskii, "he found time to be everywhere personally – in the Gypsy school, the Gypsy artel, the club, theatre, and in the nomadic camp in order to see Gypsy life in all of its diversity."[53]

The work of the Gypsy language study group moved remarkably quickly. On 10 May 1927, Narkompros issued a decree "On the Creation of the Gypsy Language Alphabet," adopting the group's recommendation that the Romani alphabet be based on the Cyrillic script with a few modifications.[54] Notably, the 1926 Soviet Census had recently estimated that only 8 per cent of the Romani population accounted for could boast even the slightest degree of literacy. This epidemic illiteracy motivated the decision to base the Romani alphabet on Cyrillic.[55] Sergievskii, Dudarova, and Pankov chose a Cyrillic-based script, in part, so that any material or book "printed in the Gypsy language might be read at first by any literate Russian person among the illiterate Gypsy masses."[56] At the time, Gypsies thus joined several other "small" and "backward" nationalities – Komi, Kalmyks, and Oirots, for example – in pragmatically adopting the Cyrillic script.[57]

In recommending the adoption of a Cyrillic-based script for Romani, Sergievskii and his cohort nonetheless departed significantly from the general Soviet tendency in the late 1920s to promote the Latinization of minority languages, as evinced most strikingly by the efforts to convert the Arabic scripts of Turkic-speaking and Muslim peoples.[58] Though the motivations for Latin alphabet conversions were typically articulated as the result of "a general striving among Eastern peoples to Latinize their orthographies," Latinization policies were also deeply rooted in the "state-sponsored evolutionism" that underpinned the early Soviet regime of nationality.[59] At its most basic level, the Latinization campaign was an early effort to distance the Soviet state from its purported Russificatory, oppressive predecessor. More broadly, the switch to Latin-based alphabets was seen as a crucial stage in the advancement of "backward" peoples whose languages were deemed "less adequate," especially in so far as new Latin-based scripts were said to "transform writing from an instrument of religious propaganda into an instrument of social progress."[60] The Latinization campaign, then, was intended primarily as a layered assault on Great Russian chauvinism, the authority of Muslim clerics and Islamic print culture, and the persistence of minority "backwardness."[61]

Sergievskii and his cohort, however, wasted little time debating the choice between a Cyrillic- and a Latin-based Romani script. Of greater practical and ideological concern for the creators of the so-called Gypsy alphabet was the question of Romani dialects. As recent experience in Moscow's Gypsy schools had already shown, it was impossible to speak of a singular Romani dialect spoken in the Soviet Union. Moreover, although ethnographers and linguists in prerevolutionary Russia had granted Roma only marginal attention in their studies, one scholar had warned of the variety of Romani dialects spoken in Russia as early as 1887. In his *Gypsies: A Few Words on the Dialects of the Transcaucasian Gypsies*, St. Petersburg University professor and Orientologist K.P. Patkanov had argued for a classificatory grid in which "the Gypsies living in Russia divide into the Russian Gypsies (of North and South Russia), the Finnish, the Transcaucasian (the Armenian Gypsies – Bosha, the Persian – Karachi, the Turkish), the Lithuanian, and the Polish Gypsies, etc."[62] Building from Patkanov's work, Professor Barannikov would soon publish his own study of Gypsies in Russia in which he bluntly maintained, "A uniformity of the language of the Gypsies of Russia, in so vast a territory as the USSR, is a fact hardly to be admitted even theoretically." Not only did Romani dialects vary by province, Barannikov explained, they also varied according to the influence of surrounding populations – be they Ukrainian, Belorussian, or Armenian.[63] Although further scholarly work on the linguistic variations among the Soviet Union's Gypsies needed to be conducted, Sergievskii, Dudarova, and Pankov could not wait for such investigations to take place. In order for the Soviet assault on "Gypsy backwardness" to succeed, they needed to codify the Romani language now.

Unsurprisingly, Sergievskii, Dudarova, and Pankov chose the "northern dialect" of the so-called "Russian Gypsies" – that is, the Russka dialect ostensibly spoken by Moscow's activist Romani elite. In choosing Russka Romani as the normative basis for the future literary language of Soviet Roma, they complied with a general tendency of early Soviet language planning. When faced with the problem of choosing among dialects in transforming the languages of "backward" minorities into modern, literary languages, linguists typically chose the dialect "spoken in the major economic and cultural centers" of the Union.[64] Although Bolshevik theory declared all dialects of unlettered languages to have "the same right to aspire to the literary language," minority elites – those who crafted the new national literatures – typically chose their own dialect as the national standard.[65] In a few cases of language standardization in the Soviet Union, efforts were made to assimilate linguistic components from all dialects and to fuse them into a single national whole potentially intelligible to all speakers of the so-called native tongue. Such was the case with the creation of Turkmen as a national language – a process that serves as an illuminating counterexample to the Soviet standardization of Romani.[66]

As Adrienne Edgar has shown, the task of creating Turkmen as a single national literary language inspired much debate and even heated controversy among Turkmen elites throughout the 1920s and 1930s. Like Romani, the Turkmen language greeted the Soviet era as "a collection of related dialects spoken by the different groups that identified themselves as Turkmen." Although Turkmen would, like Romani, need to be outfitted with an appropriate alphabet befitting its modernization under Soviet auspices, it, initially at least, went the route of a Latin script. This was a choice cemented by Turkmen participation in the Turkological Congress in Baku in 1926. It was in Baku that representatives of the Soviet Union's Turkic nationalities collectively endorsed Latinization as a linguistic policy for which they subsequently received Moscow's support.[67] Here, one can already discern a key difference in the cases of Romani and Turkmen language standardization. Decisions regarding Romani standardization came under the purview of a limited and inward-looking crowd of appointed or else self-selected specialists – Sergievskii, his graduate assistant, Pankov, Dudarova, and the Narkompros officials to whom this small clique answered. Questions regarding the Turkmen language, however, reverberated throughout the much wider circles of Turkmen cultural elites, representatives of other Turkic-speaking nationalities, and Soviet officials seeking to disarm both Islam and pan-Turkism in Central Asia.

Meanwhile, Turkmen linguists and other elites – representing each of the dialects competing for national predominance – worked and argued with one another on standardizing Turkmen through a variety of intellectual outlets: research institutes, specialized government commissions, and academic conferences. Before Moscow stepped in to wrest control over the process of Turkmen language reform from Turkmen linguists and other elites in the early 1930s, debates over a wide array of linguistic issues animated the speakers of the many Turkmen dialects. Turkmen intellectuals invested heavily into the practical and political stakes of the creation of a Turkmen national language.[68] On no side of these debates were participants willing to cede to the "linguistic hegemony" of any one Turkmen dialect. In 1930, it was thus decided at a Turkmen language conference to adopt a policy of "linguistic inclusiveness" – the Turkmen national language would "incorporate elements from all dialects and be understandable to all Turkmen."[69]

Herein, perhaps, lies the greatest difference between the processes of standardizing Romani and Turkmen. Sergievskii and his Gypsy Union colleagues did not pursue a similar project of linguistic inclusiveness in their creation of Romani as a standardized national language. If nothing else, there was the simple fact that they did not need to. Unlike the Turkmen case, there were no widespread controversies over the standardization of Romani. There were no public debates over questions of script or dialects. There were no Romani language conferences. The authority for Romani language standardization rested with a small circle of Russka Romani elites and a Narkompros appointee. The voices of Romani speakers of other dialects were neither courted nor counted. It bears repeating, also, that among the majority of Moscow's Russka activists, there were remarkably few native speakers of Romani. It was in these circumstances that Sergievskii and his activist cohort prescribed Russka Romani, the putative dialect of the Gypsy Union, to all Romani-speakers in the Soviet Union.

Once this decision was made, Gypsy Union activists assumed the responsibility for creating a national literature designed to translate Soviet values into the Romani language. Pankov and Dudarova immediately began composing the first Romani-language textbooks to be published in the USSR, Germano undertook the composition of a popular piece outlining Soviet initiatives to enlighten "backward Gypsies," and Sergievskii began work on the creation of a Romani-Russian dictionary and a treatise on Romani grammar. In 1928, Dudarova and Pankov published *Nevo drom* (*New Road*), a reading primer intended for use by Romani adults in literacy courses. Reviewing the book for Narkompros, Sergievskii lauded the authors' simple and clear portrayal of "the opposition between useful work and the parasitical existence to which Gypsies have grown accustomed." Sergievskii concluded that the primer was a striking achievement, especially given "the extraordinary poverty of the Gypsy language."[70]

Nevo drom's focus on the need for Roma to transition from "parasitism" to "socially useful" labour highlighted its intended use as an implement of both practical and political literacy.[71] As Frederick Ackerley of the Gypsy Lore Society explained, "The reading book opens with one word '*Buty*' [*rabota*, or "work"] printed on the page to itself. This strikes the keynote to the whole. It is to inculcate the virtue of work … that this literature is written."[72] According to Alaina Lemon, *Nevo drom* functioned essentially as "a parable" in which a Romani family barely surviving on the matriarch's fortune telling is hounded by starvation until the benighted protagonists discover the joys of productive labour in the socialist economy. Phrases such as "Our Romani women don't work but tell fortunes" were followed ultimately by "I want to work."[73] Its message intended as much for Romani adults as for their children, *Nevo drom* starkly demanded that Gypsies transform themselves into productive, socially useful citizens.

Nevo drom was followed in 1929 by Germano's *Nevo dzhiiben* (*New Life*) and Pankov's *Buty i dzhinaiben* (*Work and Enlightenment*). Distributed free of charge, both texts were compendia of short articles meant to appeal to and enlighten semiliterate and literate Roma. Intended to introduce Roma to Soviet industry, Pankov's work provided a variety of didactic articles that, despite their uninspiring titles, unambiguously promoted Romani integration into the Soviet industrialization drive: "Gypsies and Industry," "An Excursion to a Textile Factory," "Metals," and "In the Gypsy Club." Germano's *Nevo dzhiiben* adopted a more general tone with articles such as "Nomadic Life Is Death," "Lenin – the Great Builder of New Life," and "The Komsomol." Yet *Nevo dzhiiben* also offered readers insight into Soviet measures to educate Roma specifically in such articles as "The Romani Alphabet" and "Our Schools." Lastly, Germano's *Nevo dzhiiben* featured poetry written by Romani activists. Pankov, for example, provided two poems entitled "Towards a New Life" and "Under the Red Banner of Lenin."[74]

Pankov's, Dudarova's, and Germano's literacy primers for Romani adults were intended as the equivalent of coursework in the elementary schools for Romani children: a lesson in one's own backwardness and an exhortation to join the ranks of well-groomed, regularly bathed, conscientiously hardworking, and socially useful builders of Soviet socialism. Romani students of all ages were meant to understand that the recognition of one's own backwardness was the first key to attaining the enlightenment known to the carefully honed Soviet self and the "advanced" nationality. The new Romani alphabet thus became a favourite weapon of Romani activists who, now denied the institutional framework of the Gypsy Union, nonetheless forged ahead in their sovietizing mission as native consultants employed in the Soviet bureaucracy. For the "Gypsy masses," the new written Romani word was as much a symbol of basic national advancement as it was a constant reminder of one's own deeply rooted backwardness. Yet the Romani texts transmitted a larger lesson still: in the Soviet Union backwardness was a curable disease that theoretically entitled Roma to a range of potential opportunities for state-sponsored rehabilitation. Though diagnosed as "backward" by definition of their nationality, Roma willing to transform themselves into conscious citizens were at the very least promised a Soviet education and a stake in the building of socialism.

Educating New Soviet Gypsies

As the Soviet Union rapidly industrialized in the 1930s, Moscow's Romani activists worked to increase production of Romani-language texts. Between 1928 and 1938, several hundred Romani-language texts were published in the Soviet Union. Predictably, these works were thematically oriented to bringing "backward Gypsies" into the orbit of Sovietism. Semiliterate and literate Roma were offered simple, Romani-language tracts on Lenin, the Communist Party, Soviet nationality policy, industry, and agriculture. Many of these works tackled problems deemed specific to Roma and other "backward" peoples such as the necessity of good hygiene and of sedentarization.[75] In so far as "every citizen of the USSR had to master the heights of world culture in her mother tongue," Roma were also provided translations of the works of Pushkin, Tolstoy, Gorky, and most importantly, of Lenin and Stalin.[76]

Yet Moscow's Romani activists realized that in order for the Romani texts' message of Sovietism to take full effect, the Gypsy schools needed to rear a generation of literate Soviet citizens to consume and internalize this new national literature. In the early 1930s, activists redoubled their efforts at transforming Moscow's Gypsy schools into functioning centres of Romani-language education and Soviet enlightenment. Activists and officials focused on the creation of Romani-language textbooks and the training of Romani schoolteachers. They continued to argue that even backward Gypsy children, if properly educated, could introduce a Soviet way of life to their parents, and through them, to "the entire Gypsy population."[77]

By the early 1930s, activists and officials recognized a certain, albeit limited, progress already made in sovietizing Moscow's Romani students and parents alike. Contrary to popular depictions of Gypsy children as "filthy, grubby little savages" forever dancing and begging on urban streets, Moscow's Romani literati attempted to discursively erase this vision of a wasted, degenerate Gypsy youth from the Soviet imagination.[78] In an article entitled "An Hour in the Gypsy School," the activist Edvard Sholokh described Dudarova's students' exemplary work and active civic involvement. The schoolchildren reportedly accelerated their own program of self-improvement by entering into healthy competitions with their parents and Russian students. They encouraged other Romani children to enrol in school, helped their parents learn to read and write, tutored classmates who lagged behind, helped workers at one of the Romani artels, and exposed the truancy of those students who strayed from the path of enlightenment. These children of "the formerly backward nation of Gypsies," Sholokh insisted, were assuming the duty of their own transformation with remarkable vigour. "The

Gypsy school," Sholokh declared, "does its own modest part, making active citizens of the Soviet Union from wandering Gypsies."[79]

The enthusiastic tone adopted in the Soviet press, however, obscured the profound difficulties faced by educators, officials, and activists in the matter of schooling Romani children. When Sholokh announced that the majority of Moscow's Romani schoolchildren were enrolled in schools, for example, he deliberately distorted actual figures.[80] In 1931, approximately 150 children were enrolled in Moscow's Gypsy schools. While this official figure marked a real increase in enrolment since the schools' opening, it also underscored the limited reach of the capital's Gypsy schools.[81] Narkompros's demand that 4,000 Romani children living in Moscow Province be provided with a national elementary school education by the end of 1932 was, needless to say, never satisfied.[82] Even the children who were enrolled at Moscow's Gypsy schools, however, were still not receiving a Romani-language education. Despite the creation of a Romani alphabet and the first Romani-language primers, lessons at Moscow's Gypsy schools were still conducted in Russian with Romani studied as a separate subject.[83]

At Dudarova's school, meanwhile, students confronted not only the "anti-Gypsism" of their Russian peers, but also the threat of eviction from their classroom in the dank basement of a Russian school.[84] While Dudarova knew better than anyone the squalid conditions and hostile environment in which her students studied, she actively resisted a decision made in 1931 to expand the Russian school at the expense of her Romani students. In a letter addressed to the Nationalities Department of VTsIK, Dudarova predicted that if the Gypsy school was evicted as planned and transferred to a space within an industrial complex located twelve kilometres from her students' neighbourhood, her Gypsy school would simply disintegrate. It was better to educate children in an unsuitable basement within a hostile Russian school, Dudarova reasoned, than to transfer the school to an equally inhospitable environment located at a distance that no child or parent could reasonably be expected to travel for school. She accused regional authorities of unwisely sacrificing the education of a needy national minority for the benefit of a Russian school. Only after publicizing the Gypsy school's plight in a small newspaper story did Dudarova succeed in retaining the right for her Gypsy school to operate in the familiar squalor of the Russian school's basement.[85]

Within the Presidium of VTsIK, officials adopted an even-handed tone in appraising the development of Romani-language education.

VTsIK's resolution of 1 April 1932, "On the Condition of Work in the Service of Toiling Gypsies," announced: "With the introduction of a system of writing and the development of cultural-enlightenment work in the native language, political consciousness and activism have developed in the mass of toiling Gypsies." Long "isolated from productive life in the past," the resolution continued, Gypsies had recently "been given the opportunity to actively participate in the political, economic and cultural construction of the country." Yet, despite such progress, VTsIK admitted that state agencies – Narkompros especially – had underestimated the political importance of educating Roma. VTsIK ordered Narkompros officials to immediately accelerate the development of Romani-language schools, demanding that a Gypsy school be established wherever the "compact settlement of toiling Gypsies" could be found. VTsIK also charged Narkompros with the creation of teacher-training courses for Roma, the establishment of a "Gypsy department" within one of Moscow's teacher-training schools, and the full provision of adequate textbooks for already existing Gypsy schools. In the spirit of Stalin's Five-Year Plans, VTsIK demanded that Narkompros complete this mission by the end of 1932.[86]

By the time of the 1932 VTsIK resolution, the battle to provide Gypsy schools with adequate textbooks was already in its sixth year. Soviet publishing houses had churned out a number of enlightenment texts for a "backward" people generally assumed to be almost universally illiterate. In 1930, Pankov and Dudarova's first reading primer for Romàni school children, *Dzhidy buty* (*Vital Work*), was published and in 1931, Sergievskii's *Tsyganskii iazyk* (*The Gypsy Language*) appeared as the first grammar book composed for use in the Gypsy schools. Yet even as demands for Romani-language textbooks took a more desperate tone in the early 1930s, officials often demeaned the works produced by Pankov, Dudarova, and their Romani colleagues as flawed texts produced by insufficiently qualified authors.[87]

Criticism of these textbooks and translations, however, also arose from within the Soviet Union's small circle of Romani authors and translators themselves. Thus, in 1933 Pankov's manuscript for a fourth-year reader inspired an intense ideological debate when reviewed for Narkompros by fellow activists Dudarova, Germano, and Taranov. In addition to translations of contemporary Russian stories, Pankov's manuscript included prerevolutionary Romani folklore as well as new tales and poems penned by Pankov's fellow activists. While the reviewers generally praised Pankov's manuscript, they divided bitterly over the question of its inclusion of prerevolutionary Romani folklore. Germano supported Pankov's choice, arguing that it was ideologically useful to allow the oppressed Gypsies of Russia's capitalist past to testify in their own words to the indignity that they had suffered under the tsars. In his view, the prerevolutionary folklore perfectly complemented the contemporary Romani poetry and prose that reflected on the themes of "the transition to a settled way of life, participation in socialist construction and social life, stratification among classes, and the situation of Gypsies abroad."[88]

Dudarova, meanwhile, refused to abide other messages contained within the stories and songs of the Romani oral tradition. In explaining her dissatisfaction with Pankov's choice in Romani folklore, Dudarova prefaced her criticisms with the caveat that she, as a schoolteacher with practical experience in the shaping of young Romani minds, might prove a more discerning reader than her fellow Romani activists. In particular, Dudarova protested Pankov's inclusion of three folkloric short stories dated to prerevolutionary times. The first, "Hunger and Pain Don't Allow for Listening," recounted the tale of two drunken Gypsy thieves who were discovered by their victim and subsequently beaten for their crimes. The Russian landlord whose property was stolen succeeded in hunting down the thieves by following the sounds of the vagrants' drunken guitar playing. The second, "The Gypsy's Misfortune," was the tale of a widower who lethargically consoled himself with wine, song, and the hope of finding a new wife. The third, "The Gypsy and the Landlord," told the story of a Gypsy whose wife left him for a richer, more attractive Gypsy man. The scorned husband sought the help of his landlord, only to learn of the master's plans to take the cuckold's wife for himself. In the end, the "poor Gypsy" fled from both his heartless master and the wife who had betrayed him.

In Dudarova's view, these three stories had no place in a primer for Romani schoolchildren. "Each of these three tales that speak of theft, drunkenness, about how one Gypsy stole the wife of another is entirely without value," Dudarova explained. She surmised that the tale of the Gypsy thieves would inspire the children's "sympathy," while any depiction of drunkenness had no place in the textbook meant for the youngest representatives of a nationality prone to alcoholism. It mattered very little, Dudarova argued, that Pankov had included review questions at the conclusion of each tale that were meant to force the children to reflect upon such vices and antisocial behaviour. These review questions, Dudarova maintained, neither compensated for the unhealthy content of the stories nor increased their value as a teaching tool. The folklore, she continued, "was not an artistic description of the difficult situation of Gypsies under tsarism," and thus lacked "ideological and artistic significance." Finally, such tales were completely foreign to the interests of children and for that reason alone could justifiably be excluded from the text.[89] Taranov, too, sympathized with Dudarova's disinclination to include stories that "idealize[d] Gypsy thievery" or that otherwise contradicted the tenets of Soviet ideology.[90]

Pankov's primer forced Romani activists to consider how much they should allow the voices of the prerevolutionary Gypsy past to speak to the New Soviet Gypsies of the future. While Germano argued that the folkloric tales of drunkenness, thievery, and oppression served as valuable illustrations of "Gypsy backwardness" that children could easily assimilate, Dudarova considered the impressionability of children whose domestic lives still resembled the purported past of Gypsy vice, criminality, and deviance. Dudarova and Taranov agreed that it would be dangerous to allow Romani schoolchildren to reach their own conclusions about the ambiguous tales found in their primers. Romani children, they argued, must not be entertained by their own national "backwardness," nor moved to sympathy by the poor, ignorant Gypsy of folklore. As textbook authors, they argued, Romani activists needed to clearly explain to schoolchildren the duty to overcome their backwardness and to work at becoming Soviet.

In the end, Narkompros officials agreed with Dudarova and Taranov. They removed the three contested tales from Pankov's primer. On the basis of Dudarova's recommendation, three translations replaced the ideologically questionable Romani folklore: "Red October in Moscow," "The Childhood and School Years of Il'ich," and "A Story of the Great Plan." It was precisely this kind of material, Dudarova argued, that would provide Romani children with the "communist education" they needed. A few of the folkloric "tales and songs of poor Gypsies" were nonetheless included in Pankov's primer. It was thus considered ideologically appropriate for Romani schoolchildren to read a humorous account of a Rom "artfully" deceiving a local priest.[91] Despite Soviet revulsion for "Gypsy tricksterism," the depiction of a Rom hoodwinking a member of the clergy could nonetheless still be considered wholly appropriate. Presumably, the tale was intended not as praise of "Gypsy guile," but as denigration of religion itself and therefore still qualified as an expression of Soviet values.

In the Soviet press, meanwhile, activists continued to wax poetic on the progress made in enlightening Romani children and adults. In an article entitled "On Cultural Work among Gypsies," Germano wrote of the overwhelming impact that the creation of a Romani alphabet and the production of Romani texts had on the consciousness of his "backward" brethren. Germano quoted "one old nomad" who with tears in his eyes pronounced his great desire to see his children learn to read their native language. "Take a look, comrade," the old man shouted, pointing at a Romani text. "These are our Gypsy words." Germano quoted letters from other Roma expressing the great need for their children to learn to read and use the textbooks being printed in Moscow. Finally, he reported word from a group of provincial Roma who, upon receipt of a Romani-language primer, decided: "We always knew that Soviet power is the most popular power (*Sovetskaia vlast' – samaia narodnaia vlast'*), but when we received this book in our native language, we appreciated that this is exactly so." These letters from Roma rejoicing in the creation of Romani-language texts and celebrating the possibilities for formal, native-language education, Germano argued, revealed "the great improvement taking place among the Gypsy people" – people who had once been "benighted and broken-spirited" under tsarism.[92]

Though Germano's enthusiastic rhetoric may have captured the real desires of a few illiterate Romani nomads for a native-language education, it again masked the realities of the Soviet Union's Gypsy schools. While schools had sprouted on the new Romani kolkhozes born of Stalin's deadly collectivization drive, many were schools in name only. Narkompros officials, meanwhile, exhibited extremely limited knowledge of and seemingly little interest in the estimated thirty Gypsy schools in operation throughout the RSFSR.[93] These same officials scrambled to fulfil VTsIK's demand that Narkompros produce new cadres of trained Romani schoolteachers – a task that for years had inspired much discussion yet few practical results.[94]

Only in July 1932 did the first teaching-training courses for Roma open in Moscow's Central Institute for the Advancement of Qualified Education Cadres (TsIPKKNO). Officials invited "the best" young workers from Romani kolkhozes to apply.[95] Twenty-five students were accepted for enrolment in the courses. These students hailed predominantly from Romani kolkhozes in the Smolensk and Stalingrad regions of the RSFSR, though a few workers from Moscow's Romani cooperatives were accepted into the program as well. Six of the students were

Komsomol members while twelve identified themselves as former nomads. Although applicants were expected to have already completed at least an elementary education, two of the students could boast no further education than the completion of literacy courses.[96]

Pankov later recalled these first recruits as "undisciplined and unorganized" youths incapable of imagining "how to subordinate their own desires to the will of the collective."[97] He complained of their capricious, truant ways and disapproved of their adherence to the unsavoury culture of the nomadic camp. TsIPKKNO officials also worried about the "backwardness" of their new Romani students. In an appeal to Narkompros, one TsIPKKNO director complained that the students lacked clothing, dirtied the dormitory, and had sparked an epidemic of lice. Though the students enjoyed free boarding and a monthly stipend, TsIPKKNO officials now asked Narkompros for funding to purchase the students' shoes and clothing. Students who had arrived straight from "their tents" were completely lacking even the most basic necessities of "civilized" life.[98]

Despite the "extraordinary difficulties" faced by TsIPKKNO as it endeavoured to create new cadres of Romani schoolteachers, the recruits studied a variety of subjects, including Russian, Romani, mathematics, pedagogy, history, and civics.[99] After eight months of coursework, TsIPKKNO graduated fifteen Romani students, while those remaining needed to repeat coursework.[100] On paper at least, Narkompros planned to dispatch the graduates as Romani educators to the North Caucasus, Central Black Earth, Upper Volga, Lower Volga, Western, Leningrad, and Moscow regions.[101]

In summer 1933, however, five of the recent TsIPKKNO graduates began complaining of employment discrimination. Though they had officially been assigned to work in Moscow, city education officials refused to employ them in the capital's Gypsy schools. In written protests, the recent graduates displayed the political education they had received as TsIPKKNO students. In one letter, the students alleged that education officials in Moscow had explained that Romani schoolteachers were not needed because there were already enough Russian teachers in the city's employ. "In so far as the Gypsy schools are indigenizing," the students argued, "we consider the City Department of Education's attitude to be incorrect." In response to the city's refusal to provide them with work, the five graduates visited Moscow's Romani communities and calculated the number of children not being provided an education – an estimated 500 Romani youths. When they sent these figures to city education officials, they received no response and no new Gypsy schools were organized.

"For what are textbooks being printed?" the TsIPKKNO graduates asked in disbelief. "For what have we been left behind in Moscow to teach Gypsy children?" Astutely emphasizing their status as "the first Gypsy cadres specially sent out to re-educate our backward Gypsy generation," they inveighed against the fact that Moscow's Gypsy schools continued to be staffed – with the exception of Dudarova and Rogozhev – by Russian schoolteachers. They were ready to serve the state by enlightening their "backward" brethren, but were being rewarded not with work, but with hunger and a meaningless life on the streets. After having earned their qualifications as educators, they were left to sit idly and beg for bread – "just like dogs." Not least, the graduates sharply threatened "to return to telling fortunes in the markets."[102] Shortly thereafter, TsIPKKNO terminated its teacher-training courses for Roma.[103]

The disillusioned TsIPKKNO graduates may have been the first, but certainly were not the last of Romani teachers trained in Moscow in the 1930s and subsequently denied work in Soviet Gypsy schools. In fulfilment of Narkompros's resolution of 1 April 1932, Moscow's Timiriazev Teachers' Training College reluctantly opened the doors of its new Gypsy Department in the fall of 1933 to twenty-seven Romani students recruited primarily from Romani kolkhozes. The Romani students' arrival plunged the directorate of the Timiriazev pedagogical college into a frenzy of worried confusion and resentment as Narkompros and the Moscow City Department of Education debated their respective responsibilities for the funding of this new Gypsy Department. With both agencies refusing to assume the costs of training Romani teachers, the Timiriazev pedagogical college received "not a single kopeck" of support from either in its first three months as host to its new Romani students. The Timiriazev pedagogical college unhappily paid the new students' meager stipends from its own budget.[104]

As TsIPKKNO officials had done earlier, so too did the directorate of the Timiriazev pedagogical college quickly discover the "burden" of educating their Gypsy undesirables. With the dormitory at full occupancy, some Romani students were housed temporarily in classrooms and offices. Again, the Romani hopefuls had arrived on campus without adequate clothing and allegedly defiled the campus. Less than a month after the Gypsy Department's opening, the school's director began threatening to shut it down.[105]

In response, the Romani students quickly penned their own letter to TsIK, reporting threats of expulsion and complaining of ill treatment from the school's director. Demonstrating remarkable political acumen, the students cited Narkompros directives as they bemoaned their own lack of shoes, pleaded for stipend increases, and pointedly requested the appointment of a fellow Rom to direct the pedagogical college's Gypsy Department.[106] Upon investigation of these complaints, officials discovered that the Romani students not only lacked clothing and textbooks, but also were being taught in Russian. Illness – blamed on the students' insufficient clothing – had already forced three students to drop out.[107] To all observers, the scene at the Gypsy Department in its first months of existence was one of absolute chaos.

In its five short years of existence, the Gypsy Department of the Timiriazev pedagogical college never overcame its initial troubles. Responsibility for the department's financing was subject to constant debate while dormitory space seemed never readily available to Romani students.[108] In 1935, the department director resigned, complaining that his work had been "much too difficult and intense."[109] For the students, clothing remained scarce and stipends insufficient.[110] One student wrote home to his kolkhoz in the North Caucasus, humbly revealing the cold, hunger, and "shame" of his situation.[111] For many of the pedagogical college's Romani students, summer assignments as political-enlightenment workers on Romani kolkhozes surely came as a relief from their unenviable situation in the Soviet capital.[112]

By all accounts, the students remained unwelcome by all at the pedagogical college except for their teacher of Romani language – Pankov. Most other school officials relentlessly singled out the Romani students for their supposed propensity for theft and gambling, lack of discipline, insincere commitment, and black market activities. Even many Romani activists refused to come to the students' defence. At one meeting called by activists to discuss the situation at the pedagogical college, Germano blamed all problems on the students' lack of culture and consciousness, while another Romani leader declared the students' claims of hunger to be exaggerations.[113] In 1936, the directorate of the Timiriazev pedagogical college issued a characteristically scathing review of the school's Romani students, likening them to incorrigible children incapable of overcoming their nomadic pasts. Given their lack of culture and consciousness, the directorate insisted, the students did not understand the importance of personal hygiene, begged on the streets, squandered their stipends "irrationally," and were known to sell the clothing and shoes given them by the school. "To a significant degree," the directorate concluded, "state funds are being spent meaninglessly."[114] There was simply no point, the directorate implied, in trying to educate interminably "backward Gypsies."

Ultimately, however, it was a secret Central Committee (TsK) decree of 24 January 1938, and not complaints from officials at the Timiriazev pedagogical college, that finally sounded the death knell for early Soviet Romani educational institutions. This decree, "On the Liquidation of National Schools and National Departments within Schools," mandated the dismantling of the Gypsy schools (as well as the closure of other minority-language schools within the RSFSR: Assyrian, Vep, Izhor, Estonian, Finnish, Greek, Polish, Chinese, and others).[115] Yet the decree did more than shutter the Gypsy schools and inspire the termination of the teacher-training courses offered Roma at Moscow's Timiriazev pedagogical college. Romani-language publishing also ceased. "As a result of the implementation of this decree," V.G. Toropov has argued, "in 1938 the Gypsy language was deemed prospectless."[116] Gypsy schools and the Romani language were no longer considered desirable, expedient, or necessary messengers of Soviet values. Russian schools and the Russian language, it appeared, could do a better job of assimilating Romani students to Sovietism.

Indeed, implicit in the text of the decree is the privileging above all else of the long-term goals of what Hirsch calls Soviet "state-sponsored evolutionism." Gypsy and other minority-language schools were not afforded inherent value by the Party leadership. Rather, minority-language education and nationality policy more generally were considered tools in accomplishing the accelerated advancement of minority peoples towards the end point of socialist unity among a modern citizenry shorn of ethnic divisions.[117] Thus the TsK decree described Gypsy schools and other so-termed "special national schools" as harmful institutions that "cut the children off from Soviet life, deprived them of the opportunity to be exposed to Soviet culture and science, and blocked their path to receiving further education in technical colleges and institutions of higher education."[118] In other words, the Gypsy and other minority-language schools slated for elimination in 1938 had been deemed impediments to the long-term aims of the Soviet nationality policy that had born them. Their closure, situated against a backdrop of wider ethnic consolidation in the late Soviet 1930s, should not be seen as a retreat from Bolshevik nationality policy, but rather as the fulfilment and attempted "acceleration" of its assimilationist logic.[119]

Yet debates in the 1930s over the viability of Gypsy and other minority schools reveal that the state's long-standing commitment to "state-sponsored evolutionism" dovetailed with still more immediate, practical concerns to inspire policy changes that would affect the education not only of Roma, but also of minorities generally. The 1938 decree that shuttered Gypsy schools came on the heels of lengthy discussions within the Party leadership and among education officials that focused on broad issues of minority acculturation of Soviet values as well as on issues of cost-saving, efficiency, the educational preferences of minority peoples themselves, and even national security concerns. The closing of the Soviet Union's Gypsy schools is therefore best understood as evidence of *both* a wider push for the acceleration of "state-sponsored evolutionism" *and* a pragmatic state effort to streamline and more efficiently achieve all the varied aims of Soviet education for minorities. This policy change was at once in accord with the Soviet Union's overarching goal of "state-sponsored evolutionism" and the product of sobered bureaucratic realism in the face of the many challenges that minority education – especially for "small" and "backward" peoples such as Gypsies – posed to a state painfully aware of its own overextension and limited resources.[120]

Thus, keen contemporary observers could scarcely have been surprised by the decision to liquidate the Gypsy schools in pursuit of pragmatic educational management and Roma's smooth assimilation to Sovietism. Already in 1933, F. Krongauz, a Narkompros inspector of national schools, had concluded that the state's pained efforts to make the Gypsy schools truly Gypsy were not worth the time and resources they required. Krongauz suggested that instruction in the Gypsy schools should continue in Russian with Romani taught merely as a separate subject. After all, Krongauz concluded, it was unnecessary to teach all subjects in the native language in so far as Romani children were presumably already fluent in conversational Russian.[121] Underlying this sanguine nod to practicality was the sense that Krongauz considered "backward Gypsies" incapable of sovietizing their own children. He deemed Gypsy schools inefficient and inexpedient mechanisms of pushing Gypsies along the path towards Soviet modernity and supranational unity.

Krongauz was not alone in his retreat from the Bolshevik promise of minority native-language education for Roma and similar minority peoples. In 1933, many officials began abandoning an across-the-board commitment to minority native-language education in favour of what was now referred to as "natural assimilation" – especially for the empire's "smallest" and "most backward" nationalities. Invoking pragmatism and efficiency, many at Narkompros supported a reorganization of minority education that would prioritize native-language schooling primarily for those "relatively large peoples with more developed languages, or with the perspective of development."[122] Krongauz's practical advocacy of Russian-language schooling for Romani children was thus a candid precursor of this slightly more finessed statement made by the secretary of the Soviet of Nationalities in 1934: "In fact, we should not oppose assimilation. Our nationalities policy is absolutely clear and we can never permit forced assimilation. We won't allow that, but we should by all means welcome natural assimilation … which takes place at its own pace."[123]

The enormous difficulties and costs facing Soviet officials tasked with the creation of schools, textbooks, and native cadres of schoolteachers for Roma, let alone the prejudices that informed their decision-making, certainly contributed to "backward Gypsies" being deemed prime candidates for so-called "natural assimilation." Yet officials also seriously considered the seeming educational preferences of Roma themselves. As early as 1928, Moscow education officials had questioned the need to provide Roma and other "backward" nationalities with national-language education. In a document entitled "The Education of National Minorities," officials maintained that "backward" peoples themselves often desired their children to learn in Russian, not in their national language. "This is explained by the fact that the Russian language is more necessary [and] easier to study."[124] In time, the concept of natural assimilation proved a hardy rationalization for collapsing the native-language educational institutions designed for Roma and similarly "backward" and "small" peoples. If the end goal was forging a modern citizenry fully acculturated in Soviet values, what mattered was not the mere existence of minority schools, but their effectiveness in helping to accomplish the task. Underscoring this point in 1933, N.N. Nurmakov, chairman of VTsIK's Nationalities Department, insisted: "We open national schools not in order to provide mandatory instruction in native languages, but in order to give an education to national minorities."[125]

Official advocacy of natural assimilation became increasingly commonplace after Stalin proclaimed the Soviet Friendship of Peoples on 4 December 1935. The eradication of historic "distrust between the peoples of the USSR" had finally been achieved, Stalin declared. The antagonisms cultivated by Great Russian chauvinism under the tsars had been dissolved, replaced by harmony among all the Soviet Union's peoples.[126] As subsequent articulations of this solemn covenant of international socialist unity would make clear, there was to be no doubt in the future that "the Great Russians" deserved to be recognized by all Soviet peoples as the "first among equals."[127] Soviet officials attempting to provide quality minority education conducted in potentially 192 languages were now finally free to openly ask questions that many had been silently debating for some time now: Would it not be simplest if these friends had a common language in which they could converse? And if the Russians and their superior culture had been responsible for the forging of this friendship in the first place, did it not then make sense for Russian to be the language of socialist unity? In the end, it appeared, especially "small" and "backward" minorities such as Roma could best be educationally served not by official insistence on "national form," but rather by the most effective and even desired educational vehicles of "socialist content."[128] What mattered most of all was that Roma studied in Soviet schools. Those Soviet schools need not – and perhaps should not – be Gypsy in form.

In the wake of Stalin's historic announcement of the Friendship of Peoples, Narkompros and VTsIK officials continued to debate the future of Romani-language education. They increasingly structured their arguments around the interrelated themes of efficiency, practicality, and natural assimilation. Though the production of Romani-language textbooks had made it possible for Romani children to study every subject in the native tongue, Narkompros officials explained, Roma preferred to send their children to Russian schools.[129] As of January 1936, Narkompros estimated that "only an insignificant proportion" of Romani children in the RSFSR – 288 in all – were enrolled in Gypsy schools. All others, excluding the "neglected" children of nomadic Roma, already studied in Russian schools. Six months later, Narkompros established that of 1,470 Romani children enrolled in schools within the RSFSR, only 277 were taught in their native tongue.[130] By September, city education officials in Moscow provided further statistical evidence that across-the-board enrolment in the capital's minority schools steadily decreased with the start of each new academic year. The Soviet of Nationalities specifically noted that many of Moscow's Roma had demanded the enrolment of their children in Russian schools, justifying their choice with the belief that "as inhabitants of Moscow," their children needed to be literate in Russian, not Romani.[131] By January 1937, only thirty Romani students were enrolled in Moscow's Gypsy schools.[132] From the vantage point of officialdom, "natural assimilation" appeared the preferred route to Soviet acculturation among Roma themselves.[133] There seemed no longer any point in providing Romani children with a native-language education at all.

As this shift in thinking about Romani-language schools took place, a broader move to firmly establish Russian as the common language of the Soviet people was already underway. In late 1937, the Party leadership began discussing the great need for all Soviet citizens to become fluent in Russian, albeit as a second language. As Stalin considered the menace of Nazi Germany, he grew increasingly worried that the Red Army had become a modern-day Tower of Babel as a result of the Bolsheviks' generous nationality policies. He was particularly concerned by the inadequate Russian-language capabilities of the Soviet Union's titular nationalities. In a November speech before the Party's Central Committee, Stalin focused specifically on the problem that minorities' lack of fluency in Russian posed to the defence of the Soviet Union against foreign aggressors. Given the state of increasingly tempestuous international relations, he explained, the Soviet Union was in the process of shoring up the ranks of its Red Army. Citizens of all nationalities owed a civic duty to defend the Soviet Union, and thus were being called upon to serve. Recent conscription efforts, however, had revealed that many minority peoples – especially those from the Soviet republics – did not speak Russian capably. Clearly, such a situation imperilled the proper military defence of the Soviet Union. Thus, Stalin explained, "We have only one language in which all citizens of the USSR can make themselves understood more or less – this is the Russian language. It would be a good thing if every citizen conscripted into the army could make themselves understood in Russian."[134] In contrast to Roma, the major titular nationalities had not so readily opted for "natural assimilation." Thus, as a matter of state security no less than of "state-sponsored evolutionism," a separate solution was needed to remedy their linguistic aversion to Russian.

On 8 March 1938 the Politburo decreed mandatory Russian-language study in all non-Russian schools *as a separate subject of study*. As Peter Blitstein and Terry Martin have made clear, the decree was instituted not as a measure of Russification, but as a practical means of advancing the cultural, economic, and military goals of the Soviet state.[135] These goals no doubt included the achievement of a unified and modern Soviet citizenry. Stalin himself demanded that in the formulation and implementation of the decree, "there must be no suppression of, or limitation on, the native language, so as to warn all organizations that Russian is to be a subject of study, not a medium of instruction."[136] The 8 March decree, then, did not repudiate minority native-language education – especially as concerned the "major" nationalities – but instead mandated minority fluency in Russian.[137] For Roma, however, the TsK decree of 24 January 1938 had already rejected Romani as an acceptable "medium of instruction" and denied them native-language schools in the name of more expedient assimilation. Although Roma were still invited to the table of the Soviet Friendship of Peoples, the question of their so-called native language was no longer a topic of friendly discussion. New Soviet Gypsies, like all their fellow citizens, and like representatives of all nationalities ("big" or "small"), were expected to converse in Russian, the common Soviet language and itself a symbol of socialist modernity.

The *Natsmen's* Burden

Though exact numbers are unavailable, the Gypsy Department of Moscow's Timiriazev Teachers' Training College graduated some 120 Romani elementary school teachers, most of whom were never employed in the Soviet Union's scarce, underfunded, and short-lived Gypsy schools. Many of these graduates did serve the Soviet state in other ways – most notably as teachers of Russian in non-Russian schools. After the decree of 8 March 1938, the demand for trained teachers of Russian in autonomous regions and union republics inevitably grew, and thus "Gypsy teachers were dispatched to village schools to teach the children of very different nationalities, only not Gypsies."[138]

Over the years, Pankov maintained correspondence with his former students at the Timiriazev pedagogical college. One student wrote to Pankov in 1939 from his new position as a schoolteacher in the Smolensk region, where he taught Russian, German, and art. He did not hide his disappointment that the Gypsy schools of nearby Romani kolkhozes had been shut down. Another graduate had been sent to teach outside of Odessa, only to find professional and personal disappointment in a life alienated from her fellow Roma. In her letter to Pankov, she interrupted her Russian prose to inform her former mentor in Romani, "It is very difficult [to live] among the *gadzhe* [non-Roma], because they do not understand." The author then expressed in Russian her longing to be reunited with the students and teachers with whom she had studied in Moscow. Another student wrote Pankov from her new teaching appointment in the Chechen-Ingush ASSR, expressing support of his ongoing commitment to Romani-language education. "It's very good that Gypsy matters are moving forward," she wrote. "I have always supported and defended you as a leader of such affairs. I terribly disapprove of those … who not only do not help, but also renounce their own nation. I, in exemplary fashion, speak of the fact that I am a Gypsy wherever I find myself and take pride in this. I managed to stand on the same level as Russians and to prove that we too can be made into people (*i dokazat', chto i iz nas poluchaiutsia liudi*)."[139]

Pankov, meanwhile, descended into depression following the closing of Romani educational institutions in 1938. As he watched the schools dismantled and as he was relieved of his duties as a Romani language teacher at the pedagogical college, Pankov apparently took little delight in the long-awaited publication of the Soviet Union's first Romani-Russian dictionary. For nearly a decade, Pankov had aided Sergievskii and Barannikov in the creation of this 10,000-word tome.[140] Now that the dictionary had finally been published, there was no longer any official use or purpose seen in it. In Pankov's eyes, Gypsies again seemed doomed as an unlettered and uncivilized people. He regarded the Gypsy schools' closure as a grievously fatal blow to the mission to sovietize "backward Gypsies." While the reach of the schools had been undeniably limited, their influence over the "backward" Romani populations in Moscow and elsewhere was greater than central state officials were willing to admit. After all, he and his fellow activists had taken up the burden of enlightening their fellow Gypsies and produced Soviet citizens from the backward, seemingly hopeless Gypsy masses.

In protest of the Gypsy schools' dismantling, Pankov addressed a letter to Stalin in which he discussed the impending "decline of Gypsy culture, of the destruction of the cultural revolution's achievements." He wrote extensively of the continuing need to introduce Gypsies to socially useful labour, of the doom awaiting the Romani language, of the stranglehold placed on the Soviet Union's burgeoning Romani literature, and of his fellow activists' good faith nurturing of cadres of Romani teachers. Having sent his letter to Stalin, Pankov encouraged his former students to follow suit.[141] As he waited for a response from Stalin – either in the form of a letter or a knock at his door in the middle of the night – Pankov sunk deeper into depression. Having lost his job as a teacher responsible for the shaping of young Romani minds, Pankov was forced to take up work in a Moscow factory. In the meantime, he "stopped shaving and physically wasted away before the eyes of his beloved family." A response from Stalin, however, never arrived.[142]

Perhaps due to his own deeply personal investment in the development of Soviet Gypsy schools in the 1920s and 1930s, Pankov found little solace in what the schools had actually achieved. Pankov and his colleagues had brought a patently Soviet brand of "enlightenment" to hundreds (if not more) of Roma. Though the Gypsy schools were few and limited in their reach, Romani students had acquired reading, writing, and arithmetic skills while learning about the duties of Soviet citizenship, the necessity of a personal hygiene regime, and their expected role in the construction of socialism. The didactic Romani literature that Pankov had helped to create had transmitted these same lessons to Romani adults. Children and adults alike, Romani students had confronted the lesson intended for them by their native civilizing missionaries: that they, as Gypsies, were fundamentally backward. Although relatively few, Romani students who attended classes and engaged Romani literature were bombarded with the message that becoming Soviet entailed a deliberate mastering of one's own backwardness and a deliberate honing of one's own Soviet self.

Lenin famously stated: "The illiterate person stands outside of politics. First it is necessary to teach him the alphabet. Without it there are only rumors, fairy tales, and prejudices, but not politics."[143] Moscow's Romani activists took this message to heart. In the absence of a Romani alphabet, they first attempted to spread literacy in Russian as they raced to create a modern national language from the ostensibly impoverished dialects of their own unlettered people. They produced a slate of Romani-language texts designed to spread their message of backwardness and Sovietism far beyond the crumbling walls of Moscow's Gypsy schools and literacy centres. The ideals of labour, care of the self, and socialist solidarity were promised to those Roma who read or listened to the texts composed for them, a "backward" people, by fellow Roma who had already fashioned themselves as integrated Soviet citizens. Those Roma who engaged these lessons could no longer "stand outside of politics." They were implicated, and implicated themselves, in the Soviet civilizing mission.

Roma who participated in early Soviet Romani educational initiatives – those who attended Gypsy schools, studied at literacy centres, enrolled in teacher-training programs, engaged the didactic literature created for "backward" Gypsies, lobbied for admission into teacher-training courses, and wrestled with education officials for employment in Gypsy schools – gained training in more than literacy, arithmetic, personal health, and even pedagogy. They received a Soviet political education. Not least of all, they learned that in the early Soviet Union, the burden of ascribed backwardness – the *natsmen*'s burden – implied both duty *and* opportunity. Textbooks, teachers, activists, and officials revealed to Romani students the theoretical promises of the Soviet nationality regime – Roma's entitlement to the tangible benefits of minority "backwardness" – as much as they instructed them in their civic duty to transform themselves into literate, clean, rational, and socially useful Soviet citizens. While some, and especially the graduates of Romani teacher-training courses, would discover that many of the opportunities offered them as Gypsies were hollow promises, they learned nonetheless how to navigate the Soviet system. In learning to brush their teeth, to speak and read Russian, and to lobby the state to fulfil its promises to its "backward" minority citizens, these Roma acted not only as students of but also as participants in Soviet culture. In their performance, if not internalization, of Soviet values, they fashioned themselves as conscious, integrated citizens.

Even Roma's rejection of their own national schools in pursuit of a Russian-language education for their children must be seen as evidence that the sovietizing mission among "backward" Gypsies produced some of its intended results. The drastic decreases in enrolment at Moscow's Gypsy schools coincided with the state's campaign in the late 1930s to reassert Russian as the language of revolution, progress, and Soviet solidarity. Meanwhile, it was no secret to any Soviet citizen that social mobility required strong Russian language skills. Many Roma seem to have concluded that if the goal, or at least the demand, was to become a productive member of Soviet society, there could be little use in pursuing an education in one's own "inadequate" or "backward" national language. If it was in part the *natsmen*'s burden to properly educate one's self, some Roma seemed to have shrewdly decided that a backward Gypsy could do no better than to learn directly from and to speak the language of those who were presumably most advanced.

Finally, it must not be overlooked that the teacher-training courses offered to Roma had produced a contingent of New Soviet Men and Women qualified to preach the word of Sovietism. As students in Moscow, these Romani educators had been informed by many of their teachers that they were uncivilized and barely worth the kopecks being spent on their education. Upon graduation, however, they had been sent to all corners of the empire with a mission to educate their fellow Soviet citizens. Though some were disappointed not to be employed educating children of their own nationality, Romani schoolteachers nonetheless continued down the path of Soviet enlightenment and led others along the way. The sovietizing mission undertaken by Pankov and his fellow Gypsy Union activists in 1925 did not end with the Gypsy schools' dismantling in 1938. In ways that they had not foreseen, their mission only expanded as Romani schoolteachers brought the Soviet civilizing mission to other nationalities as well.

In still other ways that were certain not to have surprised Moscow's Romani activists by the late 1930s, however, the *natsmen*'s burden was – as defined by the state – largely to be borne by Roma and their fellow minority peoples themselves. Generous in its promises, the Soviet state all too often proved stingy in its undeniably limited resources and withholding in its commitment to transforming "backward Gypsies" into educated, productive, and conscious Soviet citizens. As in so much else, the Soviet state embraced a vision of universal and total transformation, yet struggled both desperately *and* half-heartedly to equip and staff even a handful of classrooms devoted to rearing New Soviet Gypsies – literate, clean, and civic-minded. The energy that did fuel early Soviet Romani educational initiatives was supplied primarily by Roma who, variously motivated, invested in minority education as a means of graduating themselves and others to Soviet citizenship.

As for Pankov, he never wavered in his insistence that Romani-language education had a necessary role to play in the sovietization of "backward" Gypsies. Following Stalin's death in 1953, Pankov wrote to the Party's Central Committee, arguing that after 1938 Gypsies "have once again become unlettered, deprived of the most elementary … conditions for their own development and cultural growth." The Gypsy schools' closure, Pankov maintained, had only exacerbated the marginality of his "backward" brethren. "Gypsy children in Russian schools do not succeed or do not learn at all," Pankov argued. "They are hindered by an insufficient knowledge of Russian, cultural backwardness, and ceaseless nomadism."[144] Pankov concluded his letter with a call for the restoration of the Gypsy schools and the renewed publication of Romani-language educational texts. The Central Committee rejected all of Pankov's suggestions.

3 Parasites, Pariahs, and Proletarians: Class Struggle and the Forging of a Gypsy Proletariat

In July 1931, the Nationalities Department of VTsIK hosted a conference of government officials engaged in efforts at sovietizing "backward Gypsies." Six Roma in attendance – Bezliudskii, Germano, Lebedev, Pankov, Rom-Lebedev, and Taranov – brought with them their experience as former Gypsy Union leaders as well as new insights born of their recent work helping the Soviet bureaucracy to engineer a Gypsy cultural revolution. Though more than seven years had passed since Moscow's Romani activists had announced their plan to organize "the backward proletarian Gypsy masses," attendees of the VTsIK conference were still left to wonder what a Gypsy proletariat might look like in reality.[1] Rom-Lebedev, for one, could no longer contain his frustration or impatience. After listening to his comrades discuss the relatively limited progress made in transitioning backward Gypsies to socially useful work, Rom-Lebedev interrupted the proceedings to demand not only an explanation of the phrase "toiling Gypsies" but also a justification for its use. How was it possible to speak of "toiling Gypsies," he asked, "when in the past, and in the present, the majority of [Gypsies] speculate, while the women, almost without exception, tell fortunes?"[2]

This chapter explores the distinct challenge posed by Roma to the world's first self-declared workers' state.[3] The work traditionally associated with Roma prior to the October Revolution and during NEP – trading, fortune telling, and entertaining – was not recognized by the state as socially useful or as labour at all. Roma were reviled as consummate parasitic idlers and swindlers. On the eve of Stalin's "revolution from above," Romani activists and officials therefore endeavoured to create a Romani working class from the ostensibly labour-averse backward Gypsy masses. Nationality policy provided the foundation for their efforts to organize Romani workers' cooperatives, a central

Romani club, and Romani-language periodicals that espoused the need for Roma to perform socially useful work. Yet their efforts largely failed to assimilate Moscow's Roma to the declared legitimate labour of the industrial state sector. Ultimately, the harsh realities of Stalin's First Five-Year Plan forced many Roma to seek work in the socialist economy, and especially in a variety of newly created Romani artels. The proliferation of Romani artels at the dawn of the 1930s not only coincided with but also directly resulted from the massive socio-economic dislocations caused by Stalin's tripartite campaign to ruthlessly industrialize, collectivize, and dekulakize the Soviet Union.

It was not enough, however, for so-called social parasites to labour for the state. Like their non-Romani counterparts, Romani workers were called upon to attach heartfelt meaning to their contributions to socialist construction as well as subscribe to the Soviet values of discipline, transparency, and consciousness. Therefore, when recent Vlax Romani immigrants to the Soviet Union refused to comply with the state's demand that they contribute socially useful labour to the socialist economy and to embrace Soviet values, these Roma were castigated and punished as foreign, socially alien, and as Gypsy kulaks. In Moscow, Romani activists played a pivotal role in unmasking "foreign Gypsies" (Vlax Roma) as enemies of the state. They devised a new narrative of Gypsy class struggle and invented the so-called Gypsy kulak. Moscow's nascent Romani proletarians learned by negative example that the supposed parasitism and opaqueness of traditional Gypsy culture were considered grave threats to and criminal offences against Soviet socialism and thus deserving of harsh punishment. Moscow's most celebrated Romani workers in the 1930s were those who not only laboured in the state sector, but also vocally defined themselves vis-à-vis their "foreign" and "Gypsy kulak" foils. As they joined their fellow Romani activists in trumpeting nationality policy's central message of Sovietism transcending ethnic difference, they worked, too, to defend socialism from the pernicious, alien influence of Gypsy kulaks and stubbornly foreign Gypsy malcontents. The creation of a Gypsy proletariat in Moscow proved as much a process of incorporating Roma into the urban socialist economy as of "cleansing" the Soviet capital of distinct segments of the Romani population categorized as unproductive, socially harmful, and doubly foreign.

Imagining the Gypsy Proletariat

Prior to the Revolution, many settled, urban Roma had been employed as members of professional Romani choirs. Romani service nomads meanwhile were traditionally known as itinerant horse-traders, black-smiths, tinsmiths, fortune tellers, and beggars.[4] By the time of the Gypsy Union's establishment, Roma employed in Moscow's industrial enterprises numbered only in the handfuls. Though they self-identified as proletarians, the Gypsy Union's leading members were themselves typically employed as performers in NEP's resurgent Romani choirs.[5] From the vantage point of the state, extraordinarily few Roma actually laboured – that is, performed work that contributed to socialist construction. Although they spoke often of "toiling Gypsies" and "proletarian masses" in their writings, Gypsy Union activists recognized that they projected a Soviet ideal, not reality. They therefore committed to providing Roma with all the institutional accoutrements of a proletariat on the rise: vanguard leadership, workers' clubs and schools, didactic Romani-language literature, and specialty apprentice "pilot schools and workshops in the various branches of manufacturing and craftsmanship."[6] These were to serve as the crucial ingredients of the transformation of Gypsy parasites into equal participants "in the construction of the economy and the state."[7]

Yet even for the ambitious Gypsy Union youths, the dream of forging a Gypsy proletariat seemed painfully beyond reach. Lacking confidence on the part of state officials, Gypsy Union leaders also failed to win the allegiance of Moscow's Romani service nomads – its horse-traders and fortune tellers, especially. Rom-Lebedev later recalled that although Moscow's Romani horse-traders "sensed" a nearing end for both NEP and their markets, they were loath to abandon their trades. When confronted with Gypsy Union activists' insistence that their way of life was outmoded and dangerously un-Soviet, the horse-traders obstinately refused to listen. When the activists demanded that the women of Moscow's Romani camps abandon fortune telling and begging for socially useful work, the horse-traders laughed in their faces and snarled, "And what are they capable of?! You can't tell fortunes in a factory!"[8]

Many of Moscow's Romani service nomads were not merely sceptical of the Gypsy Union, but also notoriously resentful of the Bolsheviks' reordering of social and economic life. Horse markets were no longer reliable sources of profit, while private profit itself was anathema to the architects of the socialist society in the making. Romani women could no longer survive on begging or clairvoyance. Few citizens had the resources to spare on charity or divination while professional "parasitism" and fortune telling were counter-revolutionary.[9] As one contemporary Soviet newspaper explained, "The Gypsies' trades, everyday life, and lifestyle stand in complete contradiction to the foundations

Romani woman telling fortunes. Courtesy of the State Archive of the Russian Federation.

of our socialist society ... Though the revolution brought the Gypsies a considerable improvement in their legal situation, it painfully impacted their sources of livelihood." No longer able to freely trade horses or tell fortunes, the report continued, Roma's material situation had "dramatically worsened."[10] Indeed, for many Roma, revolution and sovietization implied nothing more than their own bitter impoverishment. Moscow's so-called "camp Gypsies" thus challenged the Gypsy Union's leaders as a hostile lumpenproletariat impervious to revolutionary change.

Even those Roma newly employed in Moscow's industries posed a challenge to activists intent on proletarianizing "backward Gypsies." Germano later explained the growing pains of novice Romani proletarians in this way: "At the start of [his] life in the city, the lone camp Gypsy felt not quite himself in the unfamiliar conditions of the plants and factories. Some kind of fear seized him that he was being torn from the camp forever and that he would end up all alone among the surrounding non-Gypsies."[11] As Gypsy Union activists understood it, the best way to attract "backward Gypsies" to industrial life would be to recruit entire Romani families or camps, teach them a trade, and then help them to organize a specialized producers' cooperative. The Gypsy Union's leaders rationalized that for the time being, they would have to at least outwardly respect the legendarily secretive and closed world of the nomadic Romani camp.[12] Through the artel framework, the Gypsy Union activists would accommodate "camp Gypsies" while teaching them a productive trade and convincing them of the backwardness of their anachronistic culture. In the words of Germano, Moscow's Romani artels were designed as "levers for the organization of a new everyday culture in the Gypsy masses."[13]

The Gypsy Union thus established an industrial department devoted to "the elimination of Gypsies' existing common professions, such as fortune telling, begging, horse-trading, horse-thieving, etc." and "the introduction of [Gypsies] to the labour principle by means of assigning them work, training them in all kinds of labour specializations ... and organizing them in artels, communes, etc."[14] Gypsy Union activists coordinated a diverse array of fundraising efforts to finance the creation of workshops and artels. They organized choir concerts, hosted lecture and film series, recycled paper and rag scraps, and never ceased to petition central state and Moscow city officials for subsidies and tax relief.[15] The Gypsy Union ultimately scraped together enough resources to organize at least three workshops in central Moscow that produced printed fabrics, boots, and toys.[16] The Gypsy Union also secured contracts for Romani day labourers to work on construction sites where they could earn a living and raise their qualification levels.[17]

Although the archives remain largely silent on these ventures, one Gypsy Union enterprise attracted the attention of journalist Pavel Orlovets. Staffed almost entirely by Romani women and managed by a male Gypsy Union member, Ia.G. Dombrovskii, the Gypsy Union's textiles workshop trained women to print fabrics, manufacture stockings, and produce colourful shawls and neckties. Orlovets visited the workshop shortly after it began operations and recorded Dombrovskii's boasting about the women's progress. "Within one week they mastered the entire work," Dombrovskii bragged, "and now they give the ties their own personal design. Their taste is somehow peculiar, colourful, bright, and kind of unfashionable, but it draws in the buyer."[18]

Alongside the creation of artisanal workshops, the Gypsy Union's leaders also soon fulfilled – at least temporarily – another of their most ambitious goals: the publication of a Romani-language journal designed to aid in "the re-education of Gypsies having begun the path to labour."[19] Under the editorial lead of Taranov and Germano, *Romany zoria* (Gypsy Dawn) debuted in November 1927 with a print run of 1,500 copies and was distributed to readers free of charge. The cover of *Romany zoria*'s first issue captured the message contained within the journal's pages. Three nomadic Roma – a man, his wife, and their son – are depicted on the verge of a momentous new journey. Ready to leave all remnants of their backward life behind (including a spare cart-wheel), the three look forward – both literally and figuratively – to the possibilities of the shining Soviet future that awaits them. Before them appear two options: settled life as rational agriculturalists or settled life as industrial workers. Either of these two roads leads to the same end point of enlightenment, productivity, order, and personal salvation in Soviet civilization. Though they direct their gaze towards the smokestacks of an industrial complex, it matters little which route they choose, so long as they abandon their past lives as aimless, unproductive Gypsies divorced from Soviet society.[20]

The fledgling journal's editors and contributors had attempted to fill the thin, thirty-five-page issue with as much helpful advice and information as could possibly be of use to the backward Gypsy transitioning to the enlightened life of the Soviet citizen. Beginning with an explanatory essay outlining the tenets of Soviet nationality policy, *Romany zoria*'s first issue also featured short articles on adapting to agriculture and industrial work, the creation of the new Romani alphabet, and the organization of Moscow's Gypsy schools and club. In a feature entitled "Everything Romani in Moscow," *Romany zoria* provided information on Moscow's new artels and schools, encouraged readers to apply for seats in workers' faculties, and announced plans for the publication of the first Romani-language primer. Reflecting on the anachronism of traditional Romani professions, Rom-Lebedev's short story "Romano beng" (The Gypsy Devil) provided a satirical account of Romani fortune tellers and their questionable clientele. With bold-faced slogans, *Romany zoria* began with the salvo "Workers of the World, Unite!" and, at the turn of each page, exhorted readers to refashion themselves into productive Soviet citizens.[21]

The Soviet press enthusiastically welcomed the appearance of the world's first Romani-language journal as a successful step forward for the empire's benighted Gypsies. "The journal *Romany zoria*," *Izvestiia* declared, "must be received warmly as the harbinger of an entire people's culture being born anew."[22] Gypsy Union leaders echoed this view. Declaring the journal "a huge triumph for Soviet Gypsies," they downplayed Roma's illiteracy rates, minimized *Romany zoria*'s paltry

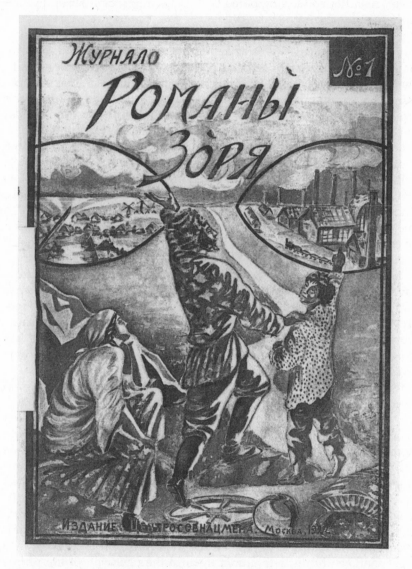

Front cover of the first issue of *Romany zoria* 1927.

circulation figures, and instead celebrated the journal as an effective mechanism for converting parasitic Gypsies into socially useful proletarians and farmers.[23]

Behind closed doors, however, excitement over the journal's publication quickly gave way to disappointment and frustration. As early as August 1927, Romani activists complained of bureaucratic impediments to the publication of their various new Romani-language propaganda materials. Although financed and published by Narkompros's Council of National Minorities (Sovnatsmen), *Romany zoria* proved an expensive venture. Months before even the first issue's printing, Gypsy Union activists were informed that they would have to "simplify" the journal "to the minimum" and endure a lengthy delay in *Romany zoria*'s initial publication.[24] Despite the purported success of the journal as both evidence of the benevolence and rationality of Soviet governance and as a mechanism for sovietizing "backward Gypsies," obstacles to the continued publication of *Romany zoria* only worsened after its first appearance in November 1927. In fact, another issue would not reach readers until 1929.

In the meantime, Gypsy Union activists also worked to create a Gypsy club that would effectively coordinate all the needs of a Gypsy proletariat in the making. They imagined the club as a counselling centre, school, housing service, labour exchange, movie house, theatre, library, lecture hall, medical office, and social meeting place for Moscow's "proletarian Gypsy masses."[25] In 1926, the Gypsy Union's leaders established the Soviet Union's first Gypsy club – named Red Star – in a former tavern on the city's northern outskirts, just paces away from Roma's notorious horse markets.[26]

As had so many of their other organizational efforts, however, Red Star disappointed the activists' quixotic visions of what their club could accomplish – at least in the short term. Resource-poor, Red Star was also located woefully far from most of Moscow's Romani neighbourhoods. While the club strategically bordered the markets of Moscow's most "backward Gypsies," its membership also suffered from its distance from the homes and workplaces of the city's activists and budding proletarians. For the horse-traders, speculators, and fortune tellers disinclined to embrace Sovietism, the mere proximity of Red Star to their markets did little to attract them to the new way of life propagated at the club. Those sympathetic to the Gypsy Union's cause but wary of the commute to Red Star, meanwhile, found it difficult "to frequently visit or actively participate in the club's work."[27] In its first year of operations, Red Star managed to recruit a mere seventy members, only twenty of whom were women.[28]

By this time, however, the Gypsy Union suffered problems greater than that of its failing journal and club. Central state authorities now charged the Gypsy Union with having completely bungled efforts to provide Roma with work training via the Gypsy Union's industrial workshops and artels. Whereas the Gypsy Union had lobbied to organize such institutions with the promise that they would "inculcate labour skills in the Gypsy masses" and train qualified Romani workers, officials found that the Gypsy Union had succeeded only in creating barely functioning workshops that sapped resources, encouraged indebtedness, and distracted the Gypsy Union from its more manageable aims.[29]

The MKK RKI inspection of March 1927 alerted officials that the Gypsy Union's industrial ventures were nothing more than a screen for the speculative interests of a few of the Gypsy Union's least sincere and most enterprising members. The Gypsy Union's textile workshop, for example, was said to have been driven to ruin by the individual profit-seeking schemes of the Gypsy Union's own comrade Dombrovskii. In the name of Soviet nationality policy, Dombrovskii had so finagled the system that the textiles workshop had come to suspiciously employ some eighteen paid service employees while the workshop's real workers – formerly nomadic Romani women – laboured without knowledge of Dombrovskii's subterfuge.[30] "Dombrovskii fell to speculation," M. Rogi later explained, "and the artel's workshop yielded a loss from month to month."[31] According to the state's narrative, Dombrovskii – the perceived consummate Gypsy – had taken advantage of Soviet nationality policy's generosity only to increase his own speculative profits.[32]

Dombrovskii's unmasking as a speculator inflicted harsh consequences on the Gypsy Union. Forced to fold its industrial enterprises and to pay off the debts that it had accrued in its industrial capacities, the Gypsy Union was accused by MKK RKI inspectors of harbouring self-interested, anti-Soviet horse-traders, stage artists, and other idlers.[33] Officials looked at the surface results of the Gypsy Union's underfunded efforts to institutionally equip an illusory Gypsy proletariat with mechanisms of self-transformation and deemed the organization incapable of transitioning Gypsy idlers to productive, socially useful labour.

At the time of the Gypsy Union's liquidation in February 1928, *Romany zoria*'s prospects also remained in doubt. Under the pretext that the club had thus far served merely as a Romani choir venue and a site of organized speculation, Red Star's doors were also closed in the wake of the Gypsy Union's dismantling.[34] Though *Romany zoria* and Red Star would both soon be resurrected, the work assumed by the Gypsy Union was transferred to Narkompros, Narkomzem, MONO, and other state agencies. Yet while the Gypsy Union had failed to provide the "Gypsy proletarian masses" with lasting, effective workers' institutions or even to win over Moscow's horse-traders and soothsayers, it had succeeded in introducing some of Moscow's Roma to labour skills and Soviet values. As would become still more clear in the era of Stalin's first Five-Year Plans, the Gypsy Union had – most importantly of all – led many Roma to the realization that minority "backwardness" was immeasurably valuable political capital in the Soviet Union. In this sense, the Gypsy Union and its shoddy workers' institutions were not merely the "prehistory to the serious cooperative movement among the Gypsy masses," but also the staging ground for both the triumphs and failures of Moscow's Romani proletariat.[35]

Learning to Labour Legitimately

In February 1928, few Soviet citizens would likely have been surprised by news of the Gypsy Union's alleged failures or shocked by the seemingly meager progress its leaders had made in fashioning a proletariat from Gypsy traders, fortune tellers, and beggars. As elsewhere in Europe, the Gypsy figured in the Soviet imagination as a meandering, beguiling swindler whose seductive powers inspired as much fear and contempt as they did desire. As in tsarist times, fascination with Gypsy freedom (*volia*) and appetite for the stereotypical Gypsy woman's licentiousness supplemented a general societal contempt for Gypsies as consummate shirkers of labour and shameless parasites.

Among popular portraits of Gypsies produced in the Soviet 1920s, the most sympathetic were still likely to delineate "Gypsies' defining feature" as "the insatiable thirst for liberty, independence, and the rejection (*nepriznanie*) of culture." Romantic visions of "Gypsy freedom," however, competed with disgust for Gypsies' allegedly stubborn refusal to work and presumed talent for subsisting on the sweat and toil of others.[36] Even those who dismissed images of Gypsies as cheats, thieves, and beggars were nonetheless willing to admit that such stereotypes contained a "certain element of truth."[37] Only the lone voice of one propagandist would go so far as to try to convince readers that

"Gypsies love to work" every bit as much as they love to trade horses or to sing and dance.[38] It was generally accepted as fact that throughout history, Gypsies could be found "neither behind a plough nor behind a factory machine."[39]

In the aftermath of the Gypsy Union's liquidation, Moscow's Romani activists faced a momentous choice. The Gypsy Union's demise, the termination of NEP, and Stalin's revolution from above left the leading propagandists among them confused as to which strategic representation of Gypsies would best serve their cause of nurturing Gypsy workers. Should they continue insisting on the existence of a Gypsy proletariat and attempt to popularize Gypsies as people unrecognized for their honest toil? Should they instead embrace prevailing stereotypes of Gypsies as work-averse parasites, and thus emphasize Gypsies' need for a carefully orchestrated cultural revolution? Or should they argue that Gypsies, though capable and willing to become heroic proletarians, had always been subjugated, isolated, and forcefully excluded from the economic, social, and political life of their oppressors? Apparently torn between these options, Moscow's Romani activists ultimately attempted to weld all three narratives into an unassailable epic of the making of the Gypsy proletariat.

Work constructing this narrative began immediately following the Gypsy Union's dissolution. In a missive addressed to the Presidium of VTsIK, Romani activists reflected bitterly on their struggle to integrate Roma into the socialist economy. In their view, one simple fact explained the urgency with which they approached the task of refashioning backward Gypsies into productive Soviet citizens: "This is the disparity between the Gypsies' everyday culture and contemporary social principles." In their immeasurable backwardness, Gypsies could not understand that only those who laboured were to enjoy the rights of Soviet citizenship. And yet it was not Gypsies' fault that they were "society's parasites." Gypsies could not be blamed for their historic poverty and oppression. Despite their overwhelming ignorance, Gypsies wanted to work in industry and till land. They were not unproductive pariahs of their own volition, but rather had become society's parasites by suffering centuries of persecution and societal alienation.[40]

During the First Five-Year Plan, activists learned to refine and nuance their narrative of national persecution. In a series of articles, for example, Germano sought to explain the "roots of anti-Gypsism" in medieval Europe. As shiftless newcomers to the superstitious villages of Europe, he explained, Gypsies had quickly realized the profits to be made in entertaining their neighbours with song, dance, fortune telling, and faith healing. Their discovery of such easy means of profit, Germano maintained, "did not dispose Gypsies to labour." Making matters worse in the long run, itinerancy further cultivated "inconstancy, laziness, and carelessness" as "defining features of Gypsies' character." Medieval Europeans grew tired, meanwhile, of fortunes that did not come true and of remedies that did not heal.[41]

Complying with popular stereotypes of Gypsies as labour-averse, shifty, and ostracized, Germano here makes no mention of sedentary Roma's history in medieval and early modern Europe as enterprising craftsmen, integrated into their local socio-economic milieus as metalworkers and artisans.[42] Nor does he acknowledge in this instance Roma's history of slavery in Romania or even of serfdom under the tsars.[43] Germano insists flatly that Gypsies quickly came to represent all that medieval Europe found threatening: foreignness, transience, an uncanny ability to profit from their own cleverness, a talent for trickery, and the "unholy" rejection of "honest" work.[44] Indeed, Germano subtly conceded, Gypsies themselves were partially responsible for becoming Europe's outcasts, confined to the socio-economic margins as beggars, swindlers, horse thieves, minstrels, and aimless wanderers. Nothing could excuse, however, the wide array of torments they suffered at the hands of their European neighbours: incarceration, torture, discriminatory laws, and even slavery.[45]

Germano and fellow Romani activists refused, however, to accept the notion that Gypsies were biologically disinclined to work or somehow innately incapable of toil. They contended that such stereotypes had been produced and popularized by none other than a European bourgeoisie drunk on visions of "Gypsies' imaginary incapacity for labour." Gluttonous connoisseurs of exotica, bourgeois men of letters had reduced Gypsies' history as starving, alienated marginals to a self-serving theory that "some kind of racial, inborn peculiarity" separated Gypsies from all other peoples.[46] These "bourgeois Gypsiologists" treated their subjects as a "dying ... tribe of degenerates, thieves, scamps, and idlers."[47] In popularizing such stereotypes, Romani activists charged, the bourgeoisie had unscrupulously provided "justification" for violent anti-Gypsism.[48]

Such dangerous and barbarous theories, Romani activists claimed, masked the fact that widespread "oppression and persecution" had isolated Gypsies and alienated them from society. It was for this reason, Germano explained, that "the illiterate and ignorant Gypsy mass" lived in "filth and poverty," having lost all stake in the economy, not to mention in cultured life. Thus halted on the evolutionary timeline of human development, Gypsies had become society's most conspicuous criminals, its "accursed tribe" of beggars, thieves, and wanderers. Yet, despite the privation and injustice they suffered, Germano maintained, many Gypsies still managed to defy both the weight of history and society's prevailing stereotypes. Although some Gypsies were indeed horse-thieves, fortune tellers, and beggars, Germano argued, others were honest toilers – metalworkers, in the main. As easy as it might be to find a Gypsy swindling on the horse market, Germano opined, it would be easier still to find honest Gypsy traders.[49]

Activists also sought to impress the public with any and all evidence that backward Gypsies were now enthusiastically joining all other nationalities in the construction of socialism. Contrary to the expectations of a public fed on the purported lies of a predatory bourgeoisie, Gypsies were proving their capacity for legitimate labour more conspicuously with every day. Not only were they settling down to collective agriculture, activists argued, they were also displaying their undeniable "attraction to industry." In the activists' telling, Gypsies were already employed as qualified workers in Moscow's factories as well as engaged in organizing a variety of artels that showcased Gypsies' long-overlooked talents. In fact, activists argued, the only obstacles preventing Gypsies from further joining the Soviet workforce in meeting the demands of the First Five-Year Plan were the "putrid" remnants of "tsarist anti-Gypsism."[50]

The fact that increasing numbers of Roma were seeking employment in Moscow's industrial sector was, to a considerable degree, grounded in the harsh realities of Stalin's revolution from above. The Soviet state's decision to abandon NEP and jump headlong into a planned economy ultimately wrought chaos, dislocation, and widespread suffering for Soviet citizens, urban and rural alike. In its rushed efforts to eradicate capitalism, the Party unleashed economic policies that trampled upon the daily lives of the Soviet citizenry. Markets were collapsed, private enterprises shuttered, and heavy industry prioritized. In urban areas, the availability of quality foodstuffs, consumer goods, and housing plummeted as the population skyrocketed and infrastructure buckled. While many Soviet urbanites may have nourished and comforted themselves with vibrant dreams of future socialist abundance, their everyday lives during the First Five-Year Plan were characterized by privation, overcrowding, and uncertainty.[51]

In the countryside, the Party's decision to pursue rapid and wholesale collectivization resulted in horror, violence, destruction, and hunger. In the view of the Stalinist leadership, the creation of state-controlled collective farms (kolkhozes) would ensure the eradication not only of private agriculture, but also of the perceived backwardness of peasant culture. Wholesale collectivization would guarantee reliable delivery of the agrarian "tribute" necessary to fuel "primitive socialist accumulation" and industrialization. It would also usher in the defeat of the stalwart rural class enemy – the kulak, or greedy capitalist farmer. Collectivization was an intended class war, and this brutal aspect of the policy was summed up neatly in Stalin's terse demand for the "liquidation of the kulak as a class." In the early 1930s, violence, hunger, and rumours of apocalypse swept through the Soviet countryside as peasants were "dekulakized," livestock was slaughtered, and harvests faltered. Very quickly, the countryside *was* radically transformed.[52] In 1930 and 1931, nearly 2 million so-called kulaks were forcibly deported to penal labour colonies euphemistically named "special settlements" and located in remote Soviet outposts.[53] As many as 12 million peasants fled the countryside for the Soviet Union's cities and nascent industrial complexes during the First Five-Year Plan.[54] By 1932–33, famine engulfed the empire's grain-producing regions, claiming as many as 5 to 7 million lives and causing painful food shortages throughout the Soviet Union.[55]

With the termination of NEP and the dizzying transition to a planned economy, many Romani service nomads found they had no sustainable option but to seek employment in urban factories or cooperatives. Though Romani fortune tellers and horse-traders had already seen their profits decline under NEP, they soon realized that Stalin's plans to rapidly reorganize the Soviet economy promised their own imminent demise. Traditional horse markets were soon replaced with state-operated ranches that could guarantee peasants "good, healthy" horses, further regulations were introduced to discourage the private sale and even ownership of horses, and horse markets themselves were shut down.[56]

The chaotic effects of Stalin's economic reordering of the country induced thousands of Roma to migrate to the empire's industrial centres during the First Five-Year Plan in the hopes of securing some kind of living. Attracted by rumours that salvation awaited them in Moscow, where officials and Romani activists were reportedly "beginning to tend to the Gypsies," Roma arrived in the capital and set up camp in its streets and outlying woods.[57] Meanwhile, not a few nomadic Romani camps starved on Moscow's outskirts as the First Five-Year Plan was furiously propelled into motion. Many Romani migrants found themselves hounded by the police, and some would later recall how relatives simply "disappeared" as a result of their efforts to obtain bread by means of fortune telling, begging, or trading.[58]

For many Roma living in Moscow and its environs, however, the answer to their problems seemed to lie not in stubbornly clinging to traditional livelihoods, but in the organization of national workers' cooperatives. By 1930, four large Romani artels operated in Moscow, and by 1931, twenty-eight artels employed approximately 1,350 Roma. Soviet officials were both shocked and eventually even worried by the rapid growth of Romani artels that seemed to spring independently from nowhere. The nationalities bureau of the All-Russian Union of Industrial Cooperatives readily admitted the initiative for creating the Romani artels had come directly from Roma themselves. While central and local bureaucracies had done no more to help the fledgling Romani artels than simply to register them in their record books, officials at VTsIK warily admitted that the entire process of organizing Romani cooperatives had taken place outside the purview of bureaucratic control or, at the very least, supervision.[59] With more Roma arriving in Moscow with each day, Soviet officials grew increasingly sceptical of the new cooperatives and the rapidity with which the "social identity of the Gypsy population" appeared to be changing.[60]

Of the twenty-eight artels operating in 1932, officials were least concerned with the four that had preceded the massive growth of the Romani cooperative movement sparked in 1931. Established in 1927–28, these four were Tsygkhimprom (Gypsy Chemical Manufacturing), Tsygpishcheprom (Gypsy Food Production), Tsygkhimlabor (Gypsy Chemical Lab), and an unnamed carpentry collective. Considered the creation of Russka Roma long established in Moscow, these cooperatives brought together new workers who, though inexperienced, had been active in or at least influenced by the Gypsy Union's sovietizing campaign.

The Soviet press hailed these four cooperatives as fragile yet effective incubators of honest Romani workers contributing, even if modestly, to the socialist economy. Workers at Tsygkhimprom, a chemical-producing cooperative, inspired an article in *Krasnaia niva* entitled "From the Gypsy Camp to the Factory." The author, S. Mar, was wildly impressed not only by Tsygkhimprom's productive capacity, but also by its workers' commitment to self-improvement. In the cooperative's own red corner, Mar reported, Romani workers gathered in the evenings to learn how to read, to discuss Stalin's wisdom, and to parse meaning from the cooperative's own Romani-language wall newspaper, *The Gypsy Worker*. Waxing poetic on the phenomenal novelty that was the Romani cooperative, Mar wrote, "How many black eyes are here! How many quick, swarthy hands disproving Gypsy indolence!"[61]

The journalist Pavel Orlovets was similarly pleased by what he discovered in his visit to the Romani carpentry collective. The artel's director, an American émigré who had once owned a furniture factory in the United States, told Orlovets, "Of course, in the early days work proceeded slowly ... But Gypsies are a sharp, receptive people and not at all lazy as is conventionally thought." As for the cooperative's members, Orlovets reported that they "bared their white teeth" in wide grins as they "cheerfully" hammered away at their work.[62] Germano, meanwhile, reported his attendance at one of the collective's production meetings and recounted a speech given by Dmitrii Shishkin, one of the collective's Romani members. While he recognized the cooperative's successes, Shishkin reprimanded his fellow artel members for talking too much on the job, taking too many smoke breaks, and thus distracting themselves from the main task of production. Another worker piped up to praise Shishkin, advocating self-criticism as the crucial ingredient for increased production and earnings.[63]

As these four cooperatives began their small but seemingly promising contribution to socialist construction, two of the Gypsy Union's other urban initiatives rebounded. In their continued effort to mentor their "backward" brethren, Moscow's Romani activists worked to reorganize Red Star and *Romany zoria* as viable institutions of Gypsy proletarianization. Under new leadership, Red Star reopened in 1928 and quickly attracted new members from the dying horse-market nearby – the same Roma who only a year ago had shunned the club completely. As before, club members organized sewing, choral, and illiteracy liquidation circles, decorated the premises with banners and wall newspapers, and suffered cramped and inhospitable conditions. Much, however, had changed since the club's opening in 1927. Recognizing that their days trading openly on the markets were over, Moscow's Romani horse-traders now looked to the club if not for entertainment or personal edification, then for assistance in finding legitimate employment. By mid-1929, two former horse-traders had even joined the club's directorate.[64]

On the surface at least, Red Star quickly came to realize the Gypsy Union leaders' original vision of a club that served as central command for the transformation of parasitic outcasts into productive citizens. "For the Gypsies," one journalist explained, "the club is everything. It is a council, a consultation office, a labour exchange, a place of study, and a place of entertainment."[65] Roma, both young and old, now attended weekly lectures on alcoholism, hygiene, atheism, the demands of socialist construction, and the privileges of Soviet citizenship. "The audience's energy during lectures is great," one MONO inspector reported. "[They] ask many questions."[66] Club leaders showed propaganda films, but also devoted special attention to aiding members in finding employment at Moscow's factories, construction sites, and Romani artels. In 1929, Red Star even opened a nursery school exclusively for the children of parents employed in Romani cooperatives.[67]

In the same year, the long-anticipated second issue of *Romany zoria* appeared, only to be followed much later, in August 1930, with its final issue. In so far as the journal's activist editors and writers continued to regard their task as providing readers with "practical solutions to questions connected to Gypsies' transition to working life," *Romany zoria*'s 1929 and 1930 issues closely resembled its first.[68] Subscribers to the free journal once again encountered articles, short stories, and poems on the themes of collectivization, industrialization, hygiene, and education. Abundant cautionary tales described how the parasitism of the anachronistic nomadic camp spelled doom for Gypsies who resisted integration into the Soviet economy.[69]

In August 1930, *Romany zoria*'s editors replaced their intermittently published journal with a more stable, monthly publication – *Nevo drom* (A New Road). With articles titled "Moscow Gypsies at Work" and "On the Cultural Revolution among Gypsies," *Nevo drom* strayed little, both in content and style, from its predecessor.[70] *Nevo drom*'s illustrated covers portrayed a Romani man symbolically surrounded by books and tractors as well as photos of proud female Romani industrial workers. Photo spreads depicted happy, satisfied, assimilated Roma in the Soviet Union and compared them to their hungry, exploited, shivering counterparts suffering in the capitalist West.[71] The short stories of the budding Romani literati, such as Bezliudskii's "Broken Whip-Handle," portrayed the misery of life in Gypsy camps and offered narrative examples of the redemption offered to horse-traders, thieves, and charlatans by Soviet nationality policy.[72]

Taking stock of all these developments at the close of the First Five-Year Plan, Mossovet officials confidently declared, "These Gypsies are citizens of the Soviet Union." There was, however, one important caveat. They spoke only of a distinct segment of Moscow's Romani population:

the activist cohort, enthusiastic club-goers, individual factory workers, and members of Moscow's most successful, Russka Romani artels – the carpentry collective, Tsygpishcheprom, and Tsygkhimprom. Mossovet officials specifically singled out Russka Romani workers who "had already mastered the skills of labour" and who "often matched the working enthusiasm of the native (*korennye*) workers of our factories." They applauded Tsygpishcheprom's workers for completing their in- dustrial and financial plan at a rate of 92 per cent despite having been set back by a small fire. They congratulated Tsygkhimprom for having completed 100 per cent of its industrial and financial plan and also for its workers' perfect attendance rates. At the Romani furniture factory, six female workers earned praise for forming their own shock brigade. "The political mood of this group of Gypsies," Mossovet officials re- joiced, "is thoroughly Soviet."[73]

Though effusive in its praise of these Russka Roma, Mossovet's re- port was almost entirely concerned with Moscow's other, reputedly dangerous Gypsies. These were the "foreign Gypsies" – Vlax Roma – who had immigrated to Russia from Central and East Europe during and since World War I.[74] Unlike Moscow's proletarian Russka Roma, these newcomers were not "of Russian extraction (*russkie poddannye*)," but itinerants arriving from Romania, Serbia, Bulgaria, and Greece.[75] These "foreign" Vlax Roma were not horse-traders or musicians, but metalworkers and mechanics who spoke an entirely different Romani dialect than that of the Russka Roma considered indigenous to the Soviet Union.[76] In the eyes of Soviet officials, the Vlax were the dark masses that seemed to be descending in droves on Moscow, bringing with them only tattered tents, disease, and caravans of backwardness. These "foreigners" were also the reason for the suspiciously sharp spike in the number of Moscow's Romani cooperatives seen in 1931. On the eve of the Second Five-Year Plan, Vlax Romani migrants seemed to threaten all the progress that officials and activists believed had been made in sovietizing Moscow's Russka Romani workers. By the end of 1932, it would be decided that most of them, like all "kulaks," would need to be unmasked, defanged, and even destroyed.

Discovering and Disarming the Gypsy Kulak

At the start of the First Five-Year Plan, the Gypsy Union's former lead- ers declared Gypsies "a propertyless class" and the "poorest segment of our population." They firmly insisted that Gypsies, "throughout their entire history, had never been exploiters."[77] According to their narrative of Romani history, centuries of exploitation and oppression had encouraged Roma to retreat into the stark isolation of their camps and to cultivate strict communal values as a shield from foreign influence. Strategically echoing the romantic views of ethnographers who claimed that Gypsies, with their "indifference towards property, material accumulation, and wealth," had escaped "the epoch of universal greed for monetary power," Romani activists claimed their backward brethren as the uncorrupted standard-bearers of primitive communism.[78]

Ever attuned to the political and cultural currents of the day, however, Moscow's Romani leaders soon rescinded claims of Gypsies' historical innocence and entirely abandoned the notion that Gypsy camps were "embryos of communism."[79] By 1930, they had decided instead that Gypsy camps were hotbeds of class struggle, dens of tyranny, nests of corruption, and a secret world of slavery. In a dizzying reversal, they redirected all blame for Gypsies' historic backwardness at the Gypsy camp (*tabor*) and, in particular, at its elders – the so-called Gypsy kulaks. In so doing, Romani activists not only dramatically altered their master narrative of the New Soviet Gypsy, but also committed themselves to unmasking Gypsy kulaks as a cancer on an otherwise thriving socialist society in the making.[80]

In 1930, Germano – the most prolific publicist of all the Romani activists – introduced the Soviet reading public to the so-called Gypsy kulak. In a short chapter entitled "The Dying Gypsy Camps," Germano contradicted his own and his fellow activists' previous accounts of the Gypsy camp as an enclave of primitive communism. "One has often heard the opinion," Germano wrote, "that there is no class division among camp Gypsies … But this is not completely true."[81] Though it was popularly believed that nomadic Gypsy camps held all property in common under the leadership of familial elders, Germano claimed instead that the camps were dens of iniquity and exploitation. In the mysterious, isolated world of the nomadic camps, kulaks owned the most valuable property (the horses) and virtually enslaved all of the camp's propertyless Gypsies. The nomadic Gypsy camp was not an "embryo of communism," but rather a screen for the cruel exploitation of poor Gypsies by their kulak elders.[82]

Germano's Gypsy kulak was not an original creation, nor was it intended to be. An ambitious nationality policy careerist, Germano was, like many of his fellow activists, demonstrably well versed in the political discourse of the day. In their efforts to narratively unmask the Gypsy kulak and to destroy the shroud of mystery that was said to obscure the cabals dominating the nomadic camps, Germano and his fellow activists were inserting themselves into a larger dialogue on the most pressing issues confronting Stalinist society in 1930: collectivization and its declared prerequisite – "the liquidation of the kulak as a class." If it was indeed true that kulaks and other saboteurs were responsible for any and all impediments to Soviet industrialization and collectivization efforts, it must only have made convenient, strategic sense to Romani activists and Soviet officials that the problems besetting the campaign to make productive workers and mindful citizens of backward Gypsies in Moscow were rooted in a stubborn, nefarious nest of Gypsy kulaks. If the Gypsy kulak could be demonized and dehumanized like all other kulaks, he, too, could be liquidated and potentially even saved. If the Gypsy kulak could be weeded out from among those Gypsies who were honestly making the transition to Soviet labour, the Gypsy proletariat could finally realize its full potential and thrive. Romani activists and their non-Romani colleagues thus committed to liquidating the Gypsy kulak as the nefarious obstacle standing in the way of Gypsy idlers becoming Soviet workers.

In 1930, such obstacles seemed to be metastasizing at a wildly fantastic rate. As urban brigades descended on the Soviet countryside to collectivize, dekulakize, and demand exorbitant "tribute" from an impoverished and increasingly famished peasantry, several million rural dwellers attempted not only to combat but also to escape marauding collectivizers and the doom of dispossession, starvation, and deportation that the brigades brought with them. At the same time, the industrial demands of the First Five-Year Plan required the massive recruitment of unskilled peasant labour to work in Soviet cities and construction sites. With millions of peasants fleeing the countryside, the populations of the Soviet Union's cities ballooned. Moscow itself swelled with in-migrants whom its infrastructure was unprepared to accommodate. Between 1929 and 1932, the capital's population nearly doubled, climbing from 2 million to 3.7 million.[83]

Alongside peasant recruits, stigmatized kulaks, escaped deportees, orphaned children, and fleeing kolkhozniks, thousands of Roma migrated to Moscow and other Soviet cities during the First Five-Year Plan. Like their fellow migrants, Roma sought employment, housing, and rations in the overcrowded and infrastructurally overburdened capital. Upon arrival in Moscow, many so-called "foreign" Vlax Roma followed the example of the Russka Romani workers whom they met at Red Star or upon being "observed" by Romani activists; they formed – on paper at least – national artels. Between May and November of 1931 alone, nearly 1,800 Roma registered with the city as members of national producers' cooperatives.[84] Though a couple of these new artels bore names such as New Way of Life and Red October, many of Moscow's Vlax Romani arrivals would undoubtedly later regret having eschewed standard Soviet style in favour of naming their cooperatives the Romanian Foreigner, the Romanian Artel, the Montenegrin Emigrant, and the First Serbo-Romanian Artel.[85]

It was not merely the foreign-sounding names of these Vlax Romani artels that aroused the suspicions of Soviet authorities. Everything about "foreign" Vlax Romani migrants seemed to scream deviance, deception, and disease. Though they had ostensibly planted themselves in Moscow, the new artel workers and their families still clung to their "nomadic lifestyle." The luckiest among them lived in "dilapidated, unheated barracks" made of plywood. [86] According to an inspection report authored by Germano, Pankov, and Tokmakov, lice, scabies, and illness spread like wildfire throughout the barracks as inhabitants had no recourse to clean water. Most, however, were not afforded the luxury of such barracks and lived instead in flimsy tents while enduring near constant harassment on the part of the police.[87] In these commentaries on Vlax Romani migrants' squalid living conditions, there was no recognition that most in-migrants to overcrowded Moscow in the early 1930s lived in wretched, dilapidated barracks on the city's barren outskirts. There was, moreover, no discussion of the *general* squalor of Soviet living conditions during these years. Instead, Vlax Roma were essentialized as filthy, primitive, and diseased as a result of their presumed nomadism and generalized ethnic backwardness.[88]

Meanwhile, the artels themselves typically lacked raw materials and equipment, while operating in fields or courtyards "under the open sky."[89] When, in 1931, Soviet authorities released funds to the new artels for the building of workshops and workers' barracks, Vlax Romani workers were said to have variously laundered the money, spent it wastefully, or to have built barracks for unemployed kin. Eighty per cent of Roma who received barracks housing as a result of these state subsidies were not legitimately employed in the artels or anywhere else. The Workers' and Peasants' Inspectorate, meanwhile, scrambled to round up all the "foreign Gypsies" who were responsible for this scandalous "criminal use" of state funds.[90]

Few of these artels appeared to be functioning in reality, and those that did nonetheless failed the Soviet ideal in nearly every imaginable way. Chaos allegedly reigned in the absence of accounting methods, labour discipline, industrial leadership, and financial and production planning. Those "foreign Gypsy" artels that did produce a final product, meanwhile, were believed capable of doing so only as a result of buying scarce raw materials on the black market.[91] Unlike Tsygkhimprom and Tsygpishcheprom, the Vlax artels did not open their ranks to any and all Roma, but instead recruited only from their own Vlax kin groups.[92] Most threatening of all, these "anti-Soviet" elements balked at the enlightenment required of Soviet citizens. They refused literacy courses and were known to make "anti-Soviet speeches" at the Gypsy club. Most avoided the club at all costs, and were even known to flee from the Romani activists who were attempting to propagandize among them.[93] The majority of Vlax Roma were soon believed to have established "pseudo-artels that were apparently created to screen the purchase and trafficking of gold." At the close of 1931, Mossovet officials concluded that the Vlax artels "serve as a concealed weapon in the hands of class enemies."[94]

Soviet officials grew increasingly convinced that the suspicious "foreign" Vlax Roma living in Moscow could not be sovietized by ordinary means – if by any means at all. They singled out Moscow's Vlax Roma as a uniquely dangerous substratum of a nationality generally assumed to be labour-averse, parasitic, and inclined to criminal activity. For their part, Romani activists – the overwhelming majority of whom were Russka Roma – served the state as investigators of the Vlax artels. In this official capacity, they advanced the idea that Vlax Roma tenaciously preserved the backward culture of nomadic camps, protected their kulak elders at any expense, and consciously refused to assimilate to Sovietism.[95] As Alaina Lemon has argued, what most concerned Russka Romani activists and Soviet bureaucrats was not simple "Gypsy backwardness," nor the actual or perceived economic and social divisions within Romani communities, but rather the perseverance of the nomadic camp – especially in its specifically "foreign" guise – as an independent, impenetrable state in miniature. Operating according to the nomadic camps' own rules and "backward" customs, so-called Gypsy kulaks were believed to lord over "the Gypsy poor" as powerful elders while the camps themselves remained sealed off from the state, illegible to officials.[96]

Romani activists did their best to unveil the culture and internal structures of the camps for Soviet officials, and the glimpse they offered revealed an isolated world of frightful deviance. As dutiful Soviet citizens, they recounted tales of bride trafficking, currency speculation, conspiracies, and murders.[97] In particular, they focused their ire on Vlax artel workers' reliance on internal structures of dispute resolution known among Roma as the *kris*, or tribunals.[98] In his *Gypsies Yesterday and Today*, Germano explained, "Among Gypsies wandering throughout the USSR … the severe power of the leader rules over all in each camp. The isolated life of the camp has its own authorities (*vlast'*), its own law, its own court. The leader settles … all disputes, offences, the division of property, weddings." The backward Gypsy of the nomadic camps, he argued, refused to bring his affairs – even his bitterest complaints – to "an official court," but instead relied on the customary law of his camp, while stealthily guarding all its secrets.[99]

The "foreign" Vlax Romani artel workers were believed to have imported the *kris* and its subversive underpinnings to Moscow. On the basis of Romani activists' findings as informants, Mossovet concluded that the Vlax Romani "pseudo-artels" functioned largely as the nerve centre for the anti-Soviet machinations of a growing network of "Gypsy kulaks" living in Moscow and its environs. Speaking of the cooperatives created in Moscow in 1931, Mossovet concluded:

> Each artel has its own Gypsy court, as well as its own supreme court, the function of which is performed by the artel "The Romanian Foreigner" in Aviation Park. Gypsies from the periphery come there and decide all disputed questions so as not to hand them over to Soviet organs. Costs are paid exclusively in gold currency. Those chosen as the chairmen of these artels and courts are the same who earlier were the camp elders or their relatives (the poor [*bedniaki*] cannot be elected).

It was no great leap from here for Soviet officials to decide, "The political mood in the majority of these artels is anti-Soviet."[100]

So-called "foreign Gypsies" were not the only "anti-Soviet elements" viewed by officials as threatening public order in Moscow or the construction of socialism in general. By the close of the First Five-Year Plan, Soviet officials confronted a widespread crisis resulting from the Party's decision to rapidly abolish capitalism and construct socialism in its place. The ongoing and massive influx of migrants from the countryside resulting from collectivization and dekulakization had disastrously overwhelmed the capital's infrastructure and rationing system. As famine swept the essential grain-growing regions of the countryside in 1932–33 and severe food shortages plagued the country, the rationing system in Moscow and other Soviet cities was brought to its already battered knees. Meanwhile, migrants seemed to be sabotaging industrial production en masse. Officials increasingly branded them as a dangerous blight on Moscow's industrial production and social order, blaming them for a marked increase in absenteeism, shoddy workmanship, alcoholism, and criminality both in the workplace and on the capital's streets. From the vantage point of the Party leadership, a "socially harmful element" had overtaken the capital and other Soviet cities, infecting them with disorder, disease, hooliganism, filth, vagrancy, and industrial sabotage.[101]

Roma – especially Vlax Roma connected to the so-called "foreign" artels – conspicuously occupied a place within Soviet officialdom's blurred vision of a "socially harmful element" threatening social order and economic advancement in the Soviet Union. In the eyes of the Party leadership, these were "superfluous" people – the unemployed, kulaks, beggars, criminals, foreign refugees, and "other anti-social elements hiding in the towns."[102] As applied to Vlax Romani migrants and their fellow social marginals in the early 1930s, "socially harmful element" functioned as a blanket bureaucratic category that both socially defined and criminalized those perceived as dangerously alien to the construction of socialism.[103]

As Soviet officials geared up for the Second Five-Year Plan, the Stalinist leadership pursued radical measures to alleviate the crisis in Soviet cities, and not least to eradicate the scourge of "socially harmful elements." Rationing systems were tightened, hooligans prosecuted, and homeless youths apprehended. Party leaders increasingly demanded that police officials vigilantly "cleanse" urban areas of all so-called "socially harmful elements."[104]

A crucial component of this campaign to purge cities of any individuals or groups seen as politically dangerous, potentially criminal, or simply déclassé was the introduction of the internal passport system in December 1932. In Moscow, Leningrad, and other closed cities, industrial complexes, and border areas, passportization required that all adult citizens have their residency as well as their class status, occupation, and ethnicity inscribed in passports whose issuance could be refused to anyone deemed suspicious by the police. All those denied passports in the closed cities were effectively defined as "socially harmful" or "socially foreign" and therefore ineligible to receive rationed goods or to claim urban residency.[105]

The passport system was designed to enable police to purge the Soviet Union's major cities of "socially harmful elements" and to prevent the future in-migration of undesirables. It was thus intended to help immunize the Soviet Union's "healthy" citizenry from disease and depravity, while also safeguarding the availability of housing, food supplies, and commodities for its "worthy" urban labourers. Equipped with the new passport regime, the police began in 1933 to vigorously cleanse major Soviet cities of what David Shearer calls the "social detritus of Stalin's industrial and agrarian revolutions from above." Suspect, passportless Roma joined hundreds of thousands of their fellow "social undesirables" and "alien elements" as the targets of policing operations intended for both the defence of social order and the purification of the Soviet body politic. Once purged of this "social detritus," Soviet cities were to become pure, undefiled beacons of socialist modernity.[106]

Yet even before the internal passport was introduced, police officials in Moscow had already begun to "cleanse" their city of Vlax Roma considered both literally and socially foreign. In 1932, several prominent Romani activists aided in a police investigation that led to the arrest, trial, and conviction of seventeen leading members of three Vlax Romani artels. Though indicted on a wide array of charges that included foreign currency speculation, money laundering, the purchase of scarce raw materials on the black market, bribery, fraud, conspiracy, and murder, the seventeen Vlax Romani defendants were essentially punished not merely for their alleged crimes or supposedly anti-Soviet inclinations, but for being too Gypsy.[107] As Alaina Lemon has rightly noted, the so-called "kulak" and "foreign Gypsy" leaders of the three Vlax Romani artels – the Romanian Foreigner, Red TransBaikal, and the Serbo-Romanian Artel – were not the real subjects of their trial. Rather, "traditional" Romani culture itself was on trial.[108] Prosecutors were less interested in the defendants' alleged statutory crimes than they were in the threat that they posed as kulak preservationists of an anachronistic culture and organizers of socio-economic deviance.

The prosecution took great pains to construe the case as a straightforward instance of the exploitation of the benighted poor by ruthless Gypsy kulaks. Deeming all the "nomadic foreign Gypsies" who had recently migrated to Moscow as afflicted by "great cultural backwardness" and "centuries-old patriarchal customs," the prosecution indicted the former-camp-leaders-cum-kulaks for blinding the Gypsy masses from the light of Soviet civilization. In fact, what made the accused so threatening to Soviet officials was not simply that they had exploited and isolated the poor, but that these so-called kulak ringleaders were not so "backward" as to not have understood their own actions as anti-Soviet. Rather, they were accused of having consciously sabotaged the construction of Soviet socialism and of having wilfully refused the state's offer to uplift Gypsies as a nationality. "All ... measures directed at the improvement of the cultural and general material welfare of the working Gypsy population," court records read:

> struck against stubborn and diverse resistance among the Gypsies, coerced by the kulaks (elders and princelings) who understood that to raise the Gypsies' cultural level and attract them to socialist construction would inevitably, in the end, result in the masses' renunciation of the old, patriarchal customs and caste distinctions of which the rich Gypsies made use.

The Vlax defendants were accused of having grown prosperous by means of sabotaging socialist construction, exploiting "the poor Gypsy masses," and manipulating nationality policy.[109]

Though trial records recount in some detail the alleged economic misdeeds of the accused in their role as the kulak ringleaders of "pseudo-artels," prosecutors and witnesses directed considerable attention to the *kris* as the ultimate manifestation of the defendants' seemingly apparent refusal to abandon the "backwardness" of nomadic camp traditions for the socio-economic integration offered them by a generous nationality policy. Whereas the "fundamental" goal of organizing Roma into industrial cooperatives had been "the attraction of the entire Gypsy mass to social labour, the improvement of their material well-being, the struggle ... against the ... ignorance and darkness among them, and chiefly, their involvement in the general course of the socialist construction of the country," the conniving kulak chiefs had stood obstinately in the way of the state's benevolent designs to transform the so-called Gypsy masses. "The Gypsy *kulachestvo*, that is, rich Gypsies, the former elders," court records explain, had easily manipulated the Gypsy masses' "lack of culture," and, in particular, their reliance on "old patriarchal customs" such as the *kris*. Contrary to the claims of the defendants, the prosecution insisted, the *kris* was not a simple mechanism for achieving social peace and reconciliation, but rather a tool of exploitation and anti-Sovietism. It was through this "so-called Gypsy court," the prosecution maintained, that the Gypsy kulaks had "held the entire Gypsy mass of the city of Moscow under [their] daily influence."[110]

The prosecution centred its accusations on five alleged instances in which a drunken revelry in the camps had led to murder. All five murders, it was claimed, had been "deliberately hidden" from the state and resolved secretly by the *kris*.[111] Making matters still worse, the *kris* had ordered each of the Romani offenders to atone for his crime by paying a fine to the sons of the deceased in none other than foreign, gold currency.[112] Once Soviet authorities had uncovered these crimes, the Gypsy kulaks had encouraged the backward Gypsies under their demonic sway to resort to any and all methods of deception and obfuscation that could possibly interfere with the state's investigation. Police investigators were forced to contend with wily, anti-Soviet Gypsies who had allegedly assumed aliases, denied relations with family members, or threatened Romani informants with false denunciations and bodily harm.[113] The prosecution interpreted all these alleged connivances in the Gypsies' "struggle against unmasking" as still further evidence that kulaks had trapped the Gypsy masses in "a special insularity."[114]

It was this dangerous insularity and kulak domination, Soviet authorities decided, that had precluded the success of any cultural-enlightenment work among the "foreign" Vlax Roma in Moscow. Tyrannical Gypsy kulaks had not only denied the poor among them to redeem themselves through participation in socialist construction, but also demanded that they outright reject Soviet power. It was primarily through the institution of the *kris*, the prosecution maintained, that so-called Gypsy kulaks were able to cement their power and to impose their "laws" and rulings as "incontestable."[115] Soviet authorities denounced the *kris* precisely because it had operated as a native source of internal cohesion that shielded "traditional" Romani culture from the state.[116] Such impenetrability simply would not be tolerated within a political culture that demanded not only transparency, but also willing assimilation to Sovietism.

The seventeen Vlax defendants charged in this case were not the only Roma in Moscow to be arrested and charged as part of a broader effort to "cleanse" Moscow of "anti-Soviet" and "foreign" Roma. Following the introduction of the internal passport in 1932, this "cleansing" gained a furious pace and did so against a backdrop of heightened Soviet demonization of class enemies masquerading in "national costume."[117] Thus, a Mossovet report tersely referenced the arrest in 1933 of another sixty-three "Gypsy kulaks" accused of ruling over several "foreign Gypsy" artels, and the expulsion of their children from one of Moscow's Romani nursery schools. In short order, the suspect Vlax artels were shut down, while many of the arrested artel workers' relatives were soon expelled from Moscow.[118] In the Soviet "cleansing state" of the First and Second Five-Year Plans, Vlax Romani artel workers were increasingly seen as dangerous "foreign elements" threatening the purity of the socialist body politic. Perceived as class enemies stubbornly refusing reinvention as New Soviet Gypsies, Vlax Roma became the targeted victims of policies, police operations, and even Russka activists seeking to isolate and remove the threat of seemingly unassimilable "foreign Gypsies" from the Soviet capital.[119]

Yet in 1933 Soviet officials faced a problem perhaps still more vexing than the dangerous Vlax artels: the existence of thousands of Roma who had set up camp on Moscow's outskirts. Officials did not know exactly how many Roma lived along the city's borders; they knew only that hundreds if not thousands of Roma had recently increased the overall number as a result of having been refused passports and legal Moscow residency. Beginning in late winter 1933, central state and Moscow city officials looked to their Russka Romani informants to investigate the Roma camped on the edge of town.[120]

One ambitious young Romani communist who had recently moved to Moscow from Smolensk, A.Ia. Gerasimov, took this duty upon himself with extraordinary vigour. In early 1933, Gerasimov frequently visited the Roma living on Moscow's outskirts and reported to Mossovet, the Nationalities Department of VTsIK, Narkomzem, and other authorities on his grim findings. On 3 May, Gerasimov reported that collectivization had deprived Romani camps of the opportunity to continue their former nomadic lifestyles and had encouraged them to descend on Moscow from all corners of the Soviet Union in search of bread. "At the present time," Gerasimov explained, "this toiling mass sits hungry, procuring meager scraps by means of begging and fortune telling. Owing to these conditions, this mass suffers from scurvy and other diseases related to hunger. The kulak takes advantage of the moment." This was particularly unfortunate, Gerasimov argued, insofar as the majority of poor nomadic Roma strived to settle on their own collective farms. Theirs was a hope, however, repeatedly trampled upon by kulaks who tried to convince the starving among them that "the poor do not receive land, that Soviet power gives nothing to Gypsies, that [their] hopes are in vain, that Gypsies do not need land, that they, the kulaks, live better without land, that their ancestors never tilled the land and lived better and did so because they obeyed" their camp elders.[121] Gerasimov further testified that the matter was yet more dangerous insofar as criminals and counterrevolutionary White Guards had recently infiltrated the nomadic camps and were now in league with Gypsy kulaks, horse-thieves, and speculators in exploiting the defenceless Gypsy poor.[122] Anticipating that the poor of the Gypsy camps languishing on Moscow's periphery would soon die from starvation, Gerasimov advised organizing national collective farms for their resettlement.[123]

Gerasimov was not alone among Romani activists in thinking that the best solution to the so-called Gypsy problem on Moscow's outskirts was to organize the starving masses on several new Romani collective farms throughout Moscow Province. As representatives of the Nationalities Department of VTsIK, the Gypsy club, and other organizations, Romani activists sought out the "backward Gypsies" of the hungry camps and compiled lists of volunteers willing to form national collective farms.[124] Some Romani families – surely with the aid of activists – even managed to submit formal requests for collective settlement to Narkomzem and the Nationalities Department of VTsIK.[125]

Seeking an easy solution to the "Gypsy problem" threatening Moscow's borders, on 21 May Narkomzem ordered Moscow Province's Agricultural Department (MOZO) to arrange for the timely settlement of nomadic Roma on collective farms and to provide them with livestock, machinery, and construction materials. For its own part, Narkomzem promised only 7,000 rubles to aid in the collectivization of nomadic Roma in Moscow Province.[126] Narkomzem next dispatched Gerasimov to scout locations potentially suitable for the creation of Romani collective farms. Gerasimov quickly mobilized all of Moscow's Romani activists in an initial effort to introduce at least 270 Romani families to their impending fate as kolkhozniks.[127]

MOZO officials, however, balked at Narkomzem's order, decrying its demands as wildly unrealistic. They complained that nomadic Roma lacked horses, machinery, seeds, and the materials necessary to build housing. They vigorously protested the notion that MOZO could afford to purchase the collective farms' material necessities and scoffed at Narkomzem's paltry contribution of 7,000 rubles. Even if MOZO had the resources to finance the massive collectivization effort assigned to it, officials explained, the task would still be made impossible by the fact that there was simply not enough free land in Moscow Province to accommodate the thousands of Roma in question. As of 1 June, MOZO would commit only to organizing one collective farm comprising fifty Romani families.[128]

Once Narkomzem's fantastical plans to rapidly collectivize nomadic Roma on farms throughout Moscow Province reached this predictable standstill, the Nationalities Department of VTsIK intervened, calling a conference to discuss the question of organizing "the Gypsy poor settled on Moscow's environs." Meeting on 22 and 23 June, the conference's bureaucrat and activist attendees generally agreed that their main task should be "to create humane conditions" for the Roma who had recently "crowded" Moscow. [129] They debated, however, whether Moscow could realistically accommodate the thousands of Roma camping on the edge of town. The majority argued that Moscow simply could not afford the great financial burden presented it by the Roma seeking employment or land there, and could absorb only a fraction of the Roma's total number. They estimated that no more than 200 families could be organized on collective farms, while handfuls of families could possibly be recruited into existing artels. For most conference attendees, the only reasonable solution seemed to be the dispersion and resettlement of "the Gypsy poor" in a variety of provinces and not merely in Moscow. For Gerasimov, however, the very suggestion of forcibly evicting nomadic Roma from Moscow was unacceptable. In his mind, the idea of herding thousands of unwitting Roma into railway cars for delivery to supposedly more accommodating provinces was nothing more than a return to the barbarity of the tsarist nineteenth century.[130] Besides, he surmised, it only made sense to collectivize the "camp Gypsies" in Moscow Province, where they could enjoy proximity to the capital's Romani activists.[131]

The conference of 22 and 23 June ended not with a resolution to the question of resettling Moscow's Romani in-migrants, but instead with a plan for all attendees to reconvene on the morning of 4 July. Yet before a 4 July meeting could take place, the OGPU had already decided on its own solution. Beginning on 28 June and ending 9 July, the OGPU conducted an operation that forcibly removed 1,008 Romani families – or 5,470 individuals – from the outskirts of Moscow. Along with "338 horses, 2 cows, and a large quantity of carts and domestic belongings," these 5,470 "so-called 'foreign' Gypsies" were organized into five echelons and sent to a Tomsk transit camp for resettlement in West Siberian labour colonies. Before departure, the Roma "were subjected to disinfection, haircuts, and smallpox vaccination." The OGPU's report on this massive "cleansing" operation tersely noted that it had been carried out "peacefully."[132]

Treated *at best* by the state as a lumpen element that could be discarded more easily than reformed, the 5,470 "so-called 'foreign Gypsies'" evicted from Moscow in the summer of 1933 suffered a gruesome fate that they shared with hundreds of thousands of fellow Soviet citizens officially categorized as "kulaks," "class enemies," and "socially foreign elements" in the early Stalinist 1930s. Treated as if livestock, these 5,470 Romani deportees were corralled into primitive and overcrowded train wagons and thereby "cleansed" from Moscow. The survivors of these 5,470 Romani deportees – malnourished and sick from the inhumane conditions of their "transfer," if not simply from the harshness of Soviet life – arrived in a Tomsk transit camp and were placed under the jurisdiction of profoundly overwhelmed OGPU agents disastrously ill-equipped to provide for their resettlement. Theoretically, the Romani deportees were expected to reforge themselves in exile as socially useful labourers. Like most special settlers in the 1930s, however, they were not provided the basic resources to construct new, productive lives in labour colonies in the distant, undeveloped landscape of the frontiers of Soviet socialism. By the fall of 1933, none of the Romani special settlers deported from Moscow and transferred to Tomsk remained within the labour colonies of the Western Siberian Krai. Survivors had all fled "at the first opportunity." The OGPU agents tasked with their resettlement, meanwhile, made little attempt to apprehend the Romani escapees.[133]

While the OGPU operation in Moscow was still underway, however, the interorganizational commission to organize the "poor Gypsy masses" settled on Moscow's outskirts did reconvene on 4 July. In the protocol drafted at the meeting's end, attendees reported that the 5,470 Roma "evicted" from Moscow had been provided bread and clothing. That being said, they then recognized the failure to organize the so-called "foreign Gypsies" in Romani kolkhozes or urban industrial collectives. This failure was attributed to MOZO, Narkomzem, and the Moscow Council of Industrial Cooperatives' "underestimation of the importance of the task." Finally, it was decided that the OGPU's "transfer of Gypsies" should in no way distract officials from continuing to work towards the further organization of Moscow's Roma and the raising of their cultural level. If anything, all parties agreed that concrete measures would soon need to be taken towards the "cleansing, rehabilitation, and strengthening" of Moscow's already existing Romani artels and, in particular, of those artels which employed "so-called foreign Gypsies."[134] Of all those in attendance, only Gerasimov seemed willing to openly admit that the 5,470 Roma "evicted" from Moscow had been treated "like hunted dogs."[135]

The ambitious demands of Stalin's First Five-Year Plan and the overwhelming socio-economic dislocations they caused necessarily impacted the course of "introducing" Moscow's Roma to "socially use-ful" labour. Between 1930 and 1932, thousands of Roma joined millions of their Soviet compatriots in escaping a devastated countryside for the illusive promised land of Moscow, thereby swelling an already over-burdened urban landscape. Within a political culture that increasingly demanded the unmasking and excising of kulaks and other harmful, anti-Soviet elements, Moscow's Romani migrants – Vlax Roma, in par-ticular – were castigated as dangerous saboteurs who prevented the assimilation of backward Gypsies to legitimate labour and civic life. Once this threat was removed from Moscow and isolated in distant la-bour colonies, it remained to be seen if the deported Roma could be redeemed by forced and penal labour and integrated as reformed citi-zens into the socialist economy. Hope nonetheless remained that in the newly cleansed Soviet capital, a robust Gypsy proletariat could now emerge unhindered by the anti-Soviet machinations of Roma deemed both literally and socially foreign.

The Gypsy Proletariat Ascendant?

In December 1933, Soviet officials appraised their diverse efforts to transform Moscow's idle Gypsies into productive workers. From one perspective, the situation appeared grim, if not altogether dire. In ad-dition to the OGPU's July "cleansing" operation, Soviet officials had liquidated another eleven Romani "pseudo-artels" in 1933. For Romani activists such as I.P. Tokmakov, a consultant employed in the Nation-alities Department of VTsIK, it was abundantly clear that Soviet offi-cialdom was to blame for failing to integrate the majority of Moscow's so-called "foreign Gypsies" into the social and economic fabric of Soviet life.[136] Most officials agreed with Tokmakov that the Vlax Roma who re-mained in Moscow after the arrests and deportations of 1932–33 were not being exposed to sufficient political-enlightenment efforts. Though Red Star continued to host lectures and literacy courses, the club was said to lack "a close connection with the masses."[137] Nevo drom, a jour-nal that activists had long found difficult to circulate among the em-pire's diverse and largely illiterate Romani populations, had been shut down in November 1932. The journal, officials concluded, had failed to adequately discuss "the class struggle among Gypsies," to "unmask Gypsy kulaks," to cater to "Gypsies' everyday life and needs," or to report meaningfully on efforts to integrate Roma as labourers in the socialist economy.[138]

Moreover, hundreds of Vlax Roma still remained in Moscow without housing, passports, or the means to make a socially useful living. Many of them had seen their relatives arrested or forcibly resettled and were now, perhaps more than ever before, distrustful of Soviet authorities.[139] Though attempts were made to absorb many of them into non-Romani artels, Soviet officials conceded that conditions had made it impossible for most "foreign Gypsies" to survive on anything but begging, fortune telling, speculation, and thievery. Recognizing the Vlax Roma still living in Moscow as skilled metalworkers, officials – as in years past – were nonetheless unable to provide them with the raw materials, tools, and housing that might allow the workers to forge successful national artels.[140] The repressive measures taken against their relatives, meanwhile, seemed to have achieved little in convincing "foreign Gypsies" of the need, or better still, the desirability of abandoning their "patriarchal customs," outmoded labour methods, and overall "cultural backwardness."[141]

Yet, from another perspective, Soviet officials had reason to be cautiously optimistic. The few remaining Romani artels in Moscow that employed Russka Roma – Tsygkhimprom and Tsygpishcheprom, in particular – seemed reliable sites not only of industrial production, but also of Roma's sovietization. At the Third All-Russian Conference of Workers among the Nationalities held in Moscow in December 1933, Grushina, a leading Romani worker at Tsygpishcheprom, delivered a report on the various successes that she and her fellow artel workers had enjoyed in previous years. If in 1931, Grushina explained, Tsygpishcheprom had completed a mere 8 per cent of its production plan, it had completed its plan at a rate of 100 per cent in 1932 and 1933. Over half of the 428 workers employed at Tsygpishcheprom, she proudly boasted, were shock workers. As a result of their labour, Tsygpishcheprom's workers now enjoyed the benefits of three dormitories, a private cafeteria, a kindergarten, and a nursery. "This is what we, Gypsies, have achieved," Grushina triumphantly declared. She and her fellow workers had achieved their industrial plan "exactly as our beloved leader Comrade Stalin directed."[142]

Tsygkhimprom's workers also had reason to congratulate themselves. In 1933, they had fulfilled their production plans at 100.2 per cent and, owing largely to the efforts of its shock workers, had increased productivity rates by 13.5 per cent in the previous year alone. Tsygkhimprom had also recently emerged as the Soviet Union's first industrial producers of "natural medical vaseline of the American type." It was with great pride that Tsygkhimprom's representatives at the conference announced the opportunity to cease importing American vaseline. "Long Live Lenin's Nationality Policy," Tsygkhimprom's conference representative declared. "Long Live the Unshakeable Wise Leader of the All-Russian Communist Party, Comrade Stalin!"[143]

As 1933 came to a close, Tsygkhimprom's workers gathered to revel in their various successes. One of the artel's Russian directors reminisced about the difficulties the workers had faced only a few years back. "Remember 1930?" he reportedly asked Tsygkhimprom's Romani workers. "When we spoke about shock work, that word was incomprehensible to you. You didn't know what a production plan was. And now we have gathered at a family meeting of the best shock workers and we recall our struggle for production and for new people." Yet the most poignant reminiscing was saved for the Romani shock workers themselves. E.K. Gracheva, a shock worker, traced the winding path of her own and her fellow workers' Soviet rebirth. "Comrades, she asked, "is it really possible to compare our present life in the artel with that which we lived in the camp? There was no life in the camp, you know, only servitude (*katorga*), especially for us women. I entered the camp at seventeen when I married. I wandered for four years. In those years I experienced enough woes to last a century."[144] Only after her husband died and she joined Tsygkhimprom, Gracheva explained, had her life truly been transformed into one worth living. At Tsygkhimprom, she had come to know the joys of socially useful labour and literacy. Once integrated into the Soviet labour force, she and her fellow Romani workers and former nomads "had understood that it was necessary to work hard (*rabotat' khorosho*) and to live a completely different life" than the one they had known "in the tents."[145]

At Tsygpishcheprom's New Year's Eve party, Grushina again reported on the artel's success in fulfilling and even surpassing the year's production plan. The impressive rise in the artel's productivity over a matter of a few years, Grushina explained, "only became possible because the fundamental backbone of the Gypsy masses comprehended that they had been called upon to work together with all the workers of the Soviet Union, that the paths of hucksterism (*torgashestvo*) and fortune telling, the paths of swindling (*obman*) and begging inherited from capitalist society had forever receded into the past." Another Romani worker, Verbitskii, shared his thoughts on the artel's prospects:

Still many difficulties await us in the future, but we must participate in the further development of the wellbeing of our country's workers ... we must tirelessly work on ourselves, [we must] uproot the roots of the past, as we open up virgin lands and create a new, shining life ... Comrades! With such pride I stand at this rostrum and look at all those in our collective. Who were we in the past (ran'she)? We know and with damnation remember our past.

It was precisely because Verbitskii and his fellow workers had realized their own backwardness that they could celebrate their achievements as Soviet citizens. "We must take pride and value the people whom we have now become," Verbitskii exhorted his fellow workers. "Gypsies," he declared, "are equal participants in the construction of [our] classless socialist society."[146]

Soviet officials joined the Romani workers of Tsygkhimprom and Tsygpishcheprom in celebrating the two artels as "an example even for ... ordinary, Russian artels."[147] All agreed that two simple explanations sufficed to account for Tsygkhimprom's and Tsygpishcheprom's success in transforming backward Gypsies into Soviet workers. The first was the international orientation of both artels; neither Tsygkhimprom nor Tsygpishcheprom exclusively employed Roma. Though Roma constituted a 65 per cent majority at Tsygpishcheprom, for example, they worked alongside representatives of at least eleven other nationalities.[148] At Tsygkhimprom, Romani workers were also in the majority at some 60–70 per cent of the artel's workforce in early 1934, and officials took note that the number of Romani employees there still continued to grow.[149] Having witnessed the progress made at the two artels during Stalin's First and Second Five-Year Plans, officials concluded that "when Gypsies work with other nationalities, they adapt to work and discipline more quickly" and "acquire ... a love for labour."[150]

Second, it was believed that Tsygpishcheprom's and Tsygkhimprom's success owed in part to the fact that the artels' workers were "Russian Gypsies" and not "foreign."[151] In the eyes of most officials in Moscow, Vlax Roma could not have been farther from the Russka on a spectrum of redeemability. Though officials recognized that the "foreign" Vlax Roma were capable, and often even quite qualified, to work, they feared that Vlax Roma would never willingly transform themselves into conscious, socially useful citizens. Many allegedly continued to live in Moscow without passports, clung to the "hellish conditions" of their dilapidated tents, and "refused to work."[152] Even some Romani workers publicly railed against their "foreign" counterparts. According to Grushina, "no use" had yet come from efforts to assimilate "foreign

Gypsies."[153] Matiushenko, a Romani activist who agitated among the "toiling Gypsy masses," agreed with Grushina that nothing could be done with them. On the suggestion made by a Mossovet official that the "foreign Gypsies" be isolated from one another and dispersed throughout a variety of Moscow's artels, Matiushenko argued that it would be impossible to successfully integrate the "foreign" idlers into any artel at all.[154] Several non-Romani officials became so frustrated with the "foreign Gypsy" problem that they began speaking of the need for another "show trial" and the possibility of sending all those who still refused to work to the GULag.[155]

Other officials still retained hope that Vlax Roma could succeed as many of their Russka counterparts had done at Tsygkhimprom and Tsygpishcheprom. It was precisely the "foreign Gypsies," one official passionately argued, who most needed to be "re-educated." Instead of sending the most recalcitrant of Moscow's Roma to the GULag, he maintained, more careful efforts needed to be made in again organizing the "foreign Gypsies" into artels.[156] Those who shared in his belief that "foreign Gypsies" could still be re-educated likewise agreed that the potential success of such an effort hinged on Soviet officials' ability to disarm the kulaks who still held sway over the "backward masses." These proponents of the further re-education of so-called "foreign Gypsies" blamed past failures on "the negligent attitude" with which various bureaucracies (especially the Moscow Council of Industrial Cooperatives) had approached the task of forging socially useful labourers of "speculators" and "swindlers" who were in fact "highly qualified" metalworkers.[157]

By late 1934, proponents of the further re-education of "foreign Gypsies" succeeded in pushing a resolution through the Moscow Council of Industrial Cooperatives that called for the establishment of a Gypsy industrial village in Krupino, a town located well outside Moscow's city limits.[158] Their express intent was to isolate the "foreign Gypsies" from the saboteurs in their midst, to physically remove them from the Soviet capital (by force, if necessary), and to resettle them in an area where they could, it was hoped, be relatively easily furnished with housing, well-equipped workshops, a school, and a club.[159] In October 1935, officials transferred twenty-eight Romani families to their new industrial village, named "The First Five-Year Plan." Upon arrival, their so-called re-education began. They were introduced to their new housing quarters and factory, but also inundated with a series of lectures and meetings of a "political-enlightenment" character.[160] By mid-November, 245 "toiling Gypsies" had been resettled to Krupino.[161] By December, 104 of the settlers were employed in the factory and 27 children matriculated in a special Romani section of the local village school.[162]

At the close of 1935, officials congratulated themselves on the great success of their "rational" and "effective" resettlement plan. The Krupino experiment, officials believed, had disproved notions that "foreign Gypsies" were beyond salvation. It had shown "that this human material, despite its distinctiveness" was "capable of work no less effective than that of … Russian workers."[163] The secret ingredient to their success, officials reasoned, had been their final victory over the so-called Gypsy kulaks. This victory had been achieved by means of providing Krupino's Roma with comfortable living conditions and replacing "camp elders" with the leadership of "disciplined workers, albeit of different nationalities."[164] This, they believed, was the key to transforming the psychology of the "foreign Gypsies" and especially the most "déclassé" among them.[165] Officials were so pleased with the initial results of their experiment that they planned to resettle still more "camp Gypsies" to Krupino.[166]

This self-congratulation proved short-lived. In February 1936, officials in Moscow learned that several groups of Romani families had abandoned Krupino to return to the capital or to move on to unknown destinations.[167] Those who remained, meanwhile, were complaining of food shortages, insufficient medical care, and the hostility of Russian neighbours.[168] Throughout the spring of 1936, Romani families settled at Krupino continued to flee their industrial village. When officials from Mossovet and VTsIK sought out the escapees in Moscow, they found a few who openly admitted that speculation in the capital afforded them a better life. Women were assumed to have returned to fortune telling, and children to their formerly truant lives on the street.[169] By May, all hope was lost, and in July Krupino's "First Five-Year Plan" settlement utterly fell apart. In October 1936, the Soviet Control Commission formally attributed the failures of Krupino to the negligence of two officials at the Moscow Council of Industrial Cooperatives.[170]

Though "The First Five-Year Plan" was ultimately reorganized, by May 1937 only thirty Romani families lived and worked at Krupino. In addition to the Vlax Roma employed there, several Russka Romani shock workers were transferred to Krupino, presumably in order to offer tutelage to their more "backward" brethren. While it was believed that the Roma living in Krupino were "gradually" acquiring labour skills, new concerns mounted daily. Suddenly officials were presented with a familiar problem. In the spring of 1937, kin of the settled Romani families unexpectedly arrived at Krupino seeking quarters and employment in the industrial village. Lacking the resources to provide for these new arrivals, Soviet officials immediately feared that the local population would be incited by predictable "unpleasantries" such as "fortune telling" and "theft."[171] Meanwhile, they admitted in frustration that the Vlax Roma in residence were still insufficiently assimilated to Soviet culture.[172] As ever before, the goal of integrating Moscow's so-called "foreign Gypsies" as labourers and conscious citizens seemed all but unattainable.

Fortunately for Moscow's officials, the Romani workers of Tsygkhimprom and Tsygpishcheprom continued to impress. At a conference organized by the Soviet of Nationalities in 1936 to discuss the "Gypsy question," Romani representatives of the two artels were excited to prove to Soviet authorities just how dedicated they were to the task of "tirelessly" improving themselves. N.E. Baranovskii, a Tsygkhimprom worker and Komsomol member, informed his audience that Soviet power had saved him from a life of miserable backwardness. Though he had been an orphan until the age of thirteen, Baranovskii explained, "The Party and state made a human being of me (*vospitali iz menia cheloveka*) and I become a useful member of society." He nonetheless wanted to make still another point very clear. In his opinion, the success of both Tsygkhimprom and Tsygpishcheprom owed largely to Moscow's labouring Roma themselves. The All-Russian Union of Industrial Cooperatives, he claimed, had done little to help "backward Gypsies" transform themselves into conscious workers in their own national artels. "We've created all of this," he said, referring to the two artels, "with our own Gypsy hands."[173]

Yet Baranovskii soon made the mistake of taking his purported enthusiasm for Soviet nationality policy too far. In a separate speech made by Grushina of Tsygpishcheprom, Baranovskii interrupted his comrade to inquire how many Roma actually worked at the artel. When Grushina revealed that 150 of Tsygpishcheprom's 400 workers were Roma, Baranovskii balked. "There's the title 'Gypsy artel,'" Baranovskii protested, "but very few Gypsies [work] there." Baranovskii's ideological faux pas, however, afforded Grushina the opportunity to shine. "Comrade Baranovskii," Grushina scolded, "our nationality policy is such that we do not create separate castes, but harmoniously work hand in hand with all other nationalities." The entire point of introducing a "backward Gypsy" to industry, she maintained, was "to re-educate, to forge him into a conscious Soviet citizen." Addressing Baranovskii's complaint directly, Grushina explained that the artel was Gypsy in so far as Gypsy workers constituted a plurality among eight other nationalities represented at Tsygpishcheprom. In a final attempt to prove that the artel was a fruitful product of Soviet nationality policy, Grushina informed her audience that five Romani workers had already been promoted within Tsygpishcheprom, a good number had graduated to larger state enterprises, and forty regularly attended literacy courses in the artel's dormitory.[174]

Zverev, another Tsygpishcheprom worker, also reprimanded Baranovskii. "Our task," Zverev argued, "is not to organize some kind of caste ... but to prepare conscious people, so that they march in step with all communists. Our task is to help Gypsies who continued to wander until yesterday learn how to work on level with other comrades." Like Grushina, Zverev also praised the Romani Stakhanovites working in his artel. Indeed, he argued that Tsygpishcheprom's Romani workers could increase their production further still if only they had a rousing work song of their very own. The kind of song he and his fellow workers needed was a high-energy march that would, he explained, "call us to a new life." For now, Romani workers sang not "cheerful, peppy tunes" as did other workers, but "very sad and outdated" songs. "I myself don't know the Gypsy language well," he admitted, "but when the songs are translated for me, I understand that all the melodies and words are outdated."[175]

What a relief it must have been for Soviet officials to hear that a Romani worker's greatest concern in 1936 was that his nationality lacked enthusiastic work songs of its own. In the face of countless obstacles to the successful introduction of recalcitrant, especially "foreign Gypsies" to socially useful labour, the Romani workers of at least two artels had demonstrated commitment to socialist labour and Soviet ideals of self. A. I. Khatskevich, Secretary of TsIK's Soviet of Nationalities, praised these "Gypsy activists" for their successes and exhorted them to continue advancing their nationality through the various mechanisms afforded them as a "backward" people by Soviet nationality policy. Though Gypsy kulaks still lingered undetected in Soviet cities and on collective farms, Khatskevich claimed, Gypsies could not be denied their achievements.[176] Though in the past Gypsies had served as "the most downtrodden, the most backward" of minority peoples, Moscow's Gypsy activists and proletarians were now "working on themselves" and had even managed to "become outstanding people not only among

Gypsies" but among all those who joined in the collective, international effort to construct Soviet socialism.[177] As for those backward Gypsies who still clung to their "slavish customs" and who mistrusted and misunderstood the Soviet civilizing mission – only their dark history of oppression could be blamed. Thus, even the most backward of backward Gypsies, Khatskevich maintained, could still be helped "to liquidate the relics of their difficult past."[178]

Idlers into Workers

When Romani activists began efforts to organize Moscow's "Gypsy masses" in 1923, they quickly realized that they had to first convince officials already troubled by the Soviet Union's shrunken proletariat that a people generally regarded as hopeless idlers, social pariahs, and backward parasites was an untapped human resource that could be reforged and integrated into the socialist economy as productive workers. From the very start of their mission, Romani activists operated according to a script that already presupposed the existence of a Gypsy proletariat. Yet their activities were much more than discursive. Through the creation of industrial workshops, artels, *Romany zoria*, and Red Star, they sought to equip the so-called Gypsy proletarian masses with labour skills and to teach them the fundamentals of Sovietism. Highlighting nationality policy as an unprecedented opportunity for Soviet self-fashioning, Moscow's Romani activists drew their peers not only into the socialist economy, but also into the performance of Soviet citizenship.

Though the Gypsy Union and its industrial enterprises were soon shuttered, Moscow's Romani activists and their protégés adapted to the rapidly changing circumstances of Stalin's First and Second Five-Year Plans. As the traditional livelihoods of Romani traders and fortune tellers were gradually effaced by the demands of Stalin's "revolution from above," the activists helped organize new national artels, expanded the activities of Red Star, and churned out didactic guides to becoming Soviet in the pages of *Romany zoria* and *Nevo drom*. In the face of a public that stubbornly doubted backward Gypsies' potential as socially useful labourers, activists revised their narrative of Romani history to account for the historically rooted obstacles that the Gypsy worker confronted on her path to the factory floor, let alone to Soviet redemption.

Romani activists dutifully tended to the exigencies of Stalin's Five-Year Plans in still other, no less important ways. They were called, in particular, to surveil the thousands of Roma who migrated to Moscow in the early 1930s, to shepherd them – when possible – into new or existing Romani artels, and to preach the tenets of Sovietism among them. When confronted by the obstinate refusal of some Roma to assimilate to the socialist economy and Soviet culture, Romani activists responded with a new narrative creation: the "Gypsy kulak." Forgoing a prior tendency to represent Gypsies as an organic, albeit backward, whole, they now defined their nationality as divided between the exploiters and the exploited. The label "Gypsy kulak" was soon joined to such equally powerful identity ascriptions as "socially harmful" and "foreign" and applied to Vlax Romani migrants to the capital. Romani activists – the majority of whom were Russka – emphasized the radical divide between "Russian Gypsies (Russka)" as loyal citizens and "foreign Gypsies (Vlax)" as stubbornly alien and anti-Soviet. Moscow's Romani activists thus worked to isolate those Gypsies whom they – no less than Soviet authorities – deemed internal enemies and threats to socio-economic order.

Armed with such powerful labelling mechanisms, Romani activists and workers distinguished themselves as vigilant citizens committed to both building socialism and protecting it from Gypsy malefactors. They informed higher Soviet authorities of the alleged economic crimes and anti-Soviet inclinations of so-called "foreign Gypsies" and participated in the trial and condemnation of their supposed kulak leaders. Most activists seemingly understood that arrests, trials, "redemptive" penal labour, and forced resettlement – even in their most violent incarnations – were tools not merely of re-education or urban "cleansing," but also, ultimately, of socialist construction itself.[179] Most among them, meanwhile, continued to promote the view that even the most backward, foreign, or intractable Gypsies could be forged into new human beings, reincarnated as socially useful labourers, and thus saved and redeemed by Soviet civilization.

Although hundreds of Moscow's so-called "foreign Gypsies" challenged and bewildered Romani activists and Soviet officials through out the Stalinist 1930s, they nonetheless remained the object of underfunded "re-education" schemes such as the experimental Romani industrial village at Krupino. While many Roma eventually fled the new life they were expected to create at Krupino, others not only settled there, but also encouraged their distant relatives to join them in their new dorm rooms, cafeteria, and workshop. Although this response to the Soviet civilizing mission may not have been the one that activists and officials were hoping for – that is, their willing transformation into New Soviet Gypsies – it was, nonetheless, evidence that even the least assimilated Roma recognized that "Gypsy backwardness" invited the material benefits of Soviet nationality policy.

The greatest victories won by efforts to proletarianize Moscow's Roma were achieved in the artels Tsygpishcheprom and Tsygkhimprom, where hundreds of Roma were employed in Soviet industry. Romani workers at Tsygpishcheprom and Tsygkhimprom advanced their labour qualifications, improved their literacy skills, submitted to political-enlightenment campaigns, and reaped the material and cultural benefits of shock work. In time, many came to understand that the work they performed on the factory or shop floor was all but meaningless if not matched by work performed towards the cultivation of their own Soviet selves. By the end of the 1930s, Tsygpishcheprom's and Tsygkhimprom's most lauded employees were those who recognized that the Bolsheviks' nationality policy was intended not simply to transform backward Gypsies into enlightened Gypsies, but to transform backward Gypsies into Soviet citizens. These Romani workers performed their duty and their right to labour as socially useful citizens of the Soviet Union. Integrated into the socialist economy, they contributed labour to the Soviet triumph over all historic backwardness – not merely their own.

4 Nomads into Farmers: Romani Activism and the Territorialization of (In)Difference

Violins weep as Gypsy women trudge through mud, leading their mournful children by hand. From the relative comfort of their coaches, self-satisfied kulaks smoke pipes and steer the wagons of their Gypsy caravan. Suddenly, the sky unleashes a torrential downpour of rain. As the ragged-clothed women and children rush to shelter themselves inside the caravan's crowded wagons, the only noise capable of over-powering the violins' plaintive wails is the miserable sound of the Gypsy children's crying. Thus begins the 1935 Soviet film, *The Last Camp* (Poslednii tabor).

Vania, a Russian activist dispatched from Moscow, attempts to convince the nomadic camp to settle on a national Romani kolkhoz. Speaking only grudgingly to the meddlesome intruder in his realm, the camp's kulak chief, Danilo, instructs Vania to "get lost." As a Russian, he explains, Vania will never understand the sacred laws of the Gypsy camp or experience the happiness of nomadic freedom. Unfazed by Danilo's menacing looks, Vania sardonically replies, "A beloved horse, a swarm of children, and long roads – that is Gypsy happiness!"

The camp soon reaches the outskirts of an idyllic kolkhoz named the Land of the Soviets. It is here, Vania hopes, that the poor nomads domineered by Danilo will "catch a glimpse of real life." To his delight, some of the Gypsies *are* impressed by the material abundance enjoyed by the kolkhozniks. The Gypsy Iudko laughingly tells Vania, "You can't scare me with work – not even with agricultural work!" Meanwhile, Iudko's daughter, Al'ta, is enchanted by an energetic young kolkhoznik named Sen'ka who demonstrates a penchant for reciting lines from Pushkin's poem *The Gypsies*.

Iudko, meanwhile, is entranced by the kolkhozniks as they happily harvest wheat in disciplined, synchronized motions. The men are strapping. The wholesome women smile. Iudko silently admires this multilayered scene of human productivity, natural beauty, material plenty, and spiritual oneness. Longingly, Iudko fingers the wheat stalks until, suddenly, he grabs hold of a bunch in a dramatic embrace. "Real grain," he whispers wistfully. Witnessing this moment of revelation, the kolkhoz chairman paternalistically invites Iudko to join the kolkhoz in reaping. Although Iudko happily obliges, the work does not come easy to this "backward Gypsy" who has never known "honest labour." With obvious frustration, he awkwardly manipulates his scythe. Yet, as a rousing Soviet work song plays in the background, the kolkhoz chairman patiently teaches Iudko to reap in deliberate, disciplined movements. Soon, Iudko is working as well as the others and happily wiping sweat from his brow.

After deciding to join the kolkhoz, Iudko feels as "free as a bird." He delights not only in his work, but also in his happy new homestead. He and his family are given a comfortable room in one of the kolkhoz houses. Humming happily to himself, Iudko smiles at the thought of his family living under a roof, of owning a cow in the future, of drinking milk at breakfast.

In celebration of Iudko's conversion to settled, agricultural labour, the kolkhoz chairman invites Danilo and the entire Romani camp to a feast. "For centuries, Gypsies have roamed the earth," the chairman says, "until the Land of the Soviets declared: 'Abandon your joyless Gypsy camps. Labour and live happily on our land in national Gypsy kolkhozes!'" As Danilo looks on bitterly, the Russians and Roma alike raise their glasses to the chairman's toast: "Comrades! To the settlement of all toiling Gypsies!"

Iudko beams with happiness. Now engaged to marry Sen'ka, Al'ta dances in celebration. Threatened by their irrepressible joy, Danilo seethes with rage as he begins to plot revenge. As the Roma and kolkhozniks are distracted by their own merrymaking, Danilo violently stabs Al'ta in the shadows, carries her limp body to Iudko, and accuses a Russian kolkhoznik of murdering Al'ta in a fit of jealousy. Decrying this horrific crime as the reason why Gypsies should never abandon their native camp for the world of perfidious Russians and their farms, Danilo triumphantly leads the bewildered Gypsies back to their camp.

Yet as Iudko cries over the body of his slain daughter, Al'ta opens her eyes, sheds a tear, and speaks weakly to him in Romani. Knowing what needs be done, Iudko races off to the camp. Arriving at daybreak, Iudko announces to his fellow Gypsies the crime of their cruel leader and challenges Danilo to a duel. Deep in the woods, the two men struggle, slashing one another with their whips. Finally, Danilo stumbles out into the camp, bloodied and dazed. Iudko stands triumphant, holding Danilo's broken whip handle. Cheered by the joyful camp as a hero, Iudko has broken not only Danilo's whip handle, but also the kulak's exploitative hold on the Gypsy poor. At the film's end, Al'ta awakens with a smile as she hears the happy singing of her fellow Gypsies. Iudko has triumphantly led them to the promised land – to the Land of the Soviets and the world of productive agricultural labour.[1]

The Last Camp portrayed the Soviet mission to sedentarize backward Gypsies as one pursued by the state with tireless vigour, but also with benevolent patience, understanding, and care. The celluloid incarnation of Soviet officialdom's hopes for a settled Romani population integrated securely in the socialist economy and assimilated to Soviet culture, *The Last Camp* also literally projected the insecurities and fears of a state ill-equipped to meet its ambitious goals. Danilo, for one, represented the perceived threat not only of the power of cunning Gypsy kulaks, but also of a Gypsy culture whose laws, language, and customs were all but inscrutable to state officials. Vania – the activist sent by Moscow to guide the camp to Soviet salvation – served as a self-conscious symbol of the state's lack of human and material investment in its listless campaign to sedentarize Roma. Lastly, the film captured the bureaucratic view of Roma as a benighted people who, while steeped in immeasurable misery, clung stubbornly to their "backward" traditions. Like sheep, the Roma of the camp begged to be guided and led – whether by Danilo or Iudko. Ultimately, Iudko and Al'ta figured as rare links in a generational chain of "backwardness" who voluntarily submitted to Soviet re-education. Their sovietization, however, required not only generous state resources, but also the paternalism of fellow citizens who were more "advanced" and ethnically Russian.

At the time of the film's release in 1935, Soviet officials charged with rationalizing the empire's nomadic Romani population were painfully aware that *The Last Camp* depicted Soviet reality only as it ought to be, not as it was. By now, Soviet officials were in their ninth year of their official campaign to sedentarize Romani nomads and organize them in collective farms. As in their wider effort to eradicate nomadism generally, Soviet officials had proved more adept at decrying the "backwardness" of "scattered" Romani nomads than they were at formulating and executing plans for Roma's sedentarization and collectivization.

Indeed, by 1935, Soviet officials openly recognized that they had thus far failed to successfully transition millions of the empire's nomadic and seminomadic peoples to sedentary, "civilized" life. They had admittedly failed to formulate a rational, cost-effective, and quick plan to immobilize the "wandering tribes" of Central Asia, the Caucasus, and Siberia and, next, to integrate them into the socialist economy and Soviet culture. The failure to successfully sedentarize nomads seemed to indicate not only the poverty of the Soviet bureaucratic imagination, but also the insufficiency of nationality policy to bring "backward" minority peoples into the Soviet fold.[2]

It was therefore no coincidence that on 9 September 1935 A.I. Khatskevich, Secretary of the Soviet of Nationalities, welcomed officials from all corners of the empire to Moscow to discuss the ever-menacing problem of nomadism within Soviet borders. The conference's task was to confront the state's failure to sedentarize the empire's nomads – its itinerant herders of goats, sheep, horses, reindeer, and camels. Once assembled, attendees dutifully recited the platitudinous hallmarks of Soviet discourse on settling nomads. They agreed, for example, that it was "through sedentarization that the backwardness of the nomadic population is liquidated." Sedentarization, one official explained, was the conduit through which "the nationality policy of the party and state fulfils itself."[3]

According to the Soviet calculus of backwardness, nomads distinguished themselves as the most economically, socially, and culturally underdeveloped of minority peoples.[4] With their seemingly stationary position on the Soviet timeline of human development, nomads' backwardness was evidenced most clearly in their low labour productivity. In the Soviet view, the economies of nomadic societies were "undifferentiated" and crudely "composite." The technology employed by pastoral nomads was "primitive, rudimentary."[5] Migration was counterintuitive to the productive spirit of the industrializing Soviet Union. Pastoral nomads exhausted and squandered their livestock, pastures, and time in their irrational pursuit of meager subsistence economies. Life was most difficult for these poor, backward nomadic and seminomadic peoples. Ever vulnerable, they were constantly exposed to the dangers of the elements: the cruel whims of weather and the indiscriminate tyranny of contagious disease. In short, the nomadic way of life was seen not only as unproductive and technologically conservative in the heroic age of Soviet socialism, but also as "wretched, primitive, and dangerous to health."[6]

It was not merely the labour of nomads that was deemed abnormal and unacceptable by Soviet policymakers in the 1920s and 1930s. Officials castigated the culture of nomadic and seminomadic peoples as deviant, backward, and inevitably antithetical to Soviet values and socialist construction. While the rare Soviet policymaker protested that there was "nothing shameful in being a nomad in the twentieth century," most essentialized nomads as patriarchal, superstitious, and dirty illiterates whose primitive culture amounted to a stubborn, premodern "survival."[7] Though formerly idealized in the Russian revolutionary tradition as primitive communists, nomads were recast during the First Five-Year Plan as peoples no less tyrannized by kulaks as were "normal," sedentary agriculturalists. No longer regarded as "noble savages," nomads were now conceptualized as backward people who clung to an irrational, inefficient, and unproductive form of economic organization while dominated by their own native, livestock-hoarding exploiters.[8]

Soviet officialdom regarded nomads as the proverbial thorn in the side of the state's plan to rationalize its population and to remould "human material" into the scientifically engineered motor of an unmistakably modern socialist economy. The modernization of Soviet agriculture and industry, after all, required that every segment of the Soviet population be rendered knowable, accounted for, productive, and ultimately reforged as conscious Soviet citizens.[9] With their mobile intractability and ability to evade the state's gaze, nomads threatened Soviet officials tasked with locating, counting, classifying, reordering, and reeducating the empire's population, not to mention extracting labour from them. Officials thus sought to immobilize the empire's nomads so that they could be known, collectivized, and remade as conscious Soviet citizens fully integrated into the socialist economy.

Without a doubt, nomadic and seminomadic peoples inspired considerable perplexity and frustration in Soviet bureaucrats already straining to make sense of an empire seemingly at odds with the socialist utopia dictated by Stalin's First Five-Year Plans. Among the empire's nomadic peoples, however, Gypsies stood out as particularly unruly, obstreperous, and inscrutable. Indeed, Gypsies seemed to have rightfully earned notoriety as the *most backward* of Soviet nomads. In the early Soviet bureaucratic imagination, Gypsies figured not merely as the archetypes of unrestrained mobility, but also as the national personification of a distinctly irrational mode of itinerancy. Gypsies alone belonged to a special category of nomadism that made them all the

Children of a nomadic Romani camp in Ukraine, circa 1935. Courtesy of the
State Archive of the Russian Federation.

more perplexing in the eyes of officials.[10] Gypsies, after all, were seen
not merely as peripatetics, but also as parasites with a deep aversion to
labour. Gypsies seemingly produced nothing of value, but instead consumed all that could be gained through deceit or self-abasement, but
never by "legitimate" labour. They lacked not only agricultural experience, but even the most rudimentary implements of cultured, settled
life.

Kazakhs were perhaps Gypsies' greatest rivals for status as the Soviet Union's "most backward" nomadic nationality in the Soviet bureaucratic imagination. Like Gypsies, Kazakhs also presented the state
with the formidable challenge of sedentarization. On the eve of Stalin's
"revolution from above," the majority of Kazakhs were pastoral nomads, illiterate, and poverty-stricken. The Soviet state wanted to transform Kazakhstan into a key grain-producing region; Kazakh herdsmen
stood in the way of such designs as pastoralists who consumed grain,
but did not produce it. As nomads, Kazakhs were presumed bereft not
only of culture, but also of the costly material prerequisites of settled
life – permanent, stationary housing not least of all. Yet the Kazakh
pastoralists did have livestock and, indeed, some among them – the

bais – appeared in officials' eyes as too wealthy, as Kazakh "kulaks."[11] Yet animal husbandry seemingly represented Kazakhs' potential for transformation into rational actors within the agricultural sector of the socialist economy – a potential greater than that of Gypsies, even if only by degree. Gypsies' stereotyped livelihoods – fortune telling, begging, crafty horse-dealing, or horse-thieving – represented, by comparison, a still greater moral and financial investment in their Soviet transformation into modern citizens.

The sedentarization of Gypsies and their transformation into farmers, moreover, was an investment that many Soviet officials doubted would produce anything but the most negligible returns. Soviet officials perceived the distinctive service nomadism of Roma as still more backward, irrational, and deviant than even the pastoral nomadism practiced by Kazakhs and other minority peoples in Siberia, Central Asia, and the Caucasus.[12] Unlike the pastoralists who essentially needed only to adapt to stationary farming in order to productively integrate into the socialist economy, Gypsies required an introduction to both settled *and* agricultural life.

Unfortunately for Soviet officials, nationality policy did not provide a clear solution to "the Gypsy problem," nor did state coffers offer unlimited resources with which to attempt the sedentarization of nomadic Roma. Their task, nonetheless, was to immobilize and refashion thousands of "scattered" Romani nomads whose very existence challenged the Soviet ideals of rationality, order, and productive labour in the socialist economy. From 1925 onward, Soviet officials struggled to devise an answer to the problem of settling a fragmented Romani population that they presumed to be dangerously backward, intractable, impoverished, and woefully inexperienced in the skills required of agriculture. Unsurprisingly, many Soviet officials gave up on the hope of fulfilling this unenviable task from the get-go.

Others, however, grasped the flimsy hope that if Roma could only be settled and collectivized on farms, the battle to de-Gypsify and sovietize them would largely be won. If, as it was believed, parasitic itinerancy was at the core of Gypsy culture, Soviet officials needed only to deprive Gypsy nomads of the ability to wander and feast off the toil of others. According to this logic, nomadic Gypsies who settled and took up agriculture also ceased to be Gypsies.[13] Thus, "backward Gypsies" were promised national territory in the form of Gypsy kolkhozes precisely because settled agriculture was seen as alien to Gypsies' national culture. Gypsy kolkhozes were intended not only to immobilize, but also to deracinate Roma. Yet in the early Soviet Union it was Roma themselves who most vigorously attempted to build stable and productive Gypsy kolkhozes. It was also Roma who, invoking nationality policy's logic, most eagerly pursued the creation of a Soviet Gypsy homeland.

The Overtasked Centre and the Peripheral Unknown

TsIK and Sovnarkom's 1926 decree "On Measures to Bring About Nomadic Gypsies' Transition to a Working, Settled Way of Life" achieved little in the matter of settling Romani nomads onto individual or collective farms. Though a few Romani families had secured plots of land as a result of the decree, its relevance to the lives of Roma rarely extended beyond the scant paper it was printed on. In February 1928, TsIK and Sovnarkom issued a second decree entitled "On the Provision of Land to Gypsies Transitioning to a Working, Settled Way of Life." All but identical to its 1926 predecessor, this new decree again obliged Narkomzem to prioritize Roma's voluntary "transition" to agricultural labour.[14] As before, Romani settlers were entitled to land, agricultural training, and various subsidies.[15] Though the 1928 decree inspired Roma throughout the empire to request land and aid in forming collective farms, their demands were largely ignored.[16] Narkomzem blamed local agricultural departments for the failure to transition nomadic Roma "to a working, settled way of life" as called for by the 1926 and 1928 decrees.[17]

Throughout the second half of the 1920s, officials and activists grasped at any evidence that Roma were voluntarily sedentarizing and taking up agriculture. They repeatedly claimed the example of the Krikunov village in the North Caucasus as proof of their success in settling Romani nomads. Yet the Krikunov villagers had organized their commune independently in 1925 and enjoyed none of the promises made to Romani settlers by the 1926 and 1928 decrees. Although propagandists trumpeted the Krikunov commune in the Soviet press, the Krikunov settlers were refused nearly all their requests for material aid and instruction.[18] By 1929, frustrated Roma had already abandoned the Krikunov settlement for unknown destinations.[19]

In the months preceding Stalin's massive collectivization drive in the winter of 1929–30, Romani activists and officials in Moscow were painfully aware that their half-hearted, armchair efforts to settle Romani nomads had produced only negligible results. Officials possessed a vague knowledge of handfuls of scattered Romani families who had received individual plots of land and even of the existence of a few Romani collective farms. Yet they also recognized that regional and local officials had followed their lead in largely avoiding the complicated task of sedentarizing Romani nomads. Though centre and periphery parroted one another's high-minded claims that sedentarization remained the fundamental method of "raising the economic and cultural level of Gypsies," both refused to confront the perceived parasitism, indolence, danger, and deviance of nomadic Gypsy life.[20]

Seeking to put an end to this stalemate, Moscow's leading Romani activists invited officials and Romani workers to discuss the dreaded "Gypsy question" at a one-day conference in October 1929. Attendees agreed that the state had thus far disastrously failed to confront Roma's nomadic challenge to the Soviet Union's all-encompassing modernization agenda. They disagreed, however, on the matter of deciding who was responsible for this momentous failure.

Romani activists blamed Narkomzem for failing to both popularize the decrees of 1926 and 1928 and to fulfil voluntary Romani settlers' requests for land. Grushina, a Romani Tsygpishcheprom worker, angrily recounted her own experience in trying to help Roma in her native province organize an agricultural commune. Only after three years of pleading and hassle, Grushina explained, had she succeeded in helping a group of rural Roma receive a plot of land through Narkomzem. Though the settlers were ultimately given a few horses and cows, they were not provided training or any other help. "In my opinion," Grushina scolded, "it is not enough to give land and to release funds for Gypsy communes." What was really needed, she explained, was for officials "to show Gypsies how to work on the land."[21] Grushina's fellow Romani worker, Baranovskii, adopted an even more indignant tone. The real problem, he claimed, was that "most say that Gypsies are capable only of singing and dancing." Narkomzem officials refused Romani settlers due to their chauvinistic belief that "Gypsies are incapable of working the land."[22]

Non-Romani officials countered the activists' complaints by attributing the failures of Romani sedentarization to the insincere schemes and general cultural backwardness of Roma themselves. One complained that many Roma who had received plots of land in one locale demanded new plots in far-off regions, or worse still, simply abandoned the land given them. He cited one instance in which Roma had petitioned for land only to terrorize neighbouring populations with thievery, fights, and other scandals. A VTsIK representative, meanwhile, insisted on an optimistic view towards the future. Like Roma, he explained, Jews had once been considered incapable of labour, but they had recently proven themselves as people who "work no worse than others." The real problem preventing the mass settlement of the empire's Roma, he argued, was logistical. In so far as Roma were a scattered population, it was difficult for officials and activists to settle, organize, and train them. Sedentarization, he opined, could proceed rationally and effectively only if "separate regions" were carved out "for the resettlement of Gypsies."[23] Shortly after this suggestion was made, however, the conference dissolved into a bitter dispute over the Gypsy Union's dismantling and the issue of Romani nomadism was sidelined.

In February 1930, two Romani activists published an article entitled "Throw the Nomadic Camps into the Past," in which they complained that the compulsory collectivization then being carried out in the Soviet village was somehow bypassing the empire's Romani nomads. "It would be utterly utopian to suppose," the authors admitted, "that it would be possible in twelve years for Soviet power to liquidate Gypsies' nomadic, wandering lifestyle and to reconstruct it on different, cultured principles." All the same, they insisted, not enough had yet been done to settle Gypsies and introduce them to socially useful, agricultural labour. Given Gypsies' "extraordinary scatteredness (*raspylennost'*)" and undeniable backwardness, they argued, only one viable solution presented itself to Soviet officials: "the compact mass settlement" of Gypsies. If only Gypsies were awarded nationality policy's most prized gift – a national territory – the matter of "carrying out cultural and Soviet work among the Gypsies" would be easy. Intimating again their anger over the Gypsy Union's closing, they asked why an organization similar to the Society for Settling Toiling Jews on the Land could not be created for Gypsies.[24] Although offered only in passing, the question was remarkably shrewd. Comparing Gypsies to a nationality similarly considered parasitic, agriculturally disinclined, and geographically dispersed throughout the empire, the activists implied unjust and unequal treatment. Gypsies, too, desired and needed a state-sponsored organization devoted to the promotion of their particularly "backward" nationality's conversion to settled, agricultural life.[25]

Although Romani activists seem wrongly to have assumed that the Soviet collectivization drive was being pursued in anything but its notoriously ad hoc, improvised, and violent incarnation, their frustration was grounded in the realities of the state's slow and unorganized manner of settling and collectivizing Romani nomads.[26] Even those officials and activists whom Stalin notoriously euphemized as "dizzy with success" seemed uninterested in settling and collectivizing Roma forcibly or otherwise.[27] Much as in the case of the formation of Moscow's Romani artels during the same period, Romani collective farms were emerging spontaneously and without state aid or oversight. Throughout 1930, central authorities thus relied only on incomplete and often contradictory reports from the provinces on the matter of integrating Roma into the agricultural sector of the state economy. The activist editors of the Romani-language journal *Nevo drom* grew so impatient with officials' confused detachment that they scoured regional newspapers for mention of Romani sedentarization and invited Romani settlers to write to them about their collective farms.[28]

The meager reports that did reach officials and activists in the capital were not encouraging. They learned of Roma who had received plots of land in accordance with the 1928 decree, but who had abandoned those same plots when faced with the absence of necessary seed, livestock, construction materials, and agricultural training.[29] Disheartening reports also trickled in from Romani settlements scattered seemingly anarchically throughout the empire. When, for example, representatives of the All-Russian Union of Agricultural Collectives (*Kolkhoztsentr*) inspected the Lebedev kolkhoz in the North Caucasus in 1930, officials found "undisciplined" Romani settlers who continued to trade horses and allegedly pocketed state subsidies intended for the farm's development. These "former nomads," Kolkhoztsentr inspectors reported, did not know how "to live culturally in [their] new conditions" and "to approach work duties." Later that year, the North Caucasus Kolkhoztsentr responded to inspectors' complaints by purging the farm of forty-five alleged saboteurs.[30] Those remaining continued "to live under the open sky" as their kolkhoz threatened to disintegrate at any time.[31]

In light of these and similar reports, the Nationalities Bureau of Kolkhoztsentr convened in January 1931 to discuss "the collectivization of toiling Gypsies." Roma, Kolkhoztsentr explained, had recently flooded bureaucratic offices with requests for land and aid to create national kolkhozes. Yet local officials refused to prioritize the creation of new Romani kolkhozes, or the strengthening of those already existing. They denied potential Romani settlers their rightful opportunity to join in socialist construction.

Kolkhoztsentr recognized, however, that problems in the locales originated in the centre. It criticized the 1926 and 1928 decrees for having "inadequately reflected toiling Gypsies' economic and national-cultural (*natsional-bytovye*) particularities (nomadic way of life, lack of housing, etc.)." It suggested that VTsIK issue a new decree outlining various incentives for Roma's settlement on collective farms, and that Narkomzem provide local authorities with detailed instructions on their obligations to create and strengthen Romani kolkhozes. Kolkhoztsentr obligated itself to inspect existing Romani kolkhozes and to aid settlers in strengthening their farms.[32]

It would ultimately take Narkomzem a full nine months and VTsIK well over a year to respond to Kolkhoztsentr's suggestions. Both agencies' responses revealed officials' bewildering lack of knowledge and stubborn refusal to take responsibility for Roma's collectivization. In a memorandum addressed to the Nationalities Department of VTsIK, Narkomzem merely summarized the sparse, laconic reports on Romani collectivization that it had received from regional affiliates and recounted its own troubling encounters with Romani nomads. Narkomzem complained of a group of Roma who had travelled from Moscow to Stalingrad, from Stalingrad to Grozny, and from Grozny to Baku – each time with free train tickets awarded them as potential Romani settlers. In closing, Narkomzem offered this banal conclusion: "Experience shows, that the transfer of Gypsies to settled life demands an especially sensitive, planned approach, taking into account the distinctive particularities characteristic ... of Gypsies who ... are not registered anywhere and who ... constantly wander."[33] Following up with a circular issued to its provincial agencies in February 1932, Narkomzem demanded an end to officials' "apparent lack of desire" to oversee Roma's sedentarization.[34]

On 1 April 1932, VTsIK issued a new resolution, "On the Condition of Work in the Service of Toiling Gypsies." Like its predecessors, the 1932 resolution offered nothing more than platitudes and marching orders. It instructed Narkomzem to devise a "concrete plan for the settling of toiling Gypsies on land" and jointly tasked Narkomzem and Kolkhoztsentr to popularize the state's sedentarization policies among Roma, to cleanse class enemies from existing Romani kolkhozes, and to strengthen new and existing Romani farms.[35] Detailed instructions for fulfilling these characteristically vague demands, however, did not follow.

In July 1932, Narkomzem's director for the organization of territory and resettlement, Comrade Murza-Galiev, admitted Narkomzem and Kolkhoztsentr's shared unpreparedness for the task of sedentarizing and collectivizing Romani nomads. The greatest difficulty facing administrators and officials, Murza-Galiev explained, lay in their

complete miscomprehension of the Soviet Union's Romani populations. Officials lacked not only precise census statistics on Roma, but
also basic understanding of their everyday life, the nature of their nomadism, or the particularities of their internal class struggle. Nomadic
Roma, he argued, were all the more inscrutable insofar as they were
"scattered across an enormous territory" and isolated from the Romani
activists upon whom officials relied in the capital. Before Narkomzem
and Kolkhoztsentr officials could begin to settle Romani nomads in fulfilment of the April 1932 decree, Murza-Galiev conceded, they first had
to uncover the results – however slim – of the 1926 and 1928 decrees.[36]

Murza-Galiev understated his case. A brief memo titled "Gypsy Kolkhozes" and dated 29 April 1932 testified that Narkomzem and Kolkhoztsentr had not yet even ascertained how many Romani collective
farms existed. They could only estimate that an approximate 368 Romani families had settled and collectivized in the Central Black Earth,
Lower Volga, Middle Volga, North Caucasus, and Western regions of
the empire.[37] Beyond this, they knew nothing of the Romani nomads
whom they ostensibly sought to settle. More than three months later,
Murza-Galiev would admit that officials were still in the process of locating Romani settlements.[38]

Throughout the summer of 1932, Narkomzem and Kolkhoztsentr
dispatched officials to investigate known Romani kolkhozes and provide settlers with training, equipment, and subsidies. They were also
to instruct local and regional officials in dealing with their Romani
charges, and to help potential settlers apply for and receive land. Narkomzem inspectors, in particular, were to encourage local officials to
seek out Romani nomads at markets and even in their own camps with
the aim of settling and collectivizing them. Perhaps most importantly,
the inspectors were to return to the capital with detailed reports on
their findings and a clear vision of how best to proceed in sedentarizing
and collectivizing Roma.[39]

Inspectors returned to Moscow, however, without a concrete plan for
integrating Romani nomads into the agricultural sector of the socialist economy. Though their fact-finding missions allowed the centre to
claim a greater understanding of the situation on the periphery, Soviet
officialdom's knowledge of Roma remained clumsily constructed from
sparse, incomplete, and sometimes contradictory reports. In characteristic response to the missions' disappointing results, the centre again
shifted blame onto the periphery for the "completely unsatisfactory"
results of the 1926, 1928, and 1932 decrees on settling Romani nomads.[40]

Such deflections of blame for past and present failures did little to mask central officials' new anxieties born of Narkomzem and Kolkhozt-sentr's inspections of Romani kolkhozes. Their concerns centred on the fact that of the twenty-five Romani kolkhozes "discovered" by the late fall of 1932, nearly all had collapsed or were on the verge of disintegration. Already in July, inspectors had reported a loss of ten Romani kolk-hozes, or a full third of collectivized Romani households accounted for in 1931. All of these kolkhozes had been located in Ukraine. Inspectors, however, did not reference the increasingly rapacious grain quotas that had already begun to reduce many peasants throughout the Soviet Union, but especially in Ukraine, to the status of starving "saboteurs." Instead, they attributed the collapse of Romani kolkhozes in Ukraine to poor harvests and the administrative failures of local officials.[41]

Of the fifteen remaining Romani kolkhozes, inspectors described all but one as isolated sites of anarchy and kulak tyranny. Inspectors charged local officials with a failure of leadership, accusing them of "great-power chauvinism" and "inattention to the needs" of Roma. They recognized only one Romani kolkhoz as having exhibited any signs of potential. Located in Smolensk Province, the "October" kolk-hoz astonished inspectors with a success that had already earned the farm multiple awards and monetary prizes. Though inspectors reported that October was home to at least nine Romani Party members and twelve Komsomol members, they offered little other insight as to why and how this Romani kolkhoz had thus far succeeded while twenty-four others failed.[42]

By summer's end, Narkomzem and Kolkhoztsentr officials – knowing little more about the empire's Romani kolkhozes than they had at the time of the 1 April 1932 decree – decided once again to relieve themselves of the burden of settling Romani nomads. They transferred the bulk of responsibility for the strengthening, expansion, and creation of Romani kolkhozes to provincial and local officials – the very same people whom they charged with negligence, inefficiency, and "great-power chauvinism."[43] Throughout the 1930s, as in the 1920s, central Soviet officials tasked with transforming backward Gypsies into settled, productive farmers would prove themselves not only ill-equipped and unwilling to do so, but also generally incompetent on matters related to Romani nomadism. Whatever failures they attached to the union-wide goal of Romani sedentarization, these central officials could not disguise that they had contributed to them. Whatever successes were enjoyed on Romani kolkhozes in the 1930s, meanwhile, belonged not only to a slim minority of provincial and local officials, but mostly to Roma themselves.

Recidivism and Rehabilitation on Romani Collective Farms

At the Third All-Russian Conference of Workers among the Nationalities held in Moscow in December 1933, Comrade Nurmakov of VTsIK's Nationalities Department implored his colleagues to take more seriously the matter of sedentarizing and collectivizing Roma. He complained that too many of them could not even consider the need to transform Romani nomads into settled farmers without cracking jokes and glancing at one another with knowing smiles.[44] Similarly frustrated, Narkomzem's Murza-Galiev demanded that officials at every administrative level recognize the ongoing campaign to sedentarize all the empire's nomads – not merely Roma – as a battle to assimilate woefully backward minorities to the socialist economy and Soviet culture.[45] While his colleagues amused themselves with distasteful jokes, Murza-Galiev chided, they neglected the state's plan to rapidly increase the number of Romani kolkhozes in the wake of the April 1932 decree. At best, they had fulfilled only 40 per cent of the target for Romani settlement in 1932, and in 1933 had achieved practically nothing at all.[46]

I.P. Tokmakov, a former nomad and Romani activist hired as a native consultant in VTsIK's Nationalities Department, detected a hollow ring to Murza-Galiev's words. In his view, Murza-Galiev's speech exemplified the state's lack of commitment to the task of Romani sedentarization and collectivization. Correcting Murza-Galiev's tally of thirteen Romani kolkhozes in the RSFSR, Tokmakov informed his audience of the existence of twenty-three such farms and one Gypsy village soviet. Had Murza-Galiev deigned to recently inquire into matters of refashioning Romani nomads into farmers, Tokmakov argued, he would have known that Romani kolkhozes had grown at a rate of 58 per cent in the previous two years alone.[47]

Murza-Galiev's artful manipulation of budgetary figures proved still more troubling for Tokmakov. Although Murza-Galiev had boasted the central state's assignation of 20 million rubles to the task of settling nomads as "enormous expenditures," he had kept silent on the relatively paltry amounts spent on Roma specifically.[48] Funds allocated specifically for the creation or expansion of Romani collective farms, Tokmakov explained, had shrunk drastically in the past year alone. Whereas 300,000 rubles had been budgeted for Romani sedentarization in 1932, a mere 100,000 were allocated in 1933. "From here we see," Tokmakov asserted, "that our agricultural organs were not adequately prepared for the settlement of Gypsies." The history of the Soviet Union's Romani kolkhozes, Tokmakov argued, was one of the Soviet state *in absentia*. Of the twenty-three existing Romani kolkhozes, he explained, twenty had been established as a result of Romani settlers' own initiative.[49] Narkomzem, he concluded, all but turned a blind eye to the Romani kolkhozniks who so desperately needed help in making their farms a success.[50] Narkomzem officials, however, stubbornly blamed the failures of Romani sedentarization on inattentive, incompetent regional authorities.[51]

Yet while centre and periphery endlessly exchanged the blame for the disasters born of little-known Romani kolkhozes, Romani kolkhozniks were largely left to fend for themselves. Throughout the 1930s, as most Soviet officials and even Moscow's Romani activists grudgingly approached the goal of settling Romani nomads, Romani settlers responded variously to the state's demand that they shed their wandering "backwardness" for a life of settled agricultural productivity and economic integration. Some fled their farms, seeing in them not a promised land of plenty, but instead a wretched site of servitude, starvation, and broken promises. Others wandered between farms, searching repeatedly for the fulfilment of the state's lofty promises, or simply the enjoyment of the temporary material rewards of announcing themselves as members of a "backward" nationality. Hundreds of Romani families did, however, build new lives on Romani collective farms. Former Romani nomads were scattered on kolkhozes from Ukraine to Siberia, from the North Caucasus to Central Asia. Some Roma settled reluctantly, refused to work on the farms, and continued to trade and tell fortunes at local markets. Others, however, struggled to develop their national farms and to reinvent themselves as Soviet kolkhozniks. The majority of these Romani settlers found the latter task considerably easier than the former. On one hand, Soviet officialdom's limp regard for the task of sedentarizing and collectivizing Roma appears a blessing in disguise, especially when Roma's experience is compared, for example, to the murderous famine that decimated the Kazakh population as a result of ruthless Soviet sedentarization and collectivization policies.[52] On the other hand, Soviet indifference no doubt frustrated and otherwise negatively impacted the efforts of those Roma who *did* attempt to integrate into the agricultural sector of the socialist economy as nomads transformed into citizen farmers.

In June 1931, the newspaper *Trud* produced a lengthy feature on "the Toiling Gypsy," a Romani kolkhoz in the North Caucasus. Its author described his task as the unveiling of "the world of nomads transitioning directly to a collective economy." Having suffered a prerevolutionary past of endless peril, privation, and tsarist persecution, the Toiling Gypsy's kolkhozniks now reputedly enjoyed the shelter and material plenty that agricultural labour earned them. "We were neglected in the past," one kolkhoznik was quoted as saying, but "Soviet power gave us new life (*rodila nas vtorichno*)." Praising the farm as evidence of Soviet nationality policy's triumphs, *Trud* described the Toiling Gypsy as an unadulterated paradise of clean homes, smiling faces, and "mountains of bread."[53]

The idyll portrayed in *Trud* could not have strayed farther from the reality of life on the Toiling Gypsy kolkhoz.[54] When the Romani activist Mikhail Bezliudskii – himself a former nomad – arrived from Moscow to inspect the farm in late 1932, he found not "mountains of bread," but rather no bread at all. Like millions of Soviet rural dwellers, the members of the Toiling Gypsy had fallen victim to the massive famine sparked by collectivization's lethal combination of rapacious grain quotas, poor harvests, and the utter demoralization of the Soviet village. Utterly appalled, Bezliudskii discovered that ten of the kolkhoz's members had recently been arrested for "theft, deviousness, and speculation," while many of those left behind abandoned their farm for weeks at a time for nearby markets. Making matters worse, neighbouring Russian kolkhozes consistently exhibited "great-power chauvinism" in their relations with the Toiling Gypsy and refused to share precious few rations doled out by regional authorities. Though Bezliudskii attempted to "cleanse" the kolkhoz of speculators, he admitted that he could accomplish little more without the help of a Kolkhoztsentr specialist. [55]

Bezliudskii's pleas went unanswered and most remaining members of the Toiling Gypsy soon deserted the farm. At the time of its establishment in 1928, the farm had united 112 households. By the end of 1932, a mere eleven remained.[56] In desperation, the farm's chairman, a Romani Party member named Ivanenko, appealed directly to VTsIK's Nationalities Department for help. Regional authorities had repeatedly refused the kolkhoz aid, and now the kolkhoz was poised to collapse – if not because of mass flight, then because those who remained would undoubtedly starve.[57]

The famine-stricken North Caucasus was home as well to at least two other struggling Romani kolkhozes, "Nevo Drom" (New Road) and

"Red Roma." Established in 1931, Nevo Drom had united forty-four households by the end of its first year.[58] Bezliudskii later remembered Nevo Drom's founder, a Rom named F.M. Danchenko, as a "young, energetic" defender of the Gypsy poor who had tirelessly recruited Romani nomads to the kolkhoz. Thanks in large part to Danchenko's efforts, several regional newspapers had praised Nevo Drom in its inaugural year as an example for nearby Russian kolkhozes. By the fall of 1932, however, Nevo Drom was falling to pieces and its members were fleeing the farm en masse. Even Danchenko had abandoned the farm for the city of Krasnodar. Alarmed by Nevo Drom's impending collapse, Bezliudskii set out to inspect the farm. Reporting back to Moscow, Bezliudskii decried the farm as "infested with criminal elements." Long-time horse-thieves had recently overtaken the kolkhoz, driving out its "active" and "honest" members such as Danchenko. It made no sense to speak of labour discipline, Bezliudskii explained, as no one who remained on the kolkhoz ever seemed to work.[59]

Comparatively, the recent settlers at the Red Roma kolkhoz were not faring as badly. In 1931, the farm's thirty-six Romani families managed to fulfil their state production quotas. By mid-1932, local officials even hoped to recruit another fifty Romani families to the farm. Red Roma's members, however, complained of abandonment by the very same officials who were known to send them work plans written in Ukrainian – a language that the kolkhozniks neither spoke nor read. The regional Kolkhoz Union ignored the farm's repeated requests for aid. Romani families soon began to flee Red Roma as well.[60]

For the few officials in Moscow paying attention – Bezliudskii, Tokmakov, and a lone Kolkhoztsentr inspector – it was clear that they were alone in their concern for the future of the North Caucasus Region's three struggling Romani kolkhozes. Instead of wasting time bothering their colleagues in the central bureaucracy, however, these three faulted North Caucasus officials for failing to fulfil the demands made of them by the decree of 1 April 1932.[61] In the midst of an unacknowledged, catastrophic famine, they reminded regional authorities of their responsibility for providing Romani kolkhozes with loans, livestock, machinery, and agricultural training.[62]

What ensued in the North Caucasus was a domino effect of bureaucratic blame allocation. In late May 1932, the Executive Committee of the North Caucasus Region (SKKIK) chided the region's agricultural departments for making no attempt to aid fledgling Romani kolkhozniks or their still nomadic counterparts as demanded of them by

VTsIK on 1 April 1932. In response, regional Kolkhoz Union officials – the very same who had recently admitted to their superiors in Moscow that they lacked plans to strengthen the region's Romani kolkhozes – reprimanded the Union's local subdepartments for underestimating the importance of Romani sedentarization and collectivization.[63] Eventually, one local Party committee reversed the blame game and chastised local Kolkhoz Union officials for straying from the "general Party line" on the importance of strengthening Romani kolkhozes.[64] Six months later, SKKIK's Nationalities Council again reprimanded regional organizations, threatening to prosecute those responsible for this blatantly "chauvinistic" approach to ministering to the needs of Romani kolkhozniks.[65] The priorities of most officials in the North Caucasus, however, continued to lie elsewhere.

In 1933 and 1934, the Toiling Gypsy reoriented itself from the path of starvation to that of bare-bones survival. Enjoying steady growth in kolkhoz membership and livestock inventory, the Toiling Gypsy fulfilled its production quotas ahead of schedule in the spring of 1934. Regional authorities celebrated ten of the farm's members as shock workers and awarded them a variety of prizes for their work.[66] In the fall of 1934, the SKKIK boastfully informed VTsIK's Nationalities Department about the Toiling Gypsy's achievements.[67]

The progress seen at the Toiling Gypsy, however, owed not to officials in the North Caucasus, but instead to Romani farmers themselves and, in particular, to one of the kolkhoz's most recent arrivals: Bezliudskii. Having witnessed the farm's chaos during his inspections of the North Caucasus's Romani kolkhozes, Bezliudskii relocated to the Toiling Gypsy in late 1932 and assumed the chairmanship of the Gypsy village soviet. Bringing his activist expertise as well as the benefits of past institutional networking with him, Bezliudskii oversaw the farm's reorganization. In 1933, the farms' members were divided into workers' brigades and joined by a Russian agronomist. They built new housing as well as separate quarters for a school, nursery, and club.[68] Bezliudskii also organized the publication of the kolkhoz's own Romani-language newspaper, For a Bolshevik Kolkhoz (Palo bolshevistsko kolkhozo) in 1934.[69] Lastly, Bezliudskii dispatched kolkhoz youth to brigadier and tractor training courses, as well as to Moscow's Timiriazev Teachers' Training College.[70]

Though Bezliudskii's leadership certainly helped the struggling kolkhoz to avoid starvation, the farm still suffered extraordinary privation. Most members suffered from poor health caused by malnutrition, bad water supply, inadequate clothing, and a lack of access to medical care.[71] Despite their repeated claims that the matter of Romani collectivization was "very important and necessary," Soviet officials at all levels refused to take responsibility for improving the Toiling Gypsy's "very poor" economic and cultural conditions.[72]

At a Soviet of Nationalities conference on Romani sedentarization held in Moscow in January 1936, Bezliudskii again accused regional officials in the North Caucasus of their "bureaucratic attitude" towards Romani kolkhozes. In the face of local officials' negligent attitude towards minority peoples, he maintained, the members of the Toiling Gypsy could depend only on themselves to improve the kolkhoz and their living conditions. In appraising the farm and its modest annual growth in crop yield, Bezliudskii admitted the Toiling Gypsy's limited productive capacity. For him, the Toiling Gypsy's success lay instead in its members having embraced Sovietism. The farm, he explained, was home to a 99 per cent "recidivist" population. Here, Bezliudskii referred explicitly to such kolkhoz members as one Rom who, having spent fifteen of his thirty-three years in prison, had recently refashioned himself into a Stakhanovite kolkhoznik. Yet when speaking of the farm's "recidivists," Bezliudskii more generally referenced all that Soviet officials fearfully associated with Gypsies: nomadism, deviance, and social foreignness. Their own nomadic Romani culture had been the farmers' past crime, but the Toiling Gypsy's members had since overcome their so-called backwardness. They had become settled, labouring citizens who now served in socialist construction as increasingly literate farmers and even Stakhanovites. Despite regional authorities' "bureaucratic attitude" towards them, the farm's members had created their own club, literacy courses, and study circles.[73]

Though the Toiling Gypsy, like most kolkhozes, never emerged as a financially stable or especially productive farm, it continued to grow throughout the remainder of the 1930s. Regionally, it attracted Roma who sought an escape from their own failed collective farms, including Nevo Drom.[74] The Toiling Gypsy also absorbed an influx of new Romani settlers with little experience in agriculture. By the late summer of 1936, it was home to seventy-five Romani households. Bezliudskii proudly reported to Moscow that these once nomadic Roma worked diligently in the fields despite the farm's overwhelming poverty.[75]

Elsewhere in the North Caucasus, Romani settlers were dealt with in an arguably even more "bureaucratic" fashion than were those working on the Toiling Gypsy. Regional officials decided that the best way to mop up the failures at Nevo Drom and Red Roma was to attach the fates of these farms to neighbouring Russian kolkhozes. In 1936, fifty-two Romani families were settled on a new Romani kolkhoz named New Road, given fifty rubles per settling family, and left to fend for themselves. Most nomadic Romani arrivals to the region, however, were not organized into new Romani kolkhozes, but instead were settled on Russian farms. Roma who were promised the comforts of productive, sedentary life found themselves instead living in tattered tents or under the open sky. Many of these Romani settlers eventually decided that nomadism afforded them greater comfort than did settled life on the farms.[76] In response to these failures, regional authorities again issued a statement in 1937 demanding that local officials do everything within their power to prevent Roma from fleeing the region's Romani kolkhozes. As before, these words rang hollow – a mere mechanical reiteration of empty promises.[77]

The affairs of Stalingrad Province's two Romani collective farms, Natsmen-Gypsy and Gypsy Dawn, in many ways mirrored those of the North Caucasus's Romani kolkhozes.[78] In Stalingrad Province, as in the North Caucasus, the emergence of Romani leaders on the farms proved the greatest factor in thwarting Romani kolkhozes' dissolution. With none of Bezliudskii's fellow Romani activists willing to abandon Moscow in pursuit of revolutionizing Romani life in the provinces, the few heroes of Stalingrad Province's Romani kolkhozes emerged instead from the ranks of newly settled "backward Gypsies."

In Stalingrad Province, no Romani kolkhoznik achieved as much as G.M. Krikunov. Though little is known about Krikunov's early years, it appears that his arrival on the Natsmen-Gypsy kolkhoz in 1931 was a turning point in his own personal life as well as in the life of the then disintegrating kolkhoz.[79] At the age of fifty-seven, Krikunov joined a farm populated by starving Roma resigned to either abandon the kolkhoz or to remain and grumble about their hunger and misery. Food supplies, clothing, and housing were scarce, and many of the farm's 114 members found it more profitable to tell fortunes in nearby villages than to labour in all-but-barren fields. Help from central or local authorities was nowhere to be found. Between 1933 and 1934, thirty-eight members fled the farm.[80]

Krikunov chose a different path. In 1932 he joined the Communist Party, enrolled in the local Party school, undertook the post of farm chairman, and joined the local village soviet administration. Under his lead, Natsmen-Gypsy's farmers built homes as well as a crèche, elementary school, and administration office. Krikunov dispatched members to training courses and established Komsomol and Pioneer cells on the farm. The children of Natsmen-Gypsy studied – albeit in Russian – in the kolkhoz's school.[81]

From the standpoint of both agricultural production and political consciousness, Natsmen-Gypsy soon enjoyed a reversal of the farm's initial years of misfortune, leading some to even hail the farm as a minor, albeit qualified, success. Despite local officials' documented negligence, Natsmen-Gypsy's farmers overfulfilled their harvest quotas in 1933. Appraising Natsmen-Gypsy in the spring of 1936, even regional officials openly admitted that Natsmen-Gypsy's economic and political advancement owed to Krikunov's Stakhanovite leadership. Inspectors noted that Krikunov built the farm's infrastructure "with his own strength and resources," regularly read newspapers to his illiterate comrades, hosted literary evenings, arranged for lectures on disease and hygiene, improved work discipline on the kolkhoz, and inspired in "former nomads" a love for agricultural labour. As a small contingent of "Stakhanovite-Gypsies" coalesced under Krikunov, officials reported, "The Gypsy-kolkhozniks have fully realized the necessity of fulfilling their obligations to the state."[82]

Although provincial officials praised the farm for its unexpected growth, they still categorized it as one of the province's most backward and impoverished kolkhozes.[83] The "vestiges" of the Romani farmers' "former nomadic life," officials noted, occasionally manifested themselves in acts that revealed their "unconscious attitude toward socialist property." This was explained as the logical "consequence of the Gypsy-kolkhozniks' lack of consciousness, illiteracy, and semiliteracy" as well as of "the inadequacy of political-enlightenment and mass-cultural work among them, and of material conditions."[84]

Meanwhile, although officials initially celebrated the integration of several Russian recruits to the kolkhoz, they soon lamented the new arrivals' "great-power chauvinism." The farm's new Russian chairman, for example, unconvincingly claimed to have "forgotten" to reward the Stakhanovite efforts of one Rom and refused to accept new Romani settlers as kolkhoz members. An "underqualified and undisciplined" Russian schoolteacher appointed to the kolkhoz aroused hostility when he forbade his pupils from speaking Romani and corporally punished them for doing so. In the scandal that ensued, Natsmen-Gypsy's school was temporarily shut down.[85]

Although Natsmen-Gypsy remained one of Stalingrad Province's most troubled kolkhozes, it nonetheless enjoyed greater success than its counterpart in the region, Gypsy Dawn. Without mention of the famine, inspectors characterized Gypsy Dawn's original settlers as conspiratorial, labour-averse parasites capable only of producing scandalous quarrels among themselves. By 1934, none of the farm's original Romani settlers remained. Regional officials responded to the chaos of Gypsy Dawn by assigning it to the responsibility of a neighbouring Russian farm.[86] Otherwise, they neglected Gypsy Dawn, a fact noted with disapproval even by the regional press. Referring to Stalingrad Province's failures at Gypsy Dawn as certain evidence of "anti-Gypsism," one VTsIK official warned in the pages of *Revoliutsiia i natsional'nosti* that such chauvinism played into the hands of Gypsy kulaks, who would be disarmed only by the successful sedentarization and sovietization of the Gypsy poor.[87]

By 1935, Gypsy Dawn united fifteen Romani families under the leadership of seven Russian families, and regional officials rested content, knowing "that the fact of the Gypsy kolkhoz's existence has great political significance, both in the matter of carrying out the correct Leninist-Stalinist nationality policy, and in the reconfiguration (*peredelka*) of nomadic Gypsies' everyday life." They ignored reports from the farm's Russian chairman that Roma were again fleeing the kolkhoz, or that nomadic Roma were rejecting recruitment on account of not wanting – as they interpreted it – to be fleeced by the state.[88]

Criminal Enthusiasm

The opposing fates of the North Caucasus's Toiling Gypsy and Red Roma farms, as well as those of Stalingrad Province's Natsmen-Gypsy and Gypsy Dawn, reveal the difference that Romani activism could make in the absence of official investment in the two regions' Romani kolkhozes. Bezliudskii and Krikunov, however, were not the only Roma dedicated to ensuring that their collective farms not only survived the harsh agricultural and political realities of the Soviet 1930s, but also produced Soviet citizens of backward Gypsy nomads. Like Bezliudskii and Krikunov, these Romani activists found their efforts unreciprocated by the state at best. In this, they were arguably fortunate – at least in comparison to the fate suffered by Mikhail Fedorovich Volkov, a Romani activist who organized Sverdlovsk Province's Red East kolkhoz in 1933 and was ultimately punished for his efforts.

In the spring of 1934, Volkov wrote to Tokmakov in Moscow with a passionate plea for help. Regional authorities, Volkov reported, adeptly published resolutions recognizing Red East's need for aid, but made no effort to provide the farm with practical or material help. They insisted, however, that Red East meet impossible state procurement quotas. If Red East's members handed over the little harvest that the farm had yielded from its combination of bad soil and lack of water and seed, Volkov explained, they would surely starve. As it was, the farm's situation was already nightmarish. "No one helps me in my work," Volkov explained:

> There is no cultural ministration and the regional executive committee approaches everything in a devil-may-care fashion, there is not one dwelling, no agricultural implements, and no bread ... The kolkhoz is very poor. You know everyone is poorly clothed, there are no clothes, all the remaining clothing has been sold for bread. I, Volkov, more than once [approached] regional organizations and nothing, I cannot obtain practical help, only words on paper.

Underscoring the unfulfilled promises of nationality policy, Volkov wrote: "To this day we live as we lived before ... and the children, poorly clothed and hungry, are freezing." Red East's Romani kolkhozniks, Volkov argued, had adapted well to agricultural life and worked diligently. As formerly oppressed minorities, they deserved the state's help.[89]

When Tokmakov wrote to officials in Sverdlovsk demanding that they assist Volkov and Red East's farmers, he received a terse and dismissive reply. Red East, the Sverdlovsk Province Executive Committee wrote, was receiving all necessary aid.[90] Nonetheless, Volkov continued to write Tokmakov and other VTsIK officials asking for help. In that Tokmakov had apparently failed to convince Sverdlovsk officials of the purported importance of the "Gypsy question," Secretary Khatskevich of VTsIK's Soviet of Nationalities next intervened on Volkov's behalf. In August 1936, Khatskevich appealed to the chairman of the Sverdlovsk Province Executive Committee: "Taking into account the attention that the state devotes to the problem of Gypsies' employment (*trudoustroistvo*), I hope that you will make the necessary efforts in order to draw the Gypsy kolkhoz into the region's number of exemplary kolkhozes."[91] In October, however, Volkov again wrote to Moscow in desperation, revealing, "The kolkhoz is in a very difficult situation, and regional organizations poorly assist [us], and [they] attempt by any means to persecute me."[92]

In a final letter dated November 1936, Volkov informed Khatskevich that he had recently been sentenced to two years of hard labour for "poor leadership" of the Red East kolkhoz. Volkov, however, expressed little interest in his own harsh fate. He begged only that the Red East kolkhoz and its members be spared of the farm's looming collapse. Though the Sverdlovsk Province Executive Committee had rightfully responded to Khatskevich's appeal by ordering regional authorities to attend to the needs of Red East, Volkov explained, those very same regional authorities had refused to comply. Rather than help Red East, they had collected all of the farm's meager harvests, leaving the farm's members with nothing.

Recognizing the farm's squalid conditions, Volkov nonetheless took great pride in the work that he and his fellow Romani kolkhozniks had achieved. "I, Volkov, organized the kolkhoz in 1933," the semiliterate kolkhoz chairman recalled:

> There was a series of difficulties, but at the present time I have achievements, several of the kolkhozniks have mastered agricultural work well, and in this year worked not badly in the sowing and harvesting, although [they] still lagged behind the Russians. Nevertheless the people are beginning to adapt to labour, the children study in school, and three adults [have enrolled] in courses.

Despite the farm's difficulties, Volkov had wanted – before his arrest, that is – to recruit more Romani nomads to the farm. A number of Roma had even appealed to regional authorities for permission to join Red East. Regional officials, however, had proven "disinterested" in accepting new recruits to the farm. "If regional organizations had helped me," Volkov maintained, "I promise I would have organized no less than 100 families."

Only after explaining the farm's straitened circumstances did Volkov finally reveal how the situation had degenerated to the point of his arrest and conviction. Volkov admitted that he had repeatedly sought help from regional officials – all to no avail. Then, in September 1935, regional officials unseated Volkov from his post of kolkhoz chairman, replacing him with a Russian of questionable ethics and poor leadership. Thirteen Romani families responded to this coup by abandoning the farm immediately. By the time Volkov was reinstated as kolkhoz chairman in the spring of 1936, only fifteen households remained on the farm – all completely unprepared for that year's sowing. "I, Volkov," he wrote, "led the kolkhoz out of this situation." By fall, the farm's membership had again risen to twenty-eight households. Volkov was soon arrested, however, on charges of failed leadership – no doubt, he admitted – due his public criticism of the same regional authorities who now sought his punishment. "I cannot lead as [they do] in Russian kolkhozes," Volkov defended himself, "because a number of the kolkhozniks are still new and do not know anything ... [and because] there are no agricultural implements ... I tried to improve the kolkhoz, but [regional authorities] underestimated my work." In a final appeal for help – not merely for himself, but also for the kolkhoz – Volkov pleaded, "If you will help me, I promise to correct all mistakes."[93]

In that same month, Khatskevich also received a petition from Red East's kolkhozniks attesting to Volkov's innocence and pleading for his release. If Soviet authorities would free Volkov from his "harsh punishment" and return him to his work on the kolkhoz, Red East's members promised, "We will work and hope, that Comrade Volkov [will be] together with us, he is very dear to us, because thanks to Comrade Volkov our kolkhoz becomes stronger and new kolkhozniks come to us, especially women. Because of Comrade Volkov's mass work we and our children have come to live better in a warm place."[94]

Clearly displeased with the reports from Volkov and Red East, Khatskevich sent an urgent memo to the chairman of the Sverdlovsk Province Executive Committee. "We have now received a new statement from ... Volkov, in which he writes that he was called to account for mismanagement and sentenced to two years of corrective labour. It is possible, that in connection with your orders to provide the kolkhoz with the greatest possible help, someone among the regional officials (*rabotniki*) decided to provide that 'help' inside out." In closing, Khatskevich recommended that the executive committee dispatch a representative to investigate the matter and reconsider Volkov's harsh punishment. [95]

In January 1937, Khatskevich finally received word from the Sverdlovsk Province Executive Committee. In a resolution titled, "On the Strengthening of the Gypsy Kolkhoz 'Red East,'" Sverdlovsk officials blamed their regional counterparts for the "full mismanagement" of the Red East farm. The executive committee demanded that all regional officials do their part to rehabilitate the kolkhoz and transform it into an example of the benevolence of Soviet nationality policy. Although no mention was made of the ill-fated Volkov directly, the decree demanded that all those responsible for the kolkhoz's past failures be brought immediately to justice.[96]

As for Volkov, his apparent crime was to have insisted that Romani nomads could be settled on successful collective farms if provided both state aid and the enlightened leadership of fellow citizens who were ostensibly more "advanced." He was punished therefore for taking Soviet nationality policy to its intended conclusion – for having traded his unproductive, nomadic, Gypsy way of life for the productive, sedentary life of the engaged Soviet citizen. Despite the apparent injustice of his situation, Volkov did not waver. In his final missive to Moscow, Volkov's stated concern rested not with the indignity of penal labour or the possibility of a still worse personal fate, but instead with transforming Red East into a successful farm and its "backward" members into productive, sedentary Soviet citizens.

Douglas Rogers has noted elsewhere the profound difference that an energetic enterprise director could make in maintaining, at the very least, the viability of even struggling Soviet collective and state farms. With their essential skills of building "wealth in people" in their loci of the rural socialist economy, Rogers explains, respected farm leaders furthered state farming in disincentivizing member flight, streamlining farm administration, organizing material and human resources, mobilizing patronage networks, and building morale among farmers.[97] Despite their divergent fates, men like Bezliudskii, Krikunov, and even Volkov not only remind us of the difference an individual citizen could make on Soviet collective farms in the 1930s, but also highlight the drawing in of former Romani nomads into the agricultural sector of a socialist economy that provided no viable opportunity for escape. It was in Smolensk Province, however, that the Soviet Union's most celebrated Romani organizer of collective farms emerged, demanding not only the dedicated agricultural labour of his peers, but also the creation of an autonomous national territory for Gypsies within Soviet borders.

October Fulfilled?

In 1927, the All-Russian Gypsy Union attracted a new member in whom they entrusted the task of both popularizing the 1926 decree on Romani sedentarization and organizing Romani kolkhozes in Smolensk Province. I.I. Gerasimov, a semiliterate Rom born in 1898, welcomed the opportunity and declared his commitment to the Gypsy Union's cause by announcing, "Our task as cultured Gypsies is to completely smash the tents and to create in their place peasant settlements on new socialist principles as our party VKP(b) dictates."[98] Gerasimov recognized the difficulties of settling, collectivizing, and integrating Romani nomads into the socialist economy. Still, in terms of relative "backwardness," he felt that the Roma of Smolensk Province were perhaps "more conscious" than their counterparts elsewhere in the empire, and therefore could be brought more easily into the Soviet fold. After all, Gerasimov's extended family had been living and farming in Smolensk Province for at least a generation.[99] His family's agricultural history thus reassured him as he vowed "to give body and soul" to the task of collectivizing Smolensk Province's Roma.[100]

Initially, it seemed, Gerasimov's most difficult task would be to convince provincial authorities that the Soviet government had indeed guaranteed land and financial aid to potential Romani settlers. As late as September 1928, officials in Smolensk remained unaware of either the 1926 or 1928 decrees on Romani sedentarization. They were thus alarmed when Romani kolkhozniks – under Gerasimov's advice – began applying for the 400 rubles promised to each settled Romani family by the 1926 decree. An official in the Nationalities Department of the Smolensk Province Executive Committee thus wrote to VTsIK seeking confirmation that such promises had, in fact, been made.[101] Upon verification, however, Smolensk officials did eventually circulate information on the 1928 decree as well as instructions as to how they were to respond to Roma's requests for land and aid.[102]

Gerasimov, meanwhile, recruited fellow activists from the Gypsy section of Smolensk's House of Culture to agitate among the province's Roma. In 1928, he organized a small Romani kolkhoz named "Worker's Road" that united six nomadic Romani families, lacked both agricultural tools and livestock, and barely managed to produce a harvest in its first two years.[103] Looking back, Gerasimov later recalled the initial failures of Worker's Road as owing to the farm's lack of proper leadership and to its members' inadequate work discipline.[104] The new kolkhozniks, Gerasimov claimed, were not yet ready to abandon their "old traditions" of horse dealing, fortune telling, and begging.[105] They lived in tents and came and left the farm as they pleased. The farm suffered from its members' "insufficient consciousness," and thus quickly degenerated into "a state of chaos."[106] Gerasimov decided that the only way to save the farm was to integrate "conscious" Roma into its ranks. He recruited several long-settled Romani families as well as his own to join the kolkhoz, now renamed "October."[107]

Only in 1931, when Gerasimov assumed the post of kolkhoz chairman, did October succeed in making a "great break" with its rather

unremarkable past. "Thanks to the good leadership of [this] commu-
nist-Gypsy," Smolensk Province officials reported to Moscow, October
emerged as the leading Romani kolkhoz in Smolensk Province, if not in
the entire Soviet Union. Gerasimov "had managed to unite the Gypsy
masses," to "reform" the farm's former nomads, and to set them upon
a path of "rapid socialist development."[108]

Under Gerasimov's lead, October's members accepted twelve new
families into their ranks and next proceeded to construct living quarters,
farm buildings, a crèche, and a communal cafeteria. They organized a
literacy centre, enrolled the farm's children in elementary school, and
dispatched its most enterprising youth to training courses held in both
Smolensk and Moscow.[109] Provincial inspectors remarked on the farm's
healthy atmosphere, noting that October's membership now included
nine party members and twelve Komsomol members.[110]

What most surprised officials in Smolensk Province, however, was
the farm's seemingly overnight transformation into a viable farm. In
1931, October's kolkhozniks overfulfilled six of their production quotas and fulfilled all others. In recognition of their efforts, the Smolensk
Region Executive Committee awarded October 300 rubles, the village
soviet presented the farm with a radio loudspeaker, and Smolensk
Province's annual agricultural exhibition celebrated several of October's kolkhozniks as shock workers.[111] Gerasimov continued to breathe
new life into the kolkhoz, reorganizing it along so-called Soviet principles. He divided the farm's members into brigades, transitioned the
kolkhoz to a piecework system, and organized various socialist competitions. He also demanded that October's members not only recognize
the political and moral value of their labour, but also publicly hold one
another to account for idling, absenteeism, or other transgressions.[112]

At a general kolkhoz meeting held in May 1931, for example, Gerasimov invited October's kolkhozniks to unmask the farm's malcontents. In this, he led by example. The kolkhoznik Ivanov, Gerasimov
alleged, had sabotaged the farm's progress while contributing no labour to the fulfilment of October's goals. Echoing Gerasimov, another
kolkhoznik inveighed against Ivanov: "He never works, but only inter-
rupts work and agitates among members, thereby contaminating the
kolkhoz. We must expel him because he is a saboteur." Another kolkhoznik, Mariia Golobatsnaia, was also defamed for taking an absence
without leave from the kolkhoz – presumably to tell fortunes and beg
in the city. Whereas October's members expelled Ivanov, Golobatsnaia
received only a "harsh reprimand" for her "passive attitude toward

work."[113] Such purges and acts of stigmatization were seen as still further evidence of the healthy discipline of October's kolkhozniks under Gerasimov's lead.

October's triumphs, however, are not sufficiently explained by the efforts of Gerasimov and his fellow Romani kolkhozniks. Geography also played a central role in the farm's success. October's location in Smolensk Province contributed to October's success in so far as officials here took seriously their state-mandated responsibility to the settled and nomadic Roma living within their jurisdiction. Given both the province's sizable non-Russian population and its relative proximity to the Soviet Union's western borders, officials in Smolensk had prioritized nationality policy long before Stalin's revolution from above imposed new demands on officials governing the Soviet periphery, and especially the empire's borderlands.[114] By the time that officials in Smolensk learned of the Soviet government's 1928 decree offering land and aid to voluntary Romani settlers, they had already been attempting to "uplift" the province's Jewish, Belorussian, Latvian, Polish, and Lithuanian citizens. Although Roma were estimated to make up a mere 0.08 per cent of the population, they were neither the numerically smallest minority population in Smolensk Province, nor the least politically significant. As one official at the Provincial Agricultural Administration made sure to note, Roma lived in the "most difficult living conditions" as a result of all they had suffered under tsarism, and were thus frighteningly "at odds" with Sovietism.[115] Realizing the "threat" that Roma posed, officials in Smolensk sought to confront rather than avoid the so-called "Gypsy problem." Aided by a growing coterie of local Romani activists, Smolensk officials adopted a more proactive stance towards sovietizing Roma than did most of their counterparts elsewhere in the empire.

In 1928, for example, officials opened a Romani elementary school in the city of Smolensk that they soon transformed into the Soviet Union's only Romani boarding school. Organized to provide children who seasonally begged for alms on Smolensk's streets with an education, the boarding school was furthermore designed to permanently liberate Romani youth from the tyranny and neglect of their parents' nomadism.[116] Yet Smolensk's boarding school soon housed the Romani children not only of persistent nomads, but also of the province's kolkhozniks. By 1934, the school – with 90 students divided among six classes – had outgrown itself and needed to be expanded to accommodate at least 120–150 pupils.[117] Awarded 50,000 rubles for its expansion, the boarding school was soon praised widely in Smolensk Province as a nearly unqualified success. A feature appearing in *Za kommunisticheskoe prosveshchenie* praised the school as effective in teaching Soviet values to "the children of Gypsy nomads" and, in particular, instilling in them "a love for labour."[118] The school's only fault seemed to lie in its reliance on the Russian language as the medium of instruction. Staffed by three Romani and three Russian schoolteachers, the school taught Romani merely as a separate subject. Highlighting the school's foremost priorities, however, inspectors were satisfied that the school's pupils were "politically developed."[119]

Smolensk Province also prioritized the training of Romani cadres. In 1930, provincial officials inaugurated a vigorous campaign to enrol promising young Roma in workers' faculties as well as in medical and teacher-training courses.[120] Given Gypsies' extraordinary "backwardness," officials in Smolensk decided that nothing should impede Roma's promotion through the ranks. In recommending a Romani candidate to the Smolensk Workers' Faculty, for example, one official even went so far as to describe Gypsies as "the only culturally backward nationality" in the province.[121] Invoking Gypsy backwardness, however, was also the bargaining method reliably adopted by young Roma themselves in their applications to educational institutions. One Rom wrote to the Provincial Education Department in January 1930 seeking admission to a local worker's faculty: "Until 1923 I was completely illiterate because my relatives are Gypsies and lived in the field ... and I did not have the opportunity to study."[122]

No Rom in Smolensk Province, however, advanced through the ranks as quickly as Gerasimov himself. After serving as a Gypsy Union plenipotentiary, leader of the Gypsy section of Smolensk's House of Culture, and chairman of the October kolkhoz, Gerasimov was appointed to the Smolensk Region Kolkhoz Union in 1931. Less than a year later, he was promoted as a leader of Gypsy affairs in the Nationalities Department of the Smolensk Province Executive Committee.[123] Responsible for the inspection and improvement of existing Romani kolkhozes as well as for the organization of new ones, Gerasimov travelled widely throughout the province in the 1930s, speaking to Roma about the blessings of nationality policy and the need for Roma to abandon their "old habits of Gypsiness (*tsyganstvo*)."[124]

As early as 1932, however, Gerasimov doubted that the mere proliferation of Romani kolkhozes in Smolensk Province or elsewhere could ensure a cultural revolution among the Soviet Union's Romani nomads.

Having helped to organize at least four other Romani kolkhozes in the region, Gerasimov conceded that October was an unprecedented success not yet likely to be replicated so long as the majority of Romani nomads continued to lead lives of "charlatanry, fortune telling, and speculation."[125] In an address to Smolensk Province's First Conference of National Minorities in August 1932, Gerasimov lamented Roma's relatively slow pace of development under Soviet nationality policy. For him, at least, the explanation for Roma's continued backwardness was obvious: they lacked territorial unity. "Scattered and fragmented," Roma had never enjoyed a territorial homeland and thus were inclined to nomadism. Even Jews, he explained, had benefited from having been clustered in the shtetls of the Pale of Settlement. Gerasimov thus suggested that the Soviet Union's "Gypsy problem" could not be solved without the establishment of a special Gypsy territory.[126]

Gerasimov's pessimism only deepened during the great famine of 1932–33. The members of October suffered the famine as did many of their fellow citizens elsewhere in the empire: most refused to even feign work; begging and so-called "pilfering" separated those who hungered from those who starved; and kolkhozniks fled the farm. As was the rule, inspectors to the farm responded to the famine by speaking only in euphemisms. What Octobers' kolkhozniks referred to as "obvious deadly famine," officials – including Gerasimov – recognized as a "natural disaster," a crushing of "enthusiasm," the kolkhozniks' "irrational" consumption of grain, and the dastardly work of "class enemies."[127] In later years, the winter of 1932–33 received no special mention in the kolkhoz's cumulative agricultural and political report card. It was better to be forgotten.[128]

In 1934, October not only rebounded, but also was proclaimed "the best among Gypsy kolkhozes in the Soviet Union."[129] Having received a new loan of 25,000 rubles and a 5,000-ruble grant for its acceptance of new nomadic families in 1934, October's members built new living quarters and expanded their livestock inventory. By year's end, October's kolkhozniks had successfully fulfilled the farm's state quotas with a surplus, thereby reearning their place on the village soviet honour roll. The Political Department of the Smolensk Region MTS rewarded the farm by opening up two seats at the Higher Communal Agricultural School in Smolensk to October's shock workers.[130] General meetings of the kolkhoz no longer centred on the unmasking of the farm's saboteurs, but instead were devoted to liquidating illiteracy and contributing to the Soviet goal of "making all nomadic Gypsies sedentary."[131]

In 1935, October superseded its achievements of the previous year, earning not only its place among the province's "leading kolkhozes," but also a truck, two bicycles, and a record player. Although Gerasimov joined Soviet officials in recognizing the farm as an exemplary national collective farm, he nonetheless struggled with the fact that Smolensk Province's other Romani kolkhozes trailed far behind October on their paths to success. While October basked in glowing praise, Gerasimov worried that the wider Soviet effort to collectivize Roma had disastrously failed. In his view, October remained an isolated success story of "backward Gypsies" becoming not only "prosperous" through agricultural labour but also integrated into the socialist economy and schooled in Soviet values. The reach of its influence did not extend beyond the farm's own borders – not to Smolensk Province's other kolkhozes, or to the potential Romani settlers whom the farm could not accommodate for lack of land. Worst of all, thousands of "backward Gypsies" either knew nothing of October's success or simply wanted no part of it.[132] Gerasimov became convinced that the answer to solving "the Gypsy problem" was for the Soviet Union to create an "administrative territorial unit" for Roma's compact settlement. In his desire to see Soviet nationality policy translate into a special Gypsy territory, Gerasimov was by no means alone.[133]

Dreams of a Soviet Gypsy Homeland

In 1935, Secretary Khatskevich of TsIK's Soviet of Nationalities chastised his colleagues for the fact that several million citizens continued to "wander" in their "extraordinary oppression (*zabitost'*) and backwardness," and thus remained immune to Soviet civilization. It was "absolutely necessary," Khatskevich claimed, "to accelerate the tempo of sedentarization."[134] Regarding Roma, a handful of officials in Moscow had recently renewed their interest in the rather negligible results of the state's half-hearted efforts to sedentarize and collectivize Romani nomads. Tokmakov and Nurmakov of VTsIK's Nationalities Department repeatedly complained of Narkomzem's intransigent negligence.[135] As early as February 1935, Tokmakov appealed to his superiors at VTSIK to plan for the "compact settlement" of Romani nomads on a territory specially delineated for that very purpose. Romani sedentarization, he maintained, had thus far proceeded only anarchically, with small groups of Roma settled on scattered bits of land that left no opportunity for the expansion of their farms.[136] Facing increased pressure from

VTsIK, Narkomzem officials began in the spring of 1935 to consider the possibilities for creating an "autonomous Gypsy region (*oblast'*)." [137]

In July, VTsIK organized a commission to discuss "the expediency of the settlement (*zemleustroistvo*) of Gypsies in one place."[138] A month later, the Nationalities Department received a letter from "a camp of nomadic Gypsies near the city of Ivanov" that underscored the significance of the commission's work. These Roma wrote:

> We, *natsmen* Gypsies, nomads, not having a defined place of residence or territory want to be sedentary, to have a defined place of residence, and our own territory in the form of a Gypsy region (*raion*) ... and when the Gypsy region is created we will also work in industry and agriculture as do other autonomous regions (*oblasti*). We nomad-Gypsies realized, that only socialist labour gives the right to be an honest citizen of the Soviet Union, and therefore we ask you to allot villages to us ... [to] all *natsmen* nomads Gypsies ... We know that our nomadic life affords us nothing good. We ask the Nationalities Department of VTsIK to appeal before the government for the allotment of a territory for Gypsies.[139]

Shortly upon receipt of this letter, the commission organized a subcommittee of representatives from VTsIK, Narkomzem, and Sovnarkom's All-Union Resettlement Committee (VPK) to investigate potential regions for the compact settlement of Roma.[140] Among themselves, however, many of these officials adamantly insisted that their intention was not to establish an "autonomous Gypsy region," but instead merely to delineate an area for nomadic Roma's compact settlement.[141] Preferably, a significant, tutelary Russian population would already be settled on such a territory.[142]

In the fall of 1935, the commission contacted officials in designated regions of interest in an attempt to locate a suitable territory for Roma's compact settlement. Officials in the North Caucasus and Azovo-Chernomorskii Krais as well as in the Crimean ASSR insisted that their regions could not accommodate the mass settlement of former Romani nomads. Officials in the Gor'kovskii and Western Siberian Krais, however, receptively invited officials to consider establishing a so-called Gypsy region within their respective borders. Yet, upon further investigation, officials in Moscow realized that neither region offered an ideal solution to the "Gypsy problem." It would be far too expensive – a modestly estimated 46 million rubles for the accommodation of 3,000

Romani families – to construct from scratch a Gypsy homeland in forests potentially unsuitable for agriculture.[143]

By November, it was clear that the commission's efforts to delineate a suitable territory for Roma's compact mass settlement had reached a dead end. VPK and Narkomzem officials, however, continued to stall. In November, the VPK announced its plan to organize brigades that would search out new territorial possibilities for Romani settlement as well as to inspect existing Romani kolkhozes throughout 1936. It hesitantly promised to devise a workable plan for the creation of a Gypsy region in 1937.[144]

Proponents of the creation of a "Gypsy homeland," however, grew increasingly impatient. Narkomzem's very own N. Voronin publicly criticized his colleagues for failing to plan effectively for Roma's sedentarization, but also clamoured for the delineation of a Gypsy territory as the answer to past failures.[145] As the petition received from Romani nomads earlier in the year had shown, word had long since begun to circulate among Romani activists that it was time to press officials for a national Gypsy territory. Meanwhile, officials in various provinces reported an increase in Romani petitions for land and membership in collective farms.[146] Worried that the VPK and Narkomzem were interested not in solving the "Gypsy problem" but instead in delaying the establishment of a Gypsy region, TsIK officials committed to still greater public advocacy of and control over "the organization of an independent national Gypsy administrative region."[147]

To this end, TsIK's Soviet of Nationalities hosted a two-day conference in Moscow in early January 1936, bringing together representatives of both Romani kolkhozes and Soviet officialdom to discuss the need to accelerate the sovietization of Roma and of Romani nomads especially. Headed by Gerasimov, Smolensk Province's Romani delegates arrived prepared to argue vigorously for the establishment of a Gypsy territory. They submitted a petition addressed to Stalin that declared: "Thanks to the correct Leninist-Stalinist nationality policy, a segment of our nation – the most downtrodden, the most uncultured and persecuted in tsarist times – has now managed to enter on level with all other workers of the Union in the construction of socialism and to build anew its happy, joyful, and prosperous life." Evidence of this historic victory over Gypsy backwardness, they argued, was abundant in Smolensk Province, where Roma happily laboured in factories, schools, and kolkhozes.[148]

They emphasized, however, that the successes seen in Smolensk did not compensate for existing impediments to the conversion of nomadic Roma to settled, agricultural life elsewhere in the Soviet Union. Though 50 per cent of its Romani population, or approximately 3,000 citizens, were settled, Smolensk Province could do nothing under present conditions for the hundreds of nomads who had recently appealed for acceptance into the province's Romani kolkhozes. Surrounded by those of other nationalities, the province's already existing Romani kolkhozes could not be expanded.[149] In the view of the Smolensk delegates, there existed only one clear solution to the problems faced in sedentarizing Roma not only in Smolensk, but throughout the empire. "Dear Comrade Stalin!" Smolensk's Romani delegates pleaded. "We ask in the name of Gypsies to allot a territory … for the compact settlement of toiling Gypsies."[150]

Representatives from struggling Romani kolkhozes were equally passionate in advocating the creation of a Soviet Gypsy homeland. Detailing a litany of troubles experienced at the Toiling Gypsy Farm, Bezliudskii concluded that the establishment of a Gypsy territory would drastically simplify efforts to sedentarize and sovietize Roma.[151] F.T. Ivanov, the chairman of the New Life kolkhoz in Gor'kovskii Krai and a former nomad, testified to the extraordinary difficulties he faced as the leader of a Romani kolkhoz neglected by Soviet officials. Ivanov earned the applause of like-minded conference attendees when he declared, "If Gypsies had their own territory, work would progress differently. With my whole soul and a clear conscience, I desire … a national Gypsy region."[152]

Still another Romani kolkhoz chairman, however, personified the Soviet failure to adequately provide for Roma's successful sedentarization and collectivization. Zhukovskii of the New Happiness kolkhoz testified: "I am the chairman of a village soviet, and am completely illiterate. In Russian village soviets and kolkhozes the chairmen are literate and, moreover, they are given help and even a Party organizer, but I [who am] completely illiterate am given no help … I am told … to lead mass work [on the kolkhoz], but how am I to carry out [such work] when I myself need to learn (uchit'sia)?" Zhukovskii's predicament represented Soviet officialdom's betrayal of nationality policy's promise. According to Bolshevik ideology, the liberation of oppressed minorities entailed the provision to them of all due help in "reforging" themselves into Soviet citizens. As "chairman of the kolkhoz, brigadier, and leader of field work," Zhukovskii insisted, "I need help." Convinced by his own experience that widespread success in sovietizing Roma would never emerge from numerous, scattered, and isolated kolkhozes, Zhukovskii concluded, "Our Gypsy kolkhozniks ask that several Gypsy kolkhozes assemble in one place so as to have their own village soviet, their own schools."[153]

Nonetheless, many of the non-Romani officials present – especially those employed in the VPK and Narkomzem – were not readily persuaded of either the necessity or desirability of a special Gypsy territory. "I completely support the creation of a Gypsy region," Narkomzem's Comrade Tsil'ko argued, "but in my opinion, we ought for starters to proceed along the line of creating smaller administrative-economic units within existing regions. Gypsies would then have their own representation in the regional executive committee, their own village soviets, their own schools, and they would be given special help. Gypsies, by virtue of their difficult past, still require a special defence of their interests."[154] Gypsies, he claimed, were exceptional in that they were entirely inexperienced in the ways of agriculture. Furthermore, Tsil'ko argued, officials would need to locate rich land in a warm climate to which Gypsies could easily adapt. Establishing a Gypsy region in Western Siberia would only predestine further failure.

Tsil'ko's preferred solution to the "Gypsy problem" was to further integrate Romani nomads into existing Russian kolkhozes. He saw no "special reasons" preventing the creation of "mixed kolkhozes." Rather, he argued that such integration would allow Gypsies – naturally inclined to metal work and raising horses – to complement the strengths of existing Russian kolkhozes. "Every kolkhoz needs such people," he concluded.[155] Nods to practicality aside, Tsil'ko's metanarrative was thinly disguised. In his view, Roma required paternalistic guidance and a still more elementary agricultural education that ethnic Russians were most capable of providing. Roma were ill-equipped to provide their own with such an apprenticeship. Once dispersed among Russian kolkhozes and isolated from the tyranny of their own "backward" culture, Roma would benefit from the tutelage of their cultural superiors, de-Gypsify, and remake themselves as Soviet citizens in the style of their Russian peers. In a Gypsy territory, he implied, the backwardness of Gypsy culture would only flourish, not subside.

Comrade Zubiitov, the VPK's representative, also rejected the immediate creation of a Gypsy territory, but advocated the expansion of existing Romani kolkhozes. The VPK, after all, could not even find suitable land for the proposed Gypsy territory. The warm, southern regions of the empire lacked land available for this purpose. Moreover, the creation of a special territory for Roma's compact mass settlement would require a huge capital investment that the state was not prepared to finance. Though willing to entertain the possibility of a Gypsy territory in the (distant) future, Comrade Zubiitov refused to formulate plans for one in the present. Invoking one of Soviet officialdom's most clichéd excuses for not satisfying the appeals of Roma, Zubiitov claimed that more precise statistics about the nomadic Romani population were needed before large-scale efforts to sedentarize Roma could be made.[156]

Officials at TsIK and VTsIK sided with those Romani activists and kolkhozniks who sought the national dignity and practical efficiency that they believed a Gypsy territory would allow them. Takoev of VTsIK's Nationalities Department repeatedly claimed that the rationalization of the Soviet Romani population was rendered impossible by its scatteredness. If only all Romani nomads could be brought to one place, enlightenment work could finally proceed rationally and effectively.[157] Tokmakov, VTsIK's native consultant for Gypsy affairs, decried Narkomzem's refusal to spend the funds necessary to establish viable Romani kolkhozes, let alone a Gypsy territory. This stinginess flew in the face of the state's supposed priority of settling Roma. The longer his colleagues stalled attempts to further collectivize Roma, Tokmakov claimed, the quicker Romani nomads grew disillusioned with the state's promise to aid their conversion to settled, agricultural labour. His office housed piles of appeals from Roma testifying to their "undoubted attraction" to settled life. To satisfy their "huge craving for sedentarization," it was "necessary to allot defined land reserves for Gypsies' resettlement (trudoustroistvo)."[158]

Tokmakov further stoked existing fears of the internal, yet hidden dangers of Roma's peculiar nomadism. With Roma "wandering from one region to the next," it was all but impossible to discern who among them were class enemies. Nomadism, he argued, shielded the Gypsy kulak from the state, and thus allowed for his machinations to proceed without restraint. Because Gypsy kulaks could not be discerned "with the naked eye," they easily took advantage of the state's gracious efforts to civilize them. As one case in the North Caucasus had shown, Gypsy kulaks were free to pocket state farm subsidies and escape unpunished into the untraceable anonymity of Gypsy nomadism.[159] Tokmakov warned that his colleagues' short-sighted and tight-fisted approach to "the Gypsy problem" portended only the further enrichment and empowerment of the Gypsy kulak and the greater oppression of the Gypsy poor.

Concluding the conference, Secretary Khatskevich lamented that "the majority of Gypsies" continued to "lead an unproductive, nomadic, uncultured way of life."[160] Underscoring the belief that Romani nomadism was infinitely more "backward" than that practiced by pastoralists, Khatskevich explained that livestock herders travelled as a means of investing in their herds, while Gypsies wandered interminably as nothing more than homeless tramps subsisting on beggary, deceit, and depravity. In so far as every Soviet citizen needed to contribute to the socialist economy, Khatskevich welcomed the creation of a "special Gypsy region." The concentrated settlement of inveterate Romani nomads would ease the difficult process of integrating them into the socialist economy and acclimating them to Soviet culture. "Let the Gypsies settle in a fixed place," Khatskevich wistfully declared, "and later there will be a Gypsy Autonomous Soviet Socialist Republic."[161]

The map of the Soviet Union was never reconfigured to include a Gypsy Autonomous Soviet Socialist Republic, nor a Gypsy autonomous region, nor even a so-called special Gypsy territory. Yet this was not so for the want of trying. Throughout the spring of 1936, Khatskevich personally campaigned on behalf of those he deemed the Soviet Union's "most backward people" and their need to be settled compactly.[162] However, by the time TsIK issued a new decree on 7 April 1936 outlining measures to improve Roma's everyday lives and to aid in nomadic Roma's transition to settled life, the question of a establishing a "special Gypsy territory" had already been muted. In addition to reiterating the need to expand existing Romani kolkhozes, TsIK's 7 April 1936 decree demanded merely that the VPK delineate "regions for the settlement of nomadic Gypsies desiring to transition to a settled way of life." In these regions, new Romani kolkhozes were to be established and fully provided for by regional and local officials.[163] Plans for the "compact settlement" of Romani nomads were once again limited to the borders of individual kolkhozes that were to remain as geographically scattered as the overall Romani population.

Dreams of a Soviet Gypsy homeland disintegrated further in the late spring of 1936 when the VPK released its own plan for ministering to the needs of Romani nomads. This plan committed the VPK to the mere physical act of delivering 1,000 nomadic Romani families for integration into existing Romani kolkhozes. Providing these new settlers with homes, livestock, or education was declared outside the domain of the VPK's responsibilities. Complicating matters further, VPK officials stipulated that they could not execute their sedentarization plan until given precise statistics on the location and number of Romani nomads wishing to settle.[164]

As VPK officials dug in their heels, it was left to VTsIK's Nationalities Department to conduct an informal census of the empire's Romani population. By the time VTsIK officials had collected all statistics available to them, however, the VPK and its responsibility for the organization of nomadic Roma's further resettlement had been transferred to the NKVD. Clearly pleased to be free from what he considered a harrowing bureaucratic nightmare, the vice chairman of Sovnarkom's now collapsed VPK flatly informed VTsIK officials in August 1936 that his office had recently been inundated with petitions from nomadic Roma seeking to settle. Otherwise, he indicated, the sedentarization of the Soviet Union's "most backward" nationality was no longer his or his office's concern.[165]

In the months following the transfer of the VPK's responsibilities to the NKVD, state plans to proceed with the expansion of existing Romani kolkhozes and the creation of new farms collapsed under the weight of Soviet red tape. The appeals of Khatskevich and his colleagues at both TsIK and VTsIK achieved little in moving matters forward towards nomadic Roma's settlement – compact or otherwise.[166] Alarmed by the inertia reigning in Moscow, Gerasimov attempted to stir new excitement in Smolensk Province about the possibility of establishing a Soviet Gypsy homeland. While lecturing Romani kolkhozniks and nomads about the new Stalin constitution of 1936, Gerasimov encouraged his brethren to appeal for the creation of a Gypsy territory on Soviet soil. In the local press, he published transcripts of speeches ostensibly given by Romani nomads camped near the city of Smolensk. One reportedly claimed, "It is shameful to continue to live in the old way. It is time to cease wandering from city to city. We must begin to work ... I propose the allocation of a region on Union territory for the settlement of Gypsies." Another declared, "I ask the government to help us settle, to help us begin to live as all people live." To no avail, Gerasimov forwarded this news clipping to officials in Moscow, again asking that the state grant these benighted nomads their request for a Soviet Gypsy homeland.[167]

At the close of the Stalinist 1930s, the Soviet state continued listlessly with vague plans to expand existing Romani kolkhozes, to create new ones, and to integrate Romani nomads into Russian kolkhozes.[168]

Officials in the NKVD's VPK complained of "the great difficulties" of securing territory on which "backward Gypsy nomads" could re-fashion themselves into productive Soviet citizens.[169] In the apparent hope that "the Gypsy problem" would either solve itself or simply disappear, Narkomzem's Comrade Tsil'ko repeatedly ignored TsIK officials' requests that his office fulfil its obligation to provide for the sedentarization of Romani nomads.[170] Disappointed officials at TsIK and VTsIK, meanwhile, again resorted to composing toothless memos detailing their colleagues' incorrigible disregard for the fate of the Soviet Union's "most backward" nomads. In their view, absolutely nothing had changed since the issuance of TsIK's 1926 decree "On Measures for the Aid of Nomadic Gypsies' Transitioning to a Working, Settled Way of Life." More than a decade later, that aid had still not materialized. These officials blamed all levels of the Soviet bureaucracy for the failure to refashion the vast majority of Romani nomads into sedentary, productive Soviet citizens integrated into the socialist economy.[171]

In part, however, these officials were mistaken. Indeed, the question of Roma's "compact mass settlement" on a "special Gypsy territory" had ultimately found no suitable answer among Soviet officials. Yet much had changed since the 1926 decree first promised Roma, as backward minority nomads, limited territorial offerings. On the eve of World War II, nearly 800 Romani families were settled on thirty Romani kolkhozes, at least one of which had been recognized as an example even for Russian farms.[172] Meanwhile, as thousands of Roma continued to lead a (semi-)nomadic life within Soviet borders, the orientation of Soviet nationality policy had shifted considerably under Stalin's reign. State priority in the Friendship of Peoples no longer insisted on the proliferation of either national or pseudo-national forms – be they territorial or otherwise, but instead on a patina of ethnocultural diversity through which the irreducibly socialist content of Soviet culture could shine in luminous triumph.

Moreover, the fate of Birobidzhan – the Jewish Autonomous Region formally established in the Soviet Far East in 1934 – had quickly proven in the eyes of many Soviet officials as a cautionary tale of failure afforded at expensive price. Much like Roma, Jews appeared in the eyes of Soviet officialdom as a "scattered nationality" with a history of "parasitism" and an aversion to "honest labour" – especially agriculture.[173] Reminiscent of much rhetoric surrounding Romani sedentarization, Mikhail Kalinin, the Soviet Union's decorative head of state, had famously declared in 1927 that "a large part of the Jewish population must be transformed into an economically stable, agriculturally compact group."[174]

With the overt aim of "productivizing the Jewish masses," the Party leadership soon publicly embraced plans to establish a "Soviet Zion" in the underdeveloped Far East as a vast agricultural colony tilled by Jewish citizens of the empire. While some even within the Jewish Sections of the Communist Party opposed the plan early on as "unfeasible" given its inevitable cost and Birobidzhan's distance from traditional areas of Jewish population, the grand colonization scheme was launched in 1928.[175] Despite the influx of sizeable financial assistance from sympathetic Jewish organizations abroad, Birobidzhan as a Soviet Jewish agricultural colony proved from its inception a disaster. Colonists arrived to this inhospitable and distant territory ill-equipped to construct new agricultural settlements, not to mention without requisite agricultural experience. Although Birobidzhan never attracted most Soviet Jews in the first place, drop-out rates among settlers to the colony were nothing short of abysmal throughout the 1930s. By 1939, only 25 per cent of the Jewish Autonomous Region's remaining Jewish residents lived in rural areas, while fewer still were productively engaged in farming.[176] Soviet officials confronting Roma's demands for a Soviet Gypsy homeland – a similarly grand project that could in no way rely on foreign financial assistance – no doubt kept Birobidzhan's depressing yet seemingly instructive example in mind. By the time that Romani activists began in the 1930s to campaign for the creation of a Soviet Gypsy homeland, Birobidzhan had already proven itself an expensive experiment whose results did not justify its costs, or the headaches it inspired in Moscow.

Thus, many Soviet officials agreed that instead of creating a special Gypsy territory, it would be best to plan for the further atomization of the nomadic Romani population on individual kolkhozes with the hope of eventually merging them with neighbouring Russian farms. In the meantime, Roma's yearnings for a Soviet Gypsy homeland would be accepted as evidence of Soviet nationality policy's successes more so than its failures. After all, Roma's dream of a Soviet Gypsy homeland provided evidence of the transformation of "backward Gypsies" into Soviet citizens in that it demonstrated their conscious belonging to the Soviet homeland they shared in common with their fellow settled, labouring Soviet citizens.

The Roots of Soviet Belonging

Throughout the 1930s, Soviet officials vacillated endlessly in their typically muddled and uninspired attempts to either solve "the Gypsy problem" or wish it into oblivion. Thousands of Roma laboured on collective farms and many among them dreamed of a Soviet Gypsy homeland. Meanwhile, Hitler crafted his own vision for the transformation of Soviet territory and for a final solution to Europe's "Gypsy problem." The Nazi invasion of the Soviet Union led to the destruction or collapse of all the Soviet Union's Romani kolkhozes, but also much more tragically to the systematic killing of Romani citizens whom the Nazis sought to exterminate with genocidal intent. Many Roma, it must be noted, also served in the war as Red Army soldiers and partisan defenders of their "fatherland."[177]

In the war's aftermath, handfuls of Romani families travelled to Smolensk Province – once the home of October, the Soviet Union's most celebrated Romani kolkhoz, and now the site of one of the most documented Nazi massacres of Romani kolkhozniks on Soviet territory. In April 1942, Nazi SS officers had arrived in the village of Aleksandrovka, whose inhabitants worked on the nearby Romani kolkhoz, "The Stalin Constitution." Established in 1937 by the leading members of October, the Stalin Constitution was created to settle the Romani nomads of Smolensk Province who could not be integrated into the October farm due to lack of land.

According to witness reports compiled in October 1943, a contingent of Nazi SS arrived in the village of Aleksandrovka on the evening of 23 April 1942, demanding of the village elder two separate lists of the inhabitants of Aleksandrovka and its neighbouring village, Devkino. One list was to include the names of Russian villagers, and the other of Roma. On the early morning of 24 April 1942, the German occupiers forced all the villagers – men, women, children, and elderly – out of their homes and onto Aleksandrovka's town square. Once assembled, a Russian-speaking Nazi officer read from his lists, demanding that the Russians and Roma separate into two groups according to nationality. While the Russians were dispatched home with strict orders not to open their doors, the Roma were ordered to march into nearby woods. Those Roma who protested – and even many of those who did not – were beaten savagely by the Germans with the butts of rifles, batons, and whips.

Once deep into the local forest, the Romani men were separated from the women and children and ordered to lie face-down on the ground. The strong among them were given shovels and ordered to dig two separate graves near a clearing by a small lake. Realizing the horrors that awaited them, many among the women began pleading with the German officers and soldiers. In desperation, they insisted that they had mistakenly been identified as Gypsies. They were Russians, they claimed, and deserved to be sent home with the others. The light-skinned among these protesters were ordered to strip naked, so that the officers could judge the purported racial characteristics of their bodies. On the basis of their thus being judged Russian, several light-haired and light-skinned women and their children were allowed to return to their village. The remaining Roma were compelled by force to await their fate. Once they had completed digging the two graves, the men were returned to their face-down position on nearby ground.

The Nazis first ordered the Roma to strip naked before they began to snatch babies and small children from their mothers' arms, throwing them mercilessly into the first of the two graves. Overwhelmed by ter-ror, several women attempted to fling themselves into the pit after their children. The SS officers next shot the remaining women, children, and elderly one by one, piling them into the mass grave, some among them still alive. After witnessing the execution of her family and neighbours, one more Romani woman was released at the last minute upon having finally convinced an officer that she was Russian. Lastly, the Germans ordered the Romani men to cover the first grave with dirt before they executed and buried them in the second mass grave. At least 180 Roma were massacred *as Roma* in the woods of Aleksandrovka that day.[178]

After the war, survivors from the October and Stalin Constitution farms alongside some new Romani arrivals to Smolensk Province at-tempted to rebuild the October kolkhoz anew. By 1950, October had reunited twenty-four Romani and eleven Russian families. In that year, all of Smolensk Province's farming Romani families – fifty-four house-holds in all – merged with neighbouring Russian farms. The children enrolled in local village schools, many of them later joining the Kom-somol and graduating to technical schools in the city of Smolensk.[179] In 1982, Smolensk Province's Roma erected a memorial statue to the Roma massacred on 24 April 1942.[180] In post-Soviet Russia, many de-scendants of Smolensk Province's celebrated Romani kolkhozniks con-tinue to work the fields of the former October and Stalin Constitution kolkhozes. According to a contemporary Romani activist, Smolensk's Roma today represent but one of several "successor communities" whose roots lie in "the remarkable era" that birthed as many as fifty-three Romani kolkhozes on Soviet territory. [181]

The era of early Soviet nationality policy is indeed remarkable, but it is not so merely for the fact that the Soviet government committed itself on paper to sedentarizing a people essentialized as peculiarly nomadic and inordinately backward and intractable. Perhaps more remarkable is the extent to which Romani citizens of the Soviet Union appropriated the reins of the Soviet mission to sedentarize them from the loose grip of officials who were largely disinterested in and cowed by the task of assimilating Romani nomads to settled, agricultural, and Soviet life. In the late 1920s and 1930s, several thousand Roma, both settled and nomadic, challenged the very same stereotype that informed Soviet policies on Romani sedentarization – that of the aimlessly wandering, rootless Gypsy who prefers to obtain her daily bread by thievery, deception, and beggary rather than by honest toil. They claimed plots of land, subsidies, and credits to which they were entitled as members of a nationality perceived to be exceptionally deviant and backward. In typically disastrous conditions, they laboured in the state economy on collective farms. Whatever their motivation, these Roma often pursued the mission to sedentarize and sovietize "backward Gypsies" with more vigour than did Soviet officials.

Meanwhile, thousands of Roma did not heed the Soviet clarion call to settle and undertake agriculture or other forms of "socially useful" labour. Most of these Roma who were aware of the Soviet Union's promises of territory and "civilization" were, it must be assumed, no less cognizant of the logic behind Soviet sedentarization policies than were their settling counterparts. Repeated state decrees on the need to "transition nomadic Gypsies to a working, settled way of life" made clear that becoming Soviet required abandoning one's traditional culture. Many Roma outright refused what was presented to them by officials and activists as a profitable exchange. Quite a few claimed their cash awards and credits as "backward Gypsy nomads" seeking to convert to Soviet life, but did so with no intention of settling permanently, if at all. Meanwhile, official efforts at eradicating the nomadism of "backward Gypsies" were so half-hearted that countless Roma undoubtedly never even received word of the recycled decrees promising them land and a glorious new Soviet life.

In the aftermath of World War II, Soviet officials reconsidered the "problem" of Romani nomadism. Recognizing the failures of earlier attempts, they opted for a new strategy. On 20 October 1956, the Supreme Soviet of the USSR issued its decree "On the Introduction of Vagrant Gypsies to Labour." Once again, Soviet officials were vaguely obliged to aid nomadic Roma in their "introduction" and "transition" to a working, settled way of life. This law, however, departed from its antecedent decrees of the 1920s and 1930s in at least one important way. The

1956 law specifically criminalized Gypsy nomadism (*brodiazhnichestvo*). It stipulated that any Gypsy who "intentionally" deviated "from socially useful work" would be punishable with as many as five years of exile and "corrective labour."[182] Although this law forced many Roma – often violently – to settle, it also ultimately failed to solve the Soviet Union's "problem" of immobilizing and thus de-Gypsifying so-called "vagrant Gypsies."[183] Thus, in the final decades of the Soviet Union, officials returned periodically to the issue of Romani nomadism. Like so many of their predecessors in the 1920s and 1930s, they resignedly issued uninspired bureaucratic reports on the need to settle Roma before returning to seemingly more important or simply more resolvable affairs of state.[184]

5 Pornography or Authenticity? Performing Gypsiness on the Soviet Stage

In early 1931, Romani activists and performers gathered in Moscow to celebrate the establishment of the Soviet Union's State Gypsy Theatre Romen. For the presumed benefit of posterity, the group solemnly posed before a camera to document the theatre's founding. The surviving photo reveals clean-shaven men sharply outfitted in suit and tie; older women in felt boots, simple blouses, and monochrome shawls; and stylishly coiffed young women wearing lipstick and heeled Mary Jane shoes. A bust of Lenin sits prominently behind the group, while *agitprop* posters decorate the walls. Absolutely nothing about the group recalls either the romantic or criminal visions of Gypsies common – both then and now – in popular imagination.

On stage in the Theatre Romen's early years, these Roma appeared and behaved much differently than in the historic photograph of the theatre's founding. The men wore caftans and tall boots, lined their eyes with kohl, buried their faces in unruly beards, and carried horse-whips. Costumed in brightly coloured and wide-flowing dresses, the women covered their heads with kerchiefs, tousled their long hair, and draped their necks with strings of jangling beads and coins. As their dances displayed the famed "Gypsy passion," the actors sang new songs of socialism. "The Gypsy sings!" announced one of the troupe's characteristic ballads, "And in his songs of labour, he glorifies his own Motherland – the land of the Soviets, where he is the happy and free son of a great family!"[1]

In the early 1930s, such performances were hailed not only as "ethnographically authentic" representations of Gypsies, but also as valuable propaganda in the struggle to transform backward Gypsies into Soviet citizens. For the Roma who wrote and performed such songs on

The founding of the State Gypsy Theatre Romen, 1931.

Romen's stage, Gypsiness was a fragile but valuable opportunity to advance themselves as professionals and to prove themselves as cultured Soviet citizens. In their performance of Gypsiness, Romen's artists simultaneously promoted Soviet stereotypes of Gypsy backwardness as ethnographically authentic and asserted themselves as authentically Soviet. Though Romen's repertoire was subject to constant debate and revision in the 1930s, the performative effect of the theatre's often contested spectacle of Gypsiness remained stable. On a stage typically adorned with horsewhips and brightly patterned tapestries, Romani performers fashioned themselves as socially useful and cultured citizens. At the same time, they authorized images of Gypsies as potentially redeemable thieves, illiterates, nomads, and whores.

Although Roma had long figured in the Russian imagination as beloved dancers and singers with a natural ability to excite audiences with their peculiarly "exotic," distinctly Gypsy brand of performance, neither the creation of the Theatre Romen in the Stalinist 1930s nor its persistence to the present day can be understood as a foregone conclusion. Due to its immense popularity among tsarist elites and merchants in imperial Russia's urban capitals, so-called Gypsy music filled many Bolsheviks with dread. They regarded the genre as a vile, corrosive, and pseudo-Gypsy element of bourgeois decadence that needed to be destroyed completely. In the 1920s, Bolsheviks located Roma's supposed backwardness not merely in nomadic camps and horse markets, but also in NEP's crowded cabarets. That a group of Romani activists and professional performers in Moscow managed to convince Narkompros that their supposedly inborn capacity to perform could be rendered socially useful on the stage of a national Gypsy theatre must therefore be considered a remarkable feat. Where others failed, Romen's founders managed not only to preserve and advance their professional and social status as performers, but also to create the only Romani institution to survive both shifting nationality policies in the Stalinist 1930s and, ultimately, the Soviet Union's collapse.

This chapter explores the sinuous fate of Romani performance in the Soviet Union from the conflicted yet boisterous days of NEP to the sober Russocentrism of the late 1930s. I focus on the Bolshevik campaign to liquidate Romani choirs in the 1920s as part of a larger NEP discussion on the imperilled morality of a new and decidedly masculine socialist culture. Although by 1930 Bolshevik critics had castigated Gypsy music and its performers as cunningly counter-revolutionary, ethnographically inauthentic, physically diseased, and ideologically poisonous, Romani performers and others in the business of performing nationality endeavoured to adapt Gypsy tropes to the Soviet stage. Both Leningrad's Ethnographic Theatre and Moscow's Gypsy Theatre Romen attempted to reconcile Russia's contested tradition of Romani performance with the ideological shifts of the Soviet 1930s.

Both theatres were tasked with replacing the so-called bourgeois decadence and ersatz Gypsiness of prerevolutionary Romani art with the socially useful staging of the ethnographically authentic Gypsy. Policymakers, activists, and performers struggled, however, to determine what ethnographically authentic Gypsies would look and sound like on stage. They could agree only that backward Gypsies need be transformed into icons of Soviet progressiveness, and that performers must sing and dance to songs that synced with Sovietism. The Ethnographic Theatre was quickly disbanded on charges that its performances subverted ethnographic authenticity and advanced kulak propaganda. Moscow's Theatre Romen adapted to both changing definitions of ethnographic authenticity and revised Soviet values, and therefore earned praise for its performances of triumphant New Soviet Gypsies in various incarnations. For Romani performers, the Soviet stage of the 1920s and 1930s proved a perilous ideological battleground, a contested institution of political enlightenment, and a productive site of their Soviet self-fashioning. For Romen's actors in particular, the stage was a place where manipulable national forms – lively music, wild dances, and colourful costumes – afforded them the socialist content of Soviet respectability. For them, performing Gypsiness meant becoming Soviet both on- and offstage.

Tsyganshchina: The Prostitution and Pornography of Gypsy Performance

Though professional Gypsy choirs enjoyed a rather confident resurgence during NEP, Romani performers once again confronted an ideological attack on their "debauched" art during the First Five-Year Plan. Whereas Romani performers and their profession had rather anonymously fallen victim to the class warfare, chaos, and poverty rampant during War Communism, they became a clearly defined target of the Bolsheviks' post-NEP campaign to liquidate all remnants of capitalism. Bolsheviks virulently sought to destroy supposedly decadent Romani choirs in an organized campaign against what was termed "tsyganshchina." The so-called debauched Gypsy genre of singing and dancing, tsyganshchina evoked in the Bolshevik imagination images of money-grubbing and slavish Gypsies catering to the egotistical and deviant sexual needs of wealthy NEPmen and vulnerable, misguided Soviet youth. Anti-tsyganshchina campaigners decried popular Gypsy music as a threatening affront to socialism and castigated Romani performers as prostituting saboteurs. For a while, it was unclear whether Romani performance could ever be assimilated into the increasingly policed and prudish Soviet culture of Stalin's Great Break.

Throughout NEP, the leaders of Moscow's two most celebrated Romani choirs – Kruchinin and Poliakov – treaded lightly through NEP society's maze of ideological contradictions. It was thanks to NEP and the ostentatious prosperity it had temporarily reintroduced to the Soviet capital that they and their choir charges were again able to profit from the business of performing Gypsy music. Yet times had dramatically changed since the fin-de-siècle apogee of elite Romani performance. Hollywood-inspired flapper fashions, casinos, dancehalls, taverns, and cabarets had eclipsed the silk evening gowns, sharp tuxedos, and luxurious restaurants known to Romani performers before the revolution.[2] The establishments where Romani choirs now performed were nouveau riche at best and seedy at worst. Even at Moscow's premier restaurants, the choirs' clients no longer represented genteel society, but instead NEP's most enterprising – and therefore politically dangerous – upstarts. Confusingly, Bolshevik ideology at the same time insisted that any manifestation of "bourgeois decadence" be considered counter-revolutionary.

As the directors of ideologically questionable Romani choirs, Kruchinin and Poliakov seemed to have perceptively understood that they were traversing a political tightrope whose end point was not yet fully discernible. Kruchinin and Poliakov, however, employed different tactics in their efforts to legitimize Gypsy art in the NEP period. An amateur ethnographer, Kruchinin adopted an "academic" approach to his choir's performances, integrating his interpretation of Romani ethnohistory into each engagement.[3] He lectured audiences on the history of Romani music and culture generally, but also provided brief historical exegeses of each individual song performed.[4] Members of Kruchinin's Studio of Old Gypsy Art also performed short, ethnographic plays such as "A Betrothal in the Gypsy Camp." Adapted from "scenes from the life of nomadic (polevykh) Gypsies," these plays were designed to educate, rather than to entertain audiences.[5] With the stated mission "to restore Gypsies' old and ... authentic (podlinnoe) musical art form and to liberate it from all that is alien and undesirable," Kruchinin's ensemble performed for nearly 600 audiences between 1920 and 1927.[6]

Rejecting Kruchinin's academic approach, Poliakov sought to resurrect the prerevolutionary popularity of so-called Gypsy romances while offering only obligatory nods to the ideological demands of the Bolsheviks' vision for a new socialist culture. Poliakov aimed to find a "respectable place among Russia's proletariat" for the Romani performers who had not been "prepared for new life" at the time of the October Revolution.[7] However, the performance program of Poliakov's choir scarcely distinguished itself from that which his prerevolutionary choir had offered various salles de la noblesse in the 1890s. While the waltzes had been excised, the "bourgeois" Gypsy romances remained.

For Bolsheviks already worried that their revolution had been betrayed, the persistence of Gypsy music's "bourgeois decadence" threatened the socialist culture they sought to create. In Bolshevik eyes, the Gypsy romances performed by Poliakov's choir fed a larger societal illness symptomized by hooliganism, philistinism, licentiousness, and petit bourgeois psychosis. With popular titles that included "I Am a Mistress of Fortune Telling and Divination," "Your Black Eyes Have Ruined Me," and "I Love You Endlessly," Gypsy romances threatened not only to infect Soviet citizens with the counter-revolutionary disease of egoism and debauchery, but also to immunize them from socialist ideals.[8] "Black Eyes" and "To Hell with You" were not Bolshevik songs, but instead the "wild" anthems of "self-satisfied" NEPmen.[9]

Yearning for NEP's end, anxious Bolsheviks increasingly lumped together these seemingly degenerate and kitschy Gypsy romances under the interchangeable rubrics "tsyganshchina" and "pseudo-tsyganshchina."[10] By 1927, however, tsyganshchina was more than cultural shorthand for decadent Gypsy music. Bolshevik crusaders employed it as a central slogan of their campaign to rescue the purity of socialist ideals from the vile, capitalist-infested cesspool of NEP popular culture.[11] They endeavoured to strangle the putrid roots of Gypsy art and to unmask the dangerous bourgeois cancer masquerading as traditional Romani folk music. In January 1927, for example, Bolshevik cultural critic Sergei Bugoslavskii decried tsyganshchina as worse than "rubbish." He declared Gypsy songs the products not of an authentic Romani culture, but instead the work of the exploitative bourgeoisie. So-called Gypsy music, he insisted, was not Gypsy at all. The "pseudo-Gypsy songs" heard in the Soviet capital, Bugoslavskii explained, were no less than the pernicious works of "semiliterate" songwriters seeking to satisfy the drunken whims of the tsarist bourgeoisie. These songwriters knew absolutely nothing of the "deep melancholy and ecstasy, the fully hot-tempered passion associated with Gypsies' everyday nomadic life." As a result, generations of Romani choirs – including those at work during NEP – sang not songs about horses or the wild steppes, but instead cheap romances about unrequited love. Only Kruchinin's ethnographic ensemble, Bugoslavskii concluded, performed "authentic (*podlinnaia*) Gypsy song."[12]

Despite having been deemed a peddler of bourgeois exotica and erotica disingenuously packaged as folk art, Poliakov fashioned himself as the director of a choir whose music synced with socialist ideals.[13] In an article published in January 1927, Poliakov joined in unleashing the anti-tsyganshchina battle cry. Emphasizing his years of Romani choir experience, he narratively positioned himself as a citizen who ostensibly knew better than most just how heinous a crime the bourgeois defilement of Gypsy art was. After all, Poliakov wrote, "Gypsy song entered me together with my mother's milk." He credited Gypsy music for allowing him to articulate the "days of joy and of woe" afforded him in his early nomadic life. Yet his deepest sorrows, he explained, were rooted not in his nomadic childhood, but rather in his adult life as a pre-revolutionary chorister. At the restaurant Iar, Poliakov maintained, he and his fellow performers became slaves to the "carousing bourgeoisie" and thus unwitting participants in the corruption of "the authentic art of Gypsy singing." As "genuine Gypsies (*podlinnye tsygane*)" on the road, Poliakov and his choir peers never sang the romances so beloved by their exploitative clients, but instead songs of "the joy and liberty of the wide open steppe." It was drunken capitalists who had created "pseudo-Gypsy art," Poliakov argued, not "genuine Gypsies."[14]

Poliakov confessed that drunken capitalists were still in the business of exploiting Romani performers and debasing their art to the point that it was "slowly dying." He recognized that Moscow teemed with performers reduced to the shame of perpetuating "pseudo-Gypsy art." Yet he also defended the "authentic" Romani performers among them. These performers, Poliakov argued, were capable of reviving "authentic" Romani art and restoring it to its precapitalist glory. They needed only a respectable theatre – not a dancehall or tavern – where they could perform for Moscow's proletariat. To this end, Poliakov announced that he had recently written a play that would allow Moscow's Romani performers to showcase the customs, songs, and dances of Roma's everyday nomadic life – indeed, to prove themselves the living repositories of "authentic" Romani culture.[15] This three-act play, *Gypsies on a New Path*, promised a rare glimpse into the authentic everyday culture of Gypsy camps, the opportunity to hear and see authentic Gypsy songs performed, and a Bolshevik-style morality tale of how prerevolutionary life afforded Roma nothing but misery.[16]

Gypsies on a New Path premiered at Moscow's Experimental Theatre on 28 February 1927. Two hundred Roma participated in bringing to life Poliakov's prerevolutionary tale of young lovers driven from their beloved nomadic camp by a predatory noble seeking to purchase the play's heroine as his wife. The two fugitives – Ivan and Masha – escape to Moscow, where Masha joins a famous Romani choir in the restaurant Iar, and Ivan trades horses on the market. Moscow, however, only disenchants the youths. Both are disgusted by the drunken atmosphere of Iar, the insolence of aristocratic "rapists," the lack of freedom they once knew in their nomadic camp, and the debasement of their musical traditions. Tragedy seems imminent once Ivan is arrested for his involvement with a student revolutionary who instils in him the dream of destroying the Russian nobility. Masha, Ivan, and the entirety of Romani culture are saved, however, by the fortuitous intervention of the Bolsheviks in October 1917.[17]

Poliakov's play aroused little excitement and received unfavourable reviews. In his brief pamphlet *Gypsies on Stage*, the cultural critic

Rostislav Bliumenau praised Poliakov as a "talented director and guitarist," but lamented his dramaturgical illiteracy. *Gypsies on a New Path*, Bliumenau concluded, was "an absolute and deserved failure." Poliakov's pitiable production of *Gypsies on a New Path* had in no way distinguished itself from tsyganshchina. Rather, Bliumenau explained, it had proved that Gypsy music was dead and putrefying in the grave of NEP's boorish culture.[18]

Poliakov's mechanically constructed portrait of Roma's prerevolutionary exploitation and default revolutionary aspirations did not suffice to quiet the growing movement to heave so-called tsyganshchina overboard from the ship of Soviet modernity. The Bolsheviks' outcry over Romani choirs and the "philistine" culture of NEP in general only became more pronounced as Stalin unleashed his cultural revolution. Yet as the anti-tsyganshchina campaign climaxed during the First Five-Year Plan, the contours of the argument for eradicating Gypsy song from Soviet culture shifted in important, if not surprising, ways. Whereas Gypsy music was first attacked for its purported lack of ethnographic authenticity, critics also began in 1928 to charge the (male) peddlers and (female) performers of tsyganshchina with pornography and prostitution. Gypsy music came to be seen not merely as a symbol of bourgeois decadence or counter-revolution, but also as a gendered and ethnicized icon of sexual deviance in an age of officially idealized prudishness.

The indexing of tsyganshchina with prostitution and pornography began quietly at first as journalists issued titillating whispers and innuendo about the dangerous debauchery of Gypsy music, and of Romani women in particular. The journal *Tsirk i estrada* published a gossipy snippet in February 1928 about a Gypsy choir director who therein was all but defamed as a pimp. The journal alleged that the director paid the women of his choir trifles for their evening services on stage. He encouraged them instead to earn their keep in the private rooms of a bar in Rostov-on-Don that, incidentally, went by the name of Riche. The journal not only alluded to the women's prostitution, but also printed the names of three women alleged to have "visited" the tavern's private rooms.[19]

In 1929, L. Lebedinskii of the journal *Proletarskii muzykant* unequivocally defined tsyganshchina as "blatant propaganda for prostitution." He described the typical female Romani performer as "all made-up ... and half-nude." It was possible, he conceded, that such a woman did not realize that she "resembled a prostitute." Yet her "hysterical shouts" and laboured breathing left little else to the audience's imagination. Lebedinskii explained that while she may have literally been singing the lyrics, "I love you, please believe me, I will love you until death," she might as well have been hissing the words, "Look at me, I'm hot, passionate: your five-ruble note will not go to waste." After decades of catering to "chauvinists," Romani women had become not only the masters of "the prostitution genre" in music, but also simple whores.[20]

Other critics, however, sought to index the purported licentiousness of Romani performers by personifying Gypsy music itself as a bewitching, manipulative, and diseased siren. In this rhetorical variant, it was not the Romani woman who figured as unbridled sexuality incarnate, but instead the grammatically feminine "Gypsy song" (*tsyganskaia pesnia*) and her twin sisters, tsyganshchina and pseudo-tsyganshchina. One critic lamented, "Shameless, erotic 'tsyganshchina,' decadent and vulgar, 'flourishes' on our stage."[21] Speaking of tsyganshchina as if of a "backward" woman, R.V. Pikel' of the Main Committee for Repertory (Glavrepertkom) explained, "The influence of the revolutionary epoch affected it least of all; it has scarcely undergone a rebirth." Meanwhile, it was precisely tsyganshchina's resistance to change that attracted NEPmen seeking "to preserve some fragments of the past" and "to forget the 'horrors' of the present." Gypsy music persisted as the trusty and beloved mistress who soothed NEPmen as they coped with the "colossal social cataclysm" of the revolution.[22]

The problem remained that tsyganshchina appealed to the proletariat as much as it did to the bourgeoisie. Despite its "reactionary essence," tsyganshchina beguiled the alcohol-prone worker seeking "to forget about his grey, bleak workdays." Combined with alcohol, Gypsy music dulled the workingman's senses and robbed him of revolutionary consciousness. "The pseudo-tsyganshchina is all the more harmful for the working class," Pikel' claimed, "because it slowly but surely deforms its psyche and consciousness." Gypsy song's "egocentric and antisocial lyrics" and "peculiar exotica" distracted the proletariat from the construction of socialism.[23] Tsyganshchina, critics claimed, polluted the proletariat's thinking with its thematic pulp of "unhealthy erotica, drunken tears, 'shattered hopes,' and 'wasted dreams.'"[24]

Critics represented Romani women as moaning sirens whose sexuality overpowered weak-willed workers, dandies, and NEPmen, infecting them with the so-called "Gypsy disease" of alcoholism, impotence, and counter-revolution. Reflecting on "the vast influence of the debauched pseudo-tsyganshchina," Bliumenau insisted on the predatory

Romani choir in the era of NEP. From Ivan Rom-Lebedev, *Ot tsyganskogo khora k teatru "Romen"* (Moscow: Iskusstvo, 1990).

nature of female Romani performers, explaining their need to secure a thoroughly drunken audience as a prerequisite of a commercially successful evening. Motivated by the desire to extract the highest possible price from alcohol-addled minds distracted by racy clothing and "exotic" beauty, he maintained, Romani women wore "short skirts ... hardly reminiscent of national Gypsy choirs" and drank immodestly alongside their clients.[25] Bliumenau and his fellow Bolshevik critics of tsyganshchina increasingly presented the women of Romani choirs not merely as enterprising prostitutes, but also as the deans of a dangerous "academy of debauchery" and the licentious guardians of a "breeding ground of philistinism."[26] They characterized Romani women as the powerful, if capricious matriarchs of the seedy NEP culture flourishing in the unproductive wasteland of the Soviet Union's taverns and restaurants.[27]

Yet no one demonized Romani choir women with as much venomous energy or unrestrained misogyny as Boris Shteinpress – a young Komsomol activist and graduate student in the Moscow State Conservatory. Beginning in 1930, Shteinpress waged war on Romani choirs – and their female performers, in particular – in the pages of the journal *Za proletarskuiu muzyku*. Explaining the origins of the dreaded tsyganshchina, Shteinpress pointed directly at the corrupting influence of Gypsy women – of the female choral performers who, in the nineteenth century, had secured their daily sustenance by "draining the pockets" of Russian merchants and aristocrats.[28] Ostensibly historicizing the "pornography" of Gypsy music, Shteinpress wrote:

> It is well known that [in tsarist times] Gypsies stole horses and Gypsy women sold their songs, dances, and love. Russian merchants and carousers liked these "hot-tempered" women with their "wild, southern blood." Gypsy women aroused their [clients'] sensuality by every means – with their appearance, wild dancing, sensual singing – so as to swindle more money from them. They therefore accentuate the unhealthy, arousing moments in their singing and dancing.[29]

Making no mention of the men who performed in the prerevolutionary Gypsy choirs, Shteinpress insisted that Gypsy women had profited from their skilled arousal of those ardent enemies of Bolshevism – crude, rich merchants and debauched aristocrats. Savouring Gypsy women's "openly-prostituted songs and dances," these men "exploited the Gypsy woman not merely as a dancer or singer, but also as a woman." Thus, Shteinpress explained, the false, prostitution-style Gypsy genre, tsyganshchina, was born. Authentic Gypsy art was bastardized, and Gypsy women reduced to whores.[30]

Crude gender dichotomies pervaded Shteinpress's writing on Gypsies and tsyganshchina, revealing much about not only his own misogyny, but also the misogyny at the heart of Bolshevik thought on questions of sex and gender. In diagnosing the historic defilement of Gypsy art and the persistent disease of tsyganshchina, Shteinpress focused on the Gypsy woman as a distinctly ethnic emblem of the seeming threat that female contamination posed to a righteous and pure Bolshevik masculinity. A self-styled and proud mouthpiece of Bolshevik morality, Shteinpress infused his analysis with rhetoric of Gypsy women's deviant sexuality, portraying them as vampires in exciting dress, well versed in the arts of seductive dance and singing and devoted to profits, no matter how vulgarly obtained. In his avowed attacks on the perniciousness of tsyganshchina, Shteinpress repeatedly counterposed the decadent, licentious, backward, counter-revolutionary Gypsy woman against the virile, productive, monogamous, and pure Soviet man of Bolshevik ideals.[31]

Thus, in Shteinpress's view, the continuing popularity of Gypsy music was a diabolic menace to the health of early Soviet society and especially of its men. As they had in the prerevolutionary past, female Gypsy performers continued to emasculate men with their "passionate, exciting singing; wild cries; fiery, sensual looks; provocative movements; [and] frenzied dancing."[32] Shaking their shoulders and breasts in sync with their "hooligan music," Gypsy women "teased" the men whom they "humiliated" and reduced to wretched, salivating beasts. As they moaned lyrics that exalted "prostitution and slavish obedience," Gypsy women contaminated their audiences with their diseased consciousness, depraved sensuality, and vile antipathy for socialism.[33] Gypsy women sapped all possibility of revolutionary energy from their male admirers, leaving them lethargic and impotent.[34]

For Shteinpress, tsyganshchina represented the gravest harm. "Alongside vodka and religion," he insisted, "tsyganshchina campaigned for the old way of life, for the old relationships between people, and against socialist construction." It was counter-revolutionary art – the kind with the dangerous propensity to "demoralize a person, to encourage (podderzhivat') philistine, petty, narrowly personal feelings, and to prompt indifference, passivity." The only possible antidote to this Gypsy malaise, Shteinpress argued, was revolutionary music that, unlike tsyganshchina, was to be "vigorous, strong, austere." Whereas Gypsy music drained its listeners of productive energy, a new proletarian music would "educate a man (*chelovek*); foster in him a new attitude towards people, towards labour; instill in him vigour, confidence, and joy."[35] While revolutionary, proletarian music could inspire in its listeners the (male) courage to march forward in the construction of socialism, Gypsy music could only destroy one's health and inspire (female) indifference to the glorious new world that New Soviet Men were creating.

Although critics had earlier focused scant attention on the culpability of Soviet consumers of Gypsy music, Shteinpress now shone a bright, accusatory light not only on bloated NEPmen, but also on young, effeminate "dandies" and promiscuous ditzes lurking among the proletariat. "Philistine" youth, Shteinpress insisted, were "entirely saturated with tsyganshchina." Under the disastrous influence of tsyganshchina, these "dandy effetes (*frantovatye zhorzhiki*)" and "girls painted with makeup" narrowly concerned themselves with their "stylish suits," "American dances," and – in the young women's case, at least – the search for a fiancé. Consumed by their "petty-bourgeois feelings," this wasted, alienated youth stood in the way of socialist construction, so intoxicated were they with the philistine siren call of tsyganshchina. Shteinpress argued that many impressionable youths – including Komsomol members – had been so seduced by the "pornography" of Gypsy romances that they did not even realize that they had become reckless, counter-revolutionary agitators.[36]

For anti-tsyganshchina crusaders, the combined effort to silence Gypsy "prostitutes" and "pornographers," to disarm gluttonous NEPmen, and to save debauched youth was but one battle in the larger Bolshevik "struggle for man's transformation."[37] In waging this battle, tsyganshchina's foes ultimately achieved more than the spreading of cultural hysteria. By 1930, the censors at Glavlit and Glavrepertkom had forbidden the publishing and sale of sheet music for "pseudo-Gypsy romances," banned the repertoires of tsyganshchina's most popular performers, cleansed Soviet radio of "the Gypsy disease," and policed clubs known to host Gypsy music concerts. Many of the Soviet Union's most popular performers of the so-called Gypsy genre again found themselves without work. Romani choirs sought hospitable venues in the provinces or simply fell apart.[38]

At the dawn of the Stalinist 1930s, Gypsy music and its demonized Romani performers seemed fated only to occupy an ignoble page in the cultural history of the Soviet Union. Tsyganshchina's critics applauded themselves for all but silencing the alleged pornography of Gypsy music. Yet for Romani activists and artists in Moscow and Leningrad – and even for tsyganshchina's most vocal critics – a series of core questions remained unanswered: Could the ethnographically authentic music of Roma's nomadic camps be resurrected on the Soviet stage? Had a purely Gypsy music ever existed at all? If so, what did it sound like? Was it even worth saving? Finally, who could be trusted to excavate the fossilized musical culture of this backward and illiterate people?

After having built his early career on the ashes of so-called tsyganshchina, Shteinpress, for one, appeared none too eager to advocate the salvaging of the purported "ethnographically authentic" musical culture of nomadic Roma. In his *Toward a History of Gypsy Song in Russia*, Shteinpress conceded merely that contemporary Romani artists' manner of singing – their "spontaneity, vivid emotionality, [and] passion verging on absurdity" – evidenced rare residual authenticity. Romani performers' wild "cries and shouts," Shteinpress surmised, were likely rooted in the "national character" of "this nomadic, 'free,' lumpen people (*narod*)."[39] All else amounted to nothing more than a disfigured cultural commodity manufactured by the tsarist ruling class and peddled by "Russified" Gypsies. Shteinpress concluded that "the connection with the genuine folk art of the camps" had been lost, perhaps forever.[40]

Roma who had both a professional and political stake in the reconciliation of so-called Gypsy music and Soviet ideological correctness, however, hoped to cleanse their art of supposed alien elements and legitimate its place in Soviet culture. Therefore, enterprising Romani activists appropriated the rhetoric of the anti-tsyganshchina campaign and styled themselves as the potential saviours of "genuine" Romani folk art. The revered Kruchinin lectured Soviet audiences on "Gypsy art and the struggle with tsyganshchina," publicly advocated the full liquidation of "dilettantism" in the sphere of Gypsy music, and continued to promote the purported ethnographic approach of his ensemble.[41] The Romani leaders born of the Gypsy Union, meanwhile, discussed the need to "revolutionize Gypsy art" and began mobilizing for the creation of a national Romani theatre.[42] In Leningrad, Romani performers sought a professional and ideological safe haven within the walls of the Ethnographic Department of the State Russian Museum. All would soon discover, however, that the battle for Roma's "ethnographic authenticity" on the Soviet stage had only just begun.

Living Ethnography? Gypsies on Display
at the Russian Museum

In 1931, a small group of Romani performers joined the troupe of Leningrad's Ethnographic Theatre. Most of them descended from St. Petersburg's prerevolutionary Romani choir dynasties. Like their colleagues in Moscow, these performers had been hounded from the Soviet stage during the preceding years of anti-tsyganshchina crusading. Now, the Ethnographic Theatre ostensibly promised them not only a future as professional performers, but also an ideological justification for their art. Given the virulence with which Bolshevik activists had recently battled tsyganshchina, these potential guarantees amounted to a considerable fortune. No longer to be regarded as counter-revolutionary prostitutes and pornographers, the Romani performers of the Ethnographic Theatre could hope to reinvent themselves as artists endowed with a special ability to bring their nationality's ethnohistory to life. Within the walls of the Russian Museum, performing Gypsiness would no longer be construed as pornography, but instead as an act of civic duty. These hopes, however, were dashed in relatively short order.

Conceived of initially as a means of animating the Russian Museum's ethnographic collections, the Ethnographic Theatre opened in 1928 only to be dismantled in 1932. During its brief run, the Ethnographic Theatre aimed "to contribute to the study of the everyday life of the peoples of the USSR and the popularization of ethnographic knowledge by means of theatrical methods."[43] Committed foremost to authenticity, the theatre promised to bring audiences "closer to the ethnographic truth" via a program that incorporated "authentic (*podlinnye*)" costumes, material culture, songs, dances, and vernaculars.[44] Although the Ethnographic Theatre faced challenges to its claims of ethnographic authenticity from the start, it was the theatre's first foray into performing Gypsiness that led to its shuttering. For a short time in Leningrad, the question of Gypsies' ethnographic authenticity provoked intense debate, inspired few definitive answers, and ultimately led Soviet authorities to doubt the mission of the Ethnographic Theatre itself.

The roots of the Ethnographic Theatre can be traced to 1922, when a small troupe of self-described Russian actors organized Leningrad's Experimental Theatre under the leadership of theatre historian V.N. Vsevolodskii-Gerngross. During NEP, the Experimental Theatre earned its greatest success for its dramatization of "ethnographic" scenes of

Russian peasant life.[45] Hailed in the Soviet press as a uniquely authentic portrait of peasant life, the theatre's widely performed play, *The Russian Peasant Wedding Ceremony*, was precisely the type of performance that the Ethnographic Department of the State Russian Museum sought as a complement to its collections in late 1927.[46] In 1928, Leningrad's Experimental Theatre joined forces with the Ethnographic Department of the State Russian Museum in its efforts to both sovietize and popularize its collections.[47]

Having been harshly criticized by political education (Politprosvet) activists and other officials for their combined failure to reflect Soviet achievements in the Russian Museum's ethnographic exhibits and to attract "the masses," scholars at the Ethnographic Department sought to defuse both criticisms simultaneously with their introduction of "ethnographic evenings" in the winter of 1927–28. Intended for worker, student, and soldier groups, ethnographic evenings featured lectures, films, slides, and live performances of Soviet nationalities marching forward in socialist progress. As such, they were meant as a corrective to the static, outdated, and uninspiring narrative of the museum's ethnographic exhibits. As Hirsch has argued, the evenings offered a stimulating "virtual tour" of the empire that allowed museumgoers to imagine themselves as members of a harmonious, multi-ethnic union speeding towards the front lines of human development.[48]

By 1929, ethnographic evenings served as a core staple of the Ethnographic Department's political enlightenment work. Members of the department's cultural-enlightenment cell congratulated themselves on the evenings' popularity.[49] Thousands of visitors were learning about "The Peoples of the USSR during the Five-Year Plan." In the evenings' ostensibly most "authentic" format, representatives of the nationality in question – typically students from the Institute of Eastern Languages or the Institute of the Peoples of the North – were on hand to perform their ethnicity.[50] These "authentic folk artists" read poems, sang songs, performed dances, and demonstrated rituals that were purported to be historically essential markers of their distinct nationality. In so far as "authentic folk artists" and other representatives of the Union's peoples were in relatively short supply, however, the Ethnographic Department often settled on performances characterized as being in "full proximity to the authentic."[51] That is, the Experimental Theatre's Russian artists performed not only Russianness, but the ethnicity of a variety of other nationalities as well.

When the Ethnographic Department decided to expand its increasingly popular program of ethnographic evenings in 1929, it found an eager partner in the Experimental Theatre.[52] Seeking a permanent home for the theatre, Vsevolodskii-Gerngross enthusiastically declared the Experimental Theatre a logical ally in the Russian Museum's efforts to propagandize "ethnographic and historical-cultural knowledge." The popularity of the museum's ethnographic evenings, he argued, had already proven the value of enlivening "the museum's objects." "Costumes worn on living people move," he explained, "domestic utensils come to life; words are heard; songs begin to ring; entire episodes from the life of the peasantry and from the life of various class groups in various epochs … play out before the audience."[53] Vsevolodskii-Gerngross promised that his troupe, reorganized as an ethnographic theatre, would fuse art and science so as to literally and "authentically" enliven the museum's artefacts.[54]

Formally ratified by Narkompros in February 1930, the Leningrad Ethnographic Theatre continued the museum's ethnographic evenings program, but aspired to much more. In so far as the Ethnographic Department depended on the new theatre to aid in reorienting the museum's collections to "reflect questions of contemporaneity," the Ethnographic Theatre articulated its primary task as "the study and popularization … of peasant art in connection with the general growth of the Russian village and the peoples of the USSR."[55] Vsevolodskii-Gerngross envisioned his theatre as a full partner in the Ethnographic Department's program of scholarly expeditions; he wanted it not only to perform the impact of collectivization and industrialization on Soviet peoples' everyday culture, but also to study said impact first-hand.[56] Authenticity required that he and the theatre's performers scrutinize the ethnographic present of revolutionary transformation with their own eyes and ears. With the modest help of the Russian Museum and the State Institute of Art History, the Ethnographic Theatre therefore organized brief expeditions to study "the Soviet village" in its various incarnations. Armed with audio recorders and cameras, the Ethnographic Theatre travelled in search of authentic material upon which to base its performances.[57]

In its first year of existence, however, the Ethnographic Theatre remained largely faithful to its tried and true repertoire of ethnographic evenings. In addition to *The Russian Peasant Wedding Ceremony*, the theatre continued to perform *Solstice* – a program of Russian peasant songs and rituals rooted in the agricultural calendar of changing seasons – and to present *The Art of the Russian North* through the media of song, dance, and documentary film.[58] Yet in an apparent effort to more perfectly complement the museum's reoriented goal of reflecting the revolution of everyday life already underway in the Soviet Union, the theatre also introduced a new concert program entitled *Four Villages*.[59] Focusing specifically on Russian peasant *byt* (way of life), *Four Villages* presented the Russian village of four historical epochs: the pre-Petrine village of Rus', the gentry-dominated serf village, the capitalist village, and the Soviet socialist village. As performed, each scene of *Four Villages* was prefaced by a lecture on the class struggles characterizing the era in question. Combined with live performance, this focus on class conflict reflected the museum's ideological mission to integrate relics of the ethnographic past into a relevant and rousing narrative of present-day socialist momentum.

In 1931, the Ethnographic Theatre was called upon to further the museum's ideological mission in still another, no less important way. At the time, scholars seated in the Ethnographic Department faced severe criticism not only for paying insufficient attention to the rapid changes then supposedly taking place among the empire's peoples, but also for not accounting for the Soviet Union's unprecedented ethnic diversity. Political education activists and museumgoers repeatedly asked why the minority peoples of the USSR were not adequately and proportionally represented.[60] The Ethnographic Department had focused much attention on Russians, but had little if anything to say about Buriats, Mari, or Roma. The scholars of the Ethnographic Department looked to the Ethnographic Theatre for help in addressing this striking deficiency.

Without sufficient resources or even the time necessary to reconstruct the entire ethnographic museum so that it represented all of the Soviet Union's nationalities, the Ethnographic Department was forced to improvise. While they planned ahead for new expeditions and exhibits, the museum's ethnographers needed in the short term to make do with what resources they had. As far as Roma were concerned, the department's ethnographers pointedly conceded, "Gypsies are absolutely overlooked (*ne zatronuty*) in the work of the Department."[61] While they hoped to finance an expedition to study Roma in Smolensk and other western provinces in 1932, Gypsies seemed fated to remain among other nontitular nationalities whose history and culture left not a trace in the museum's exhibits.[62]

The Ethnographic Theatre, however, willingly intervened on behalf of the department's ethnographers as they struggled to correct the ideological sins of their exhibits. One of the theatre's responsibilities, after all, was to provide a living ethnography for "the peoples of the

USSR who were not covered by the Museum (Gypsies, for example)."[63] Meanwhile, Roma seemed to present a particularly fruitful opportunity for the theatre to make good on this promise. In the view of the Ethnographic Theatre, the only "ethnographic material" that Gypsies seemed to offer posterity were their songs and dances. In that song and dance was "the singular type of art known" to Gypsies, an ethnography of Gypsies could – by definition – only be performed.[64] Representing Roma exclusively on stage thus seemed the perfect solution for a nationality already cast in the popular imagination as natural performers.[65]

In January 1931, Vsevolodskii-Gerngross welcomed a Romani troupe to the Ethnographic Theatre's band of performers. While half of the new artists boasted years of experience in professional Romani choirs, authenticity required that nomadic Roma also be represented at the Ethnographic Theatre.[66] A. Nikolaev-Shevyrev, a theatre manager who worked closely with the Romani troupe, later recalled these so-called "camp Gypsies" as "people lacking any understanding of theatre, of stage principles of performance. The people sat on the floor of the stage and sang and danced as they had for their whole life in the camp." This lack of experience and even of elementary culture, though, had its merits. "This was ethnography," Nikolaev-Shevyrev explained, "This was folk art." That the so-called camp Gypsies "did not know how to sing, did not know the laws of the stage, and were ... illiterate" was initially seen as a marker of the troupe's authenticity.[67]

Vsevolodskii-Gerngross focused not on remedying the camp Gypsies' lack of professional experience, but instead on determining how to harmonize the two groups in a theatrical program befitting the ideological tenets of Soviet nationality policy. Though fearful of the threatening spectre of tsyganshchina charges, Vsevolodskii-Gerngross gambled that ethnographic authenticity need not be limited to the musical culture of Roma's legendary nomadic camps. In his view, authenticity instead required that the musical culture of settled, urban, and assimilated Roma be accounted for in as much depth as that of the so-called "camp Gypsies." Marxist theory itself, he reasoned, justified such an accounting.

While granting that tsyganshchina bore "no relation to the Gypsy people's song," Vsevolodskii-Gerngross took issue with those Bolshevik critics who argued that "authentic Gypsy folk songs" simply did not exist. Surely, he explained, the songs of nomadic camp Gypsies differed from those of settled, urban Gypsies; this was the difference between "the songs of the Gypsy 'peasant'" and "the songs of the

Gypsy petit bourgeois."[68] If it was the task of the museum to show the peoples of the USSR traversing the historical timeline, then the songs of the "Gypsy petit bourgeois" needed to be performed just as much as those of "the Gypsy 'peasant.'" Each, Vsevolodskii-Gerngross claimed, was essential to authentically representing Gypsies' past and to understanding Gypsies' role in the Russian class struggle in particular. He argued that all Gypsy songs – even those born of Gypsy choirs' slavish accommodation of tsarist nobles and merchants – must be considered "ethnographic phenomena." However unsavoury these "ethnographic phenomena" were in the eyes and ears of the enlightened Soviet public, they still could not be dismissed as tsyganshchina.[69]

Vsevolodskii-Gerngross defended his claims by repeatedly invoking the standard of authenticity. When the Ethnographic Theatre premiered its Gypsy concert program in 1931, audiences were informed of tsyganshchina's fraudulent origins and content. Tsyganshchina was an "obvious forgery" of Gypsy music that reached the apogee of its development in the drunken taverns and seedy cabarets of NEP.[70] Roma, however, were not to blame for tsyganshchina. Rather, non-Romani dilettante musicians and performers had disfigured "the temperament, colour, and mood" of Gypsy songs, manipulating their rhythm in order to amplify eroticism.[71] Vsevolodskii-Gerngross defined tsyganshchina as a term properly applied only to songs not written or performed by authentic Gypsies, but instead by Russians and others who exploitatively adopted a debauched, pseudo-Gypsy style.[72] The stated task of the Ethnographic Theatre's Gypsy concert program was therefore to demonstrate "authentic Gypsy vocal and choreographic art and the authentic Gypsy national performance manner cleansed of the influence of restaurants and pleasure gardens."[73]

Composed of three parts, the program ostensibly adhered to the Marxist timeline of historical development. The presumed stage of primitive communism featured the songs and dances of nomadic Roma. These songs bore the mark of "wild, monotonous, and strange (*neponiatna*)" methodology, "a lack of harmony," and "an absurd rhythm (*nesuraznost' ritma*)." They reflected nomadic Roma's everyday life with their central themes of nature, horses, lamentable poverty, and pitiable societal alienation. During the feudal stage of Russian serfdom, it was asserted, Romani choirs became the playthings of a cunning aristocracy. The newly settled, urban Roma of these proliferating choirs transformed their art into a livelihood and altered the nature of their music in the process. While they may have been singing the same old "authentic" songs from the camps, these urban Roma adapted them to European styles of instrumentation, harmonization, and rhythm. It was at this point that the "aristocratic" guitar became associated with Gypsy music. Romani choirs increasingly performed sentimental Russian romances and their popularity soared. It was ultimately during the capitalist epoch that both nomadic and urban Roma began to assimilate and ostensibly "Gypsify" a range of Russian folk songs and romances. This is where the concert program ended.

Yet the structure of the Ethnographic Theatre's Gypsy concert program suffered from a grievously obvious ideological mistake. While purporting to bring Romani ethnohistory to life, the theatre allowed its curtains to fall immediately after the capitalist stage of development. The program did not show New Soviet Gypsies triumphantly participating in socialist construction. Recognizing the perceived fault of this omission, the Ethnographic Theatre hoped to pre-empt inevitable criticism with the admission that "for now, Gypsies lack new Soviet songs." This was the logical result of Gypsies' backwardness. In that nationality policy was steadily leading to the greater integration of Gypsies into Soviet life, the Ethnographic Theatre assured audiences that Gypsies would undoubtedly soon be singing new songs of socialism – "national in form, socialist in content."[74]

It was precisely at the time of the Gypsy concert program's premiere, meanwhile, that the museum's ethnographers came under fire for failing to adequately reflect the unassailable forward march of Soviet progress in their stationary exhibits. Political education activists and museumgoers themselves were growing increasingly impatient with the museum's stalling. It was high time, they demanded, for the Ethnographic Department to present evidence of new, Soviet culture in its full glory.[75] These demands extended to theatre performances as well. Vsevolodskii-Gerngross and the Ethnographic Theatre simply could not expect to survive for long without being able to offer audiences the purported authenticity of the ethnographic, socialist present – that is, New Soviet Gypsies singing new Soviet songs.

The Ethnographic Theatre rushed to correct its mistake. In November 1931, the theatre premiered a new, five-act play entitled *Gypsy Road*. Whereas the theatre's previous Gypsy concert program had ignored New Soviet Gypsies, *Gypsy Road* presented the path that led this "traditionally nomadic people" to sedentarization and collectivized agriculture or, alternatively, to the proletarian world of the factory. Although the theatre's performers also traced this new path's feudal and capitalist antecedents on the historical timeline (oddly, the primitive communist stage received no attention), the play climaxed in 1928 with Roma's "participation in the construction of socialism."[76] Still, there were no new Soviet Gypsy songs.

The Ethnographic Theatre advertised *Gypsy Road* as a thoroughly "realistic" play. The costumes, songs, and vernaculars were, the theatre asserted, as certifiably authentic as the class struggles that shaped them.[77] Although the play was performed in the Russian language and not in Romani, the Ethnographic Theatre argued that the very fact that many of the performers were Roma sufficed to qualify as living, breathing authenticity. Audiences were to overlook the fact that Russian actors performed the play's leading roles; according to Vsevolodskii-Gerngross, the Romani performers were simply not qualified enough to be trusted as leading actors.[78] It sufficed, the theatre decided, to display "authentic Gypsies" on stage as if they were props.

The Ethnographic Theatre opened its 1932 season with *Gypsy Road* securely placed in its repertoire. The reviews, however, were disastrous – both those penned by the critical press and those scrawled in the museum's comment books by audience members.[79] Collectively appalled by *Gypsy Road*'s lack of ethnographic authenticity, journalists and pedestrian museumgoers alike called into question the theatre's very purpose. While one museumgoer vaguely asserted that *Gypsy Road* left much to be desired, others challenged the theatre's choice in selecting Russian actors for the play's leading roles. "It seems to us that if the artists resembled Gypsies … there would be more truthfulness [in the representation], [and] the impression made would be much stronger." That the performers looked nothing like Gypsies, this visitor argued, needed to be corrected before any claim to authenticity could be made.[80] Others complained about the inauthentic costumes, one arguing that authenticity required performers to be outfitted with "long, wide skirts, earrings, and tambourines."[81] Though *Gypsy Road* attracted the rare admirer, most audience members who wrote in the response books expressed utter dissatisfaction with the theatre's performance.[82] One disappointed patron also wanted to know why the museum lacked a proper stationary exhibit devoted to Gypsies.[83]

In its scathing review of *Gypsy Road*, Leningrad's *Krasnaia gazeta* castigated the Ethnographic Theatre as a "center of political and artistic reaction, overt amateuritis (*liubitel'shchina*), hack work, and dissimulation." As a "transmitter of bourgeois influence," the paper charged, the theatre had become only more dangerous with its performances of

Gypsy Road and its Gypsy concert program. These productions scarcely reflected the "process of introducing Gypsies to production, socialist construction, and Soviet culture." Instead, they inundated Soviet audiences with scenes of Gypsies performing for nobles and merchants. The rare performance of a Komsomol song did not disguise the Ethnographic Theatre's resuscitation of the accursed tsyganshchina. While the theatre's previous productions of *The Russian Peasant Ceremony* and *Solstice* had offered audiences "truly valuable moments," its Gypsy program amounted to nothing more than "bourgeois ideology disguised as ethnography (*pod markoi etnografii*)." The paper ultimately concluded that it was "difficult to imagine any production more politically harmful, more … dramaturgically and theatrically illiterate" than *Gypsy Road*.[84] The paper *Rabochii i teatr* agreed, referring to *Gypsy Road* as "kulak propaganda," "political illiteracy," and an exemplar of "mediocrity and worthlessness."[85] Both papers recommended that the Ethnographic Theatre's entire Gypsy repertoire be eliminated at once.

These reviews seemed to confirm the doubts already entertained by the Russian Museum's ethnographers. In late 1931, Boris Kryzhanovskii raised the question of the Ethnographic Theatre's perspectives to his colleagues in the Ethnographic Department. M.A. Fride worried that the theatre occupied "an undefined place" within the museum, and that its activities went unchecked by the department. She complained that Vsevolodskii-Gerngross had organized the theatre's hack "Gypsy productions" without consulting the museum's ethnographers. The Ethnographic Department collectively agreed that the Ethnographic Theatre had "lost its way." Its value had diminished and its ability to attract audiences had declined. "Even the actors," Kryzhanovskii noted, "say that it is boring to perform."[86]

On 2 April 1932, officials from both Narkompros and the Russian Museum called upon representatives from the Ethnographic Theatre to defend its "creative path." As the theatre's spokesperson, Vsevolodskii-Gerngross hoped to impress his interlocutors with short illustrations of the "artistic strength" of both the Russian and Romani troupes.[87] Thus he called upon the Romani troupe to perform an example of both a "camp" and an "urban Gypsy" song. These, Vsevolodskii-Gerngross asserted, were representative of "Gypsy song in its pure form" and "an authentic production of Gypsy art."[88] In yet another effort to disarm his critics, Vsevolodskii-Gerngross admitted the lack of New Soviet Gypsy songs in the theatre's repertoire, but reassured his audience that these were certain to be among the new ethnographic phenomena emerging at the site of Romani kolkhozes. In time, these would also be included in the theatre's Gypsy repertoire.[89]

Following the Ethnographic Theatre's presentation, attendees discussed the theatre's past mistakes and future perspectives. Comrade Bordanian, a representative of the Treugol'nik factory, questioned the very premise of an ethnographic theatre. In Bordanian's view, the theatre's main problem was not so much that it bored the average worker (although, he claimed, this was also a real problem), but that the theatre ultimately failed the test of ethnographic authenticity. "As soon as ethnography transfers to the domain of professional actors," he argued, "it becomes a play and loses its value." Questioning the theatre's reliance on Russian artists to perform the songs, dances, and rituals of other Soviet peoples, Bordanian continued: "As soon as you become an ethnographic theatre, you lose your ethnographicness (*etnografichnost'*), because ethnography is nothing other than the demonstration of folk art, but only the people (*narod*) itself can demonstrate this." In order for the Ethnographic Theatre to serve its original purpose, Bordanian argued, it needed to extend beyond the domain of its Russian, Ukrainian, and Romani troupes to include representatives of all Soviet nationalities. Together, they could artistically commune as a Soviet Union in miniature and demonstrate the "ethnography" of how far the empire's nationalities had come since "the victory of October."

Comrade Mishchulovin of *Rabochii i teatr* located the failures of the Ethnographic Theatre more specifically in its resurrection of the reviled tsyganshchina. The theatre's "sore spot," Mishchulovin argued, was "Gypsies, tsyganshchina." Neither general audiences nor sophisticated theatre critics were fooled by the theatre's Gypsy repertoire and its attempt to mask tsyganshchina as ethnography. Vsevolodskii-Gerngross appeased no one with his empty promises of Soviet Gypsy songs being born on Romani kolkhozes. If such songs were being composed and sung (and all agreed that they must be), then the Ethnographic Theatre had no excuse for not singing them. Likewise, the theatre could not defend the inattention it paid to representing Gypsies as workers and collective farmers. Mishchulovin declared *Gypsy Road* as the ultimate evidence that "the theatre did not realize its path, did not set itself the goal to struggle for the presentation to the Soviet audience of the ethnography of the past and of Soviet ethnography." The theatre failed, Mishchulovin claimed, to display "our reality."[90]

As this verbal lashing continued, the meeting's chairman invited the Ethnographic Theatre's actors to join the discussion. Marisov, a Russian performer, defended the theatre's dependence on Russian actors, emphasizing that they were professionals. "Bitter experience" had proven time and again that "amateur" actors could not be relied upon. In his view, the Ethnographic Theatre should be lauded for its professionalism instead of being charged with chauvinism. While he and his colleagues had long since recognized the need to integrate representatives of the empire's many nationalities into their performances, Marisov maintained that the Ethnographic Theatre itself could not be blamed for the lack of qualified minority cadres.[91]

At this point, Comrade Fedorov, one of the Ethnographic Theatre's resident "camp Gypsies," chose to speak.[92] Like Marisov, he was concerned less with the issue of authenticity than he was with professionalism. Regarding *Gypsy Road*, Fedorov spoke for his fellow Romani performers when he explained that they – *as Gypsies* – found the production to be a valuable professional experience. They did not regard the play as harmful and "could not understand its mistakes." Why had they – *as Gypsies* – been so enthused about their participation in *Gypsy Road*? "The Gypsy arrived in this theatre with song and dance and nothing else," Fedorov explained. "He did not understand anything about artistic affairs." Yet thanks to the Ethnographic Theatre and its production of *Gypsy Road*, Fedorov continued: "the Gypsy sees that he stepped out on stage, that he can act and develop himself further. The Gypsy saw that he is more than a singer, that he can also be an actor, and can develop himself further." Thanks to the recent closure of *Gypsy Road*, Fedorov lamented, this same Gypsy "was denied developing himself further."[93]

For Fedorov, critics who complained about *Gypsy Road*'s lack of ethnographic authenticity had missed the point. In decrying the play's narrative, critics had failed to see the real-time chronicle of socialist triumph unfolding before their eyes – that of backward camp Gypsies transforming themselves into respectable Soviet citizens and bona fide actors. Had *Gypsy Road* not been prematurely shut down, Fedorov insisted, he and his fellow Gypsy actors "could have developed themselves further and further." The play's critics failed to appreciate "the fact that Gypsies had established for themselves the goal of developing their qualifications."

In his brief speech, Fedorov admitted a point that *Gypsy Road*'s critics were unwilling to concede. If the Ethnographic Theatre's critics were honestly seeking an "authentic" representation of the transformation of backward Gypsies into New Soviet Gypsies, they need not look any further than the theatre's stage itself. For Fedorov, the "ethnographic authenticity" of Gypsies' Sovietness rested not with costume, physical appearance, song, or even the division of leading roles, but instead with the real-time, real-life action of backward Gypsies struggling to become professional Soviet actors and cultured citizens. He argued that if this was the "authentic" transformation desired to be seen by Soviet audiences and ideologues, *Gypsy Road* should never have been shelved. Instead, the play should have been reworked so that he and his ostensibly backward colleagues could have been given "the opportunity to further develop."[94]

Fedorov's words fell largely on deaf ears. Among the meeting's discussants, only Vsevolodskii-Gerngross championed Fedorov's interpretation of *Gypsy Road* as appropriately "national in form, socialist in content."[95] Following the discussion, officials at Narkompros, the Russian Museum, and Leniskusstvo decided collectively that the Ethnographic Theatre had committed serious "methodological and political mistakes." They deemed the theatre a failed venture and shut it down.[96]

Many of the Ethnographic Theatre's artists – Russians and Roma – nonetheless went on to perform in a variety of ethnographic ensembles in the 1930s and the 1940s. Some lobbied for the Ethnographic Theatre's reorganization as a theatre of folklore.[97] Many of the theatre's Romani performers ultimately joined together to form a "Gypsy ensemble." Having learned from the Ethnographic Theatre's mistakes, they committed to the performance of "new Soviet Gypsy songs" purported as "a reflection and artistic expression of Gypsies' new socialist life."[98] Their artistic creations, however, were eclipsed by those of Moscow's State Gypsy Theatre – an institution created in 1931 with the express purpose not only of an ideologically correct staging of the New Soviet Gypsy, but also of fashioning New Soviet Gypsies themselves. It was ultimately in Moscow that Gypsies' "ethnographic authenticity" was first successfully defined on stage, only to be repeatedly redefined in line with shifts in Soviet ideology and nationality policy.

The Rebirth of Gypsy Art at Moscow's Theatre Romen

Long before Leningrad's Ethnographic Theatre debuted its Roma-themed repertoire, Moscow's Romani activists dreamed of creating the world's first national Gypsy theatre.[99] At the height of the anti-tsyganshchina crusade, the Gypsy Union's former leaders decided that the time had come for them to save Romani art from both its critics and destroyers. In late 1930, they announced themselves as "the most fervent enemies of 'tsyganshchina'" and vowed their "full readiness to participate in the merciless 'cleansing' of Indo-Romen art." Committed to endowing the national form of "Indo-Romen art" with "international, Soviet, proletarian content," they promised that a national Gypsy theatre would eradicate tsyganshchina and in its place give birth to a new, Soviet Gypsy art and to New Soviet Gypsies.[100]

On 4 October 1930, Narkompros approved the activists' plan to establish an Indo-Romen Theatre Studio in Moscow.[101] The theatre's primary tasks were to combat both tsyganshchina and anti-Gypsism, to raise Gypsies' cultural level, to introduce "the Gypsy masses to the foundations of socialist construction," to aid in the sedentarization and collectivization of Gypsy nomads, and to "acquaint the Union's Gypsy masses with the new Soviet way of life."[102] This new national theatre, however, was not to be led by Roma themselves – not even by the activist members of the theatre's original organizing committee. Instead, Narkompros invited M.I. Gol'dblat of the Moscow State Yiddish Theatre to serve as artistic director and S.M. Bugachevskii of the Bolshoi Theatre as musical director. Other non-Romani personnel soon joined Gol'dblat and Bugachevskii to take charge of stage design, choreography, and theatre administration. Though they had envisioned themselves as the theatre's administrators and artistic directors, Moscow's leading Romani activists had no choice but to yield to the tutelage of their more experienced and ostensibly more cultured comrades.[103]

Although Roma were not entrusted with the task of running their own national theatre, they were expected to contribute to its national form. While Bezliudskii, Germano, and Rom-Lebedev began work on writing ideologically appropriate and ethnographically authentic plays, they and their fellow activists also participated in selecting the troupe's performers. The theatre administration selected approximately fifteen of Moscow's veteran Romani choristers to join.[104] Most, if not all, could be traced both to prerevolutionary Russia's elite choir dynasties and to the Gypsy Union. Their merits as performers and their reputation as activists justified their inclusion in the theatre's troupe. It was nonetheless agreed that the world's first national Gypsy theatre could not depend on the artistic talents of assimilated and thus potentially deracinated stage performers. The theatre needed fresh, "authentic" blood. It needed nomadic Gypsies. The "uncivilized" Romani youth of nomadic camps and nascent kolkhozes, the theatre's organizers and administrators decided, would bring the songs, dances, rituals, and customs unknown to Moscow's Romani elites. It was through the camp youth, Rom-Lebedev later recalled in his memoirs, that the theatre expected to "discover the thoughts, dreams, and ... psychology of contemporary nomadic Gypsies." These "backward" nomads would endow the theatre with "national character (*narodnost'*)."[105]

Though Moscow's Romani elites actively sought out nomadic youths precisely for their "authentic" lack of culture, they were nonetheless shocked by the level of "backwardness" displayed by the Roma who descended upon the theatre in late 1930 for the theatre's first advertised auditions. They wondered how so many young Roma had heard of the audition in the first place; surely the notion of camp Gypsies reading *Vecherniaia Moskva*'s classifieds was pure "fantasy." Once cramped in the theatre's borrowed crawl space, the auditioners reminded Moscow's Romani elites how culturally distant they were from their benighted brethren. Rom-Lebedev mused in his memoirs, "I do not think there has ever been such an audition in any theatre studio in the world. Such would only be possible if the Neanderthals would have thought to create a theatre studio." In their interviewers' eyes, these modern-day Gypsy "Neanderthals" could not answer even the most elementary questions. With residual shock and disgust, Rom-Lebedev remembered one auditioner testifying that his birth date was – at least according to his mother – "that year when Uncle Egor traded a bay horse for a black one."[106] Likewise, Edvard Sholokh was shocked to find that most auditioners could not say whether Pushkin was a Russian or a foreign poet.[107]

Nonetheless, the camp Gypsies displayed some sense of ideological promise. All knew at least something of Lenin, Rom-Lebedev explained, and many suspected that Marx's "Gypsy beard" was evidence that the great man himself was one of their own. Beyond these muddled attempts at political literacy, the auditioners also apparently knew better than to testify to their parents' occupations. When asked about their social backgrounds, many refused to respond. They suspected that to admit their parents as fortune tellers and speculators would insure inevitable rejection.[108] One hopeful, meanwhile, astutely responded to the question of how the revolution had transformed Gypsies' lives with this "joyful" cry: "Now we are human beings!"[109] Most important of all, however, was that they delivered the desired performance. As they danced and sang, Rom-Lebedev recalled, "the room came alive with the camp atmosphere." It was happily decided that the nomads' "innate" rhythm was as "authentic" and necessary to the theatre's sovietizing mission as their illiteracy and general lack of culture. Twenty-one were chosen to join the theatre's inaugural troupe.[110]

Never intended merely as a propaganda brigade, let alone as an institution of entertainment for its own sake, the Theatre Romen was structured from the outset to function simultaneously as a school for its actors.[111] Whether rooted in Moscow's Romani choirs or in nomadic camps, Romen's actors were uniformly considered uncultured illiterates desperately in need of a disciplined enlightenment regime. Such stereotypes were seemingly confirmed by the fact that many of the theatre's new actors continued to live on Moscow's outskirts in their camp tents. Others, completely homeless, slept on park benches or in train stations. Most lacked suitable clothing, and several of the "camp Gypsies" soon fell ill with tuberculosis. In the eyes of Narkompros officials and the theatre's administrators, this aspect of the actors' wretched "authenticity" was the undeniable physical evidence of their inward poverty of consciousness and culture.[112] Systematic coursework, it was hoped, would transform them into conscious Soviet citizens qualified to carry out agitation work among their still more benighted brethren.

Beginning in January 1931, Romen's actors began coursework that ranged from practical lessons on teeth brushing to political lessons on Leninism to professional dance and voice lessons. Actors studied the Russian and Romani languages, the history of music and theatre, and the fundamentals of Soviet political literacy. These courses were designed with the goal of "raising the general cultural level of the theatre's troupe." Raising one's cultural level, meanwhile, also meant mastering one's body and assimilating acceptable techniques of movement and dance. Romen's dancers learned that the infamous (female) shimmy characteristic of tsyganshchina was to have no place in the theatre's repertoire. They were taught "the fundamental elements of classic dance" and "to develop a sense of rhythm." Gymnastics, ballet, and other methods of physical training were employed in an effort to mould the bodies of developing souls.[113]

In May 1931, Romen opened its doors to the Soviet public and premiered a two-part program entitled *Gypsy Revue*. Before the curtains rose, Rom-Lebedev stepped out onto the proscenium and shouted out to his audience in Romani, "*Romale, shunen'te tume man!*" – "Roma, listen to me!" According to Rom-Lebedev, however, no one in the audience understood him. Although the theatre intended its first program for a "backward Gypsy" audience, no Roma were in attendance to understand the Romani words spoken on stage. This non-Romani audience nonetheless curiously eyed the actors' "coffee-coloured, big-eyed faces" and their "colourful, half-worker, half-Gypsy costumes."[114] As the actors performed in Romani, audience members were to comprehend plots and meaning via the actors' expressive singing and dancing.[115]

Gypsy Revue's first part, entitled *Gypsies Yesterday and Today*, was a brief play comparing Gypsy life before and after the October Revolution. Written by Bezliudskii and Sholokh, the sketch portrayed prerevolutionary Romani life as a depressing combination of exploitation, deviance, and poverty. The usual Gypsy suspects were represented on stage as the personification of Gypsies' historic oppression: the horse-dealer, the fortune teller, the pickpocket, and the exploited chorister. On stage, these characters were victimized by the tsarist police, the predatory bourgeoisie, and finally, by their own backwardness. For the play's final scenes, however, the curtain rose to reveal the glorious Soviet present. Here, New Soviet Gypsies gathered in Moscow's Gypsy Club to bring Gypsies' old way of life – again represented by the horse-dealer, fortune teller, pickpocket, and choral singer – to trial. At the club, Gypsy workers, kolkhozniks, Communist youth, and Theatre Romen actors proved to their forbears that Soviet power had liberated them from Gypsies' outmoded, backward way of life.[116] According to Rom-Lebedev, this premiere of *Gypsies Yesterday and Today* earned the audience's resounding applause.[117]

Gypsy Revue's second part, entitled *An Ethnographic Sketch*, featured "camp folk songs and dances" that, unlike all those associated with tsyganshchina, were certified by the theatre as ethnographically authentic.[118] Under Bugachevskii's lead, the theatre had devoted much of its first months to separating elements of "authentic" Gypsy art from those of dilettantes specializing in the "pseudo-Gypsy" genre. Bugachevskii had also initiated a competition for the creation of New Soviet Gypsy songs.[119] While these new, Soviet songs were not written in time for inclusion in the theatre's premiere, *An Ethnographic Sketch* nonetheless earned praise as "authentic Gypsy art in an absolutely fresh product."[120] The theatre's "ethnographic authenticity," after all, went beyond its choice in song and dance. According to Rom-Lebedev, Romen's actors "did not sit on chairs, but on the floor – as in the camps." They did not wear stylish silk evening gowns, but instead authentic "folk, camp" dress. Rather than the foxtrot, they performed the dances of their ancestors. The Soviet press agreed, hailing the performance as the triumphant rebirth of authentic Gypsy art.[121]

Although one otherwise sympathetic foreign observer remarked that *Gypsy Revue* could not "be considered as theatrical art," she did not deny that the theatre's debut was a success. It was certainly enough "to convince Narcompros [sic] that the Gypsies were a people instinctively fitted to express themselves through the medium of the theatre."[122] Its probationary period over, the Theatre Romen began to plan ahead. Narkompros approved the theatre's plans for its first tour to Romani kolkhozes and nomadic camps in the summer of 1932.[123] The theatre, meanwhile, commissioned Germano to write Romen's first full-length play. His Romani-language *Life on Wheels* premiered in Moscow in late 1931.

"Designed for an audience who required dramatic situations presented in the simplest possible manner," *Life on Wheels* dramatized the Soviet battle to sedentarize Roma and, in particular, to liquidate the "kulaks" of nomadic camps.[124] As in *Gypsies Yesterday and Today*, Germano's play featured the typecast Gypsy characters of the Soviet imagination: horse-dealers, fortune tellers, and kulak camp chiefs. Yet *Life on Wheels* focused on the changes introduced to nomadic life when the play's hero, Kalysh, returns to his native camp after many years as an entirely changed man. Liberated from a tsarist prison after the revolution, Kalysh resurfaces after having served in the Red Army and learned to read and write. He reintroduces himself as a Gypsy Union plenipotentiary and explains the Soviet promise of land and work for Gypsies. Kalysh rails against the exploitation of Gypsy women at the hands of their husbands and chides the audience for paying benighted Gypsies for their nonsensical fortunes and erotic, cabaret performances. It is time, he declares, "to show our backward people the healthy, cheerful path of Lenin."[125] The play ends with the youth of the nomadic camp rising up against their kulak exploiter and celebrating their Soviet rebirth. Their pitiable, unenlightened "life on wheels" is over. They begin "to live as people, not as wolves."[126]

Designed by the Jewish artist A.G. Tyshler, the play's backdrop was "formed from the colorful rags and tatters of the Gypsies."[127] Tyshler represented nomadic Romani life by hanging colourful tapestries, constructing a ragged-looking cart, and littering the stage with horseshoes and bridles. Male actors sported straggly, unkempt beards and women performed in "bright, fluttering skirts" and printed shawls. Performers and audiences alike celebrated the play's set and costumes as "truly national (*narodnoe*), Gypsy, poetic."[128] According to one foreign observer, *Life on Wheels* "was feeble dramatically, but so full of colourful songs and dances ... that its fame spread far beyond Moscow."[129] Only the rare theatre critic disapproved of the theatre's "excessive admiration (*liubovanie*) for exotica and ethnography."[130]

Scene from A.V. Germano's play *Life on Wheels*, at the Theatre Romen. From Ivan Rom-Lebedev, *Ot tsyganskogo khora k teatru "Romen"* (Moscow: Iskusstvo, 1990).

Spurred by their early success, Romen's actors and administrators hurried to expand the theatre's repertoire and to prove their ideological bona fides. Yet from the theatre's very beginnings, a critical tension threatened to undermine the ideological purpose of its performances of the birth of New Soviet Gypsies. While the theatre's plays were to represent how far Roma had progressed on the evolutionary timeline since the revolution and to stress how terrible life under the tsars had been, Soviet audiences seemed to delight most of all in staged scenes of Roma's "backward" prerevolutionary past. Even Rom-Lebedev admitted in his memoirs that at the premiere of *Gypsies Yesterday and Today*, audience members twice demanded an encore of the soloist whose task it was to perform the dread exploitation and philistinism of tsyganshchina. This same audience so enjoyed the artists' representations of prerevolutionary fortune tellers that it applauded gleefully during a scene that was intended not to be cheerfully amusing, but instead sombre and serious.[131] In expanding Romen's repertoire, the theatre's artistic director and budding Romani playwrights therefore needed to be mindful not to satisfy the impolitic cravings of their audience at the expense of the plays' political message, nor to stress ideology to the point that audiences lost interest. As its rare critic had pointed out in response to *Life on Wheels*, the theatre was already in danger of crossing the line from ethnographic authenticity to crude exotica – from Gypsy art to tsyganshchina.[132]

Romen's actors and administrators were reminded of this threat again in the summer of 1932 as the theatre made its first tour of provincial capitals and Romani kolkhozes. As in Moscow, the theatre performed not only *Gypsy Revue* and *Life on Wheels*, but also a new play written by Germano. Titled *Between Two Fires*, Germano's play portrayed the struggles of a nomadic Romani camp during the Russian Civil War. *Between Two Fires'* youthful characters rejected the tyranny of both their kulak chiefs and the White Guards and volunteered to serve in the Red Army.[133] Yet as had the theatre's earlier works, *Between Two Fires* interlaced lively dances and songs into its scenes of the camp's hunger, privation, and exploitation. This contradiction of both image and tone troubled at least one constituency during its tour of Smolensk Province – home of the empire's most celebrated Romani kolkhoz. Smolensk's Komsomol newspaper, *Bol'shevistskii molodniak*, criticized the performance, citing the perplexing dissonance of a play that featured starving and benighted Gypsies dancing cheerfully as would their exploiters – the Gypsy kulaks – upon return from a successful day at the horse

Ivan Rom-Lebedev, in costume for his leading role in A.V. Germano's play *Life on Wheels*, at the Theatre Romen. From Ivan Rom-Lebedev, *Ot tsyganskogo khora k teatru "Romen"* (Moscow: Iskusstvo, 1990).

market. "Only bourgeois poets represent Gypsies in this way," the paper charged.[134]

Artistic director Gol'dblat reasoned that a safe way to disabuse the theatre of any further charges of peddling ideologically harmful exotica was to reorient Romen's repertoire – at least in part – towards the classics. It was better, he reasoned, for the theatre to interpret the works of classic authors than to have its novice Soviet playwrights accused of reproducing the ideological sins of the nineteenth century's bourgeois literati.[135] Unsurprisingly, Gol'dblat's choice to reorient the theatre towards classic dramaturgy came at a time when Soviet theatres – not merely Romen – were slowly beginning to revive the classics.[136] In terms of ideological correctness, Lenin himself had justified such a turn with his claim, "only through an exact knowledge of culture, created through the entire development of mankind, can we create a proletarian culture."[137] Rom-Lebedev later reiterated Gol'dblat's argument that a return to the classics was essential to the enlightenment of the theatre's benighted actors. They needed, he explained, to be acquainted with the great works of Russian and foreign writers as a means of becoming better performers and cultured Soviet citizens.[138]

Gol'dblat confidently chose for the theatre to interpret Prosper Mérimée's *Carmen* – the famous tale of the eponymous and enterprising Gypsy harlot who seduces, corrupts, and ultimately ruins a naïve young Spanish corporal named Don José. Not everyone, however, shared in Gol'dblat's confidence. Although most observers conceded that *Carmen* bore at least thin relevance to Romen's purpose, critics both within and without the theatre worried that *Carmen* smacked of tsyganshchina's most harmful elements. They feared that *Carmen* would return Romen's performers to the dangerously erotic moaning of the "pseudo-Gypsy" genre. Moreover, they doubted that a bourgeois tale of a swindling Gypsy whore and her emasculated lover could enlighten Soviet audiences, let alone Romen's "backward" artists.

Glavrepertkom officials strongly criticized Romen's draft of the play in the spring of 1933. One censor noted that although it was clear that Romen was attempting an interpretation of *Carmen* that reflected the social inequalities of "petit bourgeois liberalism," it had nonetheless failed to make a compelling ideological justification for the play's inclusion in the theatre's repertoire. Glavrepertkom claimed that Romen's version – no less than Mérimée's original – portrayed Carmen and her fellow smuggler Gypsies as "petty, greedy little people (*liudishki*)." Another Glavrepertkom censor took this criticism still further, and refused to recommend the theatre's production of Mérimée's "bourgeois" classic. "Instead of a serious social analysis of the reasons that gave rise to the past everyday life of Gypsies and that made smugglers, thieves, and murderers of Gypsies," the censor complained, "shades of admiration for the peculiar 'exotica' of [Gypsies'] outmoded past ... dominate the play." Romen's version of *Carmen*, he continued, did not improve upon Mérimée's original preoccupation with the exotic or his disinterest in the "economic or political."[139]

Glavrepertkom's censors were not alone. Romani activists working outside the theatre also criticized Gol'dblat's choice of repertory. At a meeting held in December 1933, several activists complained that *Carmen* had distracted Romen's actors from the theatre's real purpose: the advancement of backward Gypsies. Pankov charged the theatre administration with caring only for profits. In choosing to produce *Carmen*, he claimed, the theatre's non-Romani administrators prioritized budgetary concerns and pandered to popular appeal at the expense of the theatre's mission to educate its actors and audiences. In his view, *Carmen* offered nothing in terms of Roma's potential enlightenment, but to the contrary stunted their development as cultured Soviet citizens. In its promotion of such dramaturgical tripe, Pankov argued, "the theatre makes a variety performer of the actor, and not a Soviet actor." Tokmakov agreed, condemning *Carmen* as a cheap representation of "banditry" that offered no enlightenment to "the Gypsy masses." Tokmakov maintained that the theatre was morally obliged to offer Soviet audiences not a new interpretation of *Carmen*, but instead inspiring representations of New Soviet Gypsies and "their productive achievements ... in the city and in the kolkhozes." Romani workers representing Tsygpishcheprom and Tsygkhimprom echoed these protests. One worker captured the essence of the Romani activists' collective complaint when he declared "the ideology" of *Carmen* to be "foreign to us."[140]

Leading up to the disputed play's premiere in April 1934, Gol'dblat defended his choice in the Soviet press. In his telling, *Carmen* offered an ethnographic portrait of an era in which "the Spanish merchant bourgeoisie exploited (*ispol'zovala*) the backwardness and ignorance (*temnoty*) of the Gypsy masses." The theatre's interpretation would unveil the everyday life of the nineteenth-century Gypsy and provide an analysis of class divisions among Gypsies themselves.[141] Finally, he promised *Carmen* as evidence of the professionalization of the theatre's performers. Romen's actors were now qualified to perform one of the world's great literary classics.[142] Behind closed doors, Gol'dblat also expressed hope that a production of a popular classic would help bankroll the financially crippled theatre.[143]

Romen's production of *Carmen* earned modest press reviews. A theatre critic at *Vecherniaia Moskva* praised Romen for correcting Mérimée's mistaken "bourgeois" assumption that Gypsies' historic predilection for banditry and deceit was a biological affliction instead of a socioeconomic one. Yet this same critic would not abide what in his view were the inferior talents of Romen's actors. "With the majority arriving on the stage straight from the nomadic camp," he explained, "they are still only amateurs who have not mastered the difficult art of theatre."[144] Likewise, while the newspaper *Sovetskoe iskusstvo* congratulated Romen on having graduated to classical dramaturgy, it also advised the theatre to strive for both greater ideological clarity in its revisions of classic works and for the further elevation of its actors' qualifications.[145]

Similarly unimpressed, officials at Narkompros and the All-Russian Theatre Society convened a meeting to debate the relative merits of Romen's production of *Carmen* in early May. As the opinions of Romen's "backward" actors continued to be of little interest to officials, Gol'dblat was called upon to defend the theatre's repertoire. Explaining Romen's "repertoire crisis," Gol'dblat connected what he regarded as Roma's impoverished literary history to their purported lack of history whatsoever.[146] "It is well known," he explained, "that Gypsies lack their own written history, their own chronicle of the past ... They have nothing and know nothing of their own past." It therefore made sense, Gol'dblat argued, for Romen to adapt those classics of European literature that related in any way to Gypsies' otherwise lost history. *Carmen* justified itself by dint of the fact that it was a reflection – however problematic – of Gypsy life in nineteenth-century Spain.[147]

Furthermore, Gol'dblat argued, it was Gypsies' all-encompassing lack – lack of history, lack of culture – that required Romen's actors to be introduced to the heights of world culture. While Bezliudskii, Germano, Rom-Lebedev, and others were attempting an impressive yet decidedly slow effort to establish a repertoire composed by Roma for Roma, their plays could not hold a flame to either the theatrical greats of the bourgeois nineteenth century or the cutting edge of Soviet dramaturgy. As in all else, he claimed, Gypsies were woefully behind in developing themselves as "true artists." Romen's actors could not hope to attract audiences – be they Gypsy or otherwise – if they did not perform compelling plays in a more skilled manner. *Carmen*, Gol'dblat claimed, was therefore intended as the troupe's graduation to a more cultivated theatrical experience.[148]

Finally, Gol'dblat defended the ideology of Romen's reinterpretation of a Gypsy whore and her fellow beguiling bandits, he argued, had missed the point. "The fundamental point of our production," Gol'dblat explained, "is precisely that Gypsies are not to blame for the fact that Carmen is who she is." Romen's version of *Carmen* improved upon the bourgeois original in that it clearly demonstrated that "the pursuit of thievery, smuggling, swindling, and deceit is not a national, racial, biological characteristic of Gypsies." Rather, Gypsies were forced into leading depraved lives because they were exploited by the capitalist ruling class and by their own kulak chiefs. The play, Gol'dblat argued, served to remind Soviet audiences that "under the dictatorship of the proletariat," a modern-day Carmen was "inconceivable."[149] In Gol'dblat's reckoning, the fact that the Theatre Romen existed at all, let alone performed a piece of classic dramaturgy, proved that backward Gypsies no longer needed to resort to banditry and prostitution – at least in the Soviet Union.

In the end, Narkompros officials acquiesced to Gol'dblat's position. They decided that although *Carmen* may not have been the most ideologically suitable choice for Romen's stage, the production represented a leap forward for backward Gypsy actors and audiences alike. While Narkompros officials conceded that the Theatre Romen had still not reconciled its urge to embrace Gypsies' "exotica" with its need "to show that Gypsies can be useful in our socialist construction," they were nonetheless content with the direction in which Gol'dblat was leading his benighted charges. If anything, Gol'dblat needed to accelerate the pace of the Theatre Romen's sovietization and merge it more seamlessly with the empire's general construction of Soviet culture. In the second half of the 1930s, this sovietization would ultimately entail not merely lessons in hygiene or theatre history, but also an embrace of the Russian language and of Russian literary classics. Even more so than Gol'dblat, Romen's actors would prove eager to oblige such demands. For them, what was at stake was not the "authenticity" of their purported national identity or the preservation of their ostensible Gypsiness, but instead their professional and social futures as Soviet actors.

From Natural Performers to Soviet Actors

Carmen was not the only aspect of the theatre's early work that aroused the suspicion of Soviet officials. As early as 1932, complaints grew about the slow pace at which the theatre's actors and repertoire were maturing. Critics accused the Theatre Romen of being alienated from the "Gypsy masses," and – worse still – of failing to prioritize even the cultural and political enlightenment of its own actors. While Narkompros proved willing to excuse the theatre's production of *Carmen*, it would not abide the persistent "backwardness" of its actors. Having received reports of the troupe's low literacy rates, slovenliness, drunkenness, internal scandals, and even "foreign element" machinations, Narkompros decided that Romen needed to be cleansed and rehabilitated before matters grew still worse.[150] In order to perform the Soviet enlightenment of backward Gypsies, it was decided, Romen's actors needed first to know and to live Soviet enlightenment themselves. This meant that the theatre needed to discipline and rigorously educate its actors. As one official explained, at least 2.5 hours of each working day needed to be devoted to the actors' education in order for Romen and its troupe ever to be taken seriously as "a real (*nastoiashchii*) theatre, as real actors."[151] In 1935, the theatre's lesson plans were revised to include courses not only on "the fundamentals of Leninism," but also on the art of acting, diction, movement, and makeup. Romen's actors studied music; the Russian and Romani languages; the history of Soviet, Russian, and Western European theatre; and arithmetic. Advanced students could elect to take specialized courses in dramaturgy, directing, composing, and stage design.[152]

This enlightenment regime was deemed all the more necessary in so far as Romen's actors spent their summers touring not only provincial capitals, but also Romani kolkhozes and nomadic camps. One of the theatre's primary responsibilities remained the education of Romani workers, kolkhozniks, and nomads. Because their targets were presumably even more "backward" than they, Romen's actors could not merely "demonstrate ... man's transformation," for their Romani audiences. They needed to be a living example of that transformation.[153] Thus entrusted with the task of modelling Soviet enlightenment, the Romen troupe travelled the Soviet Union "armed with textbooks and medicinal supplies."[154] They performed their didactic plays, reported to provincial and regional authorities on the need for greater cultural-enlightenment work among Roma, and organized parades to celebrate local Romani workers and kolkhozniks.[155]

Summer tours also served to satisfy the desire shared by many of Romen's actors to be recognized as "cultured." Visits to the kolkhozes reaffirmed their sense that they themselves were not the backward Gypsies they portrayed on stage, but instead sophisticated Soviet actors whose lives little resembled those of illiterate kolkhozniks and nomads. In his memoirs, Rom-Lebedev described such tours as a valuable opportunity for playwriting. "I loved those trips to the nomadic camps," he explained. "They gave me rich material for future plays. The faces, conversations, the entire camp atmosphere remained in my memory: the tents, bonfires, wagons, the mountains of pillows, the feather beds. The songs around the fire." Rom-Lebedev also admitted the visceral delight he and his fellow actors enjoyed in their appearances before backward Gypsies as respected New Soviet Men and Women. "Among the nomad Gypsies," he wrote, "the Muscovite Gypsies, the theatre actors – appeared no less than as 'research scholars,' and every one of their words was accepted by their fellow tribesmen as wise and incontestable. This filled them with pride."[156]

Back in Moscow, such feelings of self-satisfaction and pride were far more difficult to come by for Romen's actors. To the actors' dismay, no degree of maturation or self-improvement seemed sufficient to increase their worth in the eyes of both Narkompros officials and the theatre's non-Romani personnel. Beginning in 1935, they grew increasingly vocal about the pitiable lack of respect shown them – the most cultured of a remarkably "backward" people. Yet, more often than not, they demanded respect not as New Soviet Gypsies, but as Soviet actors who faithfully fulfilled an important civic duty.

In a series of impassioned denunciations, one actress complained about the abuse heaped upon the troupe by Gol'dblat. The theatre's artistic director, she reported, was known to unjustifiably threaten her colleagues with eviction and to refer to the actors not by name but as "swine," "scoundrels," and "parasites." Gol'dblat's verbal abuse, meanwhile, matched the general insult that she and her comrades received in the form of an inexcusably paltry salary. Morale suffered, she explained, because Romen's actors knew that they were paid not only far less than their colleagues in the capital's other theatres, but also only half as much as the theatre's most humble non-Romani administrator.[157]

Many of Romen's actors were similarly discontented and for a host of different reasons. One actor dispatched a letter of protest to a variety of bureaucratic departments in which he pointedly asked, "Is it normal that in the five years of the theatre's existence, not one Gypsy has been included in the theatre's administrative personnel?"[158] His anger, he explained, was inextinguishable. He had done all that was asked of him: he had graduated from a theatrical workers' faculty, agitated among nomads, and worked to strengthen Romani kolkhozes. In turn, he had been awarded an exceptionally meagre salary and two-bit roles at the theatre. In his view, the only reasonable option remaining was for him to resign from the theatre so that his considerable talents could be put to better use elsewhere. He was an actor, after all, and not a mere Gypsy stage prop.[159]

The troupe's collective resentments spilled forth in early 1935 during a particularly contentious meeting between Narkompros officials and Romen's actors. A commission appointed by Narkompros to inspect the theatre's daily affairs had recently concluded that Romen's actors lacked a basic understanding of hygiene and discipline. Their costumes, officials complained, were filthy and the slovenly state of their theatre was an affront to audiences. One official warned Romen's actors:

> Do not forget that you are artists. We do not demand of you that you wear stylish suits, but that you have clean blouses ... This trains your artistic taste, your artistic perception. You lack this ... Bear in mind ... that the struggle for cleanliness, for a clean toothbrush, clean shirt, clean pants, an ironed costume is necessary so that it is obvious to others that you are an artist, and not a chimney sweep.[160]

Another chimed in to lecture Romen's artists on their need to strive for purity in all aspects of their lives – not merely the physical, but also the moral and artistic. "The question of cleanliness," he continued, "is also a question of the education of a new person, of a new Gypsy actor." Romen's actors needed to understand that "cleanliness depends on culture."[161]

Clearly offended, many of the actors responded bitterly to the perceived unfairness of such remarks. If they worked in filthy conditions, they argued, it was not because they themselves were uncivilized, but rather because Narkompros undervalued them as actors and thus failed to invest in their struggling, marginalized theatre. Outraged, the actor Grushin explained that Romen's costumes looked filthy on stage because they were indeed ratty and worn out with overuse. The theatre's budget did not allow for the actors' costumes to be cleaned, let alone replaced with new ones. "We will struggle for cleanliness," Grushin challenged, "but give us the capability to do so."

Tattered costumes were but one of the actors' many problems. With a salary of 190 rubles a month, Grushin bitterly complained, Romen's actors could not afford decent apartments, food, clothing, and shoes – let alone "buy and change into a fresh pair of underwear." Romen's actors often fell ill, he argued, because their basement studio was filthy, unventilated, and dangerously cold. Others chimed in, adding that although the theatre boasted its own cafeteria, Romen's actors could not afford to buy meals there. As actors, one asserted, they worked day and night and all year long without rest. Another agreed, urging Narkompros to provide the Romen troupe a dacha retreat as it did for other theatres.[162]

While Narkompros would not accept the blame for Romen's actors walking around in "crumpled rags," it did agree with Gol'dblat that the theatre's desired maturity could all but be guaranteed by adding another healthy dose of classic literature to its repertoire. After all, Gol'dblat maintained, "*Carmen* proved, that we are capable … of a more complex dramaturgy." It was thanks to *Carmen* that "we now no longer need to prove that we are capable of more than singing and dancing, that we can speak too."[163]

In 1935 the theatre began to prepare for a stage production of Pushkin's poem, *The Gypsies*. In Gol'dblat's view, the play justified itself. Not only would it allow Romen's actors to gain further experience in performing a work of "greater quality," but also it would fulfil the theatre's task as "national in form, socialist in content." That the play was "national in form" was obvious – Pushkin's poem was titled *The Gypsies*. As for the socialist content of a poem written by a nineteenth-century Russian noble recently recast as a Soviet demigod, Gol'dblat explained:

> Of all the classic authors, Pushkin more objectively approached the description of Gypsy *byt* and the description of Gypsies. I speak of his objectivity from the point of view that he knew Gypsy *byt* well, studied it in depth, and described it objectively. Pushkin is practically alone in that, in describing Gypsies, he related to them as people, not as if toward a lower caste.

Whereas the Theatre Romen had been forced to defend the fictional Carmen and her coterie of Gypsy smugglers, Gol'dblat explained, Pushkin's poem demanded no such ideological exoneration. Rather, the theatre needed only to faithfully reproduce Pushkin's image of Gypsies "as people who have the right to live and occupy a place under the sun like all others, and not like some kind of lower caste."[164]

As with his defence of *Carmen*, Gol'dblat avoided speaking directly to one of his core convictions: that the Theatre Romen needed to stop worrying about educating a Gypsy audience that – in Moscow, at least – practically did not exist. Despite the theatre's initial purpose of enlightening "backward Gypsies," Gol'dblat and Romen's actors recognized that they, for the most part, were entertaining a cosmopolitan, Soviet audience that neither understood the Romani language nor delighted in tales of how the revolution had changed Roma's lives. Gol'dblat and Romen's actors agreed on at least one thing: Romen needed to be transformed into a respected Soviet theatre – one that audiences flocked to in order to be entertained, not lectured at in an incomprehensible tongue.[165] For Gol'dblat, an embrace of spectacle instead of naïve propaganda promised the theatre's solvency. For Romen's actors, it promised Soviet respectability and perhaps, someday, even prestige.

Gol'dblat and Romen's actors also generally agreed on one of the theatre's thorniest issues: the choice between performing in the Romani or the Russian language. Up until now, the theatre had performed almost exclusively in Romani and Narkompros officials saw no reason for Romen, the Soviet Union's national Gypsy theatre, to transition to the Russian language. Gol'dblat attempted to persuade Narkompros that the theatre's adherence to the Romani language impeded the theatre's growth rather than enhanced its national character. The language was deficient, he argued, in so far as no one dialect had yet won out as the common national language. Among the theatre's troupe, actors spoke in and argued over the various dialects. On tour, they catered to Roma who spoke still different dialects. In his view, Romen's stage had been reduced to a "Babylonian chaos" that farcically confused both Russian- and Romani-speaking audiences.[166]

When Gol'dblat's argumentation failed to sway Narkompros officials, several Roma interjected with a frank admission of the theatre's real problem with performing in Romani: many of the theatre's actors were literate in Russian, not in Romani. The problem was not the supposed "backwardness" of the Romani-language, but that many of the theatre's actors were not "Gypsy" or "backward" enough to speak it fluently. As Tokmakov explained, "They cannot pronounce Gypsy words, they do not know how to pronounce them."[167] Thus, the theatre's reliance on the Romani language only served to undermine its claims of ethnographic authenticity.

Narkompros insisted that the Theatre Romen do its part to establish Romani as a "literary language" and maintain its Romani-language scripts as "national colour." The theatre's task remained "to preserve [Gypsies'] authentic, national distinctiveness, authentic national form."[168] Yet as far as "authenticity" and "national colour" went, at least one of Romen's actors failed to recognize the theatre's purported national form or content as anything but an elaborate scheme of fictions. When one Narkompros official spoke of Gypsies' "national colour" and "national sound," this actor objected forthright. "There is no such colouring," he insisted. "Gypsies sing as all people do."[169] His insightful protest, however, failed to elicit even the slightest attention, let alone censure. The show was to go on undisturbed. Narkompros stalwartly demanded from Romen's actors not only socialist content, but also national form – exotic and essential.

Romen premiered its production of Pushkin's *The Gypsies* in 1936.[170] Though the theatre's actors performed in Romani, a Russian-speaking narrator complemented them. This linguistic compromise did not spare the play its fate as a critical flop. The Soviet press was not bothered by the production's perpetuation of the image of "the Gypsy woman" as unbridled sexuality incarnate, nor did it pay much attention to Gol'dblat's insistence that the play artfully presented "the battle of two worldviews" – the "egotistical individualism" of Aleko and the "spiritual kindness" of Zemfira's camp. Rather, the press singled out the play's scene and costume design as betraying "Pushkin's simplicity and folklore" and failing to represent "Gypsies' authentic way of life (*byt*)." Describing the staging of the play as "schematic" and "simplified," the journal *Revoliutsiia i natsional'nosti* complained, "The nomadic Gypsy camp is not shown as it exists in reality."[171]

Under a barrage of criticism, Gol'dblat resigned as the theatre's artistic director in late 1936. Meanwhile, the All-Union Committee for Artistic Affairs seriously contemplated the advantages of closing the Theatre Romen's doors for good.[172] The atmosphere at the theatre turned poisonous as Romen's actors and administrators struggled to cope with the theatre's consistently failing reviews and the threat of its closure.[173] Neither the productions of plays written by novice Romani playwrights nor the adaptations of "Gypsy-themed" classics seemed to satisfy audiences or critics. Complicating matters still further, Narkompros could not find a suitable replacement for Gol'dblat. New directors were appointed and removed in quick succession, leading one of Romen's actors to comment bitterly, "We change directors here as frequently as I bartered horses in my past."[174] The theatre verged on collapse.[175]

In 1937, Narkompros decided to bring Russian culture in all its glory to the Theatre Romen in the form of a new artistic director, M.M. Ianshin. A student of Stanislavskii, a star at the prestigious Moscow Art Theatre (MKhAT), and the husband of the popular Romen actress Lialia Chernaia (Kiseleva), Ianshin was chosen by Narkompros to inject MKhAT's superior artistry into the struggling Gypsy Theatre. With his arrival, Romen's actors recognized that their "childish" years were over. In their eyes, Ianshin and MKhAT symbolized a level of talent and prestige that, for them, was seemingly "unattainable." Rom-Lebedev recalled that he and his fellow actors were awed by Ianshin's very presence and incredulous that a man of such talent would "sit next to us and attempt to persuade us that we [were] gifted people … with innate theatrical talent." Yet there he was, convincing Romen's actors that they, too, could successfully perform the plays of Tolstoy, Shakespeare, and other greats – that they, too, could master their craft if they studied and spent their "whole lives working on themselves." Soon, Rom-Leb-edev explained, he and his fellow actors began to respect themselves as professional actors. They began to imagine Romen as a filial of MKhAT, the Soviet Union's most celebrated theatre.[176]

Ianshin has long been remembered in the history of the Theatre Ro-men as its inimitable redeemer and saviour.[177] He is credited with bring-ing the stability and sophistication that the theatre had craved since its establishment, and with transforming Romen into a theatre worthy of producing the classics. Under Ianshin's lead, "the theatre began more and more to transcend the limits of a narrowly-national subject matter" and to approach the heights of "MKhAT culture."[178] As for Ianshin him-self, he saw his task as threefold: to train actors, not Gypsies; to trans-form Romen from a dance-and-song training ground of amateurs into a bona fide theatre of classical dramaturgy; and to release the Theatre Romen from the marginalization wrought by its dependence on the Ro-mani language.[179] Ianshin's style of sovietizing Romen and its actors, in other words, mirrored the revised style of Soviet nationality policy in the late 1930s. Especially for "small peoples" such as Roma, "national in form" was increasingly less a policy than a tired slogan, while social-ist content fused a lionized Russian culture to Soviet values.[180]

In reforming the theatre, Ianshin began by striking both *Carmen* and *The Gypsies* from Romen's repertoire. While *Carmen* was shelved indefi-nitely, Ianshin decided that Romen's production of *The Gypsies* could still be salvaged. Under his direction, a revised version of *The Gypsies* premiered at Romen in 1938 and marked a "turning point in the life of the theatre."[181] Performed almost entirely in the Russian language, Ianshin's version was hailed by the Soviet press as "authentic, real art." Romen's actors, it was decided, had finally begun to mature. The in-fluence of MKhAT was obvious, the newspaper *Sovetskoe iskusstvo* de-clared, as Romen had managed to create "not merely a Gypsy, but a simultaneously Gypsy and Pushkinesque performance."[182]

Ianshin's leadership was credited with having finally led the Theatre Romen to embody the dictum, "national in form, socialist in content" – at least in its revised, late-1930s variant. In other words, Romen's actors sang and danced in the ostensible Gypsy style, but spoke the immortal words of Russia's greatest poet in their Russian-language original. The actors' "national colour" was interpreted in their movements and cos-tumes while their new acting skills were borrowed and learned from Russian masters. The Romani language, meanwhile, was reserved solely for a brief introductory sketch of nomadic camp life – a sketch that could not be found in Pushkin's hallowed text. Once the Russian Aleko stepped onto the proscenium, he breathed Pushkin into the theatre and brought his superior language with him.[183]

What no one mentioned, however, was that Pushkin's "poetic image of Zemfira" had triumphantly returned Romen's actors to performing Russian favourites for Russian audiences. Though tsyganshchina had long been declared dead, Romen's actors were now performing a sacred, Pushkin-authored image of Gypsies as simultaneously and tantalizingly hot-tempered, exotic, innocent, uncivilized, freedom loving, and licentious. In the "mature" Soviet worldview, performance of this type of Gypsiness was not debauchery, but authentic art. It was not pseudo-Gypsy or even Gypsy, but Soviet.

It was thus accepted that culture had finally arrived at the Theatre Romen in the late 1930s, and that Ianshin had led Romen's actors out from the dark alley of backwardness and amateurism. As Germano explained, Romen's actors could now "display their [artistic] skill without an allowance for 'nationality.' Finally, it was time for the troupe to debunk the accepted opinion that the Gypsy theatre begins and ends with dances and songs."[184] Romen's actors had proven themselves not as Gypsies, but as authentic actors who could perform the classics with as much skill and sophistication as they could perform Gypsiness. Their artistic skill owed not to their nationality, but rather to their "raised cultural level" as Soviet citizens. If the actors had sovietized no one else with their shifting performance of Gypsiness, they had at least sovietized themselves.

From Prostitutes to People's Artists of the Soviet Union

Ianshin directed the artistic life of the Theatre Romen for five years. Following the success of his production of *The Gypsies*, Ianshin continued to revise the theatre's repertoire to include still other respected classics. On the eve of World War II, Romen's actors performed a few of the dramatic works penned by their own resident Romani playwright, Rom-Lebedev, but devoted most of their energies to new productions of Maxim Gorky's *Makar Chudra* and Federico García Lorca's *Blood Wedding*. The logic behind this reorientation was simple: the theatre needed to appeal to audiences beyond Roma and to all Soviet peoples. As Nikolai Slichenko, Romen's contemporary artistic director, would later explain, "This means that the problems that we present in our performances must be general ones that concern the widest circle of spectators. Those, for example, that are about man's purpose, about good and evil, about ethical and moral problems, about feelings of duty and responsibility."[185] Such was the content of not one national culture, but of the socialist culture shared by all Soviet peoples. Thus, Romen's actors did not need to limit themselves to performing Gypsy tropes and could only hurt themselves by speaking in Romani. Their primary task was to inflect their "national colour" into performances of works that presented universal themes and situations in the Soviet *lingua franca*. In time, it was even decided that one's passport nationality need not be Gypsy in order to perform Gypsiness or to represent Gypsies' supposed national colour on Romen's stage.[186]

None of these developments, however, should surprise. They were rooted quite firmly in the prerevolutionary soil of Russia's Romani choirs no less than of Bolshevik nationality policy. By the time of the October Revolution, entire families of Romani performers had been in the business of representing a well-crafted Gypsiness that delighted audiences seeking not merely entertainment, but also titillation. Romen's founders had learned both from their parents and from their own personal experience that Gypsiness was an "exotic" commodity for which Russian audiences hungered. A lucrative business indeed, performing Gypsiness afforded fur coats, fine china, and elite pedigree for Romani performers in the tsarist *fin de siècle*, just as it ultimately would provide an education, Moscow apartments, and honorary titles for Romen's artists in the Soviet Union.

In the performances of prerevolutionary Gypsy choirs, as in those of the Theatre Romen, Gypsiness served Roma as a national form in the most ideal, Soviet sense – that is, an elastic, colourful hollow that could be worn as if a costume, altered if need be, but, most importantly, hung up or even discarded at the end of the day. Romen's actors defined themselves not by the costumes they wore or the dances they performed, but by the very fact that they laboured on stage, entertained and educated audiences, and interpreted classics both old and new. For them, the search for ethnographic authenticity was not about defining who they or anyone else were as Gypsies, but about furthering their careers. As one of Romen's actors so aptly put it in 1935: "Gypsies sing as all people do." It was their job to sing, dance, dress, and behave on stage as people imagined Gypsies must or ought. It was precisely their performance of Gypsy tropes that evidenced their status as integrated Soviet citizens, if not yet esteemed actors.

Thus, when the Theatre Romen's curtains habitually fell and its lights dimmed, Romen's actors washed off the makeup, changed their clothes, and went about living as Soviet citizens who hoped to find their way into Moscow's most revered theatrical circles. In the summer, they arrived at Romani kolkhozes and nomadic camps with morality tales and hygiene lessons, but departed with the delightful knowledge that they were not one of those "backward Gypsies" whom they portrayed, caricatured, and invented on stage. They enjoyed the confidence that they were instead enlightened Soviet citizens waging battle with backwardness and forging a socialist culture that, like they were, was looking and sounding more and more "Russian."

As for the Theatre Romen, it ultimately withstood the test of time as an unparalleled testament to early Soviet thinking not only about Gypsies, but also about nationality in the broadest sense. Established with the express purpose of eradicating the "bourgeois decadence" of so-called tsyganshchina and replacing it with didactic folk art, the theatre throughout the 1930s served as the site of multiple reimaginings of Gypsiness as ethnographically authentic and ideologically appropriate Soviet entertainment. Long after its creation in 1930, Romen persisted as a mobilizer of Soviet ideology and a professional home for Romani actors increasingly marginalized within Moscow's wider theatrical milieu.[187] Not least of all, Romen persisted as the dependable, state-sponsored site of performances of Gypsies as fiery, excitable, tantalizing lovers of liberty – poetic, peculiar, yet capable of Soviet civilization.

Moscow's Theatre Romen exemplifies the spirit of Soviet nationality policy incarnated: national in form, socialist in content. When the Bolsheviks mandated the importance of nationality in the lives of non-Russian peoples, they facilitated both the fetishization of "authentic" national cultures as well as minority peoples' Soviet self-fashioning. In practice, Soviet nationality policy undoubtedly and crudely essentialized "national" cultures. Yet it also potentially empowered minority peoples themselves to profitably engage in the performance of both nationality and Soviet citizenship. For decades after its inception, the Theatre Romen birthed New Soviet Gypsies as reliably as it authenticated old Gypsy stereotypes.

Epilogue and Conclusion
"Am I a Gypsy or Not a Gypsy?":
Nationality and the Performance
of Soviet Selfhood

"Am I a Gypsy or not a Gypsy?" This is the question that Aleksandr Germano (1893–1955), the Soviet Union's most celebrated Gypsy writer, posed in a 1952 autobiography composed in fulfilment of his duties as a member of the Union of Soviet Writers.[1] When taken at face value, the question is surprising and puzzling. When considered in light of the history of Roma's engagement of the early Soviet nationality regime, however, the question is instead seemingly banal. Yet the question remains. Was Germano a Gypsy? As I will show, an examination of a series of Germano's autobiographic statements, written throughout his career as a Soviet writer, offers a clear answer to the question of Germano's nationality. Yet Germano's autobiographies also serve as a cipher for understanding how and why Germano's performance of nationality enabled his Soviet self-fashioning. Ultimately, Germano's evolving story of self stands as testament to the intended logic of early Soviet nationality policy as much as to one man's exemplary fulfilment of that assimilationist logic. Germano's autobiographies thus uniquely encapsulate minority people's creative capacity to self-actualize as Soviet citizens through their productive mobilization of a nationality regime that itself evolved in the early decades of the Soviet Union.

In 1952, an aging Germano sat down to the unremarkable task of completing a short questionnaire and composing an autobiography for his personnel file. He obligingly answered questions about his nationality, social origins, literary work, language proficiencies, party status, and Red Army service. Germano had performed this same routine many times previously. As required of him by the Soviet state throughout his adult lifetime, he dutifully composed both long and short versions of his life story for bureaucratic consumption.[2] As his writing career developed, Germano scrupulously updated his vita and tailored his autobiography to reflect the ideological exigencies of changing times. In 1952, however, he made one significant edit to his autobiography. His status as the Soviet Union's leading Gypsy writer notwithstanding, Germano disavowed his Gypsy nationality and instead declared himself a Russian.[3] Germano's 1952 autobiography, as well as those that preceded it, explains not only *why* he did so, but also *how* he was able to revise his nationality.

Despite its bureaucratic provenance, Germano's 1952 narrative is a remarkably compelling and inspiring tale of a provincial upstart who became a celebrated Soviet writer. It is the story of an orphaned proletarian son who became the prophetic transmitter of Soviet light to the empire's benighted Gypsies. Germano is the self-made man whose triumph became possible only thanks to the October Revolution. In 1952, he is the aging New Soviet Man. Naturally, he is Russian.

Born in 1893 in Orel, Germano described himself in his 1952 autobiography as the son of a worker father and an illiterate mother. The youngest of five children, Germano's early years were filled with sorrowful loss and crushing poverty. His father died of pneumonia while Germano was still in his mother's womb. Pregnant, uneducated, and penniless, Germano's mother sought factory work. Germano revealed little else about either parent. While mentioning that his mother lived until 1919, he credited his older sister with caring for him and ensuring his education. Looking back, Germano envisioned himself as a young boy with a passion for storytelling. Otherwise, his childhood – much like his parents – is a narrative blur.[4]

For Germano, life began anew with his enlistment in the Red Army in 1919. He quickly adapted his love of literature to his commitment to Bolshevik victory in the Civil War. In service of the army's cultural-enlightenment mission, he led political discussions and literary evenings for soldiers and civilians. Upon demobilization in 1921, Germano wrote, "I devoted myself completely to literary work." He published widely in his hometown press, volunteered at Orel's Turgenev Museum, and led the city's first workers' and soldiers' literary circle. In 1921, his satirical one-act play, *In Some Bureaucratic Office*, premiered at the Orel Metropolitan Theatre. A professional triumph for the young writer, the play was often staged locally in subsequent years. Spurred by his success, Germano devoted still more time to writing.[5]

Soon convinced that he and his literary talent had outgrown provincial Orel, Germano relocated to Moscow in 1926 with the hope of establishing himself as a great proletarian writer and Soviet literary icon. In 1952, however, he was able to recognize – with some amusement – the naiveté of his youth. "In May of 1926," Germano recalled, "I, 'a provincial classicist,' not knowing severe criticism, headed to Moscow full of high hopes … and with a dozen new and newly revised short stories in my briefcase." Moscow's editors, however, were not interested in his "provincial" talent. Germano arrived in the Soviet capital only to have his professional dreams crushed. Without money, housing, or even a reasonable chance of fulfilling his professional dreams, Germano nonetheless refused to return to Orel and instead accepted menial work in a publishing office. His pittance of a wage afforded him a room in the capital and nourished his improbable literary ambitions.[6]

Pockets empty, Germano relentlessly sought work as a writer until one day his life took a fateful turn. In 1926, Germano vaguely recalled, "Somehow someone among the Muscovites suggested that I apply to the All-Russian Gypsy Union, where there was a need for a cultural worker and organizer of a publication in the Gypsy language." Why this "someone" approached Germano "somehow" with the suggestion that he, *a Russian*, begin a career in Gypsy-language publishing at the All-Russian Gypsy Union is a question that Germano conspicuously left unanswered in his 1952 autobiography. He revealed only that he accepted an editorial position at the Gypsy Union in June of 1926 and immediately immersed himself in serving "an unlettered people" as "an organizer in every regard."

In pursuit of the Gypsy Union's enlightenment work, Germano meticulously researched Roma's language, history, and culture. Aiding the effort to construct an alphabet for the Romani language, Germano scoured the Lenin Library for any mention of Roma in the press and scholarly literature of the recent and distant past. For three years, he searched for clues on "their economy, everyday life, customs, survivals, and beliefs" while compiling his *Bibliography of Gypsies* – a reference work later published by Central Publishing in 1930. Yet Germano soon decided that the library offered him only a superficial understanding of Romani language and culture. Therefore, Germano explains, "In addition to the collection and study of published sources, I undertook the collection of the nomads' folklore and the study of the Gypsy language by ear. Reincarnated as the original 'Aleko,' I spent weeks in the camps. All of this led to my fluent mastering of the language and I began to write poetry and prose in Gypsy." It was thus only as a result of his going out to the camps to experience Gypsiness first-hand that

Germano "became well acquainted with the life and aspirations of the nomadic Gypsies and the parasitism (tsyganshchina) of the capital's choir Gypsies."[7]

The narrative manoeuvre in this passage is subtle, yet powerful in its intended effect. Germano casts himself as Pushkin's Aleko – the Russian who, disenchanted with society, seeks haven in the wild and freedom-loving nomadic Gypsy camp. Germano identifies with Aleko, however, not because he shares with this literary character a sense of societal alienation or even a romantic desire to experience what Pushkin called the Gypsies' "threadbare freedom of the road."[8] Instead, Germano casts himself as Aleko in an act of purposeful, narrative distancing. As Aleko, he is not a Gypsy, but an intrusive outsider in the Gypsies' strange world. He is a Russian.

Fearing that his sympathy with Aleko would not suffice to clarify his position as a Russian civilizer and ethnographer of Gypsies, Germano obviated any potential doubts about his own nationality. Writing as if in conversation with his readers, he insisted: "I have dwelled on this explanation so that in the future there will not be the baffled questions: am I a Gypsy or not a Gypsy? I comprehended the language (I know the northern and southern dialects) and the Gypsy soul because otherwise I would not have been able to carry out political-enlightenment work among the nomads."[9] Here again, Germano distanced himself from "the nomads" whose "Gypsy soul" became available and legible to him only once he mastered their *foreign* tongue. He emphatically storied himself as a stranger bringing enlightenment to a strange people whose consciousness he could not penetrate or change by means of his own Russian language. Germano insisted that he studied Gypsies, worked to transform them, and spoke their language, but was not one of them.

Yet, according to his own 1952 autobiography, Germano nonetheless took great pride in his professional and civic efforts to raise Gypsies' cultural level and assimilate them to Sovietism. Germano's work at the Gypsy Union, after all, propelled him to undergo a range of tasks that married his literary ambitions to his duties as a socially useful citizen. He helped create a Cyrillic-based Romani alphabet, edited the world's first Romani-language journal, and printed his stories in the pages of *Romany zoria* and *Nevo drom*. While this work aided backward Gypsies on their path to Soviet redemption, it also allowed Germano to ingratiate himself in Moscow's widening literary circles. By the end of 1928, Germano had taken his seat as secretary of the "Worker's Spring" literary circle and advanced to membership in the All-Union Society of Proletarian Writers ("Kuznitsa"). These affiliations allowed him to study literary theory – especially the tenets of socialist realism – from revered Soviet authors such as F.V. Gladkov. His networking and studying helped Germano to publish in the Soviet press an array of Russian-language articles and short stories on the theme of Gypsies' cultural revolution. This early work earned him Maxim Gorky's laconic praise – "interesting and new" – and even a first-place literary prize for one of his Russian-language stories on Soviet efforts to sedentarize Romani nomads.[10]

In 1929, Germano spearheaded the creation of a national Romani literature, organizing a minority section of the All-Union Society of Proletarian Writers named "Word of the Gypsies." He mentored a group of young Romani writers while distinguishing himself as a prolific and versatile author. He wrote and edited Romani-language textbooks, journals, and literary almanacs. As a combatant of so-called tsyganshchina and a founder of the Theatre Romen, Germano authored plays and songs for the new troupe. In addition to composing original prose and poetry in both Romani and Russian, Germano also spent the 1930s producing Romani-language translations of Russian texts that ranged from the lyrics of the *Internationale* to Pushkin's *Mozart and Salieri*. His work appeared in a number of anthologies celebrating the literary works of "the peoples of the USSR."[11] In 1934, the Union of Soviet Writers welcomed Germano into its respected ranks.

Throughout the period of socialist construction, Germano served the empire's Roma with more than his pen. His contributions to Roma's sovietization amounted to a lengthy laundry list of fulfilled duties. "As a representative of the Gypsy press," Germano explained, "I actively participated in work among toiling Gypsies." He nestled into the Soviet bureaucracy as he aided the organization of Romani collective farms, schools, and industrial cooperatives. At Moscow's Gypsy Club, Germano performed readings and offered members advice on leading new, Soviet lives. He reached out to help the nomads about whom he so often wrote in his stories. "In the aim of becoming personally acquainted on the local level with the conditions and needs of Gypsies who settled on land and in order to carry out political-enlightenment work among them," Germano wrote, "I time and again traveled to the periphery" – that is, to the nascent Romani collective farms. Saving the empire's "backward Gypsies" was not merely the Party's mission, but also Germano's personal crusade. As his words testify, Germano pursued this mission not as a Gypsy, but as a "representative of the Gypsy press."[12]

The Great Patriotic War, however, necessarily interrupted Germano's civilizing mission. During the war's bleakest days, Germano served the Soviet Information Bureau, composed a poetry cycle on Romani partisans, recited his stories and poems to injured soldiers and civilians, and read letters from the front on the radio. Though crippled by both bouts of writer's block and dwindling opportunities to publish, Germano continued to write throughout the war – about the war itself, about Roma in Russian literature, and about the Romani language.[13]

Although the Soviet Union recovered from the war, Germano's vita reveals that his publication record did not. While Germano did not comment directly on his own post-war diminishing literary returns, the final paragraphs of Germano's 1952 autobiography read superficially as a simple enumeration of works written for the Soviet public, but fated for the author's desk drawer. Read another way, Germano's list of his own post-war writings provides subtle commentary on the author's willingness and perceived need to adapt to changing times. Emerging from the war hopeful that his Russian-language writings on Soviet Roma would interest his fellow citizens, Germano worked on three manuscripts between 1945 and 1948: *Fascism and Gypsies during the Patriotic War, A Short History of Soviet Gypsies*, and *A Short History of the State Gypsy Theatre*. When these were not accepted for publication, Germano changed course. He wrote *A History of Orel Province* and collaborated on a collection of essays devoted to the history of Orel's Party organizations.[14] When it became obvious to him that Gypsies – a nontitular nationality that had long bewildered Soviet bureaucrats – were no longer even a theoretical state priority, Germano shrewdly repositioned himself as an author whose work reflected the post-war precedence of Russia, Russians, and Russianness.

Germano's autobiography also evidences his post-war refashioning of his non-professional life. Although Germano had earlier worked to transform "backward Gypsies" into enlightened workers and farmers, he endeavoured after the war to transform himself into a more knowledgeable Soviet citizen. In the absence of any public need for him to carry out further political-enlightenment work among Roma, Germano attended lectures organized by the Union of Soviet Writers on Bolshevism and socialist realism. Earlier, Germano's work educating Roma had served as his primary means of Soviet self-fashioning. After the war, Germano worked to perfect his Soviet self by trading his role as teacher of Sovietism for that of student.

At the time he wrote his 1952 autobiography, Germano could boast a life made full by his dedicated participation in the construction of Soviet socialism. He could also delight in having fulfilled his cherished dream of becoming a respected Soviet writer. Looking back on his impoverished childhood, provincial origins, and rough start in Moscow, Germano recognized the fulfilment of his professional goal as a tremendous accomplishment. In the last two decades of his life, Germano thus "carefully preserved" his prized Union of Soviet Writers membership card as a precious symbol of his achievement.[15]

Following his death in 1955, the city of Orel memorialized Germano as an accomplished native son. The Museum of Orel Writers archived many of his unpublished writings and honoured Germano alongside Turgenev, Bunin, and others.[16] His colleagues in both Orel and Moscow, meanwhile, sought to immortalize Germano as the Soviet Union's premier Gypsy writer. In 1960 and 1962, they translated Germano's Romani-language short stories into Russian and published his work in two separate anthologies. They honoured Germano not only as a pioneer of "Soviet Gypsy literature," but also as a "Russian by upbringing and education (*russkii chelovek po vospitaniiu i obrazovaniiu*)" who "devoted a large part of his work to the cause of developing and uplifting" a people that was "akin to him by birth."[17]

Germano thus posthumously entered the pantheon of Soviet literature not precisely as he had defined himself in his 1952 Union of Soviet Writers autobiography. Whereas Germano had then declared himself a Russian and explained himself as a "reincarnated Aleko," his biographers conceded that he was Russian only by dint of his "upbringing and education." They pointedly detailed the fact that Germano was the son of immigrants – a Czech father and a "Moravian Gypsy" mother.[18]

Countless times in his adult life, Germano encountered the proverbial Soviet question – Who are you by nationality? Taken as a whole, Germano's self-authored paper trail reveals that he consistently approached this question as an opportunity to define but also to revise his narrative of his own malleable, Soviet self. Ultimately, however, his varying responses to the question – silence, creative elision, Gypsy, and Russian – reveal less about Germano than they do about the critical role nationality played in the forging of Soviet subjects in both the interwar and post-war periods. They show the flexibility of Soviet nationality policy in its enabling of minority peoples to transform themselves, in both word and deed, into integrated, conscious Soviet citizens.

Germano's refusal to identify himself as a Gypsy in his 1952 autobiography was not without precedent. In an autobiography commissioned by a provincial publisher in 1925, Germano wrote about his lineage extensively without once employing the term "Gypsy." His parents, he revealed, were "foreigners who had wandered over to Russia from Austria-Hungary" as they "roamed" with a travelling camp of their metalworker and musician relatives. "Later, speaking broken Russian, they dispersed and settled in the towns of today's USSR."[19] Admitting disinterest in his own family tree, Germano laconically traced his father to a village near Prague. He provided a much less clear account of his mother's origins, however. "My mother did not sit still anywhere," Germano wrote. "She loved to travel and it was because of her that my father changed his occupation. They sold off their household junk and took aimlessly to the road."[20]

Germano's veiled references to his Romani heritage, however, morphed into full-fledged assertions of his own Gypsy nationality only once he joined the Gypsy Union. The moment at which Germano first heard that the Gypsy Union needed an organizer whose credentials included not only publishing experience but also Romani ancestors proved to be one of his life's most instructive and defining. From there, Gypsiness served as his springboard to fulfilling a professional goal that had once seemed unattainable. Germano gained work as a journal editor, ready outlets for the publication of his writings, and the cachet required for him to associate with esteemed Soviet writers. Thus, upon acceptance to the All-Union Society of Proletarian Writers as a minority littérateur in 1928, Germano did more than openly identify as a Gypsy.[21] Claiming the ultimate in purported Gypsy authenticity, Germano noted in his application that as a child he had "sometimes wandered."[22] Further underscoring the political and social value that he now attached to his minority status, he soon traded the surname officially given to him at birth, German, for its Romani equivalent, Germano. Reincarnated as a Gypsy, he embraced nationality as his guarantee of Soviet success.

In his 1934 application to the Union of Soviet Writers, Germano further revised his autobiography. Here, he claimed that his writing career began in 1926 – that is, "from the moment of the emergence of the written Gypsy language." In this retelling, Germano's professional life and socially useful work began only after he announced himself a Gypsy and joined the Gypsy Union. Although in previous statements Germano had proudly itemized his relatively modest literary accomplishments in Orel, he now struck them from his vita as if only the creations of his reborn Gypsy self mattered. In fact, Germano almost completely edited his Russian-language writings from his self-authored record in his 1934 narrative vita. Excepting his *Bibliography of Gypsies*, Germano's 1934 vita enumerated merely his Romani-language plays, poetry, stories, textbooks, and translations of various "Marxist classics."[23] Germano rendered his Russian-language publications irrelevant – a choice that would be inexplicable outside the context of Soviet nationality policy. His application represents Germano's understanding that his worthiness of membership to the Union of Soviet Writers would be judged against his credentials not simply as a writer, but as a Gypsy writer specifically. Demonstrating a fine appreciation for the Soviet nationality regime, Germano underscored that he was, first and foremost, a Gypsy writer speaking to Gypsy readers "exclusively in the Gypsy language."[24]

Germano's embrace of Gypsy nationality ultimately survived the termination of Romani-language publishing in 1938. In the spring of 1940, for example, Germano convened his fellow Romani authors under the auspices of the Union of Soviet Writers. Openly pining for the days when the state had meagrely supported their literary efforts, Germano praised his Romani colleagues for helping benighted Gypsies adapt to a settled, literate, Soviet way of life. "Gypsy writers," he maintained, "participated in the reforging of those ... who had been isolated from organized social life." Looking ahead with the hope that he and his fellow Romani writers could revive their aborted national literature, Germano agreed to organize and lead a new Gypsy section of the Union of Soviet Writers. Recognizing that his cohort's future work would necessarily be printed in Russian instead of in Romani, Germano optimistically promised that this new Russian-language Romani literature would prove a "revelation for the Soviet reader."[25]

Though the Nazi invasion interrupted his literary plans, Germano nurtured them throughout the war. In an autobiography composed after the war, Germano reiterated his long-standing commitment to the development of a Romani national literature. Reflecting on the start of his career in 1926, Germano recalled, "I gave myself completely to work among the backward Gypsy masses, and from that time forward I, as a Gypsy writer, have exclusively written in the Gypsy language. I am one of the founders of the world's only Gypsy script and an organizer of the Gypsy press. I established a core of Gypsy poets and writers." In the end, he declared, "I am happy and proud that, thanks to our party and Soviet power, I took the initiative and leading role in developing the new literature of Soviet Gypsies."[26]

Germano's shifting responses to his own personal "national question" can be understood only within the context of the evolution of the Soviet Union's ideology in general, and of its nationality policy in particular. In the 1920s, Germano and his fellow Romani activists awakened to the opportunities made available to them as representatives of a so-called "backward" nationality. By the dawn of World War II, they had seen many of those same opportunities wither and disappear. Germano's cumulative autobiographic record not only reflects this trajectory, but also provides a telescopic view of the changing priorities of the Soviet state and thus of its Romani citizens. While his development as a Soviet citizen through socially useful work remained a constant focus of Germano's autobiographies, his nationality could be and was revised. Nationality, however, was never merely incidental to the Soviet self whom Germano narrated and actively nurtured throughout his life. Rather, nationality was – as dictated by the Soviet state – a central ingredient of his Soviet subjectivity. In a variety of creative ways, Germano performed nationality as a means of achieving Sovietness. Time and again, Germano met the Soviet state's demand that he define himself in universal terms as a Soviet citizen, but also as a member of a distinctive nationality. Germano's own autobiographic statements, meanwhile, are the key to understanding why Germano variously elided, emphasized, and edited his Gypsy self in response to that demand.

As an ambitious writer steadily gaining status in his native Orel, Germano nodded briskly to his parents' shared history of "wandering" and to his mother's "love of travel." Yet in his 1925 autobiography, Germano did not prioritize his nationality as central to defining himself as a Soviet citizen or as a writer. Instead, he emphasized Red Army service as well as his efforts to educate Orel's soldiers and workers. Nearly ten years later, as an aspiring member of the Union of Soviet Writers, Germano embraced his stature as the Soviet Union's most accomplished Gypsy writer. In his 1934 autobiography, Germano enthusiastically declared himself a Gypsy devoted to his "backward" brethren. In this telling, Germano's Soviet self took his first breath only at the moment of the Romani alphabet's creation. Soon after the war, Germano recounted his accomplishments as a Gypsy writer and declared himself "happy and proud" to have served his fellow Gypsies and the cause of socialist construction.

Only upon realization that the heyday of early Soviet nationality policy had passed did Germano edit "Gypsiness" from his storied self. By 1952, the breadbasket of opportunities afforded Germano *as a Gypsy* in the 1920s and 1930s had long been emptied. According to the Soviet Union's newly revised, post-war history, the empire's "backward" Gypsies had already been "civilized" by the Soviet "first among equals" – the Russian nation. Post-war Soviet ideology celebrated Russians not only as saviours of the homeland during the Great Patriotic War, but also as the natural-born leaders of the empire's economic, cultural, political, and social development. Germano's 1952 autobiography could not have reflected these changes in Soviet ideology and nationality policy more clearly. In editing his nationality, Germano testified that for him, at least, Gypsiness no longer provided the political currency that Sovietness and now Russianness promised him. Germano sloughed off a nationality that no longer appeared to serve him as an asset, and instead embraced one that did. Here, too, his keen performance of nationality demonstrated his insistent Sovietness.

Germano's autobiographical self both personalizes and encapsulates the process by which Roma who engaged the distinctly ethnicized version of the Bolshevik civilizing mission sovietized themselves by becoming Gypsies. In Germano's case, nationality operated precisely as the Bolsheviks hoped it would: as a plastic identity that could easily be discarded once the task of Soviet self-fashioning was achieved. Although Germano's colleagues and biographers in the Soviet Union refused to posthumously grant him the exalted status of Russian nationality, they praised him, above all else, as a faithful Soviet citizen who had devoted a lifetime to the cause of uplifting "backward Gypsies" to the heights of Soviet culture.

Who was A.V. Germano by nationality? An examination of Germano's evolving autobiography provides a clear answer. At times, Germano was a Gypsy. At times, he was a Russian. The Soviet nationality regime allowed for and even encouraged such shifts in his presentation of self. Yet throughout his adult lifetime, there remained one constant in his narrative self-fashioning: Germano was a Soviet citizen – integrated, enlightened, engaged, productive, and proud. Whether identifying as a Gypsy or as a Russian, Germano presented himself as a conscious citizen who willingly devoted his life to the cause of advancing not only the Soviet people (especially the Gypsies among them), but also his own Soviet self. In his various and even contradictory manoeuvres within the framework of Soviet nationality policy, Germano fashioned himself as a New Soviet Man – indeed, as a model Soviet citizen.

Conclusion

In 1931, while still ascending to the height of his writing career, Germano published his brief survey of Romani history and culture, *Gypsies Yesterday and Today*. Although Germano trained much of his focus on the strides Romani citizens had made in becoming literate, productive, integrated citizens of the Soviet Union, he also paused to reflect on Roma's comparative history in Europe. In ways starkly reminiscent of claims made not only by the All-Russian Gypsy Union but also by tsarist-era Russian ethnographers of Roma, Germano summarized Roma's history in Europe as a bloodstained chronicle of persecution, state-sponsored violence, and societal alienation.[27] With undeniable "cruelty," Germano explained, medieval Europe had greeted the arrival of Roma to its lands with centuries of "barbarous persecution." Roma were burned at the stake, hanged, massacred, and forcibly exiled from uninviting European states. When these measures failed to rid Europe of its despised Romani populations, slavery and serfdom were introduced as corrective measures to Roma's seemingly unassimilable lifestyles. Even in the twentieth century, Germano insisted, Roma in Europe were reduced to "genuine pariahs." Denied the privilege of civic inclusion, Roma suffered impoverished lives of social alienation, cultural backwardness, and political exclusion.[28]

In Germano's view, tsarist Russia particularly excelled at persecuting its Romani populations. From the time of Roma's appearance in Russia, Germano maintained, the tsarist empire denied its Gypsy subjects even the slightest opportunity to improve themselves, engage in productive labour, and integrate into imperial Russian society. When the tsarist state did focus its attention on Gypsies, it chauvinistically refused to account for Gypsies' national "particularities." It never bothered to "listen to the voice of the downtrodden, illiterate, backward Gypsy masses and to discover how the Gypsies themselves wanted to adapt to organized life." According to Germano, the tsarist state attempted to rule its Gypsy population only through "police measures," violent coercion, and discriminatory laws. "The persecution of Gypsies," Germano argued, "continued right up until the October Revolution."[29] This persecution, in Germano's mind, manifested itself not only in serfdom, Siberian exile, and legal restrictions on Gypsies' choice of profession or domicile. The greatest crime committed by the tsarist regime against its Gypsy subjects was its refusal to them of civic inclusion. Russia's Gypsies suffered alienation, poverty, illiteracy, and backwardness as a result of this withholding.

In all of Europe, Germano maintained, only the Soviet Union dignified Gypsies with citizenship, demanding that they integrate into the social, political, cultural, and economic order of the great Soviet "family of toilers."[30] In his view, the Soviet Union's peerlessly enlightened approach to governing Gypsies owed not merely to its insistent demand that Gypsies participate in the construction of socialism as conscious citizens, but also to its liberating nationality policy. For Germano, Soviet nationality policy was the definitive and unparalleled answer to the historic and painful question of Gypsies' backwardness. Nationality policy was an invitation to integration, to citizenship. The establishment of the Gypsy Union, Gypsy schools, artels, kolkhozes, and periodicals, Germano explained, had made it possible for Gypsies themselves to actively contribute to the building of socialism and the cultural development of their nationality, as well as to their own individual advancement as Soviet citizens. For the first time in their history, Germano contended, Gypsies were given the opportunity to emerge from society's despised margins, collapse their nomadic tents, learn to read, and undertake productive labour alongside fellow citizens. Thanks to Soviet nationality policy, he proclaimed, "the emancipated backward Gypsy people is growing closer to Soviet socialist culture as an equal among equals."[31] New Soviet Gypsies were on the road to becoming New Soviet Men and Women, plain and simple.

While Germano's commentary faithfully complied with standard Soviet propaganda templates, his argument should not be entirely discounted as socialist realist hyperbole. Roma throughout Europe had suffered profoundly and variously at the hands of a variety of European states and peoples. The imperial Russian state had expended very little effort in contemplating, designing, or executing policies towards rational, informed governance of its Romani subjects. By 1931, the Soviet Union had indeed distinguished itself at the very least in its insistence that Roma participate in their own full integration into the socialist economy and Soviet culture as conscious, self-improving citizens. Although his Panglossian trumpeting of Soviet triumphs and his silence regarding the half-hearted, underfunded, biased, and coercive nature of Soviet measures towards Roma cannot be denied, Germano nonetheless made an important point. Soviet citizenship was neither denied Roma nor presented to them as a privilege that could be refused. The Soviet Union required Roma to become integrated citizens who participated in their own transformation from backward to Soviet – from unproductive to productive, chaotic to disciplined, illiterate to literate, unenlightened to conscious. It also provided them, as Gypsies, a flexible means with which to meet that demand: Soviet nationality policy.

As previous chapters have shown, early Soviet nationality policy effectively drew in many Roma to Soviet citizenship. The particular case of Roma reflects more broadly how early Soviet nationality policy aided minority peoples in refashioning themselves as New Soviet Men and Women. As participants in a state that was as coercive as it was energetic in promising affirmative action to minority peoples, Roma mobilized the Soviet nationality regime in their daily lives, transforming themselves not only into Gypsies, but also into Soviet citizens. Defined as "backward Gypsies," Roma confronted not only the inescapable politics of nationality, but also the state's unflinching demand that they transform themselves into New Soviet Men and Women – productive, settled, enlightened, and invested in the advancement of the socialist collective and their individual Soviet selves. No matter their intentions, they integrated into the socialist economy and performed their allegiance to Soviet values. With its flaws and its enticements, the early Soviet nationality regime offered Roma a foothold in the evolving socio-economic order and a plastic framework of self-sovietization. Performing their state-prescribed roles as "backward Gypsies," Roma reinvented themselves as conscious Soviet citizens. They often made Soviet nationality policy work for them and, in the process, they fulfilled the nationality regime's assimilationist logic. In becoming New Soviet Gypsies, Roma achieved Soviet citizenship.

At the time of Germano's death in 1955, Gypsies remained on the Soviet Union's roster of official nationalities, as they would until the empire's collapse in 1991. Yet as Germano himself was all too keenly aware, precious little remained of the Soviet efforts to build national Gypsy institutions and cultural forms in the 1920s and 1930s. The yellowed pages of Romani-language primers and poetry collections occupied shelves in the Lenin and Saltykov-Shchedrin libraries, mostly forgotten relics of an earlier time. Romani farmers worked the fields of decidedly non-national collective and state farms. Romani workers laboured in Soviet factories and Romani students studied in Soviet schools. Only the Theatre Romen remained – and here, Roma joined representatives of other nationalities in performing Russian-language plays devoted to enlivening Soviet themes with the purported costumes and dances of Gypsies' distant, pre-Soviet past. Though still entitled to claim special status as Gypsies, Romani citizens of the post-war Soviet Union inescapably confronted a political and social reality strikingly different from that of the interwar prime of Soviet "compensatory nation-building."[32] No longer even a theoretically abundant source of advancement or aid, Gypsy nationality now functioned in an official capacity as a state-recognized signifier of Roma's prior "backwardness" (ostensibly conquered by the early Soviet nationality regime) and primordial uniqueness.[33] Perhaps more recognizably, Gypsy nationality continued to spell Roma's exotic and potentially dangerous alterity in the popular imagination.[34] Roma themselves were expected to fulfil their obligations as Soviet citizens, now with relatively scarce allowance for their purported "peculiarities" as a nationality. New Soviet Gypsies were to have already become New Soviet Citizens.

For Germano and many of the Roma whose lives have been studied in this book, the early Soviet nationality regime had prepared them well for the reordered priorities of post-war Soviet ideology and culture. Throughout the 1920s and 1930s, Roma had encountered both the profitable possibilities and the disappointing failures of the politics of Soviet nationality. Underfunded national Gypsy institutions – from the All-Russian Gypsy Union to failed kolkhozes, from the Theatre Romen to scarce Gypsy schools, from Tsygpishcheprom to *Romany zoria* – served as more than mere decorative national "forms" attesting to the Soviet Union's purported benevolent and rational approach to liberating and sovietizing so-called backward minorities. Through them, Roma engaged the early Soviet nationality regime – whether grudgingly, forcibly, or enthusiastically. In so doing, Roma confronted their civic duty to acculturate Soviet values, to ascend to the enlightenment of Soviet modernity, and to discipline themselves as productive labourers. In their performance of Gypsiness as much as of civic consciousness, they refashioned their very selves as Soviet.

Whatever their motivations or circumstance, Roma variously confronted the Soviet state's demand that they identify as a member of a distinct nationality, but also that they transform themselves into conscious Soviet citizens – productive, literate, disciplined, and obligated to the advancement of the collective as much as to the individual self. Within the framework of early Soviet nationality policy, many Roma found a potentially productive field of play within which to claim

Soviet citizenship. In engaging the Soviet nationality regime, Roma creatively defied Gypsy stereotypes, but also reinscribed those same stereotypes into Soviet culture. In mobilizing nationality policy, Roma fashioned themselves not only as Gypsies, but also as integrated Soviet citizens. Roma's varied performance of Gypsiness, as much as of Sovietness, was central to the making of New Soviet Gypsies.

Glossary of Terms and Abbreviations

artel	producers' cooperative
byt	way of life, culture
"camp Gypsies"	Roma of nomadic or seminomadic camps, in characteristic Soviet parlance
dekulakization	process of "liquidating the kulaks as a class"
Glavrepertkom	Main Committee for Repertory
GULag	Main Administration of Corrective-Labor Camps
Gypsy Union	All-Russian Gypsy Union
kolkhoz	collective farm
kolkhoznik	collective farm worker
Kolkhoztsentr	Union of Agricultural Collectives
Komsomol	Communist Youth League
kris	Romani arbitration council
kulak	"wealthy" peasant; elastically defined in practice; deemed Soviet "class enemy"
MKhAT	Moscow Art Theatre
MKK RKI	Moscow Control Commission's Workers' and Peasants' Inspectorate
MONO	Moscow Department of Education
Mossovet	Moscow City Soviet
MOZO	Moscow Province's Agricultural Department
MTS	Machine-Tractor Station
Narkompros	People's Commissariat of Enlightenment
Narkomzem	People's Commissariat of Agriculture
natsmen	member of a national minority
NEP	New Economic Policy
NKVD	People's Commissariat of Internal Affairs

OGPU	Unified State Political Administration
Romen	State Gypsy Theatre "Romen" (Moscow)
RSFSR	Russian Soviet Federated Socialist Republic
SKKIK	Executive Committee of the North Caucasus Krai
Sovnarkom	Council of People's Commissars
Sovnatsmen	Narkompros's Council of National Minorities
TsIK	Central Executive Committee of the USSR
TsIPKKNO	Central Institute for the Advancement of Qualified Education Cadres (Moscow)
TsK	Central Committee of the Communist Party of the Soviet Union
tsyganshchina	term of opprobrium used to refer to popular Gypsy music and dance in the early Soviet Union; shorthand for the debauchery, eroticism, kitsch, and lack of authenticity that cultural critics ascribed to Gypsy artistic performance
USSR	Union of Soviet Socialist Republics
VKP(b)	All-Union Communist Party (Bolsheviks)
VPK	All-Union Resettlement Committee
VTsIK	All-Russian Central Executive Committee (of the RFSFR)

Notes

Introduction

1 Gosudarstvennyi arkhiv rossiiskoi federatsii (GARF) f. 8131 o. 11 d. 56 ll. 8–10.
2 Ibid., l. 6.
3 For a comprehensive accounting of early Soviet culture's lionized values, see David L. Hoffmann, *Stalinist Values: The Cultural Norms of Soviet Modernity, 1917–1941* (Ithaca: Cornell University Press, 2003). On the New Soviet Person in comparative context, see idem, *Cultivating the Masses: Modern State Practices and Soviet Socialism, 1914–1939* (Ithaca: Cornell University Press, 2011), 224–37.
4 Terry Martin, *The Affirmative Action Empire: Nations and Nationalism in the Soviet Union, 1923–1939* (Ithaca: Cornell University Press, 2001).
5 Alaina Lemon, *Between Two Fires: Gypsy Performance and Romani Memory from Pushkin to Postsocialism* (Durham: Duke University Press, 2000), 30–31.
6 See ibid., esp. chapter 1.
7 Yanni Kotsonis, "'Face-to-Face': The State, the Individual, and the Citizen in Russian Taxation," *Slavic Review* 63, no. 2 (2004): 221–46; and idem, "'No Place to Go': Taxation and State Transformation in Late Imperial and Early Soviet Russia," *The Journal of Modern History* 76, no. 3 (2004): 531–77. Similar to Kotsonis, Daniel Beer argues that especially after the 1905 revolution, many liberal elites became convinced that the transformation of Russian society could be achieved only through "a tutelary program of coercive modernization." See his *Renovating Russia: The Human Sciences and the Fate of Liberal Modernity, 1880–1930* (Ithaca: Cornell University Press), 206. By contrast, Eric Lohr examines some Russian liberals' search for a guarantee of individual rights and immunities from the state in natural and international

law (if not in the existing autocratic system). See his "The Ideal Citizen and Real Subject in Late Imperial Russia," *Kritika: Explorations in Russian and Eurasian History* 7, no. 2 (2006): 173–94. Aaron B. Retish has shown how participation in World War I promoted a sense of civic belonging among that segment of the population whom tsarist ministers typically conceived of as least prepared for or capable of citizenship – the peasantry. See his *Russia's Peasants in Revolution and Civil War: Citizenship, Identity, and the Creation of the Soviet State, 1914–1922* (Cambridge: Cambridge University Press, 2008).

8 This is a vision explored in Stephen Kotkin's *Magnetic Mountain: Stalinism as a Civilization* (Berkeley: University of California Press, 1995); and Cynthia V. Hooper, "Terror from Within: Participation and Coercion in Soviet Power, 1924–1964" (PhD diss., Princeton University, 2003).

9 Francine Hirsch has aptly described the Soviet civilizing mission as "state-sponsored evolutionism." See her *Empire of Nations: Ethnographic Knowledge and the Making of the Soviet Union* (Ithaca: Cornell University Press, 2005), esp. 7–10. Adeeb Khalid emphasizes the universalist nature of the Soviet civilizing mission, and the universalizing aims of the nationality policy that helped to underpin it, as key to understanding the Soviet Union as an "activist, interventionist, mobilizational state" rather than a *colonial* empire. See his "Backwardness and the Quest for Civilization: Early Soviet Central Asia in Comparative Perspective," *Slavic Review* 65, no. 2 (2006): 231–51 (quote on 232).

10 On the Bolshevik conception of "consciousness," see Katerina Clark, *The Soviet Novel: History as Ritual* (1981; Bloomington: Indiana University Press, 2000); and Oleg Kharkhordin, *The Collective and the Individual in Russia: A Study of Practices* (Berkeley: University of California Press, 1999), 55–61.

11 Yanni Kotsonis, "Introduction: A Modern Paradox – Subject and Citizen in Nineteenth- and Twentieth-Century Russia," in *Russian Modernity: Politics, Knowledge, Practices*, ed. David L. Hoffmann and Yanni Kotsonis (New York: St Martin's, 2000), esp. 9.

12 It is, moreover, participation rather than belief that can most reliably be gauged via the historical record – a point to which I will return ahead.

13 See Martin, *Affirmative Action Empire*.

14 As Yuri Slezkine has noted, the Russian peasant was considered "backward" not because he was a Russian, but because he was a peasant. He also explains, "ethnicity-based affirmative action in the national territories was an exact replica of class-based affirmative action in Russia." Yuri Slezkine, "The USSR as a Communal Apartment, or How a Socialist State Promoted Ethnic Particularism," *Slavic Review* 53, no. 2 (1994): 424, 434.

15 Ibid.

16 This historiography includes: Kate Brown, *A Biography of No Place: From Ethnic Borderland to Soviet Heartland* (Cambridge: Harvard University Press, 2004); Adrienne Lynn Edgar, *Tribal Nation: The Making of Soviet Turkmenistan* (Princeton: Princeton University Press, 2004); Bruce Grant, *In the Soviet House of Culture: A Century of Perestroikas* (Princeton: Princeton University Press, 1995); Hirsch, *Empire of Nations*; Marianne Kamp, *The New Woman in Uzbekistan: Islam, Modernity, and Unveiling under Communism* (Seattle: University of Washington Press, 2006); Khalid, "Backwardness and the Quest for Civilization"; Lemon, *Between Two Fires*; Martin, *Affirmative Action Empire*; Douglas Northrop, *Veiled Empire: Gender and Power in Stalinist Central Asia* (Ithaca: Cornell University Press, 2004); Yuri Slezkine, *Arctic Mirrors: Russia and the Small Peoples of the North* (Ithaca: Cornell University Press, 1994); and Jeremy Smith, *The Bolsheviks and the National Question, 1917–23* (New York: St Martin's, 1999).

17 See Kotkin, *Magnetic Mountain*; Kharkhordin, *Collective and the Individual*; Igal Halfin, *From Darkness to Light: Class, Consciousness, and Salvation in Revolutionary Russia* (Pittsburgh: University of Pittsburgh Press, 2000); idem, *Terror in My Soul: Communist Autobiographies on Trial* (Cambridge: Harvard University Press, 2003); Jochen Hellbeck, *Revolution on My Mind: Writing a Diary under Stalin* (Cambridge: Harvard University Press, 2006); Christina Kiaer and Eric Naiman, eds., *Everyday Life in Early Soviet Russia: Taking the Revolution Inside* (Bloomington: Indiana University Press, 2006); Eric Naiman, *Sex in Public: The Incarnation of Early Soviet Ideology* (Princeton: Princeton University Press, 1997); and Alexei Yurchak, *Everything Was Forever, Until It Was No More: The Last Soviet Generation* (Princeton: Princeton University Press, 2006). Others have noted, however, the complex inheritance bequeathed to recent scholars of Soviet subjectivity by their predecessors of the so-called totalitarian and revisionist schools. See Anna Krylova, "The Tenacious Liberal Subject in Soviet Studies," *Kritika: Explorations in Russian and Eurasian History* 1, no. 1 (2000): 119–46; and Mark Edele, "Soviet Society, Social Structure, and Everyday Life: Major Frameworks Reconsidered," *Kritika: Explorations in Russian and Eurasian History* 8, no. 2 (2007): 349–73.

18 See Slezkine, "USSR as a Communal Apartment"; and Hirsch, *Empire of Nations*, 7–10.

19 On "speaking Bolshevik," see Kotkin, *Magnetic Mountain*, chapter 5.

20 For a critique of conceptions of identity as fundamental as well as an autopsy of identity as an impoverished category of analysis, see Rogers Brubaker and Fred Cooper, "Beyond 'Identity,'" *Theory and Society* 29, no. 1 (February, 2000): 1–47. Recent explorations of national indifference have

also demonstrated immense value. See Brown, *Biography of No Place*; Tara Zahra, "Imagined Noncommunities: National Indifference as a Category of Analysis," *Slavic Review* 69, no. 1 (Spring 2010): 93–119; and idem, *Kidnapped Souls: National Indifference and the Battle for Children in the Bohemian Lands* (Ithaca: Cornell University Press, 2008).

21 Rogers Brubaker, *Ethnicity without Groups* (Cambridge: Harvard University Press, 2004), 78–79.

22 Kotkin, *Magnetic Mountain*, 220.

23 Eric Naiman has rightly cautioned against equating Soviet citizens' participation in Sovietism with belief in his review essay, "On Soviet Subjects and the Scholars Who Make Them," *Russian Review* 60, no. 3 (2001): 307–15.

24 See Kotkin, *Magnetic Mountain*, chapter 5.

25 For a concise historiographical genealogy of Western scholars' dogged focus on whether Soviet citizens "believed" in Soviet ideology, see Krylova, "Tenacious Liberal Subject."

26 Choi Chatterjee and Karen Petrone, "Models of Selfhood and Subjectivity: The Soviet Case in Historical Perspective," *Slavic Review* 67, no. 4 (2008), esp. 985. Relatedly, Mark Edele rejects a "singular 'Stalinist' subjectivity" and rightly advocates the pursuit of "the history of subjectivities in Stalinism" in his "Strange Young Men in Stalin's Moscow: The Birth and Life of the Stiliagi, 1945–1953," *Jahrbücher für Geschichte Osteuropas* 50, no. 1 (2002): 61. For a nuanced reflection on the instability of socialist, especially Soviet selves, see Douglas Rogers, *The Old Faith and the Russian Land: A Historical Ethnography of Ethics in the Urals* (Ithaca: Cornell University Press, 2009), esp. 186–9.

27 Hellbeck, *Revolution on My Mind*.

28 Kotkin, *Magnetic Mountain*, 220.

29 See, for example, Lemon, *Between Two Fires*; Kharkhordin, *Collective and the Individual*; and Yurchak, *Everything Was Forever*. For a concise and general overview of the "performative turn" in the humanities, see Peter Burke, "Performing History: The Importance of Occasions," *Rethinking History* 9, no. 1 (2005): 35–52.

30 Yurchak, *Everything Was Forever*. See also Hooper, "Terror from Within," esp. 46.

31 The quote is taken from Stephen Kotkin, "The State – Is It Us? Memoirs, Archives, and Kremlinologists," *The Russian Review* 61, no. 1 (2002): 50.

32 A.P. Barannikov, *Tsygany SSSR. Kratko-etnograficheskii ocherk* (Moscow: Tsentrizdat, 1931), 3–5.

33 The works referenced here are F. Miklosich, *Uber die Mundarten und die Wanderungen der Zigeuner Europas* (Wien: s.n., 1872–81); and A.F. Pott, *Die*

Zigeuner in Europa und Asien (Halle: Heynemann, 1845). For a selective history and critique of European studies of Roma in the nineteenth and early twentieth centuries, see Wim Willems, *In Search of the True Gypsy: From Enlightenment to Final Solution* (London: F. Cass, 1997). For an overview of past and more recent trends in Romani Studies, see David Mayall, *Gypsy Identities 1500–2000: From Egipcyans and Moon-men to the Ethnic Romany* (New York: Routledge, 2004), 23–53.

34 See, for example, Viorel Achim, *The Roma in Romanian History* (New York: Central European University Press, 2004), 7–23; and Zoltan Barany, *The East European Gypsies: Regime Change, Marginality, and Ethnopolitics* (Cambridge: Cambridge University Press, 2002), 9–12.

35 Scholars, however, have long debated what sparked the Romani diaspora from India and when, let alone the currency of tracing Romani origins in India. For brief overviews of the controversies that still attend debate on the origins of the Romani diaspora, see Ian Hancock, *Danger! Educated Gypsy: Selected Essays* (Hertfordshire: University of Hertfordshire Press, 2010), chapter 5; Radu P. Iovita and Theodore G. Schurr, "Reconstructing the Origins and Migrations of Diasporic Populations: The Case of the European Gypsies," *American Anthropologist* 106, no. 2 (2004): 267–81; and Mayall, *Gypsy Identities 1500–2000*, 219–29.

36 Ian Hancock, *A Handbook of Vlax Romani* (Columbus, OH: Slavica, 1995), 17–24; Nicolas Gheorghe, "The Origin of Roma's Slavery in the Rumanian Principalities," *Roma* 7, no. 1 (1983), esp. 14–15; and Lemon, *Between Two Fires*, 9.

37 Hancock, *Danger! Educated Gypsy*, chapter 5.

38 See Achim, *Roma in Romanian History*, 7–23; Barany, *East European Gypsies*, 9–12; and Lemon, *Between Two Fires*, 7–9.

39 See M. Bril', "Trudiashchiesia tsygane v riady stroitelei sotsializma," *Revoliutsiia i natsional'nosti*, no. 7 (1932): 60–61.

40 See, for example, Barany, *East European Gypsies*, 12–15; and Anne Sutherland, *Gypsies: The Hidden Americans* (Long Grove, IL: Waveland, 1975), 14–19. On the Romani language and its dialects, see Yaron Matras, *Romani: A Linguistic Introduction* (Cambridge: Cambridge University Press, 2002). For a valuable discussion of how Roma in the former Soviet Union have variously understood the heterogeneity of the Romani diaspora, see Lemon, *Between Two Fires*, chapter 3. Having conducted fieldwork among Roma in post-Soviet Russia, Lemon concludes, "Romani characterizations of difference are not manifestations of tribalism but ongoing engagements with European and Soviet discourses about 'civilizedness' ... They are also grounded not in 'clan' conflicts, but in political ones, and in relations to the state and its agents" (103).

41 Ibid., 7; and Nadezhda Demeter, Nikolai Bessonov, and Vladimir Kuten-
    kov, *Istoriia tsygan: Novyi vzgliad* (Voronezh: IPF "Voronezh," 2000), 78–114.
42 European states have often made distinctions between "our Gypsies"
    and "foreign Gypsies," resulting in the disadvantaging of those deemed
    "foreign" as well as the intensification of antagonisms between Romani
    groups. See, for example, Milena Hubschmannova, "Economic Stratifica-
    tion and Interaction: Roma, an Ethnic Jati in East Slovakia," in *Gypsies: An
    Interdisciplinary Reader*, ed. Diane Tong (New York: Garland, 1998), 233–67;
    and Jennifer Illuzzi, "Negotiating the 'State of Exception': Gypsies' En-
    counter with the Judiciary in Germany and Italy, 1860–1914," *Social History*
    35, no. 4 (2010): 418–38.
43 On predominant stereotypes of Roma in European history, see Katie
    Trumpener, "The Time of the Gypsies: A 'People without History' in the
    Narratives of the West," *Critical Inquiry* 18, no. 2 (1992): 843–84.
44 Paloma Gay y Blasco, *Gypsies in Madrid: Sex, Gender, and the Performance of
    Identity* (Oxford: Berg, 1999); Sarah Buckler, *Fire in the Dark: Telling Gypsiness
    in North East England* (New York: Berghahn Books, 2007); Istvan Pogany, *The
    Roma Café: Human Rights and the Plight of the Romani People* (London: Pluto,
    2004); and Michael Stewart, *The Time of the Gypsies* (Boulder: Westview,
    1997). For a thoughtful engagement of Romani Studies scholars' ongoing
    struggle to combat essentialist notions of "the true Gypsy" even in their
    own works, see Annabel Tremlett, "Bringing Hybridity to Heterogeneity in
    Romani Studies," *Romani Studies* 19, no. 2 (2009): 147–68.
45 See, for example, Belinda Cooper, "'We Have No Martin Luther King':
    Eastern Europe's Roma Minority," *World Policy Journal* 18, no. 4 (Winter
    2001/2002): 69–78; and idem, "A Pattern of Persecution," *Foreign Affairs*,
    September 28, 2010.
46 Lemon, *Between Two Fires*, 4.
47 Isabel Fonseca, *Bury Me Standing: The Gypsies and Their Journey* (New York:
    Vintage, 1995), 5.
48 Lemon, *Between Two Fires*, 3. For similar insistence that Gypsy/Romani
    accounts of rootedness and memory be taken seriously, see also Buckler,
    Fire in the Dark, esp. 12–13; and Aspasia Theodosiou, "'Be-longing' in a
    'Doubly-occupied Place': The Parakalamos Gypsy Musicians," *Romani
    Studies* 13, no. 2 (2003): 25–58.

1. Backward Gypsies, Soviet Citizens

Portions of an earlier version of this chapter were previously published
as "'Backward Gypsies,' Soviet Citizens: The All-Russian Gypsy Union,

1925–28," *Kritika: Explorations in Russian and Eurasian History* 11, no. 2 (Spring 2010): 283–312.

1 GARF f. 1235 o. 120 d. 27 l. 63.

2 See again Hirsch's apt description of "state-sponsored evolutionism" in her *Empire of Nations,* esp. 7–10. On Soviet nationality policy as "compensatory nation-building" and "Soviet affirmative action," see, respectively, Slezkine, "USSR as a Communal Apartment"; and Martin, *Affirmative Action Empire.*

3 I.I. Rom-Lebedev, *Ot tsyganskogo khora k teatru "Romen"* (Moscow: Iskusstvo', 1990), 10. Upon discovery of the benefits that Soviet nationality policy potentially offered him as a minority citizen, he changed his name to Rom-Lebedev in 1923, thereby emphasizing his Gypsy nationality.

4 Ibid., 11.

5 Ibid., 13.

6 I.V. Nest'ev, *Zvezdy russkoi estrady (Panina, Vial'tseva, Plevitskaia). Ocherki o russkikh estradnykh pevitsakh nachala XX veka* (Moscow: Sovetskii kompozitor, 1970), 20.

7 On late imperial Russia's lively and potentially democratizing restaurant culture, see Louise McReynolds, *Russia at Play: Leisure Activities at the End of the Tsarist Era* (Ithaca: Cornell University Press, 2003), esp. 193–210.

8 Rom-Lebedev, *Ot tsyganskogo khora,* 14.

9 Ibid., 15.

10 Ibid.

11 Efim Druts and Aleksei Gessler, *Tsygane Ocherki -* (Moscow: Sovetskii pisatel', 1990), 202–3.

12 B.J. Gilliat-Smith, "Russian Gypsy Singers," *Journal of the Gypsy Lore Society,* third series, no. 1 (1922): 59.

13 Rom-Lebedev, *Ot tsyganskogo khora,* 52–53. If a Romani wife, Rom-Lebedev explained, was "a famous singer or dancer, this was a great honour for her spouse." For an excellent discussion on "the Gypsy" as an image of desirous, wild freedom in Russia, see Alaina Lemon, *Between Two Fires,* esp. 31–55.

14 Quoted in K.A. Baurov, *Tsyganskie khory starogo Peterburga* (St. Petersburg: Na strazhe rodiny, 1991), 5.

15 Druts and Gessler, *Tsygane,* 209; and Baurov, *Tsyganskie khory,* 24.

16 Druts and Gessler, *Tsygane,* 212.

17 Rom-Lebedev, *Ot tsyganskogo khora,* 41–42.

18 Ibid., 48.

19 Ibid., 45.

20 Ibid., 46, 48.

21 Ibid., 42. On complaints that choir members did not dress like "real Gypsies," see also P. Stolpianskii, *Muzyka i muzitsirovanie v starom Peterburge* (Leningrad: Muzyka, 1989), 86; and Demeter, Bessonov, and Kutenkov, *Istoriia tsygan*, 180.

22 Rom-Lebedev, *Ot tsyganskogo khora*, 91–92.

23 Ibid., 99.

24 Ibid., 99–100.

25 Val'demar Kalinin, *Zagadka baltiiskikh tsygan: Ocherki istorii, kul'tury, i sotsial'nogo razvitiia baltiiskikh tsygan* (Minsk: Logvinov, 2005), 33–34.

26 Rossiiskii Institut Istorii Iskusstv (RIII) f. 1 o. 1 d. 239 ll. 134–5.

27 Born N.N. Khlebnikov, Kruchinin borrowed his pseudonym from A.N. Ostrovskii's main character in the play, *Bez viny vinovatye*. On his career, see Druts and Gessler, *Tsygane*, 237, 265–66.

28 Rom-Lebedev, *Ot tsyganskogo khora*, 100.

29 "N. N. Kruchinin," *Rabis*, no. 9 (March 1927): 10.

30 Druts and Gessler, *Tsygane*, 266.

31 RIII f. 1 o. 1 d. 239 ll. 127–30.

32 Rom-Lebedev, *Ot tsyganskogo khora*, 151.

33 Here, the young Romani activists' embrace of Soviet nationality policy's potential to service their aims of cultural and social advancement can be favorably compared to that of the Central Asian Jadids in the 1920s. As Adeeb Khalid has shown, in the wake of the October Revolution, the Jadids responded quickly to the opportunities afforded them by the early Soviet state to pursue the modernizing goals they had already long nurtured in the late tsarist empire. See his *The Politics of Muslim Cultural Reform: Jadidism in Central Asia* (Berkeley: University of California Press, 1998), esp. 281–301, as well as Kamp, *New Woman in Uzbekistan*.

34 Rom-Lebedev, *Ot tsyganskogo khora*, 160.

35 *Orlovskii ob"edinennyi gosudarstvennyi literaturnyi muzei I. S. Turgeneva* (OGLMT) f. 29 o.1 d. 49 l. 9.

36 Rom-Lebedev, *Ot tsyganskogo khora*, 160.

37 GARF f. A-259 o. 9b d. 4233 l. 21

38 Rom-Lebedev, *Ot tsyganskogo khora*, 160.

39 N.A. Pankov, quoted in Druts and Gessler, *Tsygane*, 281.

40 Rom-Lebedev, *Ot tsyganskogo khora*, 160–2.

41 GARF f. 1235 o. 119 d. 9 ll. 3–4.

42 GARF f. 1235 o. 119 d. 10 ll. 13–14.

43 GARF f. 1235 o. 119 d. 9 l. 8.

44 Ibid., ll. 11–11ob.

45 Ibid., l. 7.

46 GARF f. 1235 o.119 d. 10 l. 52.

47 Ibid.. ll. 13–13ob.

48 GARF f. 1235 o.119 d. 9 ll. 2, 52.

49 Personal papers of N. A. Pankov as quoted in Druts and Gessler, *Tsygane*, 281–82.

50 GARF f. 1235 o.120 d. 27 ll. 89–91.

51 Ibid., ll. 181–2.

52 Personal papers of N.A. Pankov as quoted in Druts and Gessler, *Tsygane*, 281.

53 GARF f. 1235 o. 120 d. 27 l. 179.

54 On early Soviet understandings of a spectrum of backwardness among minority peoples, see Martin, *Affirmative Action Empire*, esp. 126–32.

55 GARF f. 1235 o. 120 d. 27 ll. 179–80.

56 Ibid., l. 94.

57 Ibid., ll. 95–6.

58 GARF f. 1235 o. 120 d. 27 ll. 133–133ob.

59 GARF f. 1235 o. 121 d. 31 l. 40.

60 GARF f. 3316 o. 20 d. 653 l. 10.

61 GARF f. 1235 o. 120 d. 27 l. 118.

62 Ibid., ll. 133–4, 140, 151–2.

63 Ibid., l. 133ob.

64 GARF f. 3316 o. 20 d. 653 l. 22.

65 GARF f. 1235 o. 121 d. 31 l. 240.

66 See, for example, GARF f. 1235 o. 120 d. 27 l. 63.

67 On the efforts and failures of twentieth-century states to rationalize or "make legible" populations in the putative service of more effective governance, see James C. Scott, *Seeing Like a State: How Certain Schemes to Improve the Human Condition Have Failed* (New Haven: Yale University Press, 1998).

68 OGLMT f. 29 o. 1 d. 78 l. 104.

69 GARF f. 3316 o. 28 d. 793 l. 34.

70 GARF f. 1235 o. 121 d. 31 l. 193.

71 Germano, *Tsygane vchera i segodnia*, 46–7.

72 GARF f. 1235 o. 121 d. 31 l. 12.

73 Ibid., l. 221.

74 GARF f. 1235 o. 121 d. 31 ll. 299–301, 305, 313.

75 I borrow the concept of an imperial "information order" from C.A. Bayly, *Empire and Information: Intelligence Gathering and Social Communication in India, 1780–1870* (New York: Cambridge University Press, 1996).

76 A.S. Taranov, "Ot kochevki k osedlosti," *Izvestiia* , 21 January 1927.

77 GARF f. 1235 o. 121 d. 31 l. 193.

78 GARF f. A-296 o. 1 d. 46 l. 31. By 1926, Gypsy Union activists had joined with linguist M.V. Sergievskii to create a Romani-language alphabet based on the Russian Cyrillic script.

79 Ibid., l. 31.

80 GARF f. 3316 o. 20 d. 653 l. 14; OGLMT f. 29 o. 1 d. 49 l. 14.

81 GARF f. 1235 o. 120 d. 27 l. 49ob.

82 GARF f. 1235 o. 121 d. 31 ll. 110ob, 133, and 251ob.

83 Ibid., ll. 117, 131, 138, 205.

84 Ibid., ll. 103–4, 116, 122–5, 129–30, 132, 150–5, 157, 163–8.

85 See E. Popova and M. Bril', "Tsygane v Soiuze SSR," *Sovetskoe stroitel'stvo*, no. 2 (February 1932): 127–8.

86 GARF f. 1235 o. 120 d. 27 l. 49ob.

87 GARF f. 1235 o. 123 d. 27 ll. 186–7ob.

88 GARF f. 1235 o. 121 d. 31 ll. 112–13.

89 Ibid., ll. 110–11.

90 Ibid., ll. 107–107ob.

91 GARF f. 3316 o. 20 d. 653 ll. 7ob–8.

92 GARF f. 1235 o. 121 d. 31 l. 94.

93 GARF f. 3316 o. 20 d. 653 ll. 13–22, 80.

94 Ibid., ll. 19–20.

95 Ibid., ll. 16–17.

96 GARF f. 1235 o. 120 d. 27 ll. 47–47ob.

97 GARF f. 1235 o. 140 d. 752 ll. 25–25ob.

98 GARF f. 1235 o. 120 d. 27 l. 30.

99 Ibid., l. 31

100 Ibid., l. 33.

101 Romani activists inherited the trope of the "noble [minority] savage" as primitive communist from the imperial Russian ethnographic tradition. See Mark Bassin, "Inventing Siberia: Visions of the Russian East in the Early Nineteenth Century," *The American Historical Review* 96, no. 3 (June 1991): 763–94; Bruce Grant, "Empire and Savagery: The Politics of Primitivism in Late Imperial Russia," in *Russia's Orient: Imperial Borderlands and Peoples, 1700–1917*, ed. Daniel R. Brower and Edward J. Lazzerini (Bloomington: Indiana University Press, 1997): 292–310; Slezkine, *Arctic Mirrors*, esp. 113–29; and Nikolai Ssorin-Chaikov, *The Social Life of the State in Subarctic Siberia* (Stanford: Stanford University Press, 2003), esp. 44–72.

102 GARF f. 1235 o. 120 d. 27 l. 33.

103 Ibid., l. 35.

104 Ibid., l. 36.

105 Ibid., l. 34.

106 Ibid., l. 36.
107 Ibid.
108 Ibid., l. 38.
109 Kotkin, *Magnetic Mountain*, 220.
110 Tied to questions of authenticity, competing conceptions of performativity and performance are also at the heart of scholarly debates on Soviet selfhood. See, for example, Yurchak, *Everything Was Forever*; and Sheila Fitzpatrick, *Tear Off the Masks! Identity and Imposture in Twentieth-Century Russia* (Princeton: Princeton University Press, 2005).

2. A Political Education

1 Pankov's personal papers as quoted in Druts and Gessler, *Tsygane*, 282–3.
2 TsGAMO f. 966 o. 4 d. 1074 l. 23.
3 TsGAMO f. 66 o. 1 d. 6328 l. 2ᵃ. This decree is reprinted in *Narodnoe obrazovanie v SSSR. Obshcheobrazovatel'naia shkola. Sbornik dokumentov 1917–1973gg* (Moscow: Pedagogika, 1974), 145. The guarantee of native-language education was limited only by the minimum requirement of twenty-five pupils per age group. See Barbara A. Anderson and Brian D. Silver, "Equality, Efficiency, and Politics in Soviet Bilingual Education Policy, 1934–1980," *The American Political Science Review* 78, no.4 (December 1984): 1019–39; and Jeremy Smith, "The Education of National Minorities: The Early Soviet Experience," *Slavonic and East European Review* 75, no. 2 (April 1997): 281–307. On the problems and ideological conflicts that beset Narkompros in the 1920s and 1930s as it attempted to provide minority peoples with native language education, see Michael G. Smith, *Language and Power in the Creation of the USSR, 1917–1953* (New York: Mouten de Gruyter, 1998), 43–58.
4 OGLMT f. 29 o. 1 d. 49 ll. 31–32.
5 See Larry E. Holmes, *The Kremlin and the Schoolhouse: Reforming Education in Soviet Russia, 1917–1931* (Bloomington: Indiana University Press, 1991); Catriona Kelly, *Children's World: Growing Up in Russia, 1890–1991* (New Haven: Yale University Press, 2007), esp. 61–92; and Lisa A. Kirschenbaum, *Small Comrades: Revolutionizing Childhood in Soviet Russia, 1917–1932* (New York: Routledge, 2001), esp. 104–32.
6 Quoted in Tricia Starks, *The Body Soviet: Propaganda, Hygiene, and the Revolutionary State* (Madison: University of Wisconsin Press, 2008), 119.
7 TsGAMO f. 966 o.4 d. 1074 ll. 10–11.
8 GARF f. 1235 o.120 d. 27 ll. 151–2.
9 TsGAMO f. 966 o. 4 d. 1074 l. 13.

10 Germano, *Tsygane vchera i segodnia*, 94. On pollution and related taboos in Romani cultures, see Walter Otto Weyrauch and Maureen Anne Bell, "Autonomous Lawmaking: The Case of the 'Gypsies,'" *Yale Law Journal* 103, no. 2 (November 1993), esp. 342–52.

11 See TsGAMO f. 966 o. 4 d. 1074 l. 14. Though they were commonly referred to as Gypsy schools, even Narkompros officials would acknowledge that "Gypsies lack their own schools and their children study in Gypsy groups within Russian schools." TsGAMO f. 4341 o. 1 d. 270 l. 2.

12 On the schools' curriculum, see TsGAMO f. 966 o. 4 d. 1074 ll. 48–9; f. 966 o. 4 d. 1084 ll. 30–30ob; and "Tsygane uchatsia," *Ekran*, no. 20 (15 May 1927): 3.

13 OGLMT f. 29 o. 1 d. 216 l. 17. That the schoolteachers, excepting Dudarova, were Russians and not Roma should not be seen as unusual. In the 1920s and 1930s, national cadres of schoolteachers were scarce. Ethnically Russian schoolteachers were encouraged to staff the growing number of non-Russian schools and to learn minority languages on the job. It was therefore common in the early years of non-Russian Soviet education for teachers and pupils to lack a common language and for classroom instruction to be carried out primarily in Russian. See E. Thomas Ewing, "Ethnicity at School: 'Non-Russian' Education in the Soviet Union during the 1930s," *History of Education* 35, no. 4–5 (July–September 2006): 499–519.

14 GARF f. 1235 o. 120 d. 27 l. 64.

15 TsGAMO f. 966 o. 4 d. 1074 ll. 14; f. 966 o. 4 d. 1073 ll. 2ob–3.

16 GARF f. 1235 o. 123 d. 27 l. 60.

17 V. de Gila-Kochanowski, "N. A. Pankov," *Journal of the Gypsy Lore Society*, third series, vol. 38, no. 3–4 (1959): 159.

18 Kalinin, *Zagadka baltiiskikh tsygan*, 51.

19 GARF f. 1235 o. 120 d. 27ll. 63–4.

20 TsGAMO f. 966 o. 4 d. 1074 l. 14.

21 TsGAMO f. 966 o. 4 d. 1084 l. 54. Most members of this Vlax Romani community took the surname Mikhai. Writing about the school in 1931, the Romani activist A.V. Germano explained, "The surname of nearly all the children is the same – Mikhai. They are not brothers or sisters. They belong to the Mikhai clan." See his *Tsygane vchera i segodnia*, 82. In describing Vlax Roma's cultural practices, Germano and his colleagues' politically charged use of such terms as "headman" and "clan" denoted Vlax Roma's perceived social foreignness and threatening inscrutability. Distancing myself from the political inflections of activists' commentary on the "clannishness" of Vlax Roma, I therefore refer to this population simply as the Mikhai community.

22 TsGAMO f. 966 o. 4 d. 1084, l. 15
23 Ibid., l. 54; Germano, *Tsygane vchera i segodnia*, 85.
24 TsGAMO f. 966 o. 4 d. 1084 l. 54.
25 Germano, *Tsygane vchera i segodnia*, 85–6; TsGAMO f. 66 o. 11 d. 6328 l. 6. At Moscow's Gypsy schools, Roma were taught daily that only the culturally "advanced" were officially entitled to decide what was dirty, polluted, and backward in the Soviet Union, and that they – "dirty Gypsies" – needed to purify themselves physically and morally. For the classic anthropological statement on dirt as the symbolic construction of perceived social danger, cultural transgression, and both physical and moral disorder, see Mary Douglas, *Purity and Danger* (1966; New York: Routledge, 2002).
26 On the widespread challenge of living hygienically in early Soviet cities, see Starks, *Body Soviet*, 126–33.
27 E. Katerli, "Brodiachee plemia," *Leningradskaia pravda*, 28 July 1928.
28 Bolsheviks overwhelmingly conceived of the early Soviet population as dirty, diseased, and thus uncivilized and premodern. They sought to train not only Roma but also workers, peasants, and members of other so-called backward nationalities in the ways of hygiene, thereby eradicating the population's filthiness, ignorance, superstition, and moral deficiency. See Hoffmann, *Stalinist Values*, esp. chapter 1; Starks, *Body Soviet*; Slezkine, *Arctic Mirrors*, esp. chapter 7; and Northrop, *Veiled Empire*, esp. 60–4.
29 TsGAMO f. 966 o. 4 d. 1084 ll. 54–54ob.
30 Germano, *Tsygane vchera i segodnia*, 83.
31 TsGAMO f. 966 o. 4 d. 1073 l. 2ob; f. 966 o. 4 d. 1074 ll. 48–48ob; f. 966 o. 4 d. 1084 ll. 28, 72.
32 A. Cherniak, "Tsyganskie deti," *Drug detei*, no. 6–7 (June–July 1927): 29–30. For a similarly pessimistic depiction of Romani childhood, see Lebedinskii, "Tam, gde goriat kostry," *Ekran*, no. 36 (4 September 1927): 10.
33 GARF f. A-296 o. 1 d. 90 l. 47. See also "Prosveshchenie natsional'nykh men'shinstv," in Narodnyi Komissariat Prosveshcheniia RSFSR, *Narodnoe prosveshchenie v RSFSR k 1926/27 uchebnomu godu* (Moscow: 1927), 200–29. Narkompros's Council of National Minorities grouped Gypsies together with Nogais, Turkmen, Kazaks, Kirgiz, northern peoples (*severnye narodnosti*), small peoples of Siberia (*melkie sibirskie narodnosti*), Khakass, Shors, Oirots, natives of the Far Eastern Region, Altai Tatars, Assyrians, Tats, and Uigurs. Soviet distinctions between "western" and "eastern" nationalities ultimately had little to do with geography. Eastern nationalities were those defined as "culturally backward," while western nationalities were those considered, like Russians, to be relatively advanced. See Martin, *Affirmative Action Empire*, esp. 23–4, 56, and 166–7.

34 TsGAMO f. 966 o. 4 d. 1084 l. 33.

35 Ibid., l. 54ob.

36 "Tsygane uchatsia,"3, and TsGAMO f. 966 o. 4 d. 1074 l. 54.

37 TsGAMO f. 966 o. 4 d. 1073 l. 20b; f. 966 o. 4 d. 1074, ll. 6–7; 14–15; and "Tsygane uchatsia," 3.

38 TsGAMO f. 966 o. 4 d. 1084 l. 28.

39 TsGAMO f. 966 o. 4 d. 1074 l. 2.

40 Roma were not the only minority people denied access to elementary education in their native tongue as a result of practical obstacles preventing the creation of Romani-language schools. According to statistics available for the year 1927, within the RSFSR 0.9 per cent of Belorussian, 5.5 per cent of Ukrainian, 4.5 per cent of Polish, 8.0 per cent of Jewish and 19.6 per cent of Latvian schoolchildren were being taught in their native languages. By way of contrast, 77.6 per cent of Chuvash, 84.2 per cent of German, 82.3 per cent of Tatar, 88.6 per cent Kazakh, and 90.5 per cent of Kyrgyz schoolchildren studying within the RSFSR were being taught in their native languages. See Smith, "The Education of National Minorities," 305.

41 E. Glyn Lewis, *Multilingualism in the Soviet Union: Aspects of Language Policy and Its Implementation* (The Hague: Mouten, 1972), 133; and David Crowe, *A History of the Gypsies of Eastern Europe and Russia* (New York: St Martin's, 1996), 176.

42 TsGAMO f. 66 o. 11 d. 6328 ll. 6, 8.

43 TsGAMO f. 966 o. 4 d. 1084 ll. 28–28ob; "Tsygane uchatsia," 3.

44 TsGAMO f. 966 o. 4 d. 1084 l. 54.

45 Ibid., l. 33.

46 Ibid., l. 54.

47 TsGAMO f. 966 o. 4 d. 1074 l. 48ob.

48 Germano, *Tsygane vchera i segodnia*, 80.

49 Ibid., 93.

50 V.M. Papaz'ian, "Armianskie bosha (tsygane)," *Etnograficheskoe obozrenie* 49, no. 2 (1901): 144; and K.P. Patkanov, *Tsygany. Neskol'ko slov o narechiiakh zakavkazskikh tsygan: Bosha i karachi* (St. Petersburg: Tipografiia Imperatorskoi Akademii Nauk, 1887), 28–9.

51 Barannikov, *Tsygany SSSR*, 52; and idem, *The Ukrainian and South Russian Gypsy Dialects* (Leningrad: Izdatel'stvo Akademii Nauk SSSR, 1934), 13–14.

52 GARF f. 1235 o. 120 d. 27 ll. 94–95, 100, 133ob.

53 Pankov's personal papers as quoted in Druts and Gessler, *Tsygane*, 295–6.

54 OGLMT f. 29 o. 1 d. 49 l. 33.

55 GARF f. 3316 o. 22 d. 146 l. 12.

56 A.V. Germano, "O kul'turnoi rabote sredi tsygan," *Prosveshchenie natsional'nostei* no. 2 (1931): 36; and idem, *Tsygane vchera i segodnia*, 94.

57 See Martin, *Affirmative Action Empire*, 185–6, 193.

58 On Soviet language policy, see, for example, V.M. Alpatov, *150 iazykov i politika, 1917–2000* (Moscow: Kraft, Institut vostokovedeniia RAN, 2000); Leonore A. Grenoble, *Language Policy in the Soviet Union* (Dordrecht: Kluwer Academic, 2003); M.I. Isayev, *National Languages in the USSR: Problems and Solutions* (Moscow: Progress, 1977); Martin, *Affirmative Action Empire*, 182–207.

59 On "state-sponsored evolutionism," see Hirsch, *Empire of Nations*, 7–10.

60 Isayev, *National Languages*, 242.

61 In the second half of the 1930s, the Latinization campaign was abandoned when it was decided that it had impeded the cultural development of "backward" nationalities, thwarting their command of the Russian language. With few exceptions, formerly Latin-based scripts were replaced with Cyrillic-based scripts. See Smith, *Language and Power*, 156–8; and Grenoble, *Language Policy in the Soviet Union*, 51.

62 Patkanov, *Tsygany*, 47.

63 A.P. Barannikov, "About the Term 'the Gypsies of Russia,'" *Comptes Rendus de l'Academie des Sciences de l'URSS* 10 (1928): 212.

64 Isayev, *National Languages*, 231.

65 V. Lytkin, "O literaturnom iazyke natsmen'shinstv," *Prosveshchenie natsional'nostei* no. 1 (1931): 74.

66 Edgar, *Tribal Nation*, 148.

67 Ibid., chapter 5 (quote on 148).

68 Ibid., chapter 5.

69 Ibid., 152.

70 GARF f. A-296 o. 1 d. 405 l. 250.

71 Lemon, *Between Two Fires*, 134.

72 Frederick George Ackerley, "Russian Gypsies under the Soviets," *Journal of the Gypsy Lore Society*, third series, vol. 2, no. 3–4 (1932): 195.

73 Lemon, *Between Two Fires*, 134.

74 Ackerley, "Russian Gypsies under the Soviets," 195–6; A.V. Germano, *Nevo dzhiiben* (Moscow: Tsentrizdat, 1929).

75 Early Soviet Romani-language texts are archived in the department of national literatures at the Russian National Library (St Petersburg). Works published before 1931 are noted in A.V. Germano, *Bibliografiia o tsyganakh* (Moscow: Tsentrizdat, 1930).

76 Alpatov, *150 iazykov*, 49. On the reassertion of "Great Russians" as the standard-bearers of revolution and progressive culture in the Soviet Union

that began in the mid-1930s, see David Brandenberger, *National Bolshevism: Stalinist Mass Culture and the Formation of Modern Russian National Identity, 1931–1956* (Cambridge: Harvard University Press, 2002).

77 TsGAMO f. 966 o. 4 d. 1074 l. 54ob.

78 E. Katerli, "Brodiachee plemia," *Leningradskaia pravda*, 28 July 1928.

79 Edv. Sholokh, "Chas v tsyganskoi shkole," *Prosveshchenie natsional'nostei* no. 4–5 (1931): 68–9.

80 Ibid. 68.

81 GARF f. 1235 o. 123 d. 27 l. 57.

82 Ibid., l. 258.

83 GARF f. A-296 o. 1 d. 472 l. 32.

84 GARF f. 1235 o. 123 d. 27 l. 97ob.

85 Bril', "Tsygane v riady," 64–5; GARF f. 1235 o. 123 d. 27 ll. 22–3.

86 Ibid., ll. 114–15.

87 GARF f. 1235 o. 127 d. 8 l. 116.

88 GARF f. A-296 o. 1 d. 522 l. 12.

89 Ibid:, ll. 10–11.

90 Ibid., l. 13.

91 Ibid., ll. 10–11.

92 Germano, "O kul'turnoi rabote," 36–7.

93 Between 1926 and 1938, officials in Moscow remained consistently uncertain as to how many Gypsy schools operated within the empire. Between 1933 and 1938, Narkompros and VTsIK officials variously estimated the number of Gypsy schools operating within the RSFSR, although they typically cited a range of twenty-five to thirty-three schools. See, for example, GARF f. 1235 o. 127 d. 8 ll. 116, 164. The state's lack of knowledge concerning the schools was apparent at a conference hosted by the Soviet of Nationalities in January 1936 and dedicated to accelerating the assimilation of nomadic Roma in particular. Here, Secretary Khatskevich generically claimed that "Gypsy children study in dozens of schools," while Pankov complained that Narkompros officials' hazy statistics amounted to an admission that "We do not know how many Gypsy schools there are, and we do not know how many there ought to be in the future." See GARF f. 3316 o. 28 d. 793 ll. 112, 92.

94 GARF f. 1235 o. 123 d. 27 ll. 67–8, 96–7, 233 and f. A-296 o. 1 d. 472 ll. 32–4.

95 GARF f. 1235 o. 123 d. 27 l. 222.

96 GARF f. 1235 o. 127 d. 8 l. 182. That the Romani students were underqualified both for teacher training courses and ultimately for teaching itself should not be seen as unusual. Stalin's First Five-Year Plan prioritized the introduction of mandatory universal elementary education for Soviet

children despite the fact that educational officials could never hope in the short term to find enough qualified teachers to staff the rapidly expanding Soviet education system. According to statistics provided by E. Thomas Ewing for the year 1932, 44 per cent of Soviet elementary school teachers had only an elementary-level education themselves. See E. Thomas Ewing, *The Teachers of Stalinism: Policy, Practice, and Power in Soviet Schools of the 1930s* (New York: Peter Lang, 2002), 161–2.

97 Personal papers of N.A. Pankov, quoted in Druts and Gessler, *Tsygane*, 300.
98 GARF f. A-296 o. 1 d. 509 l. 23.
99 GARF f. A-296 o. 1 d. 529 l. 52; GARF f. 1235 o. 127 d. 8 l. 180.
100 GARF f. A-296 o. 1 d. 529 l. 97.
101 GARF f. 1235 o. 127 d. 8 l. 178.
102 Ibid., ll. 184–5.
103 Ibid., l. 163.
104 Ibid., l.165.
105 Ibid., ll. 146, 166, 177.
106 Ibid., ll. 151–3.
107 Ibid., l. 163.
108 Ibid., ll. 7–9, 33, 67; GARF f. 1235 o. 123 d. 28 ll. 230–230ob.
109 GARF f. 1235 o. 127 d. 8 l. 17.
110 Ibid., ll. 17; 102–3.
111 GARF f. 3316 o. 28 d. 794 l. 31.
112 On such assignments, see GARF f. 1235 o. 127 d. 8 ll. 125–34.
113 Ibid., ll. 13, 98, 102–3.
114 GARF f. 3316 o. 28 d. 793 l. 158.
115 Rossiiskii gosudarstvennyi arkhiv sotsial'no-politicheskoi istorii (RGASPI) f. 17 o. 114 d. 837 ll. 99–111.
116 V.G. Toropov, "Istoriia izucheniia tsyganskogo iazyka v Rossii," in *Tsygane: Sbornik statei*, ed. N.G. Demeter and L.I. Missonova (Moscow: IEA RAN, 1999), 20.
117 Hirsch, *Empire of Nations*, 7–9.
118 RGASPI f. 17 o. 114 d. 837 l. 100.
119 Hirsch, *Empire of Nations*, 9. Terry Martin, by contrast, promotes the interpretation of a Stalinist "great retreat" in Soviet nationality policy in the 1930s. See *Affirmative Action Empire*, esp. chapter 10.
120 Here, then, I argue that understanding of the issue is enhanced by a measured appreciation of both Hirsch's and Martin's quite different interpretive emphases in explaining the scaling back of nationality policy's tangible offerings in the mid- to late 1930s, especially for so-called "small" and "backward" minority peoples.

121 GARF f. 1235 o. 127 d. 8 l. 116.

122 Quoted in Peter Blitstein, "Stalin's Nations: Soviet Nationality Policy between Planning and Primordialism, 1936–1953" (PhD diss., University of California-Berkeley, 1999), 139.

123 Quoted in Martin, *Affirmative Action Empire*, 408.

124 TsGAMO f. 66 o. 11 d. 6328 l. 6.

125 Quoted in Martin, *Affirmative Action Empire*, 405.

126 Quoted in Martin, *Affirmative Action Empire*, 439.

127 See ibid., 451–60.

128 See Slezkine, "USSR as a Communal Apartment," 445.

129 GARF f. 3316 o. 28 d. 793 ll. 173–4.

130 GARF f. 3316 o. 28 d. 794 l. 94.

131 GARF f. 3316 o. 30 d. 843 ll. 18–19.

132 Ibid., ll. 66–7.

133 Ibid., ll. 60, 63.

134 Quoted in Martin, *Affirmative Action Empire*, 458.

135 Ibid., 459; and Peter Blitstein, "Nation Building or Russification? Obligatory Russian Instruction in the Soviet Non-Russian School, 1938–1953," in *A State of Nations: Empire and Nation Making in the Age of Lenin and Stalin*, ed. Ronald Grigor Suny and Terry Martin (New York: Oxford University Press, 2001), 258.

136 A.A. Zhdanov, quoted in Blitstein, "Nation-Building or Russification," 258.

137 Martin, *Affirmative Action Empire*, 459.

138 Druts and Gessler, *Tsygane*, 300–1. On the shortage of teachers of Russian in non-Russian schools, see Blitstein, "Nation-Building or Russification," 256.

139 Pankov's personal papers as quoted in Druts and Gessler, *Tsygane*, 301–2.

140 M.V. Sergievskii and A.P. Barannikov, *Tsygansko-russkii slovar'* (Moscow: Izdatel'stvo inostrannykh i natsional'nykh slovarei, 1938).

141 Druts and Gessler, *Tsygane*, 304.

142 Kalinin, *Zagadka baltiiskikh tsygan*, 57.

143 Quoted in Peter Kenez, *The Birth of the Modern Propaganda State: Soviet Methods of Mass Mobilization 1917–1929* (Cambridge: Cambridge University Press, 1985), 145.

144 Pankov's personal papers as quoted in Druts and Gessler, *Tsygane*, 304–5.

3. Parasites, Pariahs, and Proletarians

1 GARF f. 1235 o. 119 d. 9 l. 4.

2 GARF f. 1235 o. 123 d. 27 l. 30.

3 Roma, of course, figured merely as part of the Bolsheviks' larger challenge
to forge a robust, conscious Soviet proletariat from a shrunken, disillusioned working class. See Sheila Fitzpatrick, "The Problem of Class Identity in NEP Society," in *Russia in the Era of NEP: Explorations in Soviet Society
and Culture*, ed. Sheila Fitzpatrick, Alexander Rabinowitch, and Richard
Stites (Bloomington: Indiana University Press, 1991), esp. 12–18.
4 Barannikov, *Tsygany*, 39–49; Demeter, Bessonov, and Kutenkov, *Istoriia
tsygan*, 190–6.
5 GARF f. 1235 o. 119 d. 9 ll. 11–11ob.
6 Ibid., l. 4.
7 GARF f. 1235 o. 120 d. 27 l. 179ob.
8 Rom-Lebedev, *Ot tsyganskogo khora*, 162.
9 See Germano, *Tsygane vchera i segodnia*, 46.
10 Originally printed in *Krest'ianskaia pravda* (Luga) in 1928, this article is
quoted in Demeter, Bessonov, and Kutenkov, *Istoriia tsygan*, 199.
11 OGLMT f. 29 o. 1 d. 49 l. 23.
12 For a contemporary representation of the Romani camp as secretive, yet
internally harmonious, see M. Kosven, "Faraonovo plemia," *30 Dnei*, no. 9
(1925): 69.
13 Germano, *Tsygane vchera i segodnia*, 77.
14 GARF f. 1235 o. 121 d. 31 l. 309.
15 See ibid; GARF f. 1235 o. 120 d. 27 ll. 79, 83–4, 103–4, 140; TsGAMO f. 966 o.
4 d. 1074 l. 37.
16 OGLMT f. 29 o. 1 d. 49 l. 23; M. Rogi, *Tsygane v promkooperatsii* (Moscow:
Koiz, 1934), 24.
17 GARF f. 1235 o. 120 d. 27 l. 84
18 Germano, *Tsygane vchera i segodnia*, 70–1 (quote on 71).
19 GARF f. 4033 o. 1 d. 68 l. 237.
20 *Romany zoria*, no. 1 (November 1927).
21 *Romany zoria*, no. 1 (November 1927).
22 G.Ia., "Romany zoria," *Izvestiia*, 1 September 1928, reprinted in Germano,
Bibliografiia, 99.
23 Aleksandr German, "Sredi pisatelei-tsygan," *Chitatel' i pisatel'*, no. 47 (November 1928): 5.
24 GARF f. 1235 o. 121 d. 31 l. 110ob.
25 OGLMT f. 29 o. 1 d. 49 l. 31; and GARF f. 1235 o. 120 d. 27 l. 115.
26 Rom-Lebedev, *Ot tsyganskogo khora*, 163.
27 Germano, *Tsygane vchera i segodnia*, 90.
28 TsGAMO f. 4341 o.1 d. 271 l. 91.
29 GARF f. 1235 o. 120 d. 27 l. 80; and f. 1235 o. 123 d. 27 ll. 186–7ob.

30 Ibid., l. 186.

31 Rogi, *Tsygane v promkooperatsii*, 24.

32 GARF f. 393 o. 43a d. 1763 ll. 118–118ob.

33 GARF f. 1235 o. 123 d. 27 ll. 186–7ob.

34 E. Gard, "Loly chergen," *Vecherniaia Moskva*, 8 February 1929.

35 Rogi, *Tsygane v promkooperatsii*, 24.

36 Kosven, "Faraonovo plemia," 68–9.

37 V. Nekrasov, "Loly Chergen," *Ekran*, no. 48 (1 December 1929): 6.

38 Aleksandr Tamarin, "Rumpa shal," *Izvestiia*, 17 February 1927.

39 Nekrasov, "Loly Chergen," 6.

40 GARF f. 1235 o. 120 d. 27 ll. 30–8.

41 Aleksandr Germano, "Tsygane," *Bezbozhnik*, no. 1 (January 1928): 11.

42 See Will Guy, "Ways of Looking at Roma: The Case of Czechoslovakia," in *Gypsies: An Interdisciplinary Reader*, ed. Diane Tong (New York: Garland, 1998), esp. 17–23.

43 On Romani slavery, see Achim, *Roma in Romanian History*, esp. chapters 2–3.

44 Yuri Slezkine defines this combination as the "mercuriality" that has fundamentally defined Europe's service nomads – its Jews and Roma in particular. See Slezkine, *The Jewish Century* (Princeton: Princeton University Press, 2004), esp. 4–39.

45 Germano, "Tsygane," 11–12. Germano's claims of the historic persecution of Roma throughout Europe is not only supported but also further explored in Romani Studies scholarship. See, for example, Gheorghe, "Origin of Roma Slavery," esp. 24–25; Guy, "Ways of Looking at Roma," esp. 17–23; Ian Hancock, *The Pariah Syndrome: An Account of Gypsy Slavery and Persecution* (Ann Arbor: Karoma, 1987), esp. 11–60; Donald Kenrick and Grattan Puxon, *The Destiny of Europe's Gypsies* (New York: Basic Books, 1972), esp. 13–56; and Richard J. Pym, *The Gypsies of Early Modern Spain, 1425–1783* (New York: Palgrave MacMillan, 2007).

46 Rogi, *Tsygane v promkooperatsii*, 9.

47 Germano, *Tsygane vchera i segodnia*, 4.

48 Rogi, *Tsygane v promkooperatsii*, 9.

49 Germano, *Tsygane vchera i segodnia*, 4–5.

50 G. Lebedev and A. Germano, "Chto delat' s tsyganami," *Komsomol'skaia pravda*, 11 September 1929, 4.

51 Sheila Fitzpatrick, *Everyday Stalinism: Ordinary Life in Extraordinary Times: Soviet Russia in the 1930s* (New York: Oxford University Press, 1999), chapters 2–3.

52 On collectivization, see Lynne Viola, *Peasant Rebels under Stalin: Collectivization and the Culture of Peasant Resistance* (New York: Oxford University

Press, 1996); Lynne Viola et al., *The War against the Peasantry, 1927–1930: The Tragedy of the Soviet Countryside* (New Haven: Yale University Press, 2005); Sheila Fitzpatrick, *Stalin's Peasants: Resistance and Survival in the Russian Village after Collectivization* (New York: Oxford University Press, 1994); and R.W. Davies, *The Socialist Offensive: The Collectivization of Soviet Agriculture, 1929–1930* (Cambridge: Harvard University Press, 1980).

53 Lynne Viola, *The Unknown Gulag: The Lost World of Stalin's Special Settlements* (New York: Oxford University Press, 2007), 2.

54 Fitzpatrick, *Stalin's Peasants*, 80. On the mass rural exodus that resulted from the First Five-Year Plan's harsh industrialization and collectivization drives, see also idem, "The Great Departure: Rural-Urban Migration in the Soviet Union, 1929–1933," in *Social Dimensions of Soviet Industrialization*, ed. William G. Rosenberg and Lewis H. Siegelbaum (Bloomington: Indiana University Press, 1993); and David L. Hoffmann, *Peasant Metropolis: Social Identities in Moscow, 1929–1941* (Ithaca: Cornell University Press, 1994), esp. 32–72.

55 See, for example, Viola, *Unknown Gulag*, chapter 7; and R.W. Davies and Stephen G. Wheatcroft, *Years of Hunger: Soviet Agriculture, 1931–1933* (New York: Palgrave Macmillan, 2004), chapter 13.

56 Germano, *Tsygane vchera i segodnia*, 46; and Rogi, *Tsygane v promkooperatsii*, 17–18.

57 Popova and Bril', "Tsygane v Soiuze SSR," 134.

58 GARF f. 1235 o. 123 d. 27 l. 31; f. 1235 o. 121 d. 31 l. 381; and Demeter, Bessonov, and Kutenkov, *Istoriia tsygan*, 199–202.

59 Bril', "Tsygane v riady," 63–4; GARF f. 1235 o. 123 d. 29 l. 4.

60 GARF f. 1235 o. 123 d. 27 l. 60.

61 S. Mar, "Iz tabora k fabrike," *Krasnaia niva*, 30 August 1930, quoted in Druts and Gessler, *Tsygane*, 291.

62 P. Orlovets, "Tsygane derevoobdelochniki," *Krasnyi derevoobdelochnik*, no. 10 (15 May 1928): 9.

63 Germano, *Tsygane vchera i segodnia*, 68.

64 Z. Kupershmidt, "Po natsional'nym klubam," *Molodaia gvardiia*, no. 6 (1929): 84.

65 Nekrasov, "Loly chergen," 6.

66 TsGAMO f. 4341 o. 1 d. 271 l. 91ob.

67 TsGAMO f. 966 o. 4 d. 1074 ll. 56–7ob; "Tsyganskii detskii sad v Moskve," *Vecherniaia Moskva*, 15 January 1929.

68 Germano, "O kul'turnoi rabote," 37.

69 Germano's article "*Sovetsko sendo* [The Soviet Court]," for example, outlined the harsh punishments that would be meted criminals in Soviet

courts and shamed horse-thieves for bringing ill repute to Gypsies as a nationality. A. Germano, "Sovetsko sendo," *Romany zoria*, no. 2 (1929): 19–22. A Russian-language translation can be found in OGLMT f. 29 o. 1 d. 78 ll. 81–8.

70 Ackerley, "Russian Gypsies under the Soviets," 197.

71 *Nevo drom*, no. 1 (January 1932): 12–13.

72 OGLMT f. 29 o. 1 d. 49 l. 37.

73 GARF f. 1235 o. 123 d. 27 l. 66.

74 Ibid.

75 Ibid., l. 194.

76 Bril', "Tsygane v riady," 61.

77 GARF f. 1235 o. 120 d. 27 l. 32.

78 Kosven, "Faraonovo plemia," 69.

79 GARF f. 1235 o. 120 d. 27 l. 32.

80 As the state confronted resistance to its industrialization and collectivization programs in the early 1930s, it widely deployed class as a labelling mechanism to divide and discipline populations, to separate citizens from class enemies, and thus to force the momentum of socialist construction. See Sheila Fitzpatrick, "Ascribing Class: The Construction of Social Identity in Soviet Russia," *The Journal of Modern History* 65, no. 4 (December 1993): 745–70.

81 Germano, *Tsygane vchera i segodnia*, 53–4.

82 In the early 1930s, Soviet ethnographers struggled to make sense of nomadic societies generally, and of nomads' resistance to settle and participate in "legitimate labour" in particular. They abandoned earlier theories of pastoral nomadic societies as being stuck (rather charmingly) in the Marxist stage of primitive communism and constructed instead a vision of nomadic feudalism. Nomadic societies were thereby characterized in Marxist terms by a division between "kulak" owners of herds resistant to socialism and the poor, propertyless nomads whom they oppressed. See Ernest Gellner's "The Nomadism Debate" in his *State and Society in Soviet Thought* (Oxford: Basil Blackwell, 1988), 92–114. On how this new conceptualization of nomadic feudalism was applied to Turkmen nomads in the 1930s, see Edgar, *Tribal Nation*, esp. 193–6. On the invention of kulaks among the reindeer pastoralists and fishermen of Siberia, see Slezkine, *Arctic Mirrors*, 187–204.

83 Fitzpatrick, *Stalin's Peasants*, 80. Hoffmann places this massive peasant inmigration to Soviet cities (especially Moscow) in its wider social, cultural, economic, and political context in his *Peasant Metropolis*.

84 GARF f. 1235 o. 123 d. 27 l. 64.

85 OGLMT f. 29 o. 1 d. 49 l. 23.

86 GARF f. 1235 o. 123 d. 28 l. 222.

87 GARF f. 1235 o. 123 d. 27 ll. 16, 21, 31; f. 1235 o. 121 d. 31 l. 381.

88 On the characteristic squalor of migrant living conditions in Moscow, see
    Hoffmann, *Peasant Metropolis*, esp. 127–57. On miserable conditions as a
    defining feature of Soviet urban life in the 1930s, see Fitzpatrick, *Everyday
    Stalinism*, chapter 2. On abysmal hygienic norms in early Soviet cities, see
    Starks, *Body Soviet*, 126–33.

89 GARF f. 1235 o. 123 d. 27 l. 56; f. 1235 o. 123 d. 28 l. 222; f. 1235 o. 123 d. 29
    ll. 22, 25.

90 GARF f. 1235 o. 123 d. 27 l. 65; f. 1235 o. 123 d. 29 ll. 17–18.

91 GARF f. 1235 o. 123 d. 27 l. 65. The leaders of these artels did, however,
    publicly complain rather early on that they could not secure necessary
    materials by legal means. See ibid., ll. 74–6.

92 Alaina Lemon, "Indic Diaspora, Soviet History, Russian Home: Political
    Performances and Sincere Ironies in Romani Cultures" (PhD diss., Univer-
    sity of Chicago, 1996), 168. Lemon also notes that "Vlax Roma in Eastern
    Europe and in Russia had long been accustomed to working in 'artel-like'
    groups … which were organized according to kinship and fictive kinship
    affiliations, and to a 'socialist' ethic of splitting up profits equally among
    partners. State affiliation and subsidization changed only their official
    name." The state, however, chose to ignore the cultural roots of Vlax
    Roma's reliance on kinship in forming their "pseudo-artels." Ibid., 176.

93 GARF f. A-296 o. 1 d. 495 l. 11ob; f. 1235 o. 123 d. 27 l. 64.

94 Ibid., l. 65.

95 Ibid. On the activists' role as artel inspectors, see GARF f. 1235 o. 123 d. 29
    ll. 13–21; f. 2360 o. 1 d. 2067 l. 19.

96 Lemon, "Indic Diaspora," 179.

97 GARF f. 1235 o. 123 d. 27 l. 65. On denunciation as a form of self-fashion-
    ing, see GolfoAlexopoulos, "Victim Talk: Defense Testimony and Denun-
    ciation under Stalin," in *Russian Modernity: Politics, Knowledge, Practices*,
    ed. David Hoffman and Yanni Kotsonis (New York: St Martin's, 2000),
    204–20.

98 On the *kris*, see Lev Tcherenkov and Stéphane Laederich, *The Rroma*
    (Basel: Schwabe, 2004), 2:665–98; Weyrauch and Bell, "Autonomous
    Lawmaking"; and Ronald Lee, "The Rom-Vlach Gypsies and the Kris-
    Romani," in *Gypsy Law: Romani Legal Traditions and Culture*, ed. Walter O.
    Weyrauch (Berkeley: University of California Press, 2001), 188–230.

99 Germano, *Vchera i segodnia*, 29.

100 GARF f. 1235 o. 123 d. 27 l. 65.

101 See Paul Hagenloh, *Stalin's Police: Public Order and Mass Repression in the USSR* (Washington, DC: Woodrow Wilson Center, 2009), esp. 89–119; and David Shearer, *Policing Stalin's Socialism: Repression and Social Order in the Soviet Union, 1924–1953* (New Haven: Yale University Press, 2009), esp. 57–63, 187–92.

102 Gijs Kessler, "The Passport System and State Control over Population Flows in the Soviet Union, 1932–1940," *Cahiers du Monde russe* 42, no. 2–4 (2001): 482.

103 See Shearer, *Policing Stalin's Socialism*, esp. 57–63; and Hagenloh, *Stalin's Police*, esp. chapter 3.

104 Hagenloh, *Stalin's Police*, 103–19; Kessler, "Passport System," 479–82; and Shearer, *Stalin's Police*, esp. chapter 6.

105 On the Soviet internal passport system as a tool of population control, social discipline, police surveillance, and identity construction, see Marc Garcelon, "Colonizing the Subject: The Genealogy and Legacy of the Soviet Internal Passport," in *Documenting Individual Identity: The Development of State Practices in the Modern World*, ed. Jane Caplan and John Torpey (Princeton: Princeton University Press, 2001), 83–100; Hagenloh, *Stalin's Police*, 119–32; Kessler, "Passport System"; David Shearer, "Elements Near and Alien: Passportization, Policing, and Identity in the Stalinist State, 1932–1952," *The Journal of Modern History* 76, no. 4 (December 2004): 835–81; and idem, *Stalin's Police*, chapter 6. On the pre- and postrevolutionary intellectual heritage that informed Stalinist efforts to immunize those citizens deemed "healthy" from those deemed "socially dangerous," see Beer, *Renovating Russia*, esp. chapter 5.

106 Shearer, *Policing Stalin's Socialism*, esp. chapter 8 (quote on page 4).

107 Trial records of the case are archived in GARF f. 1235 o. 123 d. 27 ll. 195–220. I have chosen not to identify by name either the defendants or the Romani activists who testified against them.

108 Lemon, *Between Two Fires*, 171. Lemon also provides a fascinating account of sharing the details of the archival records on this case with the descendants of several of the accused in the early 1990s. See ibid., 166–93.

109 GARF f. 1235 o. 123 d. 27 ll. 219–219ob.

110 Ibid., l. 212.

111 Ibid., l. 212ob. As with nearly all aspects of the case, the prosecution relied heavily on testimony provided by those Romani activists who supplied not only accusations, but also descriptions of how the *kris* worked.

112 See, for example, ibid., ll. 211ob; 207ob.

113 Ibid., l. 209ob. For the alleged details surrounding the *kris* and the murders in question, see Ibid. ll. 198ob–212. It must be pointed out that the

features of the *kris* which Soviet authorities decried as "anti-Soviet" can be understood as traditional components of "autonomous law-making" in some Romani cultures. According to Weyrauch and Bell, the fundamental purpose of the *kris* is to avoid having private disputes resolved by state legal structures that are perceived by Romani communities as foreign, externally imposed, and devoid of decency. The function of the *kris* – as some Romani defendants in this case admitted under questioning – is to bring peace and reconciliation to the community, and one of the most common solutions to a dispute is to have the offending party pay a fine as decided upon by adjudicating *kris* elders. When faced with interference on the part of state authorities, Romani communities that adhere to the *kris* have been known to frustrate investigations, legal proceedings, and state-imposed punishments by various means. See Weyrauch and Bell, "Autonomous Lawmaking."

114 GARF f. 1235 o. 123 d. 27 ll. 206ob, 212ob. On the early Soviet obsession with "unmasking" deceivers and imposters, see Fitzpatrick, *Tear Off the Masks*.

115 GARF f. 1235 o. 123 d. 27 l. 212ob.

116 On the *kris* as a source of internal cohesion, see Weyrauch and Bell, "Autonomous Lawmaking."

117 As both Terry Martin and Amir Weiner have noted, Soviet repression of certain nationalities increased especially after Stalin's notable 1933 announcement that "The remnants of capitalism in the people's consciousness are much more dynamic in the sphere of nationality than in any other area. This is because they can mask themselves so well in national costume." Quoted in Martin, *Affirmative Action Empire*, 6. See also Amir Weiner, *Making Sense of War: The Second World War and the Fate of the Bolshevik Revolution* (Princeton: Princeton University Press, 2001), 139.

118 GARF f. 1235 o. 130 d. 5 ll. 127–28, 131. A report from the Moscow City Executive Committee reported that still another eighty Roma had been arrested in September 1932. Though exact numbers are not available, archival documents suggest that at least several hundred Romani artel workers were arrested in both Moscow and Smolensk during the early 1930s. GARF f. 1235 o. 123 d. 29 ll. 27, 75, 205, 228; and Nikolai Bessonov, "Ubity za trudoliubie," *30 Oktiabria*, no. 23 (2002): 5.

119 On the Soviet "cleansing state" and its efforts to "excise" nationalities perceived as potentially irredeemable, see Weiner, *Making Sense of War*, chapter 3; and Francine Hirsch, "Race without the Practice of Racial Politics," *Slavic Review* 61, no. 1 (Spring 2002): 30–43.

120 GARF f. 1235 o. 123 d. 28 ll. 121ob–122.

121 Ibid., l. 84.

122 Ibid., ll. 143ob–145ob.

123 Ibid., l. 83.

124 Ibid., l. 87.

125 Ibid., ll. 65–8; 364.

126 Ibid., l. 364.

127 Ibid., ll. 191–2.

128 Ibid., l. 87.

129 Ibid., l. 121ob.

130 Ibid., l. 125.

131 Ibid., l. 123.

132 GARF f. 9479 o. 1 d. 19 l. 7. In the spring and summer of 1933, the OGPU vigorously sought to "cleanse" the Soviet Union's closed cities of passportless marginals deemed "socially harmful elements." See, for example, Shearer, *Policing Stalin's Socialism*, esp. chapter 6; and Nicolas Werth, *Cannibal Island: Death in a Siberian Gulag* (Princeton: Princeton University Press, 2007).

133 Iu.A. Poliakov and V.B. Zhiromskaia, eds., *Naselenie Rossii v XX veke: Istoricheskie ocherki. Tom. 1 1900–1939* (Moscow: Rosspen, 2000), 308. On the Stalinist logic behind the special settlements and the fate of special settlers more broadly, see Viola, *Unknown Gulag*, as well as Shearer, *Policing Stalin's Socialism*, 253–60.

134 GARF f. 1235 o. 123 d. 28 l. 107.

135 Ibid., l. 163. Gerasimov made this charge in a November 1933 report addressed to the Nationalities Department of VTsIK, Narkomzem, MOZO, the Moscow Party Committee, and the Nationalities Sector of the Moscow Oblast' Executive Committee.

136 GARF f. 1235 o. 128 d. 2 l. 107.

137 P. Surozhskii, "Natsmenkluby pered smotrom," *Klub i revoliutsiia*, no. 2 (January 1931): 18–19.

138 GARF f. 1235 o. 123 d. 28 l. 332; Bril', "Tsygane v riady," 65.

139 GARF f. 1235 o. 123 d. 29 ll. 81–3, 104, 122–5, 161.

140 Ibid., l. 215.

141 Ibid., l. 233.

142 GARF f. 1235 o. 128 d. 3 ll. 212–14.

143 Ibid., l. 166.

144 Rogi, *Tsygane v promkooperatsii*, 37.

145 Ibid., 38. The majority of Tsygkhimprom's Romani employees identified themselves as former nomads. See GARF f. 3316 o. 28 d. 794 ll. 158–9.

146 Quoted in Rogi, *Tsygane v promkooperatsii*, 47–8.

147 GARF f. 1235 o. 123 d. 29 l. 179.

148 Ibid., l. 202ob.

149 Ibid., l. 200.

150 Ibid., l. 200ob, 263. Strikingly, officials also noted that Roma employed in large factories alongside other nationalities "quickly assimilate, quit going to their own club, and cease to socialize with Gypsies."

151 See the transcript of a 25 February 1934 meeting of the Moscow Council of Industrial Cooperatives for the attention paid to the fact that Tsygkhimprom and Tsygpishcheprom's Romani workers were "Russian" and not "foreign." GARF f. 1235 o. 123 d. 29 ll. 169ob–179.

152 Ibid., l. 198; GARF f. 1235 o. 123 d. 28 l. 115.

153 GARF f. 1235 o. 128 d. 3 l. 212.

154 GARF f. 1235 o. 123 d. 29 l. 198ob.

155 Ibid., ll. 170, 171ob, 197.

156 Ibid., l. 195.

157 Ibid., ll. 260–3.

158 Ibid., l. 261. The village was ultimately established 68 kilometers from the Soviet capital in the Pavlovskii Posad region of Moscow Province.

159 Ibid., ll. 219–21, 260–3.

160 GARF f. 1235 o. 131 d. 19 l. 46.

161 Ibid., l. 52.

162 Ibid., l. 69.

163 Ibid., l. 98.

164 GARF f. 1235 o. 130 d. 5 l. 129.

165 GARF f. 1235 o. 131 d. 19 l. 97.

166 Ibid., l. 98, 128; GARF f. 1235 o. 130 d. 5 l. 134.

167 GARF f. 1235 o. 131 d. 19 l. 120

168 Ibid., ll. 52, 113.

169 Ibid., l. 127.

170 GARF f. 3316 o. 28 d. 794 ll. 142–3, 186.

171 GARF f. 1235 o. 131 d. 19 ll.151–2.

172 Ibid., l. 215ob.

173 GARF f. 3316 o. 28 d. 793 l. 93.

174 Ibid., ll. 100–1. Though *Revoliutsiia i natsional'nosti* reprinted much of the transcript of this conference, Baranovskii's complaint and all direct references to it were not reproduced. See "Soveshchanie po trudoustroistvu i kul'turno-bytovomu obsluzhivaniiu tsygan," *Revoliutsiia i natsional'nosti*, no. 2 (February 1936): 61–72.

175 GARF f. 3316 o. 28 d. 793 l. 102.

176 Ibid., ll. 112–13, 116.

177 Ibid., ll. 77, 117.
178 Ibid., l. 79.
179 On state violence in the Soviet Union as a technique of refashioning Soviet citizens, "cleansing" the social body, and thereby perfecting both the
     individual and the collective, see Peter Holquist, "State Violence as Technique: The Logic of Violence in Soviet Totalitarianism," in *Landscaping the
     Human Garden: Twentieth-Century Population Management in a Comparative
     Framework*, ed. Amir Weiner (Stanford: Stanford University Press, 2003),
     19–45. David Hoffmann places Soviet excisionary violence in comparative
     perspective in *Cultivating the Masses*, chapter 5.

4. Nomads into Farmers

 1 *Poslednii tabor*, directed by E. Shneider and M. Gol'dblat (1935; Moscow:
    Vostok Video, 2006), DVD.
 2 On the failures of Soviet efforts to settle and collectivize nomadic and
    seminomadic minority citizens, see Martha Brill Olcott, "The Collectivization Drive in Kazakhstan," *Russian Review* 40, no. 2 (April 1981): 122–42;
    Niccolo Pianciola, "Famine in the Steppe: The Collectivization of Agriculture and the Kazak Herdsmen 1928–1934," *Cahiers du Monde russe* 45,
    no. 1–2 (2004): 137–92; idem, "The Collectivization Famine in Kazakhstan,
    1931–1933," *Harvard Ukrainian Studies* 25, no. 3–4 (2001): 237–51; Edgar,
    Tribal Nation, 197–220; and Slezkine, *Arctic Mirrors*, 187–217.
 3 "Soveshchanie po voprosam osedaniia kochevykh khoziastv i zemleustroistva kolkhozov natsional'nykh respublik i oblastei," *Revoliutsiia
    i natsional'nosti*, no. 10 (1935): 85. See also A. Khatskevich, "Ob osedanii
    kochevogo i polukochevogo naseleniia," *Revoliutsiia i natsional'nosti*, no. 12
    (1934): 15–24.
 4 "Soveshchanie po voprosam," 85.
 5 M.A. Sergeev, "The Building of Socialism among the Peoples of Northern
    Siberia and the Soviet Far East," in *The Peoples of Siberia*, trans. Stephen
    Dunn, ed. M.G. Levin and L.P. Potapov (Chicago: University of Chicago
    Press, 1964), 488.
 6 Ibid., 489. Soviet policymakers are not alone in their dolorous portrayal of
    pastoral nomadism. Pastoral nomadism has been castigated often, widely,
    and wrongly as economically inefficient and culturally primitive. Thomas J.
    Barfield, *The Nomadic Alternative* (Englewood Cliffs, NJ: Prentice Hall, 1993).
 7 Quoted in Slezkine, *Arctic Mirrors*, 205.
 8 See Gellner, *State and Society in Soviet Thought*, 92–114.
 9 On the "conceptual conquest" of the Soviet Union, see Hirsch, *Empire of
    Nations*. On how and why the Stalinist state faced a wider and persistent

problem of Soviet citizens' "wanderlust," see the overview provided in Mark Edele, *Stalinist Society 1928–1953* (New York: Oxford University Press, 2011), chapter 3.

10 For a contemporary articulation of Roma's "distinctive nomadism," see Barannikov, *Tsygany SSSR*, 28.

11 On the seeming challenges posed to Soviet officialdom by the Kazakhs whom they were to sedentarize and collectivize, see Pianciola, "Collectivization Famine in Kazakhstan," esp. 237–9, and idem, "Famine in the Steppe," esp. 139–47.

12 Whether Roma should be considered nomads remains a matter of dispute. In his widely influential study of pastoral nomadism, A.M. Khazanov argued that Roma do not belong to the category of nomads at all, and should instead be classified as an "ethnic-professional group." A.M. Khazanov, *Nomads and the Outside World* (Cambridge: Cambridge University Press, 1984), 15. Others, however, maintain that peripatetics who derive subsistence from commercial or other "extracting" activity, like their pastoralist counterparts, are nomads. For an articulation of this view as well as a concise history of competing definitions of "nomadism," see Aparna Rao, "The Concept of Peripatetics: An Introduction," in *The Other Nomads: Peripatetic Minorities in Cross Cultural Perspective*, ed. Aparna Rao (Köln: Böhlau Verlag, 1987), 1–32. Philip Carl Salzman is purposefully vague and inclusive in his definition of nomadism as "movement of the household during the annual round of productive activities." He intentionally refuses to specify a criteria for the "productive activities" that his definition of nomadism references. See Philip Carl Salzman, ed., *When Nomads Settle: Processes of Sedentarization as Adaptation and Response* (New York: Praeger, 1980), 10–11. More recently, Yuri Slezkine offered a still more inclusive understanding of service nomadism with his provocative argument that "Modernity was about everyone becoming a service nomad: mobile, clever, articulate, occupationally flexible, and good at being a stranger." Slezkine, *Jewish Century*, 30.

13 For a contemporary articulation of this theory, see Barannikov, *Tsygany SSSR*, 28.

14 This decree is reprinted in Germano, *Bibliografiia o tsyganakh*, 89–90.

15 GARF f. 1235 o. 121 d. 31 l. 78

16 For examples of such requests, see GARF f. 1235 o. 124 d. 25 ll. 92–3; 163–163ob.

17 Bril', "Tsygane v riady," 62.

18 GARF f. 1235 o. 121 d. 31 l. 145. For examples of press features about the Krikunov village, see P. Orlovets, "Tsyganskaia kommuna," *Pravda*, 2 October 1927, 4; D. Mallor, "Tsygane na zemle," *Izvestiia* 4 April 1928, 6.

19 Ibid., l. 56. In 1932, a Kolkhoztsentr official reported that the Krikunov
    settlement collapsed definitively only in 1931 after several of the collec-
    tive's members were arrested for horse-thieving. With their comrades
    in jail, this official reported, all those Romani settlers who still remained
    finally abandoned the commune. See Rossiiskii gosudarstvennyi arkhiv
    ekonomiki (RGAE) f. 7446 o. 13 d. 83 l. 77

20 GARF f. 1235 o. 123 d. 27 ll. 192–4ob.

21 GARF f. 1235 o. 121 d. 31 l. 51.

22 Ibid., l. 53.

23 Ibid., l. 55.

24 D. Savvov and G. Lebedev, "Otbrosit' v proshloe kochev'ia: Vkliuchim tsy-
    gan v aktivnoe stroitel'stvo sotsializma," *Komsomol'skaia pravda*, 6 February
    1930, 3.

25 On Soviet stereotypes of Jews and early Soviet efforts to promote Jews'
    compact agricultural settlement, see Robert Weinberg, *Stalin's Forgotten
    Zion: Birobidzhan and the Making of a Soviet Jewish Homeland* (Berkeley: Uni-
    versity of California Press, 1998), esp. 13–71; and Zvi Gitelman, *A Century
    of Ambivalence: The Jews of Russia and the Soviet Union, 1881 to the Present*,
    2nd ed. (Bloomington: Indiana University Press, 2001), esp. 94–108.

26 On the improvised and violent nature of the 1929–30 collectivization drive,
    see Viola, *Peasant Rebels under Stalin*; and Fitzpatrick, *Stalin's Peasants*, esp.
    chapter 2.

27 Relatedly, Pianciola argues that central and local officials similarly ap-
    proached the sedentarization and collectivization of Kazakh pastoralists
    with disastrous "indifference" during Stalin's revolution from above. This
    violently incarnated indifference resulted in famine, disease, and the over-
    whelming loss of both Kazakh lives and livestock. See Pianciola, "Famine
    in the Steppe," esp. 186–91. For a powerful personal account of dekulakiza-
    tion, collectivization, and famine in the Kazakh SSR, see Mukhamet
    Shayakhmetov, *The Silent Steppe: The Memoir of a Kazakh Nomad under Stalin*,
    trans. Jan Butler (New York: Rookery, 2006).

28 OGLMT f. 29 o. 1 d. 78 l. 41. The haphazardness of state efforts to sedenta-
    rize and collectivize nomads was witnessed among other national groups
    as well. In his discussion of the Soviet sedentarization campaign in Siberia,
    the ethnographer M.A. Sergeev noted that during the early 1930s, "the pro-
    cess of sedentarization proceeded very slowly and to a considerable degree
    exhibited an accidental nature. It sometimes proceeded by the initiative
    and efforts of the collective farms themselves." M.A. Sergeev, *Nekapitalis-
    ticheskii put' razvitiia malykh narodov severa* (Moscow: Izdatel'stvo akademii
    nauk SSSR, 1955), 456.

29 GARF f. 1235 o. 125 d. 320 ll. 1–4.

30 OGLMT f. 29 o. 1 d. 78 ll. 77–80.

31 GARF f. 1235 o. 121 d. 31 l. 21.

32 RGAE f. 7446 o. 13 d. 42 ll. 16–16ob.

33 GARF f. 1235 o. 123 d. 27 l. 38ob.

34 RGAE f. 7446 o. 13 d. 83.

35 GARF f. 1235 o. 130 d. 5 l. 40.

36 RGAE f. 7446 o. 13 d. 83 l. 111.

37 Ibid., l. 131.

38 Ibid., l. 111.

39 See ibid., ll. 121–121ob, 123; and GARF f. 1235 o. 123 d. 28 ll. 404–404ob.

40 RGAE f. 7446 o. 13 d. 83 l. 17.

41 Ibid., ll. 37–9; 43–6.

42 Ibid., ll. 45–6. Although Smolensk Province was officially designated as the Union's "Western Province" between 1929 and 1937, I refer to the region as Smolensk Province for consistency's sake.

43 Ibid., l. 113.

44 GARF f. 1235 o. 128 d. 2 l. 236.

45 Ibid., l. 174.

46 Ibid., ll. 170–1.

47 GARF f. 1235 o. 128 d. 2 l. 111.

48 Ibid., l. 173.

49 Ibid., l. 111.

50 Ibid., l. 105.

51 GARF f. 1235 o. 123 d. 28 ll. 360, 401, 403.

52 See, for example, Olcott, "Collectivization Drive in Kazakhstan"; Pianciola, "Famine in the Steppe"; idem, "Collectivization Famine in Kazakhstan"; and Shayakhmetov, *Silent Steppe*.

53 GARF f. 1235 o. 12 d. 31 l. 390ob (Pol' Vaiiana Kuriuv'e, "Tsyganskii kolkhoz," *Trud*, 6 June 1931).

54 On the "Potemkin village" as an omnipresent trope in the Stalinist press and popular culture after collectivization, see Fitzpatrick, *Stalin's Peasants*, chapter 10.

55 RGAE f. 7446 o. 13 d. 83 ll. 2–3.

56 GARF f. 1235 o. 123 d. 28 l. 421.

57 Ibid., ll. 152–152ob.

58 RGAE f. 7446 o. 13 d. 83 l. 89.

59 Ibid., l. 4.

60 Ibid., ll. 79–80; 92; 104–104ob.

61 Ibid., ll. 102–3.

62 Ibid., ll. 81–3.

63 Ibid., ll. 102, 98.

64 Ibid., ll. 89–89ob.

65 GARF f. 1235 o. 123 d. 28 l. 76.

66 Ibid., l. 421.

67 Ibid., l. 305.

68 T.F. Kiseleva, "Tsygany evropeiskoi chasti soiuza SSR i ikh perekhod ot kochevaniia k osedlosti," (PhD diss., Moscow State University, 1952), 159.

69 The 24 May 1934 issue is archived in GARF f. 1235 o. 123 d. 28 ll. 255–255ob. Only two issues were published.

70 GARF f. 3316 o. 28 d. 793 l. 90.

71 GARF f. 1235 o. 123 d. 28 ll. 417–18.

72 GARF f. 3316 o. 28 d. 793 ll. 209, 210.

73 Ibid., ll. 90–1.

74 GARF f. 1235 o. 123 d. 28 l. 417.

75 GARF f. 3316 o. 28 d. 794 ll. 97–9.

76 GARF f. 1235 o. 123 d. 28 l. 415–16, and GARF f. 1235 o. 130 d. 5 ll. 267–71.

77 Gosudarstvennyi arkhiv Krasnodarskogo kraia (GAKK) f. R-580 o. 1 d. 636 ll. 67ob.

78 Stalingrad Province was home to as many as thirty nationalities, which together comprised an approximate 12 per cent of the province's population. Relative to larger Kalmyk, Tatar, and Kazak populations in the province, Roma were considered numerically insignificant by provincial authorities. See Anver Tazhurizin, "Obsluzhivanie natsional'nostei v Stalingradskom krae," *Revoliutsiia i natsional'nosti*, no. 6 (1935): 63–72; and idem, "O rabote sredi natsmen'shinstv Stalingradskoi oblasti," *Revoliutsiia i natsional'nosti*, no. 8 (1937): 74–80.

79 Gosudarstvennyi arkhiv Volgogradskoi oblasti (GAVO) f. 2059 o. 2 d. 186 l. 5. G.M. Krikunov likely relocated to "Natsmen Gypsy" from the North Caucasus's "Krikunov village" following its collapse in 1931.

80 GARF f. 1235 o. 123 d. 28 ll. 1–2, 382; GAVO f. R-2059 o. 2 d. 11 l. 106.

81 GARF f. 1235 o. 123 d. 28 l. 382; GAVO f. R-2059 o. 2 d. 11 ll. 106–7ob.

82 GAVO f. R-2059 o. 2 d. 186 ll. 5, 50–2; f. R-2059 o. 2 d. 468 ll. 107, 109–109ob; f. R-2059 o. 2 d. 345 l. 121.

83 GAVO f. R-2059 o. 2 d. 345 l. 120.

84 GAVO f. R-2059 o. 2 d. 186 l. 5

85 Ibid., ll. 6–6ob.

86 GARF f. 1235 o. 123 d. 27 ll. 5–6; GAVO f. R-2059 o. 2 d. 619 l. 156.

87 See M. Bril', "Tsygane v riady," 63.

88 GAVO f. R-2059 o. 2 d. 619 ll. 155–6.

89 GARF f. 1235 o. 123 d. 28 l. 320.

90 Ibid., l. 246.

91 GARF f. 3316 o. 28 d. 794 l. 117.

92 Ibid., l. 193.

93 Ibid., l. 191.

94 Ibid., l. 192.

95 Ibid., l. 190.

96 Ibid., ll. 212–13.

97 Rogers, *Old Faith and the Russian Land*, esp. chapter 3. On a related note, Tracy McDonald has shown how rural soviet chairmen often "represented a voice of reason" in the countryside during collectivization, defending peasants' interests, helping to moderate the blunt force of state policies on village life, and potentially even staving off violent peasant resistance to collectivization. See her *Face to the Village: The Riazan Countryside under Soviet Rule, 1921–1930* (Toronto: University of Toronto Press, 2011), esp. 270–8 (quote on 275).

98 Quoted in Germano, *Tsygane vchera i segodnia*, 5.

99 Kiseleva, "Tsygane evropeiskoi chasti," 166.

100 Quoted in Germano, *Tsygane vchera i segodnia*, 6.

101 GARF f. 1235 o. 123 d. 109 ll. 1–2.

102 GASO f. R-2360 o. 1 d. 194 l. 36.

103 GASO f. R-2360 o. 2 d. 2069 l. 12; RGAE f. 7446 o. 13 d. 83 l. 65.

104 GASO f. R-2360 o. 2 d. 2069 l. 20.

105 GARF f. 3316 o. 28 d. 793 l. 120.

106 RGAE f. 7446 o. 13 d. 83 l. 65.

107 GASO f. R-2360 o. 1 d. 2069 ll. 12, 52.

108 RGAE f. 7446 o. 13 d. 83 l. 66.

109 GASO f. R-2360 o. 1 d. 2069 ll. 52–3; f. R-2360 o. 2 d. 2069 l. 12; f. R-2360 o. 1 d. 1478 ll. 74–6.

110 RGAE f. 7446 o. 13 d. 83 l. 21.

111 GASO f. R-2360 o. 1 d. 2069 ll. 52–3.

112 GASO f. R-2360 o. 1 d. 1478 l. 74.

113 Ibid., l.74ob.

114 For an excellent collection of documents chronicling Smolensk Province's administering of early Soviet nationality policy, see G.N. Mozgunova, ed., *Sudby natsional'nykh men'shinstv na Smolenshchine 1918–1938 gody: Dokumenty i materialy* (Smolensk: 1994).

115 GARF f. 1235 o. 125 d. 60 l. 35.

116 GASO f. R-2350 o. 2 d. 44 l. 88; f. R-2350 o. 2 d. 46 l. 72.

117 GASO f. R-2350 o. 4 d. 90 ll. 452–452ob. Across the board, Romani el-
     ementary school enrolment in Smolensk Province had grown by a rate of
     118.6 per cent in the 1933–34 academic year. See GASO f. R-2350 o. 5 d.
     179 l. 88.

118 GARF f. 3316 o. 28 d. 793, unnumbered document (M. Rogi, "Novaia
     zhizn'," *Za kommunisticheskoe prosveshchenie*, 30 October 1934).

119 GASO f. R-2350 o. 3 d. 138 l. 64ob.

120 GASO f. R-2360 o. 1 d. 817 ll. 13, 75ob; GASO f. R-2350 o. 2 d. 46 ll. 119,
     121.

121 GASO f. R-2350 o. 2 d. 46 l. 119.

122 Ibid., l. 109.

123 GASO f. R-2360 o. 1 d. 1482 l. 34 and f. R-2360 o. 1 d. 2068 l. 25.

124 GASO f. R-2360 o. 1 d. 2067 l. 4.

125 GASO f. R-2360 o. 2 d. 2069 l. 23.

126 Ibid., l. 38.

127 GASO f. R-2360 o. 1 d. 2067 ll. 13–16; f. R-2360 o. 1 d. 2697 ll. 24–6ob; f.
     R-2360 o. 1 d. 2068 ll. 66, 68, 128; f. R-2360 o. 2 d. 2069 ll. 58–62, 73,79.

128 GARF f. 1235 o. 123 d. 28 ll. 367–367ob.

129 GASO f. R-2360 o. 2 d. 432 l. 113.

130 GARF f. 3316 o. 28 d. 793 ll. 8, 120; GASO f. R-2360 o. 1 d. 2073 l. 93.

131 GASO f. R-2360 o. 2 d. 432 l. 74.

132 GASO f. R-2360 o. 2 d. 1524 ll. 73–4; GARF f. 3316 o. 28 d. 793 ll. 119–23.

133 GARF f. 1235 o. 28 d. 793 l. 368.

134 "Soveshchanie po voprosam osedaniia," 85–7.

135 GARF f. 1235 o. 123 d. 28 ll. 242, 283, 300.

136 GARF f. 3316 o. 28 d. 793 l. 9.

137 GARF f. 1235 o. 130 d. 5 l. 85.

138 Ibid., l. 77.

139 Ibid., l. 84.

140 Ibid., l. 90

141 Ibid., l. 100.

142 Ibid., l. 85.

143 Ibid., l. 136. For the results of the commission's expedition to the Mari
     Autonomous Oblast' in Gor'kovskii Krai, see GARF f. 1235 o. 130 d. 5 ll.
     113–15. On the possibility of establishing a Gypsy region in the Western
     Siberian Krai, see GARF f. 1235 o. 130 d. 9 ("Delo ob organizatsii v pre-
     delakh Zapadno-Sibirskogo kraia avtonomnoi oblasti tsygan").

144 GARF f. 1235 o. 130 d. 5 l. 136.

145 N. Voronin, "Voprosy trudoustroistva kochuiuishchikh tsygan," *Vlast'
     sovetov*, no. 19 (15 October 1935): 14–16.

146 GARF f. 3316 o. 28 d. 793 l. 57.

147 Ibid., l. 154.

148 GARF f. 3316 o. 28 d. 793 l. 131.

149 Ibid., l. 89.

150 Ibid., l. 131ob.

151 Ibid., ll. 90–2.

152 Ibid., l. 94.

153 Ibid., ll. 95–6.

154 Ibid., l. 88.

155 Ibid., l. 89.

156 Ibid., l. 88.

157 Ibid., ll. 85–6.

158 Ibid., ll. 105–6.

159 Ibid., ll. 106–7.

160 Ibid., l. 81.

161 Ibid., ll. 113–16.

162 GARF f. 3316 o. 28 d. 794 ll. 10, 12–13.

163 GARF f. 1235 o. 130 d. 5 l. 216.

164 GARF f. 3316 o. 28 d. 794 ll. 70–6.

165 Ibid., ll. 141, 148, 178, 180–2, 184–204, 210–12, 222.

166 Ibid., ll. 110, 122, 149; f. 1235 o. 130 d. 5 ll. 246–7.

167 Ibid., ll. 215, 253–4.

168 RGAE f. 5675 o. 1 d. 168 ll. 1–2; f. 5675 o.1 d. 179 ll. 24–6, 36–9, 59; f. 5675 o.1 d. 180 ll. 104–10; f. 5675 o. 1 d. 218 ll. 2, 4–5ob, 15; GARF f. 5446 o. 18 d. 916 ll. 5–9.

169 GARF f. 1235 o. 130 d. 5 l. 264; GARF f. 3316 o. 28 d. 794 l. 218.

170 GARF f. 3316 o. 28 d. 794 ll. 219–22.

171 GARF f. 1235 o. 130 d. 5 ll. 230–7.

172 Ibid., l. 235.

173 See Weinberg, *Stalin's Forgotten Zion*, esp. 13–21.

174 Quoted in Gitelman, *Century of Ambivalence*, 98.

175 Ibid., 98–104.

176 See Weinberg, *Stalin's Forgotten Zion*, esp. 21–58.

177 On the Nazi genocide of Roma, see Martin Holler, "Like Jews? The Nazi Persecution and Extermination of Soviet Roma under the German Military Administration: A New Interpretation, Based on Soviet Sources," *DAPIM Studies on the Shoah* 24 (2010): 137–76; Michael Zimmerman, "The National Socialist 'Solution of the Gypsy Question,'" in *National Socialist Extermination Policies: Contemporary German Perspectives and Controversies*, ed. Ulrich Herbert (New York: Berghahn, 2000), 186–209; and Gilad

Margalit, *Germany and Its Gypsies: A Post-Auschwitz Ordeal* (Madison: University of Wisconsin Press, 2002), esp. chapter 2. Kenrick and Puxon estimated that 30,000 Romani citizens of the Soviet Union "were killed by the Einsatzgruppen army units and in the [Nazi] extermination camps." See their *Destiny of Europe's Gypsies*, 150. On Roma's service as Red Army soldiers and partisans, see Nikolai Bessonov, *Tsyganskaia tragediia, 1941–1945. Fakty, dokumenty, vospominaniia. Tom 2: Vooruzhennyi otpor* (St. Petersburg: Shatra, 2010).

178 GARF f. 7021 o. 44 d. 1091 ll. 1–44. As Martin Holler has demonstrated, Nazi "persecution of Roma in the Smolensk territory was … systematic, and the intention was the complete obliteration of this ethnic group." On other Nazi genocidal actions against Roma in Smolensk Province, see his "Like Jews?" 151–5 (quote on 155).

179 Kiseleva, "Tsygane evropeiskoi chasti," 175–8.

180 Druts and Gessler, *Tsygane*, 331–2.

181 Valdemar Kalinin, "Oh This Russian Spirit Abides Everywhere," in *Scholarship and the Gypsy Struggle: Commitment in Romani Studies*, ed. Thomas Acton (Hertfordshire: University of Hertfordshire Press, 2000), 146.

182 "O priobshchenii k trudu tsygan, zanimaiushchikhsia brodiazhnichestvom," *Vedomosti Verkhovnogo Soveta SSSR*, no. 21 (1956): 450.

183 On the 1956 decree's failures, see Crowe, *History of the Gypsies*, 188; and Druts and Gessler, *Tsygane*, 306–7.

184 See, for example, GARF A-259 o. 46 d. 980 ll. 1–72.

5. Pornography or Authenticity?

1 Rossiiskii gosudarstvennyi arkhiv literatury i iskusstva (RGALI) f. 2928 o. 1 d. 279 l. 1.

2 Anne E. Gorsuch, *Flappers and Foxtrotters: Soviet Youth in the "Roaring Twenties"* (Pittsburgh: Center for Russian & East European studies, University of Pittsburgh, 1994); and S. Frederick Starr, *Red and Hot: The Fate of Jazz in the Soviet Union* (New York: Limelight Editions, 1994), esp. chapter 4.

3 "N. N. Kruchinin," *Rabis*, no. 9 (15 March 1927): 10.

4 RGALI f. 656 o. 2 d. 1115 ll. 14–22ob.

5 RGALI f. 2684 o. 1 d. 16 l. 3.

6 "Etnograficheskii ansambl' starinnoi tsyganskoi pesni," *Rabis*, no. 2 (January 1928): 11.

7 RGALI f. 2684 o. 1 d. 12 l. 1.

8 These songs were among many romances that the Main Committee for the Control of Repertory (Glavrepertkom) vigorously censored at the close of

NEP. RGALI f. 656 o. 1 d. 3986 l. 2, 4–4ob. On the rhetoric of contamination and disease in Bolshevik social criticism during NEP, see Naiman, *Sex in Public.*

9 Rom-Lebedev, *Ot tsyganskogo khora*, 151.

10 For an insightful history of "tsyganshchina," see Lemon, *Between Two Fires*, 140–3.

11 The anti-tsyganshchina campaign corresponded to wider Bolshevik efforts to stamp out popular "mass songs" and dances, and jazz music. See Robert A. Rothstein, "The Quiet Rehabilitation of the Brick Factory: Early Soviet Popular Music and Its Critics," *Slavic Review* 39, no. 3 (September 1980): 373–88; and Starr, *Red and Hot*, esp. chapter 5.

12 Sergei Bugoslavskii, "Tsyganshchina," *Novyi zritel'*, no. 2 (11 January 1927): 2.

13 "'Tsyganshchina' i tsyganskaia pesnia," *Rabis*, no. 14 (April 1927): 8.

14 Egor Poliakov, "Pesn' tsyganskaia," *Tsirk*, no. 9 (January 1927): 9.

15 Ibid.

16 "'Tysgane na novom puti' (Beseda s Egorom Poliakovom)" *Tsirk*, no. 10 (February 1927): 16.

17 RGALI f. 2684 o. 1 d. 12 ll. 1–17.

18 Rostislav Bliumenau, *Tsygane na estrade* (Moscow: Kinopechat', 1927), 29–30.

19 Vozniukov, "Rukovoditel' tsyganskikh khorov," *Tsirk i estrada*, no. 3–4 (February 1928): 15.

20 K. Blagoveshchenskii, ed., *Dovesti do kontsa bor'bu s nepmanskoi muzykoi* (Moscow: Gosudarstvennoe muzykal'noe izdatel'stvo, 1931), 13–15.

21 R. Bliumenau, "Umiraushchaia tsyganshchina," *Tsirk i estrada*, no. 2 (February 1928): 2.

22 R. Pikel', "'Zadvorki' zrelishchnogo iskusstva," *Zhizn' iskusstva* (Leningrad), 23 September 1928. On the Bolsheviks' vision of men as the standard-bearers of progress and of women as "backward," see Eliot Borenstein, *Men without Women: Masculinity and Revolution in Russian Fiction, 1917–1929* (Durham: Duke University Press, 2000); and Elizabeth A. Wood, *The Baba and the Comrade: Gender and Politics in Revolutionary Russia* (Bloomington: Indiana University Press, 1997).

23 Pikel', "'Zadvorki' zrelishchnogo iskusstva."

24 R. Bliumenau, "Za tsyganskuiu pesniu," *Novyi zritel'*, no. 39 (23 September 1928): 11.

25 R. Bliumenau, "Tsyganskaia bolezn': Na soveshchanii tsyganskikh khorakh," *Tsirk i estrada*, no. 14 (September 1928): 13.

26 V. Manukhin, "Akademiia poshlosti," *Ekran*, no. 7 (17 February 1929): 12.

27 Bliumenau, "Tsyganskaia bolezn'," 13.

28 Boris Shteinpress, "Proiskhozhdenie 'tsyganshchiny,'" *Za proletarskuiu muzyku*, no. 10 (1930): 12.

29 Boris Shteinpress, "Chem plokha 'tsyganochka,'" *Za proletarskuiu muzyku*, no. 4 (1930): 9–10.

30 Shteinpress, "Proiskhozhdenie," 10, 12.

31 On Bolshevik thinking on sexuality and gender, see Frances Lee Bernstein, *The Dictatorship of Sex: Lifestyle Advice for the Soviet Masses* (Dekalb: Northern Illinois University Press, 2007); Borenstein, *Men without Women*; Naiman, *Sex in Public*; and Wood, *Baba and the Comrade*.

32 Shteinpress, "Proiskhozhdenie," 12.

33 Shteinpress, "Chem plokha," 6–8.

34 On Bolshevik fears that sexuality robbed citizens of energy better devoted to production and other social useful tasks, see Bernstein, *Dictatorship of Sex*, chapter 5.

35 Shteinpress, "Chem plokha," 7–9.

36 Ibid., 10. See also "Ataka s negodnymi sredstvami," *Za proletarskuiu muzyku*, no. 3 (February 1931): 1–2.

37 D.V. Zhitomorskii, "B'em nepmanskuiu muzyku," *Rost*, no. 13 (1930): 26.

38 Anna Orlova, "Gde zhe vykhod? Golos proizvodstvennika," *Tsirk i estrada*, no. 3 (January 1930): 10; and Vaitsenfel'd and Nisanelis, "Privlech k otvetstvennosti," 19.

39 B. Shteinpress, *K istorii "tsyganskogo peniia" v Rossii* (Moscow: Gosudarstvennoe muzykal'noe izdatel'stvo, 1934), 21.

40 Ibid., 61.

41 Anna Goldberg, "Teper' – perestroika," *Novyi zritel'*, no. 38 (16 September 1928): 5; R. Bliumenau, "Tsyganshchina pered sudom obshchestvennosti," *Tsirk i estrada*, no. 20–1 (December 1929): 10; OGLMT f. 29 o. 1 d. 49 ll. 57–8; and RGALI f. 2668 o. 1 d. 4 ll. 1–3.

42 OGLMT f. 29 o. 1 d. 49 ll. 45–62.

43 [Gosudarstvennyi russkii muzei], *Leningradskii gosudarstvennyi etnograficheskii teatr Russkogo muzeia* (Leningrad: 1931), 1.

44 Gosudarstvennyi russkii muzei], *Etnograficheskii teatr* (Leningrad: 1930), 3.

45 RGALI f. 2310 o. 1 d. 10 l. 5ob–6. Vsevolodskii-Gerngross was a scholar based at the State Institute of Art History. On the Experimental Theatre, see Z.V. Stepanov, *Kul'turnaia zhizn' Leningrada 20-kh – 30-kh godov* (Leningrad: Nauka, 1976), 36–7.

46 [Gosudarstvennyi russkii muzei], *Etnograficheskii teatr*, 5; and RGALI f. 2310 o. 1 d. 10 ll. 6–7.

47 In her richly contextualized account, Hirsch analyses the Ethnographic Department as a pivotal "cultural technology of rule" that brought together scholars, activists, and patrons together in the process of "knowing" and "transforming" Soviet nationalities in the 1920s and 1930s. See Hirsch, *Empire of Nations*, chapter 5.

48 See ibid., esp. 201–4.

49 *Rossiiskii etnograficheskii muzei* (REM) f. 2 o. 1 d. 284 l. 8.

50 RGALI f. 2310 o. 1 d. 10 ll. 6ob–7.

51 REM f. 2 o. 1 d. 299 l. 6.

52 Ibid., ll. 1–1ob; 5–6ob.

53 Ibid., l. 2.

54 [Gosudarstvennyi russkii muzei], *Etnograficheskii teatr*, 1.

55 REM f. 2 o. 1 d. 299 ll. 19, 20.

56 Ibid., l. 5.

57 REM f. 2 o. 2 d. 117 ll. 9–9ob.

58 [Gosudarstvennyi russkii muzei], *Etnograficheskii teatr*, 3–8.

59 On the museum's efforts to transform its ethnographic exhibits to account for socialist construction, see Hirsch, *Empire of Nations*, esp. 211–21.

60 See ibid., esp. 204–11.

61 REM f. 2 o. 1 d. 264 l. 6. Under the auspices of the Ethnographic Department, however, A.P. Barannikov had undertaken an expedition to study Roma in the Kursk and Voronezh provinces in 1928, and in Ukraine in 1930. His studies resulted not in a museum exhibit, but instead in his monograph, *The Ukrainian and South Russian Gypsy Dialects* (1934). See REM f. 2 o. 1 d. 233 ll. 138–9; 174.

62 Fieldwork had been proposed for 1931–2 with the explicit aim to obtain ethnographic material for the museum. The archival files provide no further record of such an expedition. See REM f. 2 o. 1 d. 264 l. 13.

63 REM f. 2 o. 2 d. 117 l. 4.

64 REM f. 2 o. 2 d. 113 l. 9. For a similar view, see Barannikov, *Tsygany*, 64.

65 See Lemon, *Between Two Fires*.

66 REM f. 2 o. 2 d. 113 l. 10

67 REM, uncatalogued delo, "Materialy tsyganskogo ansamblia rabotavshego v sostave Etnograficheskogo teatra GME," sheets 16–17.

68 REM f. 2 o. 2 d. 117 l. 5ob.

69 Ibid., l. 6ob.

70 Ibid., l. 7.

71 REM f. 2 o. 2 d. 113 l. 19

72 RGALI f. 2310 o. 1 d. 10 l. 8ob.

73 REM f. 2 o. 2 d. 117 l. 10ob.

74 REM f. 2 o. 2 d. 113 ll. 19ob–20ob.

75 On the failed Ukrainian exhibit of 1931, see Hirsch, *Empire of Nations*, 208–15.

76 REM f. 2 o. 2 d. 117 l. 12ob.

77 REM f. 2 o. 2 d. 113 l. 21ob.

78 REM f. 2 o. 2 d. 117 l. 12ob.

79 A. Dorokhov, "Barskie zabavy pod muzeinoi sen'iu," *Rabochii i teatr*, no. 6 (1932): 17; R. Ganin, "Tabor teatral'noi reaktsii v stenakh Russkogo Muzeia," *Krasnaia gazeta* (Leningrad), 27 February 1932; and Stepanov, *Kul'turnaia zhizn'*, 37. A rare exception proved to be Barannikov's English-language review of the Ethnographic Theatre's work. This review, however, was intended for foreign readers abroad. See A. Barannikov, "On the Russian Gypsy Singers of Today," *Journal of the Gypsy Lore Society*, 3rd series, 11 (1932): 187–92.

80 REM f. 2 o. 1 d. 424 ll. 12ob–13.

81 Ibid., l. 16ob.

82 Ibid., ll. 10, 20.

83 Ibid., l. 19ob.

84 Ganin, "Tabor teatral'noi reaktsii."

85 Dorokhov, "Barskie zabavy," 17.

86 REM f. 2 o. 1 d. 355 ll. 91ob–92.

87 Ibid., l. 5.

88 Ibid., l. 8ob.

89 Ibid., l. 9.

90 Ibid., ll. 15–16ob.

91 Ibid., l. 18ob–19.

92 On Fedorov's origins, see REM, uncatalogued delo, "Materialy tsyganskogo ansamblia rabotavshego v sostave Etnograficheskogo Teatra GME," sheet 16ob.

93 RGALI f. 2310 o. 1 d. 10 l. 19.

94 Ibid., l. 19.

95 Ibid., l. 20ob.

96 REM f. 2 o. 1 d. 299 l. 29.

97 Ibid., ll. 30–46.

98 REM, uncatalogued delo, "Materialy tsyganskogo ansamblia rabotavshego v sostave Etnograficheskogo teatra GME," sheet 17.

99 GARF f. 1235 o. 120 d. 27 ll. 89, 100.

100 E.K., "Ot nochnogo kabaka k proletarskomu teatru. Tsygane ob"iavili bor'bu protiv 'tsyganshchiny,'" *Rabochii i iskusstvo*, 5 September 1930.

101 RGALI f. 645 o. 1 d. 240 l. 57.

102 RGALI f. 645 o. 1 d. 241 l. 18; GARF f. 1235 o. 123 d. 27 l. 227

103 RGALI f. 2928 o. 1 d. 1 l. 4.

104 Ibid., l. 6.

105 Rom-Lebedev, *Ot tsyganskogo khora*, 167.

106 Ibid., 167–8.

107 E. Sholokh, "Tsyganskii teatr 'Romen,'" *Narodnoe tvorchestvo*, no. 5 (1938): 50.

108 Rom-Lebedev, *Ot tsyganskogo khora*, 168.

109 Sholokh, "Tsyganskii teatr," 50.

110 Rom-Lebedev, *Ot tsyganskogo khora*, 169.

111 The theatre's name was officially changed from the Indo-Romen Theatre Studio to the State Gypsy Theatre "Romen" in the spring of 1931.

112 GARF f. 1235 o. 123 d. 27 l. 26; RGALI f. 2928 o. 1 d. 3 l 6ob and f. 2928 o. 1 d. 65 l. 3; and Rom-Lebedev, *Ot tsyganskogo khora*, 173.

113 RGALI f. 645 o. 1 d. 240 ll. 52–4. See also A. Shakh, "Tsyganskoe iskusstvo v proshlom i nastoiashchem," *Natsional'naia kniga*, no. 7 (1931): 33–4; Marie Seton, "The Evolution of the Gypsy Theatre in the USSR," *Journal of the Gypsy Lore Society*, 3rd series, 14, no. 2 (1935): 67; and Rom-Lebedev, *Ot tsyganskogo khora*, 169–72.

114 Rom-Lebedev, *Ot tsyganskogo khora*, 174–5.

115 In January 1931, one of the theatre's Romani organizers, Andreev, advised that actors should perform in Russian, not in Romani. He reasoned that the theatre could not live long if it could not hold the attention of non-Romani audiences. The theatre could not subsist only on tickets sold to Roma. His fellow Romani activists accused Andreev of not understanding the theatre's mission. See RGALI f. 645 o. 1 d. 240 ll. 53ob–54.

116 RGALI f. 656 o. 1 d. 3147 ll. 1–14.

117 Rom-Lebedev, *Ot tsyganskogo khora*, 175.

118 GARF f. 1235 o. 121 d. 31 l. 271ob.

119 RGALI f. 2928 o. 1 d. 64 ll. 1–2; and "Organizuetsia tsyganskii teatr," *Rabis*, no. 8 (March 1931): 24.

120 Shakh, "Tsyganskoe iskusstvo," 33.

121 Rom-Lebedev, *Ot tsyganskogo khora*, 175.

122 Seton, "Evolution," 67.

123 RGALI f. 645 o. 1 d. 257 l. 104.

124 Seton, "Evolution," 69. Germano later justified the mechanical and simplistic text of his play, arguing that Romen's troupe at that time was incapable of mastering a more sophisticated work. OGLMT f. 29 o. 1 d. 49 l. 68.

125　RGALI f. 656 o. 1 d. 754 l. 9.

126　Ibid., l. 46.

127　Seton, "Evolution," 70.

128　Rom-Lebedev, *Ot tsyganskogo khora*, 177.

129　Joseph Macleod, *The New Soviet Theatre* (London: George Allen & Unwin, 1943), 79.

130　RGALI f. 2928 o. 1 d. 65 l. 10.

131　Rom-Lebedev, *Ot tsyganskogo khora*, 175.

132　On paper at least, Narkompros committed itself in late 1932 to the "struggle with abuse of ethnography and 'exotica'" in the repertoires of the Union's national theatres. GARF f. 1235 o. 125 d. 31 l. 414.

133　RGALI f. 656 o. 1 d. 755 ll. 24–58.

134　RGALI f. 2928 o.1 d. 66 l. 12.

135　RGALI f. 2928 o. 1 d. 6 ll. 11–13

136　On the Stalinist co-optation of Russian classics in particular, see Brandenberger, *National Bolshevism*, esp. 77–94; and Kevin M.F. Platt and David Brandenberger, ed., *Epic Revisionism: Russian History and Literature as Stalinist Propaganda* (Madison: University of Wisconsin Press, 2006).

137　Quoted in Seton, "Evolution," 70.

138　Rom-Lebedev, *Ot tsyganskogo khora*, 178.

139　RGALI f. 656 o. 1 d. 1610 ll. 2–3.

140　GARF f. 1235 o. 123 d. 28 ll. 184–6. See also Lemon, *Between Two Fires*, 145.

141　RGALI f. 2928 o. 1 d. 68 l. 24.

142　RGALI f. 2928 o. 1 d. 69 l. 4.

143　GARF f. 1235 o. 123 d. 28 l. 183.

144　RGALI f. 2928 o. 1 d. 69 l. 8.

145　Ibid., l. 10.

146　RGALI f. 2310 o. 1 d. 99 l. 61.

147　Ibid., l. 63.

148　Ibid., ll. 61–2.

149　Ibid., ll. 68–9..

150　RGALI f. 645 o. 1 d. 257 l. 61; f. 2310 o. 1 d. 98 ll. 19, 27–9ob; and GARF f. 1235 o. 123 d. 28 ll. 98–9ob, 182ob–186.

151　RGALI f. 2928 o. 1 d. 473 l. 17

152　RGALI f. 2310 o. 1 1 d. 99 ll. 21–3; and f. 2310 o. 1 d. 160 ll. 1–4.

153　RGALI f. 2310 o. 1 d. 98 l. 22ob.

154　Seton, "Evolution," 67.

155　GARF f. 1235 o. 127 d. 8 ll. 30–2; RGALI f. 2928 o. 1 d. 71 l. 9, 14, 18; and GASO f. R-2360 o. 2 d. 433 l. 27–8.

156　Rom-Lebedev, *Ot tsyganskogo khora*, 192–3.

157 RGALI f. 2310 o. 1 d. 99 ll. 4–7, 9–14.
158 Ibid., ll. 17–18. Others also complained that Roma's lack of representation in the theatre's administrative hierarchy was chauvinistic. Pankov alleged that the theatre's reliance on Russians displayed a lack of concern for the development of minority cadres. In early 1936, Tokmakov complained that of the ninety-seven people serving as the theatre's administrative and technical personnel, only five were Roma. He advocated that the theatre's personnel be "Gypsified." See GARF f. 1235 o. 28 d. 793 ll. 92, 99, 108; and f. 3316 o. 28 d. 794 l. 16.
159 RGALI f. 2310 o. 1 d. 99 ll. 17–18. This actor unhappily stayed on at the theatre, but regarded his fellow Romen actors as semiliterate, untrained amateurs. See GARF f. 3316 o. 28 d. 794 ll. 84–8.
160 RGALI f. 2928 o. 1 d. 473 ll. 18–18ob.
161 Ibid., l. 33ob.
162 Ibid., ll. 25–25ob.
163 Ibid., ll. 6, 8.
164 RGALI f. 2928 o. 1 d. 473 l. 11ob–12. With the choice of Pushkin's *The Gypsies*, Gol'dblat looked ahead to the Pushkin Jubilee of 1937, which in part celebrated Pushkin's purported wise and sensitive approach to representing non-Russians in his poems.
165 Lemon, *Between Two Fires*, 144. For an account of similar dilemmas facing another minority theatre in the 1930s, see Jeffrey Veidlinger, *The Moscow State Yiddish Theater: Jewish Culture on the Soviet Stage* (Bloomington: Indiana University Press, 2000), esp. chapter 4.
166 RGALI f. 2928 o. 1 d. 473 l. 13. On how debates over dialects among the Theatre's Romani performers served to scaffold their perceptions of cultural distance from other Roma, see Lemon, "'Form' and 'Function,'" esp. 40–4.
167 RGALI f. 2928 o. 1 d. 473 l. 30.
168 Ibid., l. 31ob.
169 Ibid., l. 29.
170 Romen's adapted script of Pushkin's *Tsygany* is archived in RGALI f. 656 o. 3 d. 2277 ll. 5–21.
171 S. Even'ev, "Tsyganskii teatr 'Romen,'" *Revoliutsiia i natsional'nosti*, no. 4 (1937): 89.
172 GARF f. 5446 o. 18 d. 2613 ll. 2, 13–14, 16, 18, 20, 23.
173 OGLMT f. 29 o. 1 d. 49 ll. 97–102.
174 GARF f. 3316 o. 28 d. 793 l. 99.
175 RGALI f. 2310 o. 1 d. 99 l. 55.
176 Rom-Lebedev, *Ot tsyganskogo khora*, 179–82.

177 Ibid., 179–91; N. Slichenko, *Rodilsia ia v tabore* (Moscow: Molodaia gvardia, 1980), 22–6; Elena Sizenko, "Ochi chernye: Nikolai Slichenko o tsyganakh, tsyganskom iskusstve i o 'tsyganshchine' v iskusstve," *Itogi*, 13 February 2005; and OGLMT f. 29 o. 1 d. 49 ll. 108–15.

178 Slichenko, *Rodilsia ia v tabore*, 21; OGLMT f. 29 o.1 d. 49 l. 108.

179 Slichenko, *Rodilsia ia v tabore*, 21–4.

180 See Slezkine, "USSR as a Communal Apartment," esp. 445–52; and Brandenberger, *National Bolshevism*.

181 Sholokh, "Tsyganskii teatr," 51.

182 RGALI f. 2668 o. 1 d. 7 l. 4.

183 RGALI f. 2928 o. 1 d. 76 l. 2. On the post-1938 deployment of Soviet "Stage Romani" as itself a script of the impoverishment of Romani as compared to Russian, see Lemon, "'Form' and 'Function.'"

184 OGLMT f. 29 o. 1 d. 49 l. 115.

185 Slichenko, *Rodilsia ia v tabore*, 21.

186 Rom-Lebedev introduced several of the theatre's non-Romani performers in his *Ot tsyganskogo khora*, 227–8.

187 During late and postsocialism, Alaina Lemon has shown, Romen and its performers continued to be dogged by the issue of authenticity and its attendant anxieties, both professional and personal. And, while the Theatre Romen remained the only Gypsy institution born of early Soviet affirmative action still standing, its actors ultimately found themselves both professionally trapped and redeemed by it. Long before the Soviet Union's dissolution, Lemon explains, "the Romani Theater was an ethnic 'ghetto' and there were no other theaters where Romani performers could find work." Romen's actors have feared their own permanent estrangement from "authentic" Romani culture while continuing to profit from performances of Gypsy stereotypes. Among fellow Roma in Russia, they have derived from their work both prestige and scorn. Lemon, *Between Two Fires*, esp. chapter 4 (quote on 13).

Epilogue and Conclusions

* Portions of an earlier version of this epilogue were previously published as "Aleksandr Germano, 1893–1955" in *Russia's People of Empire: Life Stories from Eurasia, 1500 to the Present*, ed. Stephen M. Norris and Willard Sunderland (Bloomington: Indiana University Press, 2012): 265–73.

1 OGLMT f. 29 o. 1 d. 156 ll. 4ob.

2 On the centrality of autobiography to Soviet self-fashioning, see Kotkin, *Magnetic Mountain*, esp. 215–25; Fitzpatrick, *Tear off the Masks*, esp. chapters

1, 5, and 6; Halfin, *Terror in My Soul*, esp. chapters 2 and 5; and Hellbeck, *Revolution on the Mind*.

3 OGLMT f. 29 o. 1 d. 156 ll. 1–8ob.

4 Ibid., l. 2ob.

5 Ibid., ll. 3–3ob.

6 Ibid., l. 4.

7 Ibid., l. 4ob.

8 Alexander Pushkin, *The Gypsies and Other Narrative Poems*, trans. Antony Wood (Boston: David R. Godine, 2006), 5.

9 OGLMT f. 29 o. 1 d. 156 ll. 4ob–5.

10 Ibid., ll. 5–5ob.

11 OGLMT f. 29 o. 1 d. 156 ll. 5ob–7.

12 Ibid., l. 7. The archives are categorically silent on Germano's said visits to the Union's Romani kolkhozes.

13 Ibid., l. 7ob.

14 Ibid., ll. 7ob–8.

15 A.V. Germano, *Povesti i rasskazy* (Orel: Orlovskoe knizhnoe izdatel'stvo, 1962), 6.

16 Ibid.

17 Ibid., 236.

18 See ibid., 237; Germano, *Povesti i rasskazy* (1962), 3; E. Sholokh, "A. V. Germano," in *Literaturnaia entsiklopediia*, vol. 2 (Moscow: Izdatel'stvo kommunisticheskoi akademii, 1964), 138; and OGLMT f. 29 o. 1 d. 214 l. 1.

19 OGLMT f. 29 o. 1 d. 137 l. 1.

20 Ibid., l. 2.

21 RGALI f. 1638 o. 1 d. 92 ll. 2, 56.

22 RGALI f. 1638 o. 1 d. 83 l. 76.

23 OGLMT f. 29 o. 1 d. 136 ll. 1–2.

24 OGLMT f. 29 o. 1 d. 137 l. 4.

25 RGALI f. 631 o. 6 d. 426 ll. 8–10.

26 Ibid., l. 2.

27 These tsarist-era ethnographies include: Papaz'ian, "Armianskie bosha (tsygane)"; Patkanov, *Tsygany*; M. Plokhinskii, "Tsygane staroi Malorossii (po arkhivnym dokumentam)," *Etnograficheskoe obozrenie* 7, no. 4 (1890): 95–117; N.G. Shtiber, "Russkie Tsygany: Etnograficheskii ocherk," *Ezhemesiachnye literaturnye prilozheniia k zhurnalu "Niva,"* no. 11 (1895): 519–54; and V.V., "Iuridicheskoe polozhenie tsygan v Rossii," *Iuridicheskoe obozrenie* (Tiflis), no. 60 (1882): 67–87.

28 Germano, *Tsygane vchera i segodnia*, 14–21.

29 Ibid., 22–7.

30 Ibid., 44.
31 Ibid., 53.
32 Slezkine, "USSR as a Communal Apartment," 414.
33 On the gradual turn from constructivist to primordial understandings of nationality in Soviet ideology that began as early as the 1930s, see Slezkine, "USSR as a Communal Apartment"; and Terry Martin, Modernization or Neo-traditionalism? Ascribed Nationality and Soviet Primordialism," in *Stalinism: New Directions*, ed. Sheila Fitzpatrick (New York: Routledge, 2000): 348–67.
34 See Lemon, *Between Two Fires*.

Bibliography

I. Archival Sources

Gosudarstvennyi Arkhiv Krasnodarskogo Kraia (GAKK). Krasnodar.

Fond R-580:	Ispol'nitel'nyi komitet slavianskogo raionnogo soveta deputatov trudiashchikhsia za 1922–37 godov
Fond R-687:	Ispol'nitel'nyi komitet krasnodarskogo soveta deputatov trudiashchikhsia

Gosudartsvennyi Arkhiv Rossiiskoi Federatsii (GARF). Moscow.

Fond A-259:	Sovet ministrov RSFSR
Fond A-296:	Komitet po prosveshcheniiu natsional'nykh men'shinstv pri Narkompros RSFSR
Fond 1235:	Vserossiiskii tsentral'nyi ispolnitel'nyi komitet RSFSR
Fond 3316:	Tsentral'nyi ispolnitel'nyi komitet SSSR
Fond 4033:	Tsentral'noe izdatel'stvo narodov SSSR (Tsentroizdat) pri tsentral'nom ispolnitel'nom komitete SSSR
Fond 5446:	Sovet ministrov SSSR
Fond 7021:	Chrezvychainaia gosudarstvennaia komissiia po ustanov-leniiu i rassledovaniiu zlodeianii nemetsko-fashistskikh zakhvatchikov i ikh soobshchnikov i prichinennogo imi ushcherba grazhdanam, kollektivnym khoziaistvam (kolk-hozam), obshchestvennym organizatsiiam, gosudarstven-nym predpriiatiiam i uchrezhdeniiam SSSR
Fond 8131:	Prokuratura SSSR
Fond 9479:	Chetvertyi spetsotdel ministerstva vnutrennikh del SSSR, 1931–59

Gosudarstvennyi Arkhiv Smolenskoi Oblasti (GASO). Smolensk.

Fond R-2350:	Otdel narodnogo obrazovaniia zapadnogo oblispolkoma 1929–37gg
Fond R-2360:	Ispol'nitel'nyi komitet zapadnogo oblastnogo soveta rabochikh, krest'ianskikh i krasnoarmeiskikh deputatov, 1923–41gg
Fond R-2361:	Ispol'nitel'nyi komitet Smolenskogo oblastnogo soveta deputatov trudiashchikhsia (oblispolkom) 1933–74gg
Fond R-2555:	El'inskii raiispolkom 1930–5, 1937gg
Fond R-2529:	Iartsevskii raiispolkom 1930–7gg

Gosudarstvennyi Arkhiv Volgogradskoi Oblasti (GAVO). Volgograd.

Fond 313:	Nizhne-Volzhskoi kraevoi ispolnitel'nyi komitet sovetov (Kraiispolkom) gor. Saratov, 1928–32; Nizhne-Volzhskoi kraevoi ispolnitel'nyi komitet sovetov (Kraiispolkom) gor. Stalingrad, 1932–4
Fond R-2059:	Stalingradskii kraevoi ispolnitel'nyi komitet sovetov rabochikh, krest'ianskikh, i krasnoarmeiskikh deputatov

Orlovskii Ob"edinennyi Gosudarstvennyi Literaturnyi Muzei I.S. Turgeneva (OGLMT). Orel.

Fond 29:	Germano, A.V.

Rossiiskii Etnograficheskii Muzei (REM). St. Petersburg.

Fond 2:	Gosudarstvennyi muzei etnografii narodov SSSR

Rossiiskii Gosudarstvennyi Arkhiv Ekonomiki (RGAE). Moscow.

Fond 5675:	Uchrezhdeniia po rukovodstvu pereseleniem v SSSR
Fond 7446:	Kolkhoztsentr SSSR i RSFSR
Fond 7486:	Narodnyi komissariat zemledeliia SSSR

Rossiiskii Gosudarstvennyi Arkhiv Literatury i Iskusstva (RGALI). Moscow.

Fond 631:	Soiuz pisatelei SSSR
Fond 645:	Glaviskusstvo

Fond 656:   Glavnoe upravlenie po kontroliu za repertuarom pri
                   Komitete po delam iskusstv pri SNK SSSR
Fond 1638:   Vsesoiuznoe obshchestvo proletarskikh pisatelei
                   "Kuznitsa"
Fond 2310:   Upravlenie teatral'no-zrelishchnymi predpriiatimi Nar-
                   komprosa RSFSR
Fond 2668:   Skvortsova, M.V.
Fond 2684:   Akimov, I.N.
Fond 2928:   Moskovskii tsyganskii teatr "Romen"

*Rossiiskii Gosudarstvennyi Arkhiv Sotsial'no-Politicheskoi
Istorii (RGASPI). Moscow.*

Fond 17:   Tsentral'nyi Komitet KPSS

Rossiiskii Institut Istorii Iskusstv (RIII). St. Petersburg.

Fond 1:   Sobranie rukopisei i pisem deiatelei muzyki i teatra

*Tsentral'nyi Gosudarstvennyi Arkhiv Moskovskoi Oblasti (TsGAMO).
Moscow.*

Fond 966:   Otdel narodnogo obrazovaniia Mossoveta (MONO)
Fond 4341:   Otdel narodnogo obrazovaniia Mosoblispolkoma
                   (MOONO)

II. Published Primary Sources

a. Newspapers

Izvestiia
Komsomol'skaia pravda
Krasnaia gazeta
Leningradskaia pravda
Pionerskaia pravda
Pravda
Rabochii i iskusstvo
Sovetskoe iskusstvo
Trud
Vecherniaia Moskva

b. Journals

Bezbozhnik
Chitatel' i pisatel'
Drug detei
Druzhba narodov
Ekran
Klub i revoliutsiia
Krasnyi derevoobdelochnik
Molodaia gvardiia
Narodnoe tvorchestvo
Natsional'naia kniga
Nevo drom
Novyi zritel'
Ogonek
Prosveshchenie natsional'nostei
Rabis
Rabochii i teatr
Revoliutsiia i natsional'nosti
Romany zoria
Sovetskoe stroitel'stvo
30 Dnei
30 Oktiabria
Tsirk
Tsirk i estrada
Vedomosti Verkhovnogo Soveta SSSR
Vlast' sovetov
Zhizn' iskusstva

c. Articles, Books, Pamphlets, and Document Collections

Ackerley, Frederick George. "Russian Gypsies under the Soviets." *Journal of the Gypsy Lore Society*, 3rd series, 2, no. 3–4 (1932): 192–9.

Barannikov, A.P. "About the Term 'the Gypsies of Russia.'" *Comptes Rendus de l'Academie des Sciences de l'URSS* 10 (1928): 211–17.

Barannikov, A.P. "Ob izuchenii tsygan SSSR." *Izvestiia Akademiia Nauk SSSR*, no. 6 (1929): 369–478.

Barannikov, A.P. "The Russian Gypsy Singers of Today." *Journal of the Gypsy Lore Society*, 3rd series 11, no. 3–4 (1932): 187–90.

Barannikov, A.P. *Tsygany SSSR: Kratkii istoriko-etnograficheskii ocherk*. Moscow: Tsentrizdat, 1931.

Barannikov, A.P. *The Ukrainian and South Russian Gypsy Dialects*. Leningrad: Izdatel'stvo Akademii Nauk SSSR, 1934.

Blagoveshchenskii, K., ed. *Dovesti do kontsa bor'bu s nepmanskoi muzykoi*. Moscow: Gosudarstvennoe muzykal'noe izdatel'stvo, 1931.

Bliumenau, Rostislav. *Tsygane na estrade*. Moscow: Kinopechat, 1927.

Germano, A.V. *Bibliografiia o tsyganakh*. Moscow: Tsentrizdat, 1930.

Germano, A.V. *Nevo dzhiiben*. Moscow: Tsentrizdat, 1929.

Germano, A.V. *Povesti i rasskazy*. Moscow: Sovetskii pisatel', 1960.

Germano, A.V. *Povesti i rasskazy*. Orel: Orlovskoe knizhnoe izdatel'stvo, 1962.

Germano, A.V. *Tsygane vchera i segodnia*. Moscow: Uchpedgiz, 1931.

Gilliat-Smith, B.J. "Russian Gypsy Singers." *Journal of the Gypsy Lore Society*, 3rd series, 1 (1922): 58–64.

[Gosudarstvennyi russkii muzei]. *Etnograficheskii teatr*. Leningrad, 1930.

[Gosudarstvennyi russkii muzei]. *Leningradskii gosudarstvennyi etnograficheskii teatr Russkogo Muzeia*. Leningrad, 1931.

Isayev, M.I. *National Languages in the USSR: Problems and Solutions*. Moscow: Progress, 1977.

Kiseleva, T.F. "Tsygany evropeiskoi chasti soiuza SSR i ikh perekhod ot kochevaniia k osedlosti." PhD diss., Moscow State University, 1952.

Macleod, Joseph. *The New Soviet Theatre*. London: George Allen & Unwin, 1943.

Mozgunova, G.N., ed. *Sudby natsional'nykh men'shinstv na Smolenshchine 1918–1938 gody: Dokumenty i materialy*. Smolensk: 1994.

Narodnoe obrazovanie v SSSR. Obshcheobrazovatel'naia shkola. Sbornik dokumentov 1917–1973gg. Moscow: Pedagogika, 1974.

Narodnyi Komissariat Prosveshcheniia RSFSR. *Narodnoe prosveshchenie v RSFSR k 1926/27 uchebnomu godu*. Moscow: Narodnyi Komissariat Prosveshcheniia RSFSR, 1927.

Papaz'ian, V.M. "Armianskie bosha (tsygane)." *Etnograficheskoe obozrenie* 49, no. 2 (1901): 93–158.

Patkanov, K.P. *Tsygany: Neskol'ko slov o narechiiakh zakavkaskikh tsygan: Bosha i karachi*. St. Petersburg: Imperial Academy of Sciences, 1887.

Plokhinskii, M. "Tsygane staroi Malorossii (po arkhivnym dokumentam)." *Etnograficheskoe obozrenie* 7, no. 4 (1890): 95–117.

Pushkin, Aleksandr Sergeevich. *The Gypsies and Other Narrative Poems*. Translated by Antony Wood. Boston: David R. Godine, 2006.

Rogi, M. *Tsygane v promkooperatsii*. Moscow: Koiz, 1934.

Rom-Lebedev, I.I. *Ot tsyganskogo khora k teatru "Romen."* Moscow: Iskusstvo', 1990.

Sergievskii, M.V. *Tsyganskii iazyk: Kratkoe rukovodstvo po grammatike i pravopisaniiu.* Moscow: Tsentrizdat, 1931.

Sergievskii, M.V., and A.P. Barannikov. *Tsygansko-russkii slovar'.* Moscow: Izdatel'stvo inostrannykh i natsional'nykh slovarei, 1938.

Seton, Marie. "The Evolution of the Gypsy Theatre in the U.S.S.R." *Journal of the Gypsy Lore Society,* 3rd series, 14, no. 2 (1935): 65–73.

Shayakhmetov, Mukhamet. *The Silent Steppe: The Memoir of a Kazakh Nomad under Stalin.* Translated by Jan Butler. New York: Rookery, 2006.

Sholokh, E. "A. V. Germano." In *Literaturnaia entsiklopediia,* vol. 2. Moscow: Izdatel'stvo kommunisticheskoi akademii, 1964.

Shteinpress, B. *K istorii "tsyganskogo peniia" v Rossii.* Moscow: Gosudarstvennoe muzykal'noe izdatel'stvo, 1934.

Shtiber, N.G. "Russkie Tsygany: Etnograficheskii ocherk." *Ezhemesiachnye literaturnye prilozheniia k zhurnalu "Niva",* no. 11 (1895): 519–54.

Slichenko, Nikolai. *Rodilsia ia v tabore.* Moscow: Molodaia gvardiia, 1980.

V.V. "Iuridicheskoe polozhenie tsygan v Rossii." *Iuridicheskoe obozrenie* (Tiflis) 60 (1882): 67–87.

III. Secondary Literature

Achim, Viorel. *The Roma in Romanian History.* Budapest: Central European University Press, 2004.

Alexopoulos, Golfo. "Victim Talk: Defense Testimony and Denunciation under Stalin." In *Russian Modernity: Politics, Knowledge, Practices,* edited by David Hoffman and Yanni Kotsonis, 204–220. New York: St Martin's, 2000.

Alpatov, V.M. *150 iazykov i politika, 1917–2000.* Moscow: Kraft, Institut vostokovedeniia RAN, 2000.

Anderson, Barbara A., and Brian D. Silver. "Equality, Efficiency, and Politics in Soviet Bilingual Education Policy, 1934–1980." *American Political Science Review* 78, no. 4 (December 1984): 1019–39. http://dx.doi.org/10.2307/1955805.

Barany, Zoltan. *The East European Gypsies: Regime Change, Marginality, and Ethnopolitics.* Cambridge: Cambridge University Press, 2002.

Barfield, Thomas. *The Nomadic Alternative.* Englewood Cliffs, NJ: Prentice Hall, 1993.

Bassin, Mark. "Inventing Siberia: Visions of the Russian East in the Early Nineteenth Century." *American Historical Review* 96, no. 3 (June 1991): 763–94. http://dx.doi.org/10.2307/2162430.

Baurov, Konstantin Aleksandrovich. *Tsyganskie khory starogo Peterburga.* St. Petersburg: Na strazhe rodiny, 1991.

Bayly, C.A. *Empire and Information: Intelligence Gathering and Social Communication in India, 1780–1870.* New York: Cambridge University Press, 1996.

Beer, Daniel. *Renovating Russia: The Human Sciences and the Fate of Liberal Modernity, 1880–1930.* Ithaca: Cornell University Press, 2008.

Bernstein, Frances Lee. *The Dictatorship of Sex: Lifestyle Advice for the Soviet Masses.* Dekalb: Northern Illinois University Press, 2007.

Bessonov, Nikolai. *Tsyganskaia tragediia, 1941–1945. Fakty, dokumenty, vospominaniia. Tom 2: Vooruzhennyi otpor.* St.Petersburg: Shatra, 2010.

Blitstein, Peter. "Nation Building or Russification? Obligatory Russian Instruction in the Soviet Non-Russian School, 1938–1953." In *A State of Nations: Empire and Nation-Making in the Age of Lenin and Stalin,* edited by Ronald Grigor Suny and Terry Martin, 253–74. New York: Oxford University Press, 2001.

Blitstein, Peter. "Stalin's Nations: Soviet Nationality Policy between Planning and Primordialism, 1936–1953." PhD diss., University of California-Berkeley, 1999.

Borenstein, Eliot. *Men without Women: Masculinity and Revolution in Russian Fiction, 1917–1929.* Durham: Duke University Press, 2000.

Brandenberger, David. *National Bolshevism: Stalinist Mass Culture and the Formation of Modern Russian National Identity, 1931–1956.* Cambridge: Harvard University Press, 2002.

Brown, Kate. *A Biography of No Place: From Ethnic Borderland to Soviet Heartland.* Cambridge: Harvard University Press, 2004.

Brubaker, Rogers. *Ethnicity without Groups.* Cambridge: Harvard University Press, 2004.

Brubaker, Rogers, and Frederick Cooper. "Beyond Identity." *Theory and Society* 29, no. 1 (February 2000): 1–47. http://dx.doi.org/10.1023/A:1007068714468.

Buckler, Sarah. *Fire in the Dark: Telling Gypsiness in North East England.* New York: Berghahn Books, 2007.

Burke, Peter. "Performing History: The Importance of Occasions." *Rethinking History* 9, no. 1 (2005): 35–52.

Chatterjee, Choi, and Karen Petrone. "Models of Selfhood and Subjectivity: The Soviet Case in Historical Perspective." *Slavic Review* 67, no. 4 (Winter 2008): 967–86. http://dx.doi.org/10.2307/27653033.

Clark, Katerina. *The Soviet Novel: History as Ritual.* 1981. Bloomington: Indiana University Press, 2000.

Cooper, Belinda. "A Pattern of Persecution." *Foreign Affairs,* 28 September 2010.

Cooper, Belinda. "'We Have No Martin Luther King': Eastern Europe's Roma Minority." *World Policy Journal* 18, no. 4 (Winter 2001/2002): 69–78.

Crowe, David. *A History of the Gypsies of Eastern Europe and Russia*. New York: St Martin's, 1996.

Davies, R. W. *The Socialist Offensive: The Collectivization of Soviet Agriculture, 1929–1930*. Cambridge, MA: Harvard University Press, 1980.

Davies, R. W., and Stephen G. Wheatcroft. *Years of Hunger: Soviet Agriculture, 1931–1933*. New York: Palgrave Macmillan, 2004.

Demeter, Nadezhda, Nikolai Bessonov, and Vladimir Kutenkov. *Istoriia tsygan: Novyi vzgliad*. Voronezh: IPF "Voronezh," 2000.

Demeter, N.G. *Tsygane: Mif i real'nost'*. Moscow: Institut etnologii i antropologii RAN, 1995.

Demeter, N.G., and L.I. Missonova, eds. *Tsygane: Sbornik statei*. Moscow: Institut etnologii i antropologii RAN, 1999.

Douglas, Mary. *Purity and Danger*. 1966. New York: Routledge, 2002.

Druts, Efim, and Aleksei Gessler. *Tsygane: Ocherki*. Moscow: Sovetskii pisatel', 1990.

Edele, Mark. "Soviet Society, Social Structure, and Everyday Life: Major Frameworks Reconsidered." *Kritika: Explorations in Russian and Eurasian History* 8, no. 2 (2007): 349–73. http://dx.doi.org/10.1353/kri.2007.0025.

Edele, Mark. *Stalinist Society 1928–1953*. New York: Oxford University Press, 2011.

Edele, Mark. "Strange Young Men in Stalin's Moscow: The Birth and Life of the Stiliagi, 1945–1953." *Jahrbücher für Geschichte Osteuropas* 50, no.1 (2002): 37–61.

Edgar, Adrienne. *Tribal Nation: The Making of Soviet Turkmenistan*. Princeton: Princeton University Press, 2004.

Ewing, E. Thomas. "Ethnicity at School: 'Non-Russian' Education in the Soviet Union during the 1930s." *History of Education* 35, no. 4–5 (July–September 2006): 499–519. http://dx.doi.org/10.1080/00467600600715018.

Ewing, E. Thomas. *The Teachers of Stalinism: Policy, Practice, and Power in Soviet Schools of the 1930s*. New York: Peter Lang, 2002.

Fitzpatrick, Sheila. "Ascribing Class: The Construction of Social Identity in Soviet Russia." *Journal of Modern History* 65, no. 4 (December 1993): 745–70. http://dx.doi.org/10.1086/244724.

Fitzpatrick, Sheila. *Everyday Stalinism: Ordinary Life in Extraordinary Times: Soviet Russia in the 1930s*. New York: Oxford University Press, 1999.

Fitzpatrick, Sheila. "The Great Departure: Rural-Urban Migration in the Soviet Union, 1929–1933." In *Social Dimensions of Soviet Industrialization*, edited by William G. Rosenberg and Lewis H. Siegelbaum, 15–40. Bloomington: Indiana University Press, 1993.

Fitzpatrick, Sheila. "The Problem of Class Identity in NEP Society." In *Russia in the Era of NEP: Explorations in Soviet Society and Culture*, edited by Sheila Fitzpatrick, Alexander Rabinowitch, and Richard Stites, 12–33. Bloomington: Indiana University Press, 1991.

Fitzpatrick, Sheila. *Stalin's Peasants: Resistance and Survival in the Russian Village after Collectivization*. New York: Oxford University Press, 1994.

Fitzpatrick, Sheila. *Tear Off the Masks! Identity and Imposture in Twentieth-Century Russia*. Princeton: Princeton University Press, 2005.

Fitzpatrick, Sheila, Alexander Rabinowitch, and Richard Stites, eds. *Russia in the Era of NEP: Explorations in Soviet Society and Culture*. Bloomington: Indiana University Press, 1991.

Fonseca, Isabel. *Bury Me Standing: The Gypsies and Their Journey*. New York: Vintage, 1995.

Fraser, Angus. *The Gypsies*. Oxford: Blackwell, 1995.

Garcelon, Marc. "Colonizing the Subject: The Genealogy and Legacy of the Soviet Internal Passport." In *Documenting Individual Identity: The Development of State Practices in the Modern World*, edited by Jane Caplan and John Torpey, 83–100. Princeton: Princeton University Press, 2001.

Gay y Blasco, Paloma. *Gypsies in Madrid: Sex, Gender, and the Performance of Identity*. Oxford: Berg, 1999.

Gellner, Ernest. *State and Society in Soviet Thought*. Oxford: Basil Blackwell, 1988.

Gheorghe, Nicolas. "The Origin of Roma Slavery in the Rumanian Provinces." *Roma* 7, no. 1 (1983): 12–27.

Gila-Kochanowski, V. "N. A. Pankov." *Journal of the Gypsy Lore Society*, 3rd series, 38, no. 3–4 (1959): 159–60.

Gitelman, Zvi. *A Century of Ambivalence: The Jews of Russia and the Soviet Union, 1881 to the Present*. 2nd ed. Bloomington: Indiana University Press, 2001.

Gorsuch, Anne E. *Flappers and Foxtrotters: Soviet Youth in the "Roaring Twenties."* Pittsburgh: Center for Russian & East European Studies, University of Pittsburgh, 1994. http://dx.doi.org/10.5195/cbp.1994.59

Grant, Bruce. "Empire and Savagery: The Politics of Primitivism in Late Imperial Russia." In *Russia's Orient: Imperial Borderlands and Peoples, 1700–1917*, edited by Daniel R. Brower and Edward J. Lazzerini, 292–310. Bloomington: Indiana University Press, 1997.

Grant, Bruce. *In the Soviet House of Culture: A Century of Perestroikas*. Princeton: Princeton University Press, 1995.

Grenoble, Leonore A. *Language Policy in the Soviet Union*. Dordrecht: Kluwer Academic, 2003.

Guy, Will, ed. *Between Past and Future: The Roma of Central and Eastern Europe*. Hertfordshire: University of Hertfordshire Press, 2001.

Guy, Will. "Ways of Looking at Roma: The Case of Czechoslovakia." In *Gypsies: An Interdisciplinary Reader*, edited by Will Guy, 13–68. New York: Garland, 1998.

Hagenloh, Paul. *Stalin's Police: Public Order and Mass Repression in the USSR, 1926–1941*. Washington, DC: Woodrow Wilson Center, 2009.

Halfin, Igal. *From Darkness to Light: Class, Consciousness, and Salvation in Revolutionary Russia*. Pittsburgh: University of Pittsburgh Press, 2000.

Halfin, Igal. *Terror in My Soul: Communist Autobiographies on Trial*. Cambridge: Harvard University Press, 2003.

Hancock, Ian. *Danger! Educated Gypsy: Selected Essays*. Hertfordshire: University of Hertfordshire Press, 2010.

Hancock, Ian. *A Handbook of Vlax Romani*. Columbus, OH: Slavica, 1995.

Hancock, Ian. *The Pariah Syndrome: An Account of Gypsy Slavery and Persecution*. Ann Arbor: Karoma, 1987.

Hellbeck, Jochen. *Revolution on My Mind: Writing a Diary under Stalin*. Cambridge: Harvard University Press, 2006.

Hirsch, Francine. *Empire of Nations: Ethnographic Knowledge and the Making of the Soviet Union*. Ithaca: Cornell University Press, 2005.

Hirsch, Francine. "Race without the Practice of Racial Politics." *Slavic Review* 61, no. 1 (Spring 2002): 30–43. http://dx.doi.org/10.2307/2696979.

Hoffmann, David L. *Cultivating the Masses: Modern State Practices and Soviet Socialism, 1914–1939*. Ithaca: Cornell University Press, 2011.

Hoffmann, David L. *Peasant Metropolis: Social Identities in Moscow, 1929–1941*. Ithaca: Cornell University Press, 1994.

Hoffmann, David L. *Stalinist Values: The Cultural Norms of Soviet Modernity, 1917–1941*. Ithaca: Cornell University Press, 2003.

Holler, Martin. "Like Jews? The Nazi Persecution and Extermination of Soviet Roma under the German Military Administration: A New Interpretation, Based on Soviet Sources." *DAPIM Studies on the Shoah* 24 (2010): 137–76.

Holmes, Larry. *The Kremlin and the Schoolhouse: Reforming Education in Soviet Russia, 1917–1931*. Bloomington: Indiana University Press, 1991.

Holquist, Peter. "State Violence as Technique: The Logic of Violence in Soviet Totalitarianism." In *Landscaping the Human Garden: Twentieth-Century Population Management in a Comparative Framework*, edited by Amir Weiner, 19–45. Stanford: Stanford University Press, 2003.http://dx.doi.org/10.1002/9780470758380.ch6

Hooper, Cynthia V. "Terror from Within: Participation and Coercion in Soviet Power, 1924–1964." PhD diss., Princeton University, 2003.

Hubschmannova, Milena. "Economic Stratification and Interaction: Roma, and Ethnic Jati in East Slovakia." In *Gypsies: An Interdisciplinary Reader*, edited by Diane Tong, 233–67. New York: Garland, 1998.

Illuzzi, J. "Negotiating the 'State of Exception': Gypsies' Encounter with the Judiciary in Germany and Italy, 1860–1914." *Social History* 35, no. 4 (2010): 418–38. http://dx.doi.org/10.1080/03071022.2010.515707. Medline:21348176

Iovita, Radu P., and Theodore G. Schurr. "Reconstructing the Origins and Migrations of Diasporic Populations: The Case of the European Gypsies." *American Anthropologist* 106, no. 2 (2004): 267–81. http://dx.doi. org/10.1525/aa.2004.106.2.267.

Kalinin, Valdemar. "Oh This Russian Spirit Abides Everywhere." In *Scholarship and the Gypsy Struggle: Commitment in Romani Studies*, edited by Thomas Acton, 140–9. Hertfordshire: University of Hertfordshire Press, 2000.

Kalinin, Val'demar. *Zagadka Baltiiskikh tsygan: Ocherki istorii, kul'tury, i sotsial'nogo razvitiia Baltiiskikh tsygan*. Minsk: Logvinov, 2005.

Kamp, Marianne. *The New Woman in Uzbekistan: Islam, Modernity, and Unveiling Under Communism*. Seattle: University of Washington Press, 2006.

Kelly, Catriona. *Children's World: Growing Up in Russia, 1890–1991*. New Haven: Yale University Press, 2007.

Kenez, Peter. *The Birth of the Modern Propaganda State: Soviet Methods of Mass Mobilization 1917–1929*. Cambridge: Cambridge University Press, 1985. http://dx.doi.org/10.1017/CBO9780511572623

Kenrick, Donald, and Grattan Puxon. *The Destiny of Europe's Gypsies*. New York: Basic Books, 1972.

Kessler, Gijs. "The Passport System and State Control over Population Flows in the Soviet Union, 1932–1940." *Cahiers du Monde russe* 42, no. 2–4 (2001): 477–503. Medline:20020566

Khalid, Adeeb. "Backwardness and the Quest for Civilization: Early Soviet Central Asia in Comparative Perspective." *Slavic Review* 65, no. 2 (2006): 231–51. http://dx.doi.org/10.2307/4148591.

Khalid, Adeeb. *The Politics of Muslim Cultural Reform: Jadidism in Central Asia*. Berkeley: University of California Press, 1998.

Kharkhordin, Oleg. *The Collective and the Individual in Russia: A Study of Practices*. Berkeley: University of California Press, 1999.

Khazanov, A.M. *Nomads and the Outside World*. Cambridge: Cambridge University Press, 1984.

Kiaer, Christina, and Eric Naiman, eds. *Everyday Life in Early Soviet Russia: Taking the Revolution Inside*. Bloomington: Indiana University Press, 2006.

Kirschenbaum, Lisa A. *Small Comrades: Revolutionizing Childhood in Soviet Russia, 1917–1932*. New York: Routledge, 2001.

Kotkin, Stephen. *Magnetic Mountain: Stalinism as Civilization*. Berkeley: University of California Press, 1995.

Kotkin, Stephen. "The State – Is It Us? Memoirs, Archives, and Kremlinologists." *Russian Review* 61, no. 1 (2002): 35–51. http://dx.doi.org/10.1111/1467-9434.00204.

Kotsonis, Yanni. "'Face-to-Face': The State, the Individual, and the Citizen in Russian Taxation." *Slavic Review* 63, no. 2 (Summer 2004): 221–46. http://dx.doi.org/10.2307/3185727.

Kotsonis, Yanni. "Introduction: A Modern Paradox – Subject and Citizen in Nineteenth- and Twentieth-Century Russia." In *Russian Modernity: Politics, Knowledge, Practices*, edited by David L. Hoffmann and Yanni Kotsonis, 1–16. New York: St Martin's, 2000.

Kotsonis, Yanni. "'No Place to Go': Taxation and State Transformation in Late Imperial and Early Soviet Russia." *Journal of Modern History* 76, no. 3 (September 2004): 531–77. http://dx.doi.org/10.1086/425440.

Krylova, Anna. "The Tenacious Liberal Subject in Soviet Studies." *Kritika: Explorations in Russian and Eurasian History* 1, no. 1 (Winter 2000): 119–46. http://dx.doi.org/10.1353/kri.2008.0092.

Lee, Ronald. "The Rom-Vlach Gypsies and the Kris-Romani." In *Gypsy Law: Romani Legal Traditions and Culture*, edited by Walter O. Weyrauch, 188–230. Berkeley: University of California Press, 2001.

Lemon, Alaina. *Between Two Fires: Gypsy Performance and Romani Memory from Pushkin to Postsocialism*. Durham: Duke University Press, 2000.

Lemon, Alaina. "'Form' and 'Function' in Soviet Stage Romani: Modeling Metapragmatics through Performance Institutions." *Language in Society* 31, no. 1 (2002): 29–64. http://dx.doi.org/10.1017/S0047404502001021.

Lemon, Alaina. "Hot Blood and Black Pearls: Socialism, Society, and Authenticity at the Moscow Teatr Romen." *Theatre Journal* 48, no. 4 (1996): 479–94. http://dx.doi.org/10.1353/tj.1996.0086.

Lemon, Alaina. "Indic Diaspora, Soviet History, Russian Home: Political Performances and Sincere Ironies in Romani Cultures." PhD diss., University of Chicago, 1996.

Lemon, Alaina. "Roma (Gypsies) in the Soviet Union and the Moscow Teatr 'Romen.'" *Nationalities Papers* 19, no. 3 (Winter 1991): 359–72. http://dx.doi.org/10.1080/00905999108408208.

Lewis, E. Glyn. *Multilingualism in the Soviet Union: Aspects of Language Policy and Its Implementation*. The Hague: Mouten, 1972.

Lohr, Eric. "The Ideal Citizen and Real Subject in Late Imperial Russia." *Kritika: Explorations in Russian and Eurasian History* 7, no. 2 (2006): 173–94. http://dx.doi.org/10.1353/kri.2006.0021.

Margalit, Gilad. *Germany and Its Gypsies: A Post-Auschwitz Ordeal*. Madison: University of Wisconsin Press, 2002.

Martin, Terry. *The Affirmative Action Empire: Nations and Nationalism in the Soviet Union, 1923–1939*. Ithaca: Cornell University Press, 2001.

Martin, Terry. "Modernization or Neo-Traditionalism? Ascribed Nationality and Soviet Primordialism." In *Stalinism: New Directions*, edited by Sheila Fitzpatrick, 348–67. New York: Routledge, 1999.

Matras, Yaron. *Romani: A Linguistic Introduction*. Cambridge: Cambridge University Press, 2002. http://dx.doi.org/10.1017/CBO9780511486791

Mayall, David. *Gypsy Identities 1500–2000: From Egipcyans and Moon-men to the Ethnic Romany*. New York: Routledge, 2004.

McDonald, Tracy. *Face to the Village: The Riazan Countryside under Soviet Rule, 1921–1930*. Toronto: University of Toronto Press, 2011.

McReynolds, Louise. *Russia at Play: Leisure Activities at the End of the Tsarist Era*. Ithaca: Cornell University Press, 2003.

Naiman, Eric. "On Soviet Subjects and the Scholars Who Make Them." *Slavic Review* 60 (July 2001): 307–15.

Naiman, Eric. *Sex in Public: The Incarnation of Early Soviet Ideology*. Princeton: Princeton University Press, 1997.

Nest'ev, I.V. *Zvezdy russkoi estrady (Panina, Vial'tseva, Plevitskaia): Ocherki o russkikh estradnykh pevitsakh nachala XX veka*. Moscow: Sovetskii kompositor, 1970.

Northrop, Douglas. *Veiled Empire: Gender and Power in Stalinist Central Asia*. Ithaca: Cornell University Press, 2004.

Olcott, Martha Brill. "The Collectivization Drive in Kazakhstan." *Russian Review* 40, no. 2 (April 1981): 122–42. http://dx.doi.org/10.2307/129204.

Pianciola, Niccolo. "The Collectivization Famine in Kazakhstan, 1931–1933." *Harvard Ukrainian Studies* 25, no. 3–4 (2001): 237–51. Medline:20034146

Pianciola, Niccolo. "Famine in the Steppe: The Collectivization of Agriculture and the Kazak Herdsmen 1928–1934." *Cahiers du Monde russe* 45, no. 1–2 (2004): 137–92.

Platt, Kevin M.F., and David Brandenberger, eds. *Epic Revisionism: Russian History and Literature as Stalinist Propaganda*. Madison: University of Wisconsin Press, 2006.

Pogany, Istvan. *The Roma Café: Human Rights and the Plight of the Romani People.* London: Pluto, 2004.

Poliakov, Iu.A., and V.B. Zhiromskaia, eds. *Naselenie Rossii v XX veke: Istoricheskie ocherki. Tom. 1 1900–1939.* Moscow: Rosspen, 2000.

Pym, Richard J. *The Gypsies of Early Modern Spain, 1425–1783.* New York: Palgrave MacMillan, 2007. http://dx.doi.org/10.1057/9780230625327.

Rao, Aparna. "The Concept of Peripatetics: An Introduction." In *The Other Nomads: Peripatetic Minorities in Cross Cultural Perspective*, edited by Aparna Rao, 1–32. Köln: Böhlau Verlag, 1987.

Rao, Aparna, ed. *The Other Nomads: Peripatetic Minorities in Cross Cultural Perspective.* Köln: Böhlau Verlag, 1987.

Retish, Aaron B. *Russia's Peasants in Revolution and Civil War: Citizenship, Identity, and the Creation of the Soviet State, 1914–1922.* Cambridge: Cambridge University Press, 2008.

Rogers, Douglas. *The Old Faith and the Russian Land: A Historical Ethnography of the Urals.* Ithaca: Cornell University Press, 2009.

Rothstein, Robert A. "The Quiet Rehabilitation of the Brick Factory: Early Soviet Popular Music and Its Critics." *Slavic Review* 39, no. 3 (September 1980): 373–88. http://dx.doi.org/10.2307/2497160.

Salzman, Philip Carl, ed. *When Nomads Settle: Processes of Sedentarization as Adaptation and Response.* New York: Praeger, 1980.

Scott, James C. *Seeing Like a State: How Certain Schemes to Improve the Human Condition Have Failed.* New Haven: Yale University Press, 1998.

Sergeev, M.A. "The Building of Socialism among the Peoples of Northern Siberia and the Soviet Far East." In *The Peoples of Siberia*, translated by Stephen Dunn, edited by M.G. Levin and L.P. Potapov, 487–510. Chicago: University of Chicago Press, 1964.

Sergeev, M.A. *Nekapitalisticheskii put' razvitiia malykh narodov severa.* Moscow: Izdatel'stvo akademii nauk SSSR, 1955.

Shearer, David. "Elements Near and Alien: Passportization, Policing, and Identity in the Stalinist State, 1932–1952." *The Journal of Modern History* 76, no. 4 (December 2004): 835–81.

Shearer, David. *Policing Stalin's Socialism: Repression and Social Order in the Soviet Union, 1924–1953.* New Haven: Yale University Press, 2009.

Slezkine, Yuri. *Arctic Mirrors: Russia and the Small Peoples of the North.* Ithaca: Cornell University Press, 1994.

Slezkine, Yuri. *The Jewish Century.* Princeton: Princeton University Press, 2004.

Slezkine, Yuri. "The USSR as a Communal Apartment, or How a Socialist State Promoted Ethnic Particularism." *Slavic Review* 52, no. 2 (1994): 52–76.

Smith, Jeremy. *The Bolsheviks and the National Question, 1917–23*. New York: St Martin's, 1999. http://dx.doi.org/10.1057/9780230377370.

Smith, Jeremy. "The Education of National Minorities: The Early Soviet Experience." *Slavonic and East European Review* 75, no. 2 (April 1997): 281–307.

Smith, Michael G. *Language and Power in the Creation of the USSR, 1917–1953*. New York: Mouten de Gruyter, 1998. http://dx.doi.org/10.1515/9783110805581.

Ssorin-Chaikov, Nikolai. *The Social Life of the State in Subarctic Siberia*. Stanford: Stanford University Press, 2003.

Starks, Tricia. *The Body Soviet: Propaganda, Hygiene, and the Revolutionary State*. Madison: University of Wisconsin Press, 2008.

Starr, S. Frederick. *Red and Hot: The Fate of Jazz in the Soviet Union*. New York: Limelight Editions, 1994.

Stepanov, Z.V. *Kul'turnaia zhizn' Leningrada 20-kh – 30-kh godov*. Leningrad: Nauka, 1976.

Stewart, Michael. *The Time of the Gypsies*. Boulder: Westview, 1997.

Stolpianskii, P. *Muzyka i muzitsirovanie v starom Peterburge*. Leningrad: Muzyka, 1989.

Suny, Ronald, and Terry Martin, eds. *A State of Nations: Empire and Nation-Making in the Age of Lenin and Stalin*. Oxford: Oxford University Press, 2001.

Sutherland, Anne. *Gypsies: The Hidden Americans*. New York: Free Press, 1975.

Tcherenkov, Lev, and Stéphane Laederich. *The Rroma*. Basel: Schwabe, 2004.

Theodosiou, Aspasia. "'Be-longing' in a 'Doubly-occupied Place': The Parakalamos Gypsy Musicians." *Romani Studies* 13, no. 2 (2003): 25–58.

Tremlett, Annabel. "Bringing Hybridity to Heterogeneity in Romani Studies." *Romani Studies* 19, no. 2 (2009): 147–68. http://dx.doi.org/10.3828/rs.2009.8.

Trumpener, Katie. "The Time of the Gypsies: A 'People without History' in the Narratives of the West." *Critical Inquiry* 18, no. 4 (Summer 1992): 843–84. http://dx.doi.org/10.1086/448659.

Veidlinger, Jeffrey. *The Moscow State Yiddish Theater: Jewish Culture on the Soviet Stage*. Bloomington: Indiana University Press, 2000.

Viola, Lynne. *Peasant Rebels under Stalin: Collectivization and the Culture of Peasant Resistance*. New York: Oxford University Press, 1996.

Viola, Lynne. *The Unknown Gulag: The Lost World of Stalin's Special Settlements*. New York: Oxford University Press, 2007.

Viola, Lynne, V.P. Danilov, N.A. Ivnitskii, and Denis Kozlov, eds. *The War against the Peasantry, 1927–1930: The Tragedy of the Soviet Countryside*. New Haven: Yale University Press, 2005.

Weinberg, Robert. *Stalin's Forgotten Zion: Birobidzhan and the Making of a Soviet Jewish Homeland*. Berkeley: University of California Press, 1998.

Weiner, Amir. *Making Sense of War: The Second World War and the Fate of the Bolshevik Revolution*. Princeton: Princeton University Press, 2001.

Werth, Nicolas. *Cannibal Island: Death in a Siberian Gulag*. Princeton: Princeton University Press, 2007.

Weyrauch, Walter Otto, and Maureen Anne Bell. "Autonomous Lawmaking: The Case of the 'Gypsies.'" *Yale Law Journal* 103, no. 2 (November 1993): 323–99. http://dx.doi.org/10.2307/797098.

Willems, Wim. *In Search of the True Gypsy: From Enlightenment to Final Solution*. London: Frank Cass, 1997.

Wood, Elizabeth A. *The Baba and the Comrade: Gender and Politics in Revolutionary Russia*. Bloomington: Indiana University Press, 1997.

Yurchak, Alexei. *Everything Was Forever, Until It Was No More: The Last Soviet Generation*. Princeton: Princeton University Press, 2006.

Zahra, Tara. "Imagined Noncommunities: National Indifference as a Category of Analysis." *Slavic Review* 69, no. 1 (Spring 2010): 93–119.

Zahra, Tara. *Kidnapped Souls: National Indifference and the Battle for Children in the Bohemian Lands*. Ithaca: Cornell University Press, 2008.

Zimmerman, Michael. "The National Socialist 'Solution of the Gypsy Question.'" In *National Socialist Extermination Policies: Contemporary German Perspectives and Controversies*, edited by Ulrich Herbert, 186–209. New York: Berghahn Books, 2000.

Index

"affirmative action," 6, 10, 252, 258n14. *See also* nationality policy

All-Russian Gypsy Union. *See* Gypsy Union

All-Union Resettlement Committee (VPK), 178–9, 181–5

alphabet, Romani, 52, 66, 78–9, 83, 85, 89, 241, 242. *See also* Romani language

artels, Romani: alleged criminal activities of 111, 123–5, 127–30; and Gypsy Union, 39, 40, 52, 54, 65, 105–7, 111–12; Krupino industrial village, 138–40, 143; 117; praise of, 117–18, 119–20, 135–7, 139, 140, 141–2; proliferation during the First Five-Year Plan, 104, 115–17, 122–3; shortages of raw materials, 123, 124, 140, 279n91; surveillance of, 123, 124–5, 127, 143; textiles production, 107, 111; Tsygkhimprom, 117, 120, 124, 135–8, 140, 144, 226, 282n145; Tsygpishcheprom, 117, 120, 124, 135, 137–8, 140–1, 144, 153, 226, 253; Vlax compared to Russka, 104, 119–20, 123, 124, 134, 137–8, 143

backwardness: attributes of 12; blamed on tsarist oppression of minorities, 4, 5, 10, 28, 42, 43; Bolshevik fear of, 5, 7–8; and claims of Gypsies as "most backward" nationality, 7–8, 141, 149–51, 183, 184; and distinction between so-called "eastern" and "western" nationalities, 73, 269n33; sociohistorical origins of Gypsies, 4, 42–4, 49, 57–8, 113–15, 161, 250–1; spectrum of, 43, 95, 265n54; as strategy for minority self-advancement and claim-making, 4–5, 6–7, 8, 13–14, 24, 28–9, 40, 42, 63–5, 112, 175, 248–9, 252–4

Barannikov, A. P., 17–18, 77–8, 80, 99, 295n61

Bezliudskii, M. T., 47, 48, 103, 119, 161–4, 165, 167, 171, 180, 217, 220, 227

Birobidzhan, 185–6

Blitstein, Peter, 97

Brubaker, Rogers, 14

Bugachevskii, S. M., 217, 220

"camp Gypsies," 106–7, 121, 130–1, 132, 139, 209, 215, 217–19, 220. *See also* Gypsy camps

Carmen, 225–8, 232, 235

choirs. *See* Gypsy choirs

citizenship: nationality policy as a pathway for achieving, 5, 6–7, 10–14, 251–4; and performativity, 10, 15–17; prerevolutionary views of, 8–9, 257n7; Soviet views of, 9–10

collective farms, Romani: and bureaucratic indifference, 56–7, 152–60, 161–3, 164–5, 167–71, 182–4; and famine, 158, 161, 162, 167, 176; "Gypsy Dawn" farm, 165, 167; material conditions of, 161, 163–4, 165–6, 168, 172–3, 176; mergers with Russian farms, 165, 167; "Natsmen-Gypsy" farm, 165–7; "Nevo Drom" farm, 161–2, 164, 165; "October" farm, 158, 172–4, 175, 176–7, 187, 188; postwar reconsolidation of, 188; "Red East" farm, 167–71; "Red Roma" farm, 162, 165, 167; and Romani activism, 158–9, 163–4, 165–74, 175–7, 179–81, 189; and Russian tutelage, 166, 167, 169, 181; "Stalin Constitution" farm, 187–8; "Toiling Gypsy" farm, 161, 163–4, 167, 180; wartime collapse and destruction of, 187. *See also* sedentarization

collectivization, 89, 116–17, 122, 125, 130, 152, 154, 160, 161, 278n80, 289n97. *See also* collective farms, Romani; Famine (1932–33)

Commission on the Settlement of Toiling Gypsies, 48, 52–3, 56, 58–9

"compensatory nation-building," 253, 263n2. *See also* "affirmative action"; nationality policy

cooperatives. *See* artels, Romani

dance: as distinctively "Gypsy," 7, 191, 192, 194, 209, 210, 219, 235; and question of authenticity, 25, 209, 210, 217, 218, 220; and tsyganshchina, 201–2, 203, 219, 293n11

deportation (resettlement), 126–7, 129–30, 131–4, 138–9, 143, 166. *See also* All-Union Resettlement Committee

dialects. *See* Romani language

Dombrovskii, Ia.G., 107, 111

dress: and portrayal of "Gypsiness" at Theatre Romen, 191, 202, 237; as prerevolutionary measure of civilizedness, 32, 34; as Soviet measure of civilizedness, 68–9, 72, 90, 91–2, 145, 164, 165, 168, 191, 201–2, 219, 230–1

Dudarova, N. A., 69, 74–5, 76, 78–88, 91

Edgar, Adrienne, 80

education. *See* Gypsy schools; non-Russian schools

Ethnographic Department (of Russian Museum), 204, 206–9, 211, 213, 295n47, 295n61

Ethnographic Theatre (Leningrad): closure, 205, 216; costumes, 205, 212; and debates over "ethnographic authenticity," 209–16; establishment, 205–7; Gypsy Road performance, 205, 211–16; propaganda function of, 205–6, 207; relationship with Ethnographic Department of Russian Museum, 206–9, 211, 213, 216; repertoire, 207, 210–13; Romani performers, 205, 209, 212, 213, 214, 215–16

ethnography: prerevolutionary
study of Gypsies, 77, 79–80, 114,
121, 250, 301n27; Soviet study of
Gypsies, 208, 242, 295n61, 295n62.
See also Ethnographic Department
(of Russian Museum); Ethnographic Theatre (Leningrad);
tsyganshchina

Europe: and the "bourgeois" study
of Gypsies, 18, 114; and common Gypsy stereotypes, 22, 112;
narratives of Romani history in,
42–3, 113–15, 250–1, 276n45; and
Romani diaspora, 17–20, 120

Experimental Theatre (Leningrad),
205–7

Famine (1932–33), 116, 125, 158,
160–2, 167, 176, 286n27

"foreign Gypsies," 21–2, 76, 104, 120,
122–7, 129–30, 132–4, 135, 137–40,
141, 143, 262n42. *See also* Vlax
Roma

fortune telling: and "backwardness,"
34, 35, 37, 41, 43, 44, 49, 51, 59, 82,
105–6, 130, 135, 136, 172, 176; and
stereotypes of Romani women, 44,
82, 103, 139; as traditional Romani
profession, 25, 39, 103, 105–7, 114,
117, 142, 151, 160, 165

gender, 198–204, 293n22, 294n31

Gerasimov, A.Ia., 130–3

Gerasimov, I. I., 171–7, 179, 184

Germano, A. V., 92, 103, 123, 252,
253: autobiographic texts of, 25–6,
239–50; commemoration of, 245;
disavowal of Gypsy nationality,
240, 241–2, 245–6, 248–50; ethno-
historical and journalistic writings

on Roma, 48, 72–3, 77, 89, 106–7,
113–15, 118, 121–2, 125, 250–2,
276n45, 277n69; literary career,
239, 240–1, 242–4, 245, 246–8; 250;
and Romani-language textbooks,
82–3, 86–9, 243; and Theatre
Romen, 217, 221–3, 227, 236, 243,
297n124

Gilliat-Smith, Bernard, 33

Glavrepertkom (Main Committee for
Repertory), 199, 203, 225, 292n8

Gol'dblat, M. I., 217, 224–5, 226,
227–8, 230, 231–3, 234

Gypsies, The (Pushkin), 7, 145, 232,
233–6, 242

Gypsy autonomous region: bureaucratic opposition to, 178–9, 181–2,
183–4, 185–6; failure to material-
ize, 183–6; support for, 154, 171,
176, 177–8, 179–81, 182–3, 184;
surveying of potential territory
for, 178–9, 290n143

Gypsy camps: "authenticity" and,
197, 204, 209–11, 213, 217–19, 220,
229–30; demonization of, 121–2,
124–5, 127–9; depicted in Theatre
Romen performances, 220, 221,
223, 229; as "embryos of communism," 60, 121; migration to
Moscow during First Five-Year
Plan, 116, 130, 134; as preservers of
"backward" Gypsy culture, 106–7,
119, 121, 124, 127–9, 218; surveillance of, 124–5, 127, 130–1. *See also*
"camp Gypsies"; Gypsy kulaks

Gypsy choirs: association with Russka Roma, 21; costumes, 34, 194;
and debates over "ethnographic
authenticity," 193, 195–7, 204,
209–11; demonization of, 35, 193,

194, 195–6, 198–204; dynasties, 33, 41–2, 63, 205, 217; and Gypsy Union, 37–8, 40, 41–2, 63, 105, 216–7; popularity of before the October Revolution, 21, 30, 32–3, 191; and prerevolutionary restaurant culture, 30, 32–3, 35, 194, 196–7; repertoires of, 32–3, 36, 195–7; revitalization during NEP, 36–7, 194–7; and Romani women, 33–4, 198–202; and social distinction, 30, 31, 34–5, 36, 63, 237; and War Communism, 35–6, 194. *See also* Gypsy music; tsyganshchina

Gypsy club (Red Star), 108, 110–12, 118–19, 122, 124, 131, 134, 142, 220, 243, 283n150

Gypsy kulaks: arrest and prosecution of, 127–30; depicted in Soviet film, 145–7; as depicted in Theatre Romen performances, 221, 223–4, 227; descriptions of, 121, 124–5, 127–30, 182; as foil for Romani activists, 104, 143; invention of, 104, 121–2, 143; and Romani collective farms, 158, 167, 182–3; and Vlax Romani artels, 104, 124–5, 127–30, 134, 138–9, 143

Gypsy music: censorship of, 203, 292n8; as counter-revolutionary, 35–6, 40, 193, 194, 195–6, 198–201, 202–3; gendered critique of, 198–202; popularity of, 30, 32–3, 37, 192, 195, 199, 211; and question of authenticity, 34, 193, 196, 197, 204, 209–11, 213–14, 216. *See also* Gypsy choirs; tsyganshchina

Gypsy schools: adult literacy courses, 39, 44, 45, 52, 54, 70, 74–5, 82, 90, 100, 118, 124, 141, 164, 173;

assimilationist aims of, 66–7, 68, 83, 84, 86, 93–8, 100; boarding school in Smolensk Province, 174–5; curricular emphasis on hygiene, 66–7, 68, 71–3, 83; curriculum, 68, 69; enrolment, 69, 85, 96, 101, 174, 290n117; establishment, 67–9, 77, 174; Gypsy Union involvement in, 66–70; liquidation of, 93–8, 99, 102; other non-Russian schools compared to, 73, 76, 93, 270n40; and perceived threat of epidemic disease, 72–3, 75; physical conditions of, 67, 69, 74, 85; relationships with Romani parents, 68, 69, 70–4, 84, 96, 101; relationships with Russian schools, 69, 74–5, 84, 85, 268n11; on Romani collective farms, 89; 85, 89, 166, 175; Romani-language instruction in, 76–7, 85, 94–5, 175; Russian-language instruction in, 69, 70, 75, 76–7, 85, 93, 94–5, 97–8, 100, 166, 175; staffing problems, 73, 75, 76–7, 90–1, 95, 268n13; teachers of, 68, 69, 70, 74, 91, 166, 175; and textbook scarcity, 69, 73, 74, 75, 86, 95; unknown number of, 89, 272n93. *See also* teacher-training courses; textbooks, Romani-language

Gypsy theatre. *See* Theatre Romen

Gypsy Union (All-Russian Gypsy Union): anti-tsyganshchina campaign, 216–17; bureaucratic scepticism of, 28, 41, 53–5, 57 59, 111–12; career advancement and political education of its activist leaders, 28–9, 62–5; closure, 59–60, 62, 66, 111–12, 113; and Commission on the Settlement of Toiling Gypsies,

48–9, 53–4, 58–9; correspondence with Soviet Roma, 45–6, 55, 56–7, 61–2; and creation of Gypsy alphabet, 52, 66, 78–9, 266n78; as dominated by Russka Roma, 76, 77, 80, 82, 117; establishment, 37–41; financial difficulties of, 46–7, 55, 57; goals of, 38, 39, 40–1, 43, 44–5, 49; industrial activities of, 54–5, 106–7, 111–12, 142; membership statistics, 45, 54; MKK RKI inspection of, 54, 111; narratives of Romani history, 42–3, 49, 58, 60–1; organization of Gypsy schools, 66–70; propaganda efforts of, 49–53; rhetorical emphasis on "Gypsy backwardness," 28–9, 40, 42–3, 44, 46, 49, 51–2, 56, 57–9, 62–4; and Romani women, 44; ties to Gypsy choirs, 38, 41–2, 63

Hancock, Ian, 18–19
Hellbeck, Jochen, 16
Hirsch, Francine, 93, 206, 258n9, 273n120, 295n47
Hoffmann, David L., 257n3, 278n83
horse-trading, 35, 39, 51, 105–6, 107, 116, 118, 151, 172
hygiene: as curricular unit in Gypsy schools, 66–7, 68, 71–3, 83, 269n25; as general, early Soviet problem, 71–2, 123, 269n28, 279n88; Gypsies' perceived aversion to, 123, 230–1; and Lenin's teachings, 68; as Soviet value, 67, 68, 72, 231, 269n28

Ianshin, M. M., 234–6
ideology: historiographic treatment of, 11–12, 16, 260n23, 260n25;

and question of authenticity, 12, 15–17, 64; and subjectivity, 12, 15–17, 64
India, 18, 19, 58, 261n35
industrialization: First-Five Year Plan, 104, 115–17, 122, 125, 126, 130, 133–4, 278n80; and passportization, 126–7, 129; and Romani in-migration to Moscow, 116–17, 120, 122, 123, 125–6, 130–2, 134

Jews, 154, 174, 176, 185–6

Kazakhs, 150–1, 160, 270n40, 285n11, 286n27
Khalid, Adeeb, 258n9, 264n33
Khatskevich, A. I., 141–2, 148, 168–70, 177, 183–4, 272n93
Khlebnikov, N. I., 35–6
kolkhozes. See collective farms, Romani
Kolkhoztsentr (Union of Agricultural Collectives), 155–6, 157–8, 161, 162
Komsomol, 37–8, 40, 54, 89–90, 158, 166, 173, 188, 201, 203
Kotkin, Stephen, 16
Kotsonis, Yanni, 8
Krikunov, A. P., 56–7
Krikunov commune, 56–7, 152, 286n19, 288n79
Krikunov, G. M., 165–6, 167, 171, 288n79
kris, 125, 128–9, 280n113
Krongauz, F., 94–5
Kruchinin, N. N., 35–6, 194–6, 204

Last Camp, The (film), 145–7
Latinization, 79, 81, 271n61
Lebedev, I. G., 29–32, 34–5, 37

Lemon, Alaina, 7, 22, 23, 82, 124, 127,
    261n40, 279n92, 280n108, 300n187
Lenin, V. I., 28, 36, 42, 68, 75, 83, 84,
    100, 136, 191, 218, 221, 224–5
Life on Wheels, 221–3

Martin, Terry, 97, 273n119, 273n120,
    281n117
McDonald, Tracy, 289n97
migration, rural-urban, 115–17, 120,
    122–3, 125–7, 130, 134, 277n54,
    278n83
MONO (Moscow Department of
    Education), 67–9, 71, 73, 74, 75,
    112, 119
Moscow Art Theatre, 234–5
Mossovet (Moscow City Soviet), 39,
    40, 41, 119–20, 124, 125, 129, 130,
    138, 139
music. See Gypsy music

Naiman, Eric, 260n23
Narkompros (People's Commissariat
    of Enlightenment), 27, 110, 112,
    267n3; and Ethnographic Theatre
    207, 213, 216; and Gypsy choirs
    36; and Gypsy schools 67, 68, 70,
    73, 76, 82, 85, 86, 88, 89, 90, 91, 92,
    94–5, 96, 268n11, 269n33, 272n93;
    and Romani language standard-
    ization 78–9, 81, 82; and Theatre
    Romen 193, 217, 219, 221, 227–8,
    230–2, 233, 234
Narkomzem (People's Commissariat
    of Agriculture), 45, 48, 55, 59,
    112, 130, 131, 133, 152, 153, 156–8,
    159–60, 177–9, 181, 182, 185
nationality policy: assimilationist
    logic of, 6–7, 11, 13–14, 27–8, 67,
    93–8, 100–2, 142–4, 148, 151–2, 216,
219, 238, 239, 245, 249, 251–4; and
    distinction between "backward
    and "advanced" nationalities, 10,
    12, 43, 269n33; as framework for
    self-sovietization, 6–7, 8, 10–11,
    13–14, 15, 28–9, 62–5, 67, 100–2,
    142–4, 236, 237–8, 239, 245, 248–54;
    historiographical treatment of, 11;
    mutability of and shifts in, 24–6,
    93–8, 185, 193, 235, 248–9, 252–3;
    reliance on minority participation,
    6, 10–11, 13, 64, 102, 152, 189; as
    restitution for tsarist oppression,
    5, 6, 10, 28. See also "affirmative
    action"; "compensatory nation-
    building"; "state-sponsored
    evolutionism"
"natural assimilation," 95–7
Nevo drom (periodical), 119, 134,
    142, 155, 242
New Economic Policy (NEP), 36–7,
    60, 103, 105, 113, 115, 116, 193–6,
    198–201, 203, 205, 210
New Soviet Person, 5, 9, 12–13, 63,
    252
NKVD, 41, 59–60, 184–5. See also
    OGPU
nomads and nomadism: competing
    scholarly definitions of, 285n12;
    and egalitarianism, 60, 121, 149;
    Gypsies defined as exceptional
    compared to others, 8, 47, 60,
    149–51, 157, 181, 182–3, 188–9,
    285n10, 285n12; and kulaks, 121,
    149, 151, 278n82; pastoral, 148,
    150–1, 183, 278n82, 284n6, 285n12,
    286n27; service, 25, 151, 285n12;
    Soviet state's attitude towards, 25,
    50–1, 148–51, 159, 177, 190. See also
    sedentarization

non-Russian schools: debates over,
73, 76, 93–8; legislation regarding, 67, 93, 97–8 267n3; Russian-
language instruction in, 76, 97–8,
268n13, 270n40; staffing challenges,
73, 98, 268n13, 274n138
North Caucasus Krai, 56–7, 90, 92,
152, 155, 157, 161–5, 167, 178, 182
Nurmakov, N. N., 95, 159, 177

OGPU, 132–3, 134, 282n132. *See also*
NKVD
Orlov, A. G., 32

Pankov, N. A., 103, 123; advocacy for
Gypsy schools, 69–70, 98–100, 102,
272n93; authorship of Romani-
language texts, 82–3, 86–8; biography of, 70; Gypsy Union activism,
41, 66, 103; letter to Stalin, 99; and
standardization of the Romani
language, 78–82; teaching career,
90, 92, 98–100; and Theatre
Romen, 226, 299n158
passportization, 126–7, 129
pastoral nomadism, 148, 150–1, 183,
278n82, 284n6, 285n12, 286n27.
See also nomads and nomadism
Patkanov, K. P., 80
performativity: historiographic
treatments of, 17, 64, 267n110; and
subjectivity, 10, 15–17, 64
Poliakov, E. A., 36–8, 194–8
pollution (taboos), 69, 71
primordialism, 7, 253, 302n33
Pushkin, A. S., 7, 33, 84, 218, 232,
233, 234, 235, 236, 242, 299n164

Red Star. *See* Gypsy club (Red Star)
Rogers, Douglas, 171

Rogozhev, N. P., 74, 76–7, 91
Romani diaspora, 17–21, 261n35,
261n40
Romani Holocaust, 187–8, 291n177,
292n178
Romani intelligentsia: displacement
in the aftermath of the October
Revolution, 35, 36; prerevolutionary history of, 30–4; and social
striving, 32, 63, 237
Romani language: alphabet creation,
78–9; and "backwardness," 77, 78,
79, 83; dialects, 18, 19, 20, 21, 77–8,
79–80, 81–2; dictionary, 82, 99;
in Gypsy schools, 76–7, 85, 94–5,
175; periodicals, 78, 104, 107–12,
118–19, 134, 142, 155, 163, 242, 251,
253; and philological study of the
Romani diaspora, 18–19, 79–80;
and question of native fluency,
20, 21, 30, 75, 77–8, 94; standardization of, 78–82; termination of
publishing in, 93, 247; Theatre
Romen debates about, 228, 232–3,
235–6, 237; in Theatre Romen performances, 233–6, 237, 299n166,
300n183; Turkmen language compared to, 80–2. *See also* textbooks,
Romani-language
Romani literature, 40, 65, 66, 82–4,
99, 100, 105, 108, 119, 241, 242–3,
245, 247–8, 271n45. *See also* textbooks, Romani-language
Romani Studies, 18–19, 22–3, 262n44,
276n45
Romany zoria, 107–12, 118–19, 142,
242, 253
Rom-Lebedev, I. I., 103, 105, 263n3;
career at Theatre Romen, 217–18,
219–20, 223, 225, 227, 229–30,

234–5, 236; childhood, 29–30, 32, 34–5; Gypsy Union leadership, 37–8, 41–2, 55, 103; literary career, 108, 217, 227, 229, 236

"Russian Gypsies." *See* Russka Roma

Russian language: in Gypsy schools, 69, 70, 75, 76–7, 85, 93, 94–5, 97–8, 100, 166, 175; in non-Russian schools, 76, 93, 95, 97–8; as Soviet lingua franca, 96, 97–8, 101; Theatre Romen debates about, 228, 232–3, 235–6; in Theatre Romen performances, 219, 228, 233–4, 235–6, 237, 238, 253

Russian literature, 7, 33, 84

Russka Roma, 23, 77, 80, 82, 117, 122, 124, 130, 135; compared to Vlax Roma, 20–2, 76–7, 119–20, 137–8, 139, 143; defined, 20–1; described as "Russian Gypsies" by the Soviet state, 21, 80, 137, 143

Russocentrism, 96, 98, 193, 235, 238, 244, 249, 271n76

sedentarization: and bureaucratic indifference, 55, 147–8, 151–61, 162, 164–5, 168–70, 177, 184–5, 189–90, 286n27, 286n28; and bureaucratic infighting, 152–3, 155–61, 162–3, 168–70, 179, 182, 183–4; and Commission on the Settlement of Toiling Gypsies, 48, 52–3, 56, 58–9; and lack of material investment in, 131, 147–8, 151–3, 155, 159–60, 165, 182; and legislation regarding Gypsies, 48, 152–3, 155–7, 159, 162–3, 172, 183, 189–90; logistical challenges of, 131, 149–51, 154, 156–7, 176, 178–9; policy

rationale for, 147–52, 159, 188–9; and question of Gypsies' "compact mass settlement," 176–86. *See also* collective farms, Romani; Gypsy autonomous region; nomads and nomadism

Sergievskii, M. V., 78–82, 86, 99

service nomadism, 25, 151, 285n12. *See also* nomads and nomadism

Shearer, David, 127

Sholokh, E., 84–5, 218, 220

Shteinpress, Boris, 201–4

Slezkine, Yuri, 11, 258n14, 263n2, 276n44, 285n12

Slichenko, Nikolai, 236–7

Smolensk Province: management of ethnic difference within, 61–2, 172, 174–5, 289n114; Romani boarding school in, 174–5; Romani collective farms in, 89, 158, 171–7, 179–80, 184; and Romani Holocaust, 187–8, 292n178; Theatre Romen tours of, 223–4

"socially harmful elements," 126–7, 134, 143, 282n132

Sovietism, 6

Sovnarkom (Council of People's Commissars), 46, 48, 54, 55, 73, 152, 178, 184

special settlements, 116, 132–3, 282n133

Stalin, I. V., 84, 95–8, 99, 102, 118, 135, 136, 155, 179, 180, 185, 281n117; and "Great Retreat," 93, 273n119; and "revolution from above" (Great Break), 75, 86, 89, 103–4, 112, 113, 115–17, 126–7, 133–4, 142, 150, 155, 174, 194, 198, 286n27

Stalingrad (Volgograd) Province, 165–7, 288n78

"state-sponsored evolutionism," 79, 93–4, 97, 258n9

stereotypes of Gypsies: as averse to labour, 7–8, 39, 103, 112–15, 124, 150, 167, 185, 189; as averse to hygiene, 8, 21, 42, 67, 71–3, 84, 123; as communal, 54, 60–1, 121; as criminals, 4, 5, 21, 112, 114–15, 124 151, 189; as diseased, 8, 22, 58, 67, 71–2, 73, 75, 76, 120, 123, 193, 219; as freedom-loving, 7–8, 22, 23, 112, 145, 236, 238, 242 263n13; as licentious, 22, 112, 198–9, 201–2, 236; as marginal, 5, 7–8, 21, 22, 23, 43–4, 58, 70, 113, 114–15, 219; as natural performers, 192, 193, 209, 221; as nomads, 7–8, 18, 22, 23, 40, 47, 60, 114–15, 149–51, 154, 155–6, 159, 164, 182–3, 188–9, 204; as "people without history," 7, 23, 209, 227; pan-European, 22; reproduction through the everyday performance of, 63, 192, 238, 254; in Romani Studies, 22–3; in Theatre Romen performances, 25, 191–2, 238; as tools of self-sovietization, 4–5, 8, 39, 63, 113, 238, 254

Studio of Old Gypsy Art, 36, 195

subjectivity: and centrality of nationality to Soviet self-fashioning, 6–7, 8, 10–11, 12–16, 23–4, 64, 238, 239, 245, 248–9, 253–4; historiographic treatment of, 12, 15–17, 64, 259n17, 260n23, 260n26, 267n110, 300n2; performative achievement of, 10, 15, 17, 64–5

Sverdlovsk Province, 167–70

Taranov, A. S., 39, 41, 47, 48, 49, 50, 86, 88, 103, 107

teacher-training courses, 24, 86, 89–93, 100, 101, 175

textbooks, Romani-language: Buty i dzhinaiben, 82–3; debates over content of, 86–8; Nevo drom, 82; Nevo dzhiiben, 82–3; production of, 82–4, 86; scarcity in Gypsy schools, 69, 73, 74, 75, 86, 95; termination of publication, 93

Theatre Romen: actors' complaints about, 230–1, 233; Carmen performance, 225–8, 232, 235; costumes, 191, 194, 217, 220, 221, 230–1, 234, 235; criticism of, 221, 223–4, 225–8, 234; education of actors, 219, 229; establishment, 191, 216–17; financial difficulties of, 226, 231, 232, 297n115; Gypsy Revue performance, 219–21, 223; internal scandals, 230, 234; Life on Wheels performance, 221–3; non-Romani actors, 237, 252–3; non-Romani administration, 217, 230, 234–6; praise for, 220–1, 225, 235; propaganda function of, 217, 226, 229, 232, 237; and question of "authenticity," 191–2, 193, 217–9, 220, 225, 233–4, 235–8, 300n187; relationship with Moscow Art Theatre, 234–5; repertoire concerns and crises, 217, 223–5, 227–8, 232, 235–7; and Romani language, 219–20, 232–3, 235–6, 237; and Russian language, 233–4, 235–6, 237; Soviet legacy of, 238, 300n187; stage designs, 192, 221, 234; and threat of closure, 234; ties to prerevolutionary Romani intelligentsia, 217, 237; tours of provinces and collective farms, 221, 223, 229–30,

238; and tsyganshchina, 216–17, 219, 220, 223, 225, 236, 237
Tokmakov, I. P., 123, 134, 159–60, 162, 167–8, 177, 182, 226, 233, 299n158
Tolstoy, Lev, 7, 33, 84, 234
TsIK (Central Executive Committee), 40, 48, 57, 152, 177, 179, 182, 183, 184, 185
tsyganshchina, 194, 196–205, 209–10, 213, 214, 216–17, 219, 220, 223, 225, 236, 238, 242, 293n11
Tsygkhimprom, 117, 120, 124, 135–8, 140, 144, 226, 282n145
Tsygpishcheprom,117, 120, 124, 135, 137–8, 140–1, 144, 153, 226, 253
Turkmen language, 80–1

Vlax Roma, 71, 76–7, 268n21, 279n92; compared to Russka Roma, 20–1, 76, 120, 124, 137–8, 139, 143; criminalization of, 104, 120, 123–30, 143; defined, 20; and industrialization, 104, 120, 122–5, 129, 135, 137–40; labeled by the state as "foreign Gypsies," 21–2, 104, 120, 124, 126, 143; resettlement of, 132–3, 135, 138–40
Volkov, M. F., 167–71

VPK. *See* All-Union Resettlement Committee (VPK)
Vsevolodskii-Gerngross, V. N., 205, 207, 209–10, 211, 212, 213–14, 216, 294n45
VTsIK (All-Russian Central Executive Committee), 95, 103, 113, 117, 130, 131, 134, 139; and Gypsy schools, 68–9, 85–6, 89, 96, 272n93; and Gypsy Union, 40, 41, 42, 47, 48, 53, 54, 55, 57, 60, 68–9; and sedentarization, 153–4, 156, 159, 161, 163, 167, 168, 172, 177–8, 182, 184, 185

women, Romani, 34, 44, 82, 103, 105, 107, 111, 136, 139, 170; association with tsyganschina, 198–9, 201–3, 225; depicted in Theatre Romen performances, 191, 221, 225, 227–8, 234, 236, 238; as prerevolutionary elite fetish, 7, 33, 34, 35, 201–2, 263n13

Yurchak, Alexei, 17

Zemfira (literary character), 7, 234, 236
Zhvigur, E., 67, 71–4, 77